THE HISTORICAL DEVELOPMENT OF FUNDAMENTAL MORAL THEOLOGY IN THE UNITED STATES

Readings in Moral Theology No. 11

Edited by
Charles E. Curran
and
Richard A. McCormick, S.J.

PAULIST PRESS
New York / Mahwah, N.J.

Acknowledgments
"The Moral Act in *Veritatis Splendor* and Aquinas's *Summa Theologiae*" by Jean Porter and *"Veritatis Splendor*: A Revisionist Perspective" by Charles E. Curran are taken from *Veritatis Splendor: American Responses*, edited by Michael E. Alsopp, with permission of Sheed & Ward, an apostolate of the Priests of the Sacred Heart, 7373 South Lovers Lane Road, Franklin, Wisconsin 53132, 1800-558-0580. "The Duty and Right to Follow One's Judgement of Conscience" by Germain Grisez is reprinted by permission from *The Linacre Quarterly*. "Moral Theology in the United States: An Analysis of the Last Twenty-Five Years" by Charles E. Curran is reprinted from *Toward an American Catholic Moral Theology* by Charles E. Curran, © 1987 by the University of Notre Dame Press and is used by permission of the publisher. "Church Teaching Authority: Problems and Perspectives" by John P. Boyle is reprinted by permission from his book *Church Teaching Authority*, © 1995 by University of Notre Dame Press. Margaret Farley's "How Shall We Love in a Postmodern World?" is reprinted from *The Annual of the Society of Christian Ethics* (1994): 3–19, by permission of the editors. "Seventy-Five Years of Moral Theology in America" by Paul E. McKeever is reprinted from *American Ecclesiastical Review* by permission of The Catholic University of America Press. "A Sounder Theory of Morality" by John Finnis, Joseph M. Boyle, Jr. and Germain Grisez is reprinted from *Nuclear Deterrence, Morality and Realism*, Clarendon Press, Oxford.

Cover design by Tim McKeen

Library of Congress Cataloging-in-Publication Data

The historical development of fundamental moral theology in the United States / edited by Charles E. Curran and Richard A. McCormick.
   p. cm.—(Readings in moral theology : no. 11)
   Includes bibliographical references.
   ISBN 0-8091-3879-4 (alk. paper)
   1. Christian ethics—Catholic authors. 2. Catholic Church—Doctrines. I. Curran, Charles E. II. McCormick, Richard A., 1922- . III. Series.
BJ1249.H565   1999
241´.04273—DC21   99-32353
                                                                        CIP

Published by Paulist Press
997 Macarthur Boulevard
Mahwah, New Jersey 07430

www.paulistpress.com

Printed and bound in the
United States of America

Contents

PART THREE:
POST-VATICAN II

Foreword

Moral theology, like every other theological discipline, has roots in the past. These roots reveal the concerns, emphases, and priorities of a different historical era. It might seem fruitless to retreat to a past we have by and large abandoned.

We do not think so. The past both shapes and constrains us far more than we realize. Revisiting it, therefore, can bring into sharper focus the qualities and cultural limitations of the present work of moral theologians. Knowing our past may give us some inkling of how others to come may judge our work. History is an instructor.

For this reason we first present several historical overviews of moral theology in the United States to set the stage. We then enter, one by one, the *dramatis personae* of the pre-Vatican II period. Many other articles could have been chosen. We believe, however, that our choices convey the structure and spirit of fundamental moral theology of the time.

The names of August Lehmkuhl, Thomas J. Bouquillon, John A. Ryan, Henry Davis, John A. McHugh, Francis J. Connell, Edwin F. Healy, John C. Ford, and Gerald Kelly were well known to students of moral theology in the United States in the past, but contemporary theologians are often not familiar with them. In this section we have included two chapters highlighting the preoccupation with confessional practice that shaped the approach to moral theology.

Our third and final section assembles some post-Vatican II literature. The selection process here has been more difficult. The previous ten volumes in this series have discussed this period in great depth. Here we have tried to show the major controversies existing in moral theology (the moral act, moral norms, conscience, church teaching authority) and also indicate some new developments (virtue theory, dialogue with postmodernism).

Our hope is that a better knowledge of the past and present will help the discipline of moral theology deal more adequately with the future.

Charles E. Curran
Richard A. McCormick, S.J.

Part One

HISTORICAL OVERVIEW

1. Seventy-Five Years of Moral Theology in America

Paul E. McKeever

This chapter first appeared in *American Ecclesiastical Review* 152 (1965).

This article will be divided into two parts, the first dealing with factors and events which have influenced the development of moral theology in this country, the second dealing with the substantive content of that development. Under "factors and events" we will discuss in order, texts and manuals, The Catholic University of America, periodical literature, *The Catholic Encyclopedia,* and the Catholic Theological Society of America.

Under substantive content, we will discuss those areas of moral theology in which American theologians have made notable contributions. This will entail the following subjects: the nature of moral theology, evaluative cognition, conscience, law, virtue and pseudo-virtue, intercredal co-operation, business ethics, medico-moral problems, warfare, temperance and prudence, and marriage. It will be necessary, and in a sense inevitable, to discuss content, at least to a minimal degree, when dealing with texts and manuals produced either by American theologians or for the American scene. Since most of the texts to be mentioned are not in actual use in American seminaries today, they have, for the most part, only historical interest. One distinctly historical purpose they serve is to reveal that the whole question of methodology is not new. That question, if one may indulge in understatement, is still with us. Seeing the divergent opinions expressed in these various American manuals, and the reasons behind them, may serve to help in the evaluation of similar opinions which have come to the fore in the immediate past. American texts, furthermore, still serve the very helpful purpose of indicating attitudes toward the whole problem of the force of American law on the American Christian conscience.

I. TEXT BOOKS

Although their texts appeared before 1889, I think it important to mention the works of Kenrick, Konings, and Sabetti, since each continued to have considerable influence well into the 20th century.

The first completed moral text by an American author was Francis Patrick Kenrick's *Theologia Moralis.*[1] Written in a difficult classical Latin style, it followed the "virtue" approach to moral theology, defended probabilism, and incorporated materials from American law and customs, especially in the tract on justice. As Arthur Preuss said, this text "did splendid service to the American clergy during the latter half of the nineteenth century."[2] It still serves as a reference for American materials,[3] and has assumed historical significance for its modified and reluctant defense of maintaining the *status quo* with respect to the pre-Civil War slavery issue.[4]

The next manual of importance was written by the renowned Redemptorist, Anthony Konings (+1884). Coming to this country from Holland, he eventually exercised an enormous influence on the American church. His work *De Absolutione Parentibus etc.*, on the Catholic school issue, was most influential on the legislation of the Third Council of Baltimore (1884), and his commentary on Episcopal faculties, later revised by Joseph Putzer, C.SS.R., became a classic for American bishops. Here, however, we are more concerned with his *Theologiae Moralis S. Alphonsi Compendium,* which went into seven editions, the last appearing in 1888. Konings was a moralist and a canonist, and his work reflected both disciplines. He presented moral principles in accordance with the mind of St. Alphonsus, gave a methodical exposition of equiprobabilism,[5] and incorporated materials from American law, both civil and ecclesiastical.[6] Though written in Latin, Konings made the deliberate attempt in his work to improve on what he regarded as the difficult and obscure style of Archbishop Kenrick.[7] Konings's work was based on the method of J. P. Gury, S.J. (+1866).[8] This fact was duly noted by the European Jesuit Sigé, whose reaction was expressed in an article entitled, "La théologie Dury-

Ballerini recommandée par un disciple de Saint Alphonse."[9] One would expect, however, certain affinities between Gury and St. Alphonsus, since both based their method on the enormously influential *Medulla Theologiae Moralis* of Herman Busembaum (+1688). Although Konings adopted Gury's method, he retained the usual Redemptorist positions with respect to moral doctrine.

Gury was also the basis for the *Compendium Theologiae Moralis* of Aloysius Sabetti, S.J. (+1898).[10] First published by Pustet in 1884, revised and re-edited by Timothy Barrett, S.J. (+1935), it became the most widely used American manual, going into at least thirty-four editions, the most recent under the editorship of Daniel F. Creeden, S.J. Clear, concise, and well organized, it followed the traditional Jesuit defense of probabilism, used the "precept" approach, and included specifically American elements, especially in the tract on justice. Sabetti-Barrett is still quoted for its tendency toward leniency with respect to a penitent who has not payed his income taxes,[11] and also for the lenient opinion that a *bona fide* bankrupt who has received a discharge in bankruptcy can consider himself free of further moral obligation in strict justice toward his creditor.[12]

This summary of Konings and Sabetti helps to make clear the influence of the Busembaum-Gury tradition in the United States. This textbook tradition in general, and Sabetti and Konings in particular, undoubtedly served well the purpose of training confessors. The time was to come in the United States, however, and had already arrived in Germany, when this kind of presentation of moral theology would be seriously questioned. It was criticized because it followed the "precept" approach, rather than the more positive "virtue" approach, did not forge strong enough links between dogma and moral, and did not sufficiently emphasize the virtue of charity. This questioning of methodology appears before the turn of the century in the work of Thomas J. Bouquillon.

Bouquillon (+1902) was the first Professor of Moral Theology at the Catholic University of America. Trained at the Gregorian University, he had taught moral theology for ten years at Bruges.[13] While still in Europe Bouquillon published his *Institutiones Theologiae Moralis Fundamentalis* in 1873, *De Virtutibus Theologicis* in 1875, and *De Virtute Religionis* in 1880.[14] *The Theologia Moralis Fundamentalis* went through two more editions, one appearing in 1890, after

Bouquillon had arrived in Washington, the other in 1903. A second edition of *De Virtutibus Theologicis* appeared in 1890. Bouquillon was most concerned with the problem of method. Three methods are possible in the presentation of moral theology, he reflected. One would concentrate on the moral rectitude and goodness of moral actions, and therefore divide the material of moral theology according to the cardinal virtues. Another would follow the order of the precepts of the Decalogue and the Church, and the third would consider man according to his threefold character, *"ens individuum," "ens religiosum"* and *"ens sociale."* After giving due respect to the merits of the first two methods, he chose the third because "it corresponds more intelligibly to the natural order of love, and the supernatural order of charity."[15]

At the turn of the century, we meet the almost incredibly energetic Father Adolf Tanquerey, S.S. (+1932). A European theologian who had taught philosophy and dogma in Europe, he came to St. Mary's Seminary in Baltimore, where, from 1887 until 1895, he taught dogmatic theology. In 1896 he became Professor of Moral Theology, and in 1902 published his work *Synopsis Theologiae Moralis et Pastoralis.* It was not until he returned to Europe that he published the third volume, *De Virtute Justitiae,* in 1905. Although used in many American seminaries, its treatment of specifically American materials was spotty. Edited by F. Cimetier, it contained, at least in its tenth edition, a supplement for America and Great Britain pertaining to legal-moral issues.

In 1908 a book was published in English entitled *A Manual of Moral Theology for English-Speaking Catholics.* It is important for us not only because its English author gained a wide public in the United States, but also because it included in volume one "Notes on American Legislation" by the Irish born and educated Michael Martin, S.J. The author was Thomas Slater, S.J. (+1928), whose other works, popular in America, included *A Short History of Moral Theology,* 1909; *Questions of Moral Theology,* 1915; *The Foundations of True Morality,* 1920 *Cases of Conscience,* in two volumes, 1911, 1912; and *On Morals Today,* 1920. He also wrote extensively for the *Catholic Encyclopedia.* The Slater-Martin manual followed the precepts, taught probabilism, and with reference to the bankrupt's obligation to pay his debts after receiving a discharge, argued *late et longe* for the view that the obligation ceased. Referring to the American theologians who preceded him, viz. Kenrick, Konings, and Sabetti, Martin states, "If these authors were now, after the Bankrupt Act has been in operation for over nine years, to express their opinion, it would scarcely be rash to say that they would hold the debtor's obligation extinguished, either on the ground of full remission being granted under the Act, or by the consent of the creditor."[16]

Slater's introduction is important because of the attitude toward moral theology it manifested. It will be interesting to contrast the following ideas with those of Koch-Preuss, which we will see presently. Slater forthrightly requested his readers to bear in mind "that manuals of moral theology are technical works intended to help the confessor and the parish priest in the discharge of their duties. They are as technical as the text-books of the lawyer and the doctor. They are not intended for edification, nor do they hold up a high ideal of Christian perfection for the imitation of the faithful. They deal with what is of obligation under pain of sin; they are books of moral pathology."[17]

Between 1918 and 1924 there appeared in translation a remarkable five volume work on moral theology by Anton Koch, a theologian of the famous university at Tübingen. Koch was in the tradition of the German moralists Sailer, Hirscher and Linsenmann. Arthur Preuss (+1934), a Catholic layman, who had founded the *Fortnightly Review* in 1896, translated Koch's work with the title *A Handbook of Moral Theology*. In rather direct contrast with Slater, Koch-Preuss stated that, "Moral Theology is an independent science, with a well defined scope and object, and it is neither its sole nor its principal aim to train preachers or confessors."[18] With reference to casuistry: "This method (casuistical) may be defined as technical instruction in the application of the general principles of morality to special conditions and events, real or imaginary....Thus defined casuistry is a legitimate, nay an indispensable instrument for testing the morality of human acts....Employed prudently, i.e., with due regard for the principles of morality, the casuistic method is undoubtedly useful. However, it embraces only a narrow sector of life, and appraises human conduct mainly from the external juridical, and legal point of view, and hence easily leads either to excessive rigorism or undue laxity."[19]

The first volume deals most adequately with the history of moral theology and treats succinctly the sources of the science. Among the latter are revelation, reason, ecclesiastical tradition, the lives of the saints, and the teaching of Catholic moralists. With respect to the latter, "There is a clear cut distinction between an author's testimony to the teaching of the church, and his private opinions."[20] These five volumes contain many quotations from American legal sources, and at the end of each chapter there is appended a helpful list of suggested supplementary readings.

Between 1906 and 1917 a series of books called *The Casuist* were published by the Joseph F. Wagner Company of New York. These were "cases" in the traditional sense of the word, with especial application to the American scene. Four of the volumes bore no names of editor or authors, but the fifth volume was "prepared and edited" by another of those ardent laborers, John A. McHugh, O.P. (+1950). Later in the twenties McHugh, together with Charles J. Callan, O.P. (+1962), published a two-volume work in English entitled *Moral Theology*. Following traditional lines of development, it had the merit of giving concrete examples, or brief cases, within the text itself. In 1958 a new edition "revised and enlarged" by E. P. Farrell, O.P., was published by its original publisher, Joseph F. Wagner, Inc.

In more recent years two books have appeared in English which summarize the fundamentals of moral theology, either for the laity[21] or for those "engaged in parish work."[22] In these works both Father Connell and Father Adelman make references to various aspects of American law, especially when dealing with such matters as income taxes, bankruptcy, copyright and patent laws, prescription, etc.

All these "American" texts, both new and old, still serve the useful purpose of forming certain or at least probable opinions with respect to conscience obligation of various typically American moral problems, especially those arising from American laws and customs. It must be noted, however, that no American text has ever attempted a complete correlation of moral theology and pertinent aspects of American law. If I remember correctly, a project of this nature was once suggested as a task for the Catholic Theological Society of America, but to date nothing has come of it.

In 1964 none of these texts, to my knowledge, is in classroom use, except perhaps for supplementary reading. American seminaries have turned more and more toward European manuals like Noldin-Schmitt,[23] Zalba, Genicot-Salsman, Aertnys-Damen, Jorio, Merkelbach, Prümmer, and recently Bernard Häring. Each of these works inculcates its own method. As we will see, the whole question of method is still being ardently discussed, not only by contemporary European theologians, but also by Americans.

II. INFLUENCES ON THE DEVELOPMENT OF MORAL THEOLOGY IN THE UNITED STATES

1. *Catholic University of America*

Catholic University has played a significant role in the development of moral theology in this country because of the influence of outstanding professors like Thomas J. Bouquillon, Monsignor John A. Ryan, Francis J. Connell, C.SS.R., and John C. Ford, S.J.

Bouquillon's work we have already mentioned. His influence on John A. Ryan we have not. Ryan was sent to Catholic University in the fall of 1898 by Archbishop John Ireland in order to study moral theology. While there he audited courses in economics and sociology. His doctoral dissertation, not published until 1906, was entitled *A Living Wage: Its Ethical and Economic Aspects.* This was the beginning of Ryan's major interest in the field of moral theology—the attempt to make Catholic social principles pertinent to the contemporary world. He studied deeply in the field of economics, sociology, and political science.

Ryan's indebtedness to his graduate moral professor is clearly expressed in this quotation from Patrick Gearty's scholarly book, *The Economic Thought of Monsignor John A. Ryan.*

> But Ryan considered that his greatest fortune at the University was to be able to pursue his major subject, moral theology, under the Belgian-born Very Reverend Dr. Thomas Bouquillon, who, Ryan said, was "the most erudite man I have ever known." One of the things that Ryan prized most in being able to study under Bouquillon was his method or his approach to moral problems involving economics or sociology. In these matters Bouquillon insisted on a precise description of the social factors involved and was "not satisfied with merely general knowledge"; and he had a "passion for exactness, for accuracy, and for thoroughness." "My indebtedness to him," said Ryan, "because

of his devotion to and exemplification of this method is greater than I can describe."[24]

Ryan taught moral theology at the St. Paul Seminary from 1902 until 1915, and then, with the encouragement and assistance of Cardinal Gibbons, joined the faculty at the Catholic University. In his first year he taught political science, and the following year became a member of the theology faculty, where he taught moral theology and industrial relations until 1937.[25]

Ryan's writings were extensive as Gearty's complete bibliography shows.[26] Perhaps his most important book was *Distributive Justice,* published in 1916, and revised in 1927 and 1942. In it he gave a moral evaluation of "rent from land, interest on capital, profits from enterprise, and wages for labor."[27] Other important titles included *Social Reconstruction,* 1920; *The Church and Labor,* 1920 (Joseph Husslein, co-author); *The State and the Church,* 1922 (F. X. Moorhouse Millar, co-author); *A Better Economic Order,* 1935; *Social Doctrine in Action,* 1941, and *The Norm of Morality,* 1944.

One of Ryan's personal triumphs was the Bishops' Program of Social Reconstruction of 1919. This was the program Ryan had submitted to the National Catholic War Council. As Gearty says, "This group adopted the program as its own....Since this document bore the signatures of the executive committee representing the American Hierarchy, it came to be known as the 'Bishops' Program for Social Reconstruction,' or was referred to simply as 'The Bishops' Program.'" The program included the following points: legislation for a minimum wage and child labor, social insurance against unemployment, sickness, accidents, and old age, public housing projects, legal enforcements of the right of labor to organize, the control of monopolies, and curtailment of excess profits. Almost every aspect of Ryan's program is law today.

Ryan not only taught in the classroom, not only wrote a vast body of literature in his chosen field, but also became concretely involved in the efforts of the nation to improve its social and economic condition. Thus Gearty writes:

John A. Ryan's abiding interest in the case of the working people was by no means limited to his support of labor unions. He realized very well that it was the unorganized, unskilled workers who were most often the subject of harsh employment policies and the recipients of extremely low wages. It was largely for this reason that he became a strong advocate of minimum wage laws, for through these laws the legislative power of the state would be invoked to protect the basic right of unorganized workers who had no other means of protection.[28]

Ryan was a firm supporter of the New Deal because he thought it was prepared to put into practice the principles of social reform he had been advocating for years. He acted as an adviser to Roosevelt, and served on many committees established by the government under Roosevelt's administration. It is reported that when he was once asked whether the New Deal influenced his thinking he retorted somewhat irreverently, "Before the *New Deal was I am.*"

When he died in 1945 he received many tributes, including one from President Truman. His fellow moralist Father John C. Ford paid tribute to "a courageous moralist who for so many years championed the Catholic cause in public in the United States, not fearing to say unpopular things, and not fearing to make an occasional mistake. He always spoke the truth as he saw it, and he was always ready to admit, and profit by, the few errors into which he was thus honestly led."[29]

In 1940 Father Francis J. Connell, C.SS.R., went to Catholic University to join the graduate faculty, and immediately began to teach moral theology. He had had twenty-two years' experience teaching dogmatic theology, during the course of which he published a tract *De Sacramentis Ecclesiae.*[30] Between then and 1957 Father Connell became a national figure, not only because of his extensive writings in *The American Ecclesiastical Review* and elsewhere, but because of the many dissertations he directed on important and contemporary moral problems. During this period he wrote not only *Outlines of Moral Theology,* already mentioned, but also *Morals in Politics and Professions.*[31] Many of Father Connell's responses to moral questions were published in book form under the editorship of Eugene J. Weitzel, C.S.V. It is entitled *Father Connell Answers Moral Questions,* and was published in 1959 by The Catholic University of America Press.

Among the many dissertations that were published in the field of moral theology during his tenure the following are worthy of special note: M. Crowe, C.SS.R., *The Moral Obligation of Paying Just Taxes*, 1944; B. J. Cunningham, C.M., *The Morality of Organic Transplanation*, 1944; V.P. O'Brien, C.M., *The Measure of Responsibility in Persons Influenced by Emotion*, 1948; W. K. Glover, S.M., *Artificial Insemination Among Human Beings*, 1948; J. A. Dorszynski, *Catholic Teaching About the Morality of Falsehood*, 1948; L. J. Riley, *The History, Nature and Use of Epikeia in Moral Theology*, 1948; A. J. Falanga, C.M., *Charity the Form of the Virtues According to Saint Thomas*, 1948; J. A. Sullivan, *Catholic Teaching on the Morality of Euthanasia*, 1949; J. A. Costello, S.M., *Moral Obligation of Fraternal Correction*, 1949; W. J. King, *Moral Aspects of Dishonesty in Public Office*, 1949; J. F. Doherty, *Moral Problems of Interracial Marriage*, 1949; K. B. Moore, O.Carm., *The Moral Principles Governing the Sin of Detraction and an Application of These Principles to Specific Cases*, 1950; G. C. Bernard, C.S.C., *The Morality of Prizefighting*, 1952; J. D. Davis, *The Moral Obligation of Catholic Civil Judges*, 1953; M. F. McAuliffe, *Catholic Moral Teaching on the Nature and Object of Conjugal Love*, 1954; J. D. Brokhage, *Francis Patrick Kenrick's Opinion on Slavery*, 1955; N. L. Lohkamp, O.F.M., *The Morality of Hysterectomy Operations*, 1956; J. A. Prah, O.C.D., *Communication of Non-Catholics in Catholic Religious Rites*, 1956; A. F. Zimmerman, S.V.D., *"Overpopulation" – A Study of Papal Teaching on the Problem with Special Reference to Japan*, 1956; J. Shinners, *The Morality of Medical Experimentation on Living Human Subjects in the Light of Recent Papal Pronouncements*, 1958.

Father Connell's own writings, in which he dealt with the problems of average persons, clerical and lay, were very diversified. A bibliography of many works was prepared by Robert Sullivan, C.F.X., and appeared in *The American Ecclesiastical Review* for June, 1958. Freedom of conscience, evaluative cognition, medico-moral problems, problems involving co-operation, marriage and the family, dating habits among American youth, prize-fighting, privileged communication, modern warfare, and many other questions, some of major importance, others of interest perhaps only to the person who asked advice, all received careful and succinct treatment in a style very much valued for its clarity and exactness. We will see the content of these various opinions later.

In September, 1958, following Father Connell's retirement, Father

John C. Ford, S.J., joined the faculty of the School of Sacred Theology, thereby assuring Catholic University's continued prominence in the field of moral theology. From the New England Province of the Society of Jesus, Father Ford had enjoyed many years of teaching experience in moral theology, not only at the Gregorian University, but also at Weston College, and other theologates in this country. Starting in 1941 Father Ford became a familiar contributor to *Theological Studies,* presenting not only the results of his own scholarly research, but also, in the feature "Current Theology," which he many times wrote, giving perceptive and critical evaluations of the writings of others. Deeply interested in depth psychology, a careful expositor of the idea of evaluative cognition, a recognized authority on alcoholism, devoted to the study of the theology of marriage, and a noted canonist, Father Ford has recently won wide acclaim for the two-volume *Contemporary Moral Theology,* which he co-authored with the late and beloved Gerald Kelly, S.J.[32]

2. Periodical Literature

There seems to be little reason for repeating the names and data of the various rather well-known American theological periodicals.[33] Each has made many notable contributions, as we will see later. Special mention should be given *Theological Studies* because of the feature "Current Theology: Notes on Moral Theology." Once, and often twice a year, this feature has reviewed and evaluated books and articles, published both here and abroad, in the field of moral theology. These critical reflections by eminent Jesuit moralists have contributed immensely to theological discussion, and have made an impact abroad. Sometimes as long as fifty pages, they now constitute a veritable dossier of moral-theological activity throughout the world for the years 1940–1964. The names of the theologians who wrote this outstanding feature are enough to guarantee its value: John C. Ford, S.J.;[34] Gerald Kelly, S.J.;[35] John R. Connery, S.J.;[36] Joseph J. Farraher, S.J.;[37] and John J. Lynch, S.J.[38]

Of course other important articles on moral theology appeared in *Theological Studies,* but these will be discussed later together with the more important articles in the other American theological periodicals.

3. The Catholic Encyclopedia

The *Catholic Encyclopedia* devoted considerable space to moral theology,[39] including a very useful and reflective history of the subject by Augustine Lehmkuhl, S.J.,[40] and short biographies of famous moralists. Rather famous moralists also wrote for the *Catholic Encyclopedia,* including Lehmkuhl himself,[41] Arthur Vermeersch, S.J.;[42] John A. Ryan;[43] and Thomas Slater, S.J.[44]

We have already seen the differences of opinion between Slater and Koch-Preuss on the nature and method of presenting moral theology. Lemhkuhl was well aware of the contemporary criticisms of casuistry as a method, and expressed his own point of view in the *Catholic Encyclopedia* as follows:

> The reformers assert that the casuistical method has choked every other and that it must give place to a more scientific systematic treatment. It is evident that a merely casuistical treatment does not come up to the demands of moral theology, and as a matter of fact, during the last decades the speculative element was more and more insisted on even in works chiefly casuistic. Whether the one or the other element should prevail, must be determined according to the proximate aim which the work intends to satisfy. If there is question of a purely scientific explanation of moral theology... casuistry then serves only to illustrate the theoretical explanations. But if there is a question of a manual which is intended for the practical needs of a pastor and confessor and for their education, then the solid scientific portion of general moral-theological questions must be supplemented by an extensive casuistry. Nay, when time and leisure are wanting to add ample theoretical explanation to an extensive casuistical drill, we should not criticize him who under these circumstances insists on the latter at the expense of the former; it is the more necessary in actual practice.[45]

4. The Catholic Theological Society of America

The CTSA is today an integral part of the American theological scene. From its annual meetings have come not only papers of scholarly quality, later published in the *Proceedings,* but also the opportunity for discussion and dialogue among priests actively engaged in the work of theology. The Society has helped take the theologian out of his isolation, and brought him into contact with many other minds sharing the same interests and problems. There can be no question of the benefit it has been to the development of moral theology in this country.

The founding of the CTSA is linked to the Catholic University, and *The American Ecclesiastical Review,* and had for its first president the Catholic University moralist, Francis J. Connell, C.SS.R. The story of its founding is told by Monsignor Joseph C. Fenton:

> The decision which really resulted in the formation of this Society was made, however, in the course of a discussion that took place immediately after a meeting of the Board of Editors of *The American Ecclesiastical Review.* One night in October, 1945, The Rev. Dr. Eugene M. Burke, C.S.P., insisted upon the need of such a society. The only other members of the Board then present in the editorial office, the Rev. Dr. Edmund D. Benard and the Rev. Dr. Joseph C. Fenton, both priests of the Diocese of Springfield, and both like Dr. Burke, members of the faculty of Sacred Theology at the Catholic University of America, agreed wholeheartedly with their confrere. All three were convinced that the Rev. Dr. Francis J. Connell, C.SS.R., also a member of the Catholic University theological faculty, was particularly well fitted to take the lead in preparing the formation of an American Catholic theological association.[46]

From the beginning the Society has published its annual *Proceedings,* the size of which has grown with its membership. Drawing from all elements of the theological community in the United States, the pages of the *Proceedings* contain the following items of interest to the moral theologian: F. J. Connell, C.SS.R., "The Catholic Doctrine on the Ends of Marriage" (1946), 34–45; T. O. Martin,

"Problems in the Morality of Warfare" (1947), 47–71; F. J. Connell, C.SS.R, "Governmental Repression of Heresy" (1948), 26–101; T. W. Smiddy, "Current Medico-Moral Problems" (1950), 157–158; J. C. Ford, S.J., "The New Psychology, Moral Responsibility and Alcoholism" (1950), 64–149; J. E. Murphy, "Detraction in Public Life" (1953), 131–142; J. A. Duhamel, S.J., and J. Hayden, O.S.B., "Theological and Psychiatric Aspects of Habitual Sin" (1956), 130–167; A. Carr. O.F.M. Conv., "The Morality of Situation Ethics" (1957), 75–102; J. F. Cronin, S.S., and F. W. Carney, "The Morality of Right to Work Laws" (1957), 193–216; H. C. Gardiner, S.J., "Moral Principles for Discerning the Obscene" (1954), 126–139; P. Bussard, O. Bennett, O.F.M., and J. R. Connery, S.J., "The Role of Prudence in the Right to Censor in Literature and Arts" (1958), 149–177; F. J. Gilligan, "Moral Aspects of Segregation in Education" (1958), 51–64; J. J. Lynch, S.J., "Moral Aspects of Pharmaceutical Fertility Control" (1958), 127–138; A. F. Zimmerman, S.V.D., "Morality and the Problem of Overpopulation" (1959), 5–27; J. L. Thomas, S.J., "Contemporary Protestant Attitudes on Contraception" (1960), 51–62; A. H. Hayes and D. Lowery, C.SS.R., "Moral Problems in Business Practice" (1961), 121–146; G. Kelly, S.J., "Contraception and the Natural Law" (1963), 25–46; J. J. Lynch, S.J., "Changing Pastoral Emphases on the Practice of Periodic Continence" (1963), 107–116; G. Rooney and P. O'Brien, C.M., "The Right of Workers to Share in Ownership, Management, and Profits" (1963), 151–156.

Notes

1. Philadelphia, Vol 1, 1841; vol. 2, 1842; vol. 3, 1843; also Malines, Belgium, 1860. Kenrick became Archbishop of Baltimore in 1851, and died in 1863.

2. Koch-Preuss, *Handbook of Moral Theology,* B. Herder, 1918–1924, 1. 71.

3. For example he quotes Kent's *Commentaries,* the laws of Delaware, Pennsylvania, Maryland, Illinois, Ohio, Massachusetts, New York, Alabama, and others.

4. "Id quaeri potest utrum heri possint servos retinere, quum eorum

majores injuria videantur ex Africa huc traducti. Nobis affirmandum videtur: nam tituli vitium longissimi temporis lapsu sanatum habendum est, quum societatis conditio alias incerta semper foret, cum gravissimo turbarum periculo." 1. no. 40; see Brokhage, J. D., *Francis Patrick Kenrick's Opinion on Slavery* (Catholic University dissertation), 1955.

5. "He was the first to give a methodical exposition of the views of St. Alphonsus regarding the vexed question of equiprobabilism." *Catholic Encyclopedia,* VIII, 690.

6. The Ecclesiastical law he incorporated was that of the Second Baltimore Council.

7. "...quae ad res nostras pertinent maximam partem desumpsi ex Actis et Decretis Concilii Plen. Balt. II, et ex Theologiae Morali, quam bonae et clarae memoriae Kenrick conscripsit, difficiliori et aliquoties obscuriori stylo ejus aliquantulum immutato." Konings, *Theologiae Moralis S. Alphonsi Compendium,* "Monitum Necessario Legendum."

8. "In plurimis *Compendium Theologiae Moralis* P. Gury, cujus praeclarissima methodus vix non omnibus theologiae moralis tum Professoribus, tum alumnis probatur, et quam secutus sum, propemodum exscripsi, illud prae caeteris conatus, ut ad Alphonsianam doctrinam, quam integerrime, illud exigerem." *Ibid.,* "Monitum."

9. De Meulemeester, Collet, and Henze, *Bibliographie Général des Ecrivains Redemptorists,* Deuxième Partie, Louvain, 1935, under "Konings."

10. Sabetti, *Compendium Theologiae Moralis A Joanne Petro Gury S.J. conscriptum et ab Antonio Ballerini, ejusdem Societatis, adnotationibus auctum.*

11. 29th ed.: "Colligis ex dictis, 1. non posse confessarium absolute loquendo et subpoena denegandae absolutionis indiscriminatim urgere obligationem solvendi tributa ista in futurum, quamvis adhortari debeat fideles, ut ea diligenter solvant et ab omni eorum defraudatione abstineant." *Ibid.,* n. 416.

12. To the question, "An cessio bonorum in perpetuum excuset a restitutione facienda?", the response is given: "Probabilis est sententia affirmativa. Nam lex nunc vigens lataque I Julii 1898 pro omnibus Statibus et Territoriis nostris manifesta hanc interpretationem patitur." *Ibid.,* n. 463.

13. P. H. Ahern, *The Catholic University of America – 1887–1896 – The Rectorship of John J. Keane* (Washington, D. C.: The Catholic University of America Press, 1948), p. 22.

14. H. Hurter, *Nomenclator Litterarius,* V. 2057.

15. Bouquillon. "Caeteri actus dicuntur simpliciter morales, in oppositione ad theologales. In explicanda autem eorum natura cum regulis quibus reguntur, alii attendunt diversam speciem rectitudinis, seu bonitatis quae ipsis inest, et materiam dividunt secundum virtutes cardinales; alii sequuntur

ordinem praeceptorum Decalogi et Ecclesiae; alii considerant hominem juxta triplicem suum characterem, ut est ens individuum, ut est ens religiousum et ut est ens sociale. Primus distributionis modus, qui est S. Thomae et aliorum plurimorum, in Secunda secundae, q. 47–170, favet expositioni rerum scientificae, ac practice multum prodest concionatori; alter distributionis modus, quem secuti sunt tum antiqui tractatores, tum recentiores moralistae multi, inter quos S. Alphonsus, valde convenire videtur catechistis et confessariis, licet vix permittat sufficientem explicationem virtutum; tertius distributionis modus, apud recentiores non raro usurpatus, nobis praeferendus videtur, quia planior est et ordini naturali amoris atque ordini supernaturali charitatis respondet; caeterum duorum aliorum commoda simul in se conjungit." *Theologia Moralis,* 15–16.

16. Slater-Martin, *A Manual of Moral Theology,* vol. 1, 447–448.

17. Ibid., vol. 1, 5–6.

18. Koch-Preuss, *Handbook of Moral Theology,* vol. 1, 2–3.

19. Ibid., vol. 1, 37–38.

20. Ibid., vol. 1, 33.

21. F. J. Connell, C.SS.R., *Outlines of Moral Theology,* Bruce, 1953.

22. H. Jone, O.F.M.Cap., Englished and Adapted to the Code and Customs of the United States of America by U. Adelman, O.F.M.Cap., *Moral Theology,* Newman, 1953.

23. "The author who undoubtedly has the greatest influence in the construction of a course of study in this subject (Moral Theology) is H. Noldin, whose manual is entitled, *Summa Theologiae Moralis,* formerly revised by A. Schmitt, and the newest editions are brought up to date by G. Heinzel." *Seminary Newsletter, The National Catholic Education Association* (Sept. 1964), volume 6, n. 1, 13.

24. The Catholic University of America Press, 1953, p. 23.

25. Ibid., 35.

26. Ibid., 316–321.

27. Ibid., 35 f.

28. Ibid., 33 f.

29. *Theological Studies,* VI (1945), 524.

30. Apud Carolum Beyaert, Bruges, et Fridericum Pustet, New York, 1933.

31. Newman Press, 1946.

32. Volume 1, 1960; volume 2, 1963.

33. See G. W. Shea, "Seventy-Five Years of Dogmatic Theology in America," *AER,* CLI (1964)165.

34. II (1941) 525 ff.; VI (1945) 524 ff.

35. VIII (1947) 97 ff.; IX (1948) 85 ff.; X (1949) 67 ff.; XII (1951) 52 ff.;

XIII (1952) 59 ff.; XIV (1953) 31 ff.; XXIV (1963) 626 ff. (Note: Kelly and Ford together did the "Current Theology" XV (1954) 52 ff.)

36. XV (1954) 594 ff.; XVI (1955) 558 ff.; XVII (1956) 549 ff.; XVIII (1957) 560 ff.; XIX (1958) 533 ff.; XX (1959) 590 ff.

37. XVI (1955) 233 ff.; XXI (1960) 581 ff.; XXII (1961) 610 ff.; XXIV (1963) 53 ff.

38. XVII (1956) 167 ff.; XVIII (1957) 216 ff.; XIX (1958) 165 ff.; XX (1959) 231 ff.; XXI (1960) 221 ff.; XXIII (1962) 233 ff.; XXIV (1963) 213 ff.; XXV (1964) 232 ff.

39. A detailed outline with references to articles in the *Encyclopedia* is given in volume XVI, pp. 924–927.

40. XIV, 611.

41. "Theology, Moral, History of"; "Divorce."

42. "Cloister," "Congo," "Interest," "Modernism," "Novice," "Nun," "Obedience," "Religious," "Poverty," "Religious Life," "Postulant," "Virginity," and "Vows," among others.

43. "Collectivism," "Communism," "Compensation," "Conciliation," "The Family," "Individualism," "Insanity," "Labour (sic) and Labour Relations," "Legislation," "Labor Unions," "Marriage," "Monopoly," "Population Theories," "Poverty and Pauperism," *"Rerum Novarum,"* "Social Communities."

44. "Contracts," "Debts," "Fraud," "Gambling," "Honor," "Justice," "Divine Law, Moral Aspects of," "Lottery," "Lying," "Mental Reservations," "Obligation," "Reparation," "Restitution," "Speculation," "Sunday," "Synderesis."

45. *Catholic Encyclopedia,* XIV, 611. b.

46. *Proceedings of the First Annual Meeting of the Catholic Theological Society,* 1946.

2. Moral Theology in the United States: An Analysis of the Last Twenty Years (1965–1985)

Charles E. Curran

This chapter first appeared in Charles E. Curran, *Toward an American Catholic Moral Theology* (Notre Dame, Ind.: University of Notre Dame Press, 1987).

To analyze the development of moral theology in the United States in the twenty years since the end of the Second Vatican Council is no simple task. To facilitate such a study this chapter will consider the contexts of Catholic moral theology in the United States and will give a brief overview of its content. The context within which moral theology is done obviously has a great influence on the approach and the very content of moral theology. There are four important contexts of moral theology in the United States that help to explain what has happened in the last twenty years—the ecclesial, the societal, the ecumenical, and the academic.

I. The Contexts of Moral Theology

Ecclesial Context

Since moral theology like all theology is in the service of the church, it is only natural that what happens in the life of the church will have a significant impact on moral theology. The Second Vatican Council and its aftermath have had a great influence on Catholic moral theology throughout the world and in the United States.

In general, moral theology in the United States was unaware of the renewal of moral theology that was brought to a head by the Second Vatican Council. There were no leading figures in moral theology in the United States at the time who were really calling for a change in the basic orientation and method of the discipline. The primary purpose in teaching moral theology was to train confessors for the sacrament of penance, especially in terms of the role of judge, and the method of the manuals of moral theology was generally followed.

The renewal of moral theology that began in Europe and was encouraged by Vatican II called for both a new orientation and a somewhat different methodology. Moral theology could no longer view its function primarily as training priests to be confessors in the sacrament of penance. Within the context of this narrow orientation moral theology was basically interested in determining what was sinful and the degree of sinfulness involved in particular acts. The renewal of moral theology called for a life-oriented moral theology that reflects on the totality of the Christian life, including the gospel call to perfection and holiness. The newer methodological approach above all stressed the important role of the scriptures, the need to overcome the gulf between faith and daily life, as well as between the supernatural and the natural, the importance of historicity, and the necessity for moral theology to be in dialogue with other theological disciplines.

One of the first and most significant consequences of the renewal in moral theology was the fact that the leading moral theologians in the United States before the council were not prepared to deal well with the newer developments in orientation and methodology. As a result the leadership in post-Vatican II moral theology in the United States passed to a new group of younger theologians who were just beginning to teach moral theology in the 1960s. Throughout the period after the council there were no real leaders in Catholic moral theology who had been in the field for a great number of years. The generation teaching moral theology before the council generally found it very difficult to adapt to the changes brought about by the renewal, and many of them withdrew from the field of moral theology.

Moral theology in the United States could not avoid the practical issues which confronted the church in this period. The North American penchant for dealing with practical problems also influenced moral theology in this country. The most significant issue in the early post-Vatican II period was that of contraception for married couples.

At the time a number of revisionist theologians were calling for a change in the teaching on artificial contraception, and a great many disagreed with the conclusions of the 1968 encyclical *Humanae vitae* condemning this practice. The revisionist theologians appealed to newer insights found in Vatican II and in the renewal of moral theology to support their position. Historical consciousness was a very important concept for revisionist theologians. It is fair to say that in general the United States made little or no contribution to the theology of Vatican II except in the area of religious liberty. John Courtney Murray's work had been a major, if not the major, influence on the new teaching on religious freedom proposed at Vatican II. The American Jesuit appealed above all to historical consciousness to argue for the need to change the older condemnation of religious liberty and to justify the fact that such change could be understood in terms of a true development.[1] In the same way many moral theologians maintained that changed circumstances and changing knowledge in the biological and medical area called for a change in the teaching on artificial contraception. Revisionist theologians also appealed to the renewal of moral theology to put greater stress on the person and the subject rather than on human nature. Personalism and historical consciousness called for a change in the old understanding of natural law, especially as applied to artificial contraception and other issues of sexuality.[2]

After *Humanae vitae* the moral question of artificial contraception became intimately involved with the ecclesiological issue of the teaching role of the hierarchical magisterium and the proper response of the faithful. In theory and practice revisionist Catholic theologians have accepted the possibility of responsible dissent from authoritative, authentic, noninfallible hierarchical teaching. Again the revisionists appealed to a changing understanding of the church proposed in Vatican II to justify the possibility of dissent. The church is the whole people of God. An older absolute division between the *ecclesia docens* and the *ecclesia discens* can no longer be accepted. The noninfallible teaching of the hierarchical magisterium on specific moral issues cannot claim to have absolute certitude. One can speak of a presumption in favor of this teaching, but the presumption always cedes to the truth. Again the appeal to historical consciousness calls for a hermeneutic, or interpretation, of past formulations of hierarchical teaching.

However, a minority of moral theologians defended the teaching of *Humanae vitae* and strongly opposed at least in practice the possibility of dissent from such teaching. Germain Grisez, who was trained in philosophy, published in 1964 a defense of the official teaching on contraception that in its own way involved a revision of the accepted Catholic arguments against artificial contraception.[3] Grisez rejects the argument from a conventional natural law approach that contraception is intrinsically immoral because by it one engaging in intercourse prevents the act from attaining its natural end. The natural teleology of human functions does not necessarily require absolute moral respect.[4] Grisez also denies the validity of the phenomenological argument against artificial contraception based on sexual intercourse as an experience of love as a total giving because it is connected with a very questionable philosophical theory of human beings and of the marital society.[5] In opposition to conventional natural law theory and situationism Grisez develops his own theory of practical principles based on the moral obligation never to go against essential or basic human goods. In subsequent years Grisez has further elaborated his fundamental theory. Grisez also holds that the teaching condemning artificial contraception is infallibly proposed by the ordinary magisterium.[6]

The lively debate sparked by *Humanae vitae* in 1968 heavily influenced the course of moral theology in the United States and in the world. The two questions of the existence of absolute norms and the proper response to the noninfallible hierarchical church teaching have dominated the concerns of moral theology since that time.

There can be no doubt that a strong division exists among United States theologians in general and moral theologians in particular on these two issues that are very closely intertwined. Most Catholic theologians in the United States belonged to the Catholic Theological Society of America that came into existence in 1946. Until the late 1960s this was a clerical organization consisting mostly of seminary professors. However, the complexion of the membership began to change in the late 60s, and many of the older members no longer attended the meetings. In 1955 the first national meeting of the Society of Catholic College Teachers of Sacred Doctrine was held with the purpose of strengthening the teaching of theology in Catholic colleges. Later this society changed its name to the College Theology Society and became ecumenical, but it still remains a predominately Catholic group.[7]

The vast majority of the membership of these two academic societies became generally associated in the 70s with the revisionist and progressive trends in Catholic theology, although obviously all the members did not accept these positions. Perhaps the most publicized illustration of this development was the publication in 1977 of *Human Sexuality: New Directions in American Catholic Thought.*[8] This volume was actually the report of a committee established by the Board of Directors of the Catholic Theological Society of America in 1972. The committee report like all other previous reports was received by the Board of Directors and never actually approved by the board or by the membership at large. *Human Sexuality* evoked a significant debate, thus fulfilling one of its intended purposes. The methodological approach and the solution of particular problems proposed in the book were criticized by many revisionists. Although the majority of contributing moral theologians take some revisionist positions, there are differences and debates among them.

To counteract this growing tendency among Roman Catholic theologians and to defend the need for adherence to the hierarchical magisterium a number of more conservative Catholic scholars founded the Fellowship of Catholic Scholars in 1977. Unfortunately the relationships between the two different approaches and the two different groups have not always been cordial and dialogical. These tensions and divisions continue to mark Catholic theology and especially Catholic moral theology in the United States today. In the judgment of some these tensions are often exacerbated by ultraconservative groups and newspapers.[9] However, all concerned should strive for a greater openness to dialogue and mutual respect.

The two questions posed in the wake of the discussion over artificial contraception have continued to be two of the most important concerns addressed by Catholic moral theology in the United States. This issue of the existence and grounding of specific concrete norms has continued to be debated at great length. The revisionist position is often characterized by a proportionalist theory that argues that premoral evil can be done for proportionate reasons.[10] Germain Grisez has tended to be the leading figure in the position upholding the fact that human responsibility means that human beings can never directly go against a basic human good. Such an understanding of responsibility definitely grounds some specific absolute moral norms. In addition, both sides have continued to debate the question of the proper response due by theologians and by the faithful at large to the noninfallible teaching of the hierarchical magisterium. Here revisionist theologians have had support from a good number of ecclesiologists who have generally supported the right to dissent in certain circumstances.

The fact that there exist two generic positions called, for lack of better terms, the conservative and the revisionist, should not hide the fact that there are also many differences within these approaches. In the future it will be beneficial for all concerned to recognize these rather significant differences within each group. Such a recognition will avoid overly simplistic characterizations and should facilitate dialogue and criticism not only between the two groups but also within the two general positions.

Not only the life of the universal church but also the life of the local church has affected moral theology in the United States. Perhaps the most distinctive aspect of this local church influence has been the recent involvement of the American Catholic bishops in social issues especially through their two pastoral letters on peace and the economy. American theologians had been giving some attention to these areas, but the leadership taken by the bishops has focused attention on both issues. As a result, Catholic moral theologians have devoted more attention to these two very significant questions and to the whole area of social ethics.

Societal Context

A second important context for moral theology is the societal influence. A number of factors in the United States in the last twenty years have emphasized the importance of ethics. In the 1960s the struggle against poverty, racial discrimination, and war raised the consciousness of the society at large to the importance of ethics. The shock of Watergate in the 1970s only increased the importance of ethical considerations. Questions of law, conscience, and public policy have been discussed at great length. Concerns about population growth, energy resources, especially nuclear energy, ecology, and the role of women in society have all contributed to the heightened awareness of the need for ethics.

Within this atmosphere so conducive to the role of ethics a number of significant developments have occurred. Perhaps the most important from the academic perspective has been the interest of philosophy in substantive ethical questions. Until recently this country's philosophical ethics was dominated by the linguistic analysis approach and primarily interested in metaethical questions. But now philosophical journals and books are dealing with all the many ethical questions facing society. Contemporary philosophical work has stimulated moral theology and become an important dialogue partner with moral theology.

Another result of the widespread interest in ethics has been the establishment of different commissions by the government to study problems especially in the area of recent developments in bioethics. The best known and most productive commission is "The President's Commission for the Study of Ethical Problems in Medicine and Biomedical and Behavioral Research," which was active from January 1980 to March 31, 1983. The commission, whose power was only advisory, produced ten reports, five appendix volumes, and a guidebook for institutional review boards. The reports dealt with such topics as defining death, deciding to forego life-sustaining treatment, making health-care decisions, protecting human subjects, screening and counseling for genetic choices, securing access to health care, splicing life, and whistle-blowing in biomedical research.[11]

Support for ethical studies has come not only from the government but also from private-sector funding. Think-tanks and research institutions have sprung up to study and assess the ethical aspects of the many different questions facing society. Sometimes theologians, philosophers, and ethicists are part of larger interdisciplinary groups, whereas at other times the institutes tend to be primarily composed of ethicists. This widespread interest in ethics with the resulting growth in institutional support for ethical concerns is a great help to ethics in general, but in my judgment the contribution to moral theology is somewhat ambivalent.

Moral theology and Christian ethics reflect on the moral life in the light of the Christian and Catholic self-understandings. The United States, however, is a pluralistic country in which many people do not share these Christian beliefs. Questions that arise from these differences have both theoretical and practical dimensions. From the theoretical perspective the question concerns whether there exists one moral order which is the same for Christians and for all others or whether there is a unique morality for Christians and another morality for non-Christians. The question has often been addressed in this country in terms of the distinctiveness of Christian ethics and Christian morality. On the basis of both contemporary and traditional Catholic theological insights I maintain there is only one moral order and that the specific content of Christian morality does not differ from what human morality calls for. However, the fact that the explicit material content of Christian morality is *per se* available to all human beings does not mean that moral theology, or Christian ethics, and philosophical ethics are the same. Moral theology explicitly reflects on the Christian life and the one human moral order in the light of explicitly Christian realities.[12]

The recognition that the specific moral content is the same, but that moral theology and philosophical ethics are not the same because of their different sources, should guide reaction to what is often happening in the United States today. The American Catholic bishops have recognized in their pastoral letters that they are addressing two different audiences— their fellow believers in the church and the broader public that does not necessarily share their beliefs. In addressing the public at large the pastoral letters prescind from the appeal to specifically Christian sources.[13] Such an approach is certainly legitimate and appropriate.

There exists, however, a danger in some institutes and commissions dealing with public policy. Here the tendency is often to prescind from any Christian sources and to discuss issues in a purely philosophical manner. There is a very apparent problem here for the discipline of moral theology as such. Within such institutes and commissions often there is no room for Christian ethics or Jewish ethics or Muslim ethics. As a result the discipline of moral theology is not helped by such commissions and institutes. At times I can understand why public commissions especially should prescind from religious differences; but, on the other hand, pluralism does not always require that everything should be reduced to the least common denominator. Perhaps even here efforts could be made to show how different religious perceptions can agree but also even disagree on particular issues facing society. The problem is very difficult, but it should be noted that the broad support for ethical institutes and commissions has not necessarily had a positive effect on the development of the discipline of moral theology as such.

The societal context has also brought to the fore the differences between the moral order and the legal order. Catholic moral theology as illustrated in the approach of Thomas Aquinas has always distinguished between the two orders. The emergence of constitutional government, especially as it appeared in the United States with the emphasis given to the freedom of the citizen, has stressed even more the differences between the moral order and the legal order. In my judgment the best approach to this question in theory is found in the principles enshrined in Vatican II's Declaration on Religious Freedom. This document recognizes that the freedom of individuals should be respected as far as possible and curtailed only when and insofar as necessary. Public order with its threefold aspect of justice, peace, and public morality is the criterion that justifies the proper intervention of the state. In addition, laws must be just and enforceable, and also the feasibility of passing such legislation is most significant in supporting possible laws. Unfortunately, it seems that many Catholics in the United States do not consciously realize the practical scope of the difference between the two orders.

In practice, discussions about law and morality have quite frequently occurred in the United States. In the last three presidential elections the question of abortion law has come to the fore in the light of the liberal law now existing in this country. In my judgment the criteria proposed above can justify a more strict law or even the existing law depending on whether one gives more importance to the criterion stressing justice and the need to protect the rights of the innocent or the criteria giving the benefit of the doubt to the freedom of individuals and invoking feasibility. Despite some significant statements to the contrary there is no basis for saying that there is only one Catholic position on the legal aspects of abortion in this country.

The role of the United States in the contemporary world has become, especially since the Vietnam era, an important object of discussion and criticism within the society at large. Without a doubt the two most significant questions today involve peace and economy. Both these issues have important domestic and international aspects, especially in terms of relationships with the third world and with the nations of the southern hemisphere. Catholic ethicists in dialogue with many others of differing backgrounds have been discussing the issues of war and peace. Some Catholic moralists have used the just-war principles in an effort to limit the possible use of nuclear weapons and the arms race. Some have become nuclear pacifists, while a comparatively small but growing and determined group have embraced a total pacifism.[14] As mentioned earlier, the recent pastoral letter of the United States bishops has given a very significant impulse for further study in this area. Catholic moral theologians have given less sustained attention to the issues of economics and the relationship of the United States to the world economic order. Here the American bishops have provided important leadership. The process leading to a pastoral letter on the economy has stimulated much study in this area. Human rights has been an important area of concern both domestically and internationally, and Catholic scholars have been addressing this issue out of the context of the developing Catholic tradition.[15]

The role of women in society and feminism have become very significant issues in the United States. Some feminists have declared that Christianity is opposed to feminism and have moved beyond Christianity. Christian feminists strive to show that feminism and Christianity are compatible. Christian feminist ethics is already emerging as a special approach in Christian ethics.[16] There is a growing number of women writing today in the area of moral theology. Feminism is much more than merely a women's issue, but the ever-increasing number of well-trained women theologians will insure that the feminist approach receives its proper place in ethics. Catholic feminists often feel that the institutional church is not open and sympathetic. In practice I think that the most crucial, and unfortunately divisive, issue facing the Catholic Church in the United States is the role of women in church and society. The rightful role and function of women in society and the church is not simply a women's issue but truly a human issue involving human rights and the good of humanity in general, and a Christian issue concerning the community of equal disciples of Jesus.

Ecumenical Context

A third important context for moral theology in the United States is the ecumenical context. This is an entirely new phenomenon that has only emerged in the last twenty years but is very characteristic of the contemporary discipline of moral theology. This ecumenical aspect is now present in such a way that it cannot be dismissed as merely a passing fad.

There are various ways in which the ecumenical emphasis has been institutionalized. There is no society of Catholic moral theologians in the United States. Moral theologians before 1965 belonged almost exclusively to the Catholic Theological Society of America and to the College Theology Society, as it is now called. The Society of Christian Ethics, as it is now called, was founded in 1959 primarily by Protestant seminary professors of Christian social ethics. This society itself has grown considerably from 117 members in 1960–61 to 664 in 1983. In its earliest years the society, which meets once a year and now publishes an annual, was predominantly male, white, and Protestant. Since then there has been a marked increase in the number of female, black, and Roman Catholic members. According to the recently published history of the society, beginning with the year 1965 Roman Catholics began joining the society at the rate of about five or six per year through the 60s. The first Roman Catholic became president of the society in 1971. By 1983 145 Catholics belonged. The programs and the new history of the society bear out the ecumenical aspect of the group.[17]

There are other significant ways in which the ecumenical aspect of moral theology has been institutionalized. Some Catholic moral theologians now teach in denominational, private, and state institutions. A good number of somewhat younger Catholic moral theologians have been trained in and received their degrees from Protestant or independent institutions. The literature in moral theology in the last few years in the United States well illustrates the ecumenical dimension of the discipline. With encouragement from the Society of Christian Ethics and others the *Journal of Religious Ethics* began publishing in 1973 as an independent, ecumenical, academic enterprise dealing with all aspects of religious ethics. The ecumenical character of moral theology is nowhere better illustrated than in the literature reviewed in the "Notes on Moral Theology" that have regularly appeared at least once a year in *Theological Studies.* "Notes on Moral Theology" critically reviews the most important articles that have appeared in the preceding year. Before 1965 the literature reviewed was almost totally Roman Catholic, but now the "Notes" are truly ecumenical without losing their Catholic bases. The contemporary authority, success, and importance of these

"Notes" is due to the incisive and penetrating work of Richard A. McCormick, who composed them for nineteen years before passing on the role to others in 1984.

There can be no doubt that the ecumenical aspect has had an impact on Catholic moral theology in the United States, but this has also been a two-way influence, with Catholic ethics also affecting Protestant ethics. One must also remember that the ecumenical dialogue occurs as part of a larger context within which Catholic moral theology is being renewed.

There has been a growing rapprochement between Protestant and Roman Catholic ethics. James M. Gustafson, a University Professor at the University of Chicago and a most respected analyst of Christian ethics, has aided this growing rapprochement in his study of these developments. In the area of practical moral reason Protestantism has been consciously moving away from a "wasteland of relativism," whereas Roman Catholics coming from the opposite pole have been searching for responsible openness. To strengthen the discipline Protestantism has been seeking some philosophical base to overcoming the seeming vagaries of historicism and existentialism, whereas Roman Catholics have been revising natural law to overcome its excessive rigidity. From a theological viewpoint Christological concerns and a striving to overcome an extrinsic understanding of nature and grace within the Catholic tradition have brought the two approaches closer together.[18]

Gustafson's analysis is quite accurate, but there is one important aspect missing in his book which the Chicago professor himself has recognized in his study. Gustafson considers only the revisionist moral theologians. The more conservative moral theologians are not mentioned or discussed. As a general rule it is true that the ecumenical aspect is more pronounced among revisionist Catholics than among the more conservative Catholic moral theologians.

However, this general statement must be properly nuanced. A number of more conservative Catholic moral theologians frequently appeal to more conservative Protestants such as Paul Ramsey. Ramsey's positions in medical ethics have often echoed the conclusions of conservative Catholic positions. The *Linacre Quarterly* is the official journal of the National Federation of Catholic Physicians' Guilds, which every year presents its Linacre Quarterly Award for the best article that appeared in the journal in the previous year. The 1978 award was presented to Paul Ramsey for his article "Euthanasia and Dying Well Enough" that appeared in the February 1977 issue.[19] It is interesting to note that Ramsey and two other somewhat conservative religious ethicists are members of the editorial advisory board of this journal, but there are no longer any Catholic revisionist moral theologians on the board.

There can be no doubt that especially in areas of sexual and medical ethics Ramsey's conclusions are generally congenial to more conservative Roman Catholics. However, all should recognize that from a methodological viewpoint a great difference exists between Ramsey's approach and traditional Catholic emphases. Ramsey adopts a deontological methodology based on faithful, covenant love. The Thomistic tradition has an entirely different methodological approach with its emphasis on the ultimate end of human beings and the good. The retired Princeton University professor is strongly opposed to any teleology. It is true that Ramsey has often dealt favorably with the Catholic tradition in areas such as just war and medical ethics, especially the care for the dying. In addition Ramsey has at times spoken favorably about Catholic natural law methodology. However, Ramsey has never really accepted the Catholic concept of natural law. From a theological perspective Ramsey's heavy emphasis on *agape* and his unwillingness to accept the Catholic concept of mediation have always made it somewhat difficult for him to ground theologically an understanding of natural law. From a philosophical viewpoint, even when Ramsey was speaking favorably of Jacques Maritain's approach to natural law, the American Methodist never really accepted the ontological aspect of natural law proposed by the French Thomist. While it is true that Ramsey has dealt extensively with traditional Catholic issues such as just war and ordinary-extraordinary means to preserve life, his treatment of these issues is from his own *agape*-based deontological methodology. Although Ramsey's conclusions are often in agreement with the teachings of the hierarchical magisterium, his methodology considerably differs from traditional Catholic approaches.[20]

In my view the ecumenical dialogue shows the primary differences between Roman Catholic and Protestant ethicists to center on the characteristic Catholic acceptance of mediation. Mediation is distinctive of Catholic theology and is manifested in all aspects of that theology. The revelation of God is mediated through scripture and tradition. The word and work of God are mediated in and through Jesus, and in and through the human instrumentality of the church. The moral call to follow Jesus is mediated in and through the human and human experience. From a theological perspective traditional Catholic natural law theory illustrates the reality of mediation. Catholic ethics appeals, not immediately to the will or word of God, but rather to the human that mediates the divine will and word. It is necessary to remember that one danger in mediation is to absolutize what is only a mediation, and this has often occurred, as exemplified in Catholic ecclesiology.

It is precisely the Catholic insistence on mediation which I see as the critical difference between the Catholic tradition and the theocentric ethics recently proposed by James M. Gustafson. Recall that Gustafson has been quite appreciative of many of the recent developments among Catholic moral theologians. However, his new two-volume study shows again that mediation is often the continuing point of difference between Protestant ethicists of all types and Catholics be they liberal or conservative. Gustafson claims to be following the Reformed tradition in emphasizing the glory of God. The Chicago professor rejects most of contemporary Christian ethics as being too anthropocentric and too much based on the human. God, and not human beings, is the center of meaning. Human fulfillment or human happiness cannot be the primary concern of Christian ethics. Human experience itself underscores the tragic aspects of human existence, and at times human beings must be angry with the God who brings this about. Gustafson also cannot accept the reality of an afterlife.[21] However, in the Catholic tradition there has never been the need to choose between the glory of God and human fulfillment. The glory of God is the human person come alive. The glory of God is seen in and through human fulfillment and happiness. Thus the contemporary dialogue indicates that Protestant and Catholic ethicists often differ over the methodological significance of mediation, whereas Catholics of all different stripes are usually in agreement on this important theological issue.

The analysis given of the ecumenical aspect of moral theology in the United States indicates that the ecumenism involved is a true ecumenism and not just a watering down of one's own Catholic tradition. The integrity of the moral theologians themselves would insure that this is the case. One further illustration of the more substantive differences between Protestant and Catholic ethicists came to the fore in a dispute over abortion occasioned by "A Call to Concern" signed by 209 scholars mostly from the field of Christian ethics and including many well-known Protestant ethicists but noticeably lacking in Catholic support. The document rejected the absolutist position on abortion, supported the 1973 Supreme Court rulings, called for the government to fund abortions for poor people, and expressed sorrow at the heavy institutional involvement of the bishops of the Roman Catholic Church in favor of the absolutist position.[22] It is true that there is a great diversity among Catholic theologians on the question of the legal aspect of abortion and even some diversity on the moral question itself. However, "A Call to Concern" was rejected by the vast majority of Roman Catholic moral theologians. In his recent history of the Society of Christian Ethics Edward LeRoy Long maintains that one of the most valuable meetings in the life of the society involved an honest and frank discussion over "A Call to Concern" at the 1978 meeting.[23]

Academic Context

A fourth significant context of moral theology in the United States is the academic context. For all practical purposes moral theology and all Catholic theology in the United States were not looked on as academic disciplines before the 1960s. Theology was primarily identified with seminary education, which in the pre-Vatican II period meant separation from all other worlds. It is true that theology was taught at all Catholic colleges, but for the most part it was treated as a catechetical rather than an academic enterprise. The professors were usually clerics, many of whom did not have advanced degrees. The very fact of priestly ordination was often judged to be sufficient preparation for teaching theology.

The beginning of the College Theology Society in 1954 indicates an incipient move toward a greater professionalization in the teaching of what was then called sacred doctrine. At the time only priests and brothers were admitted into the Catholic Theological Society of America. Women religious and laity with advanced degrees in theology were looking for a professional organization. This declericalization and continued professionalization of theology began to grow especially in the 1960s. Corresponding to this was the increase in the number of Catholic universities offering a doctorate degree in theology. Theology both in its undergraduate and graduate setting was striving for academic respectability alongside all the other academic disciplines. Vatican II only heightened the interest in and concern for theology as a respected academic discipline in the Catholic college and university.

At the same time the self-understanding of Catholic colleges and universities began to change. Academic freedom had been a hallmark of American higher education throughout its existence. Colleges and universities must be free and autonomous centers of study with no external constraints limiting their autonomy or their freedom.[24] In the post-World War II period Catholic colleges and universities realized that they were more and more a part of American higher education in general. Before 1960 most Catholic educators still thought there was a basic incompatibility between the Catholic institution of higher learning and the American understanding of a college or university with its autonomy and freedom. However, with a growing understanding on the part of American Catholic educators, they realized they should be and could be an integral part of American higher education, and the theological developments highlighted at Vatican Council II also influenced a new approach.[25] The most significant illustration of the new approach was the so-called "Land O' Lakes Statement" issued by 26 leaders in Catholic higher education in the United States and Canada in 1967. The statement makes its point succinctly and forcefully:

> The Catholic university today must be a university in the full modern sense of the word with a strong commitment to and concern for academic excellence. To perform its teaching and research functions effectively, the Catholic university must have a true autonomy and academic freedom in the face of authority of whatever kind, lay or clerical, external to the academic community itself. To say this is simply to assert that institutional autonomy and academic freedom are essential conditions of life and growth and indeed of survival for Catholic universities as for all universities.[26]

The Catholic literature on academic freedom before the 1960s was invariably negative and defensive. However, the middle 1960s saw a growing acceptance of the place for and need of academic freedom in

American Catholic higher education. A dissertation accepted at The Catholic University of America in 1969 made the case for the full acceptance of academic freedom for Catholic institutions of higher learning and for Catholic theology,[27] even though a dissertation published in 1958 held the exact opposite position.[28] Perhaps the contemporary scene is best illustrated by the fact that in 1984 a Roman Catholic layman defended a doctoral dissertation "Academic Freedom in the American Roman Catholic University" at Drew University, a graduate school with ties to the Methodist Church![29]

In this context Roman Catholic theology in general and moral theology in particular are looked upon as academic disciplines like other academic disciplines existing within Catholic institutions of higher learning that claim for themselves academic freedom and autonomy. Such a context does not deny anything that is essential to Catholic theology and moral theology as such. Catholic theology can and must recognize the role of the hierarchical teaching office in the church. However, judgments about the competency of Catholic scholars that affect their right to teach in Catholic institutions can only be made by academic peers and not by any authority, clerical or lay, which is external to the academic community itself. Such judgments about competency to teach Catholic theology must give due weight to the teaching of the hierarchical magisterium. The academic freedom of the Catholic institution and of Catholic theology is in the eyes of most United States theologians compatible with a Catholic understanding of the proper role of the hierarchical magisterium and of theologians within the church. Archbishop Weakland of Milwaukee maintains that the acceptance of academic freedom is not merely a compromise with secular reality but makes Catholic institutions of higher learning more effective in their service to the church.[30] A minority of Catholic scholars, in particular those associated with the Fellowship of Catholic Scholars, would not accept such an understanding of academic freedom as applied to Catholic institutions and theology.

The academic context of Catholic theology in the United States means that the theologian cannot see one's role and function in terms of a commissioning to teach given by the hierarchical magisterium in the church. Theology very definitely is in the service of the church, but it is also an academic discipline as such. Recent canonical legislation has been viewed by many as threatening the understanding of theology as an academic discipline and as questioning whether Catholic institutions of higher learning can belong to the mainstream of American higher education.

The academic context of Catholic moral theology comes primarily from the place, the academy, in which theology is done. However, there are different places where theology is being done today. Commissions and think-tanks or institutes have already been mentioned. Very often these institutes are ecumenical and multidisciplinary in their approach. Theologians of various denominations work together with other humanists and scholars in debating the problems facing society and the world. One of the best known of such institutes is the Institute of Society, Ethics, and the Life Sciences, commonly called the Hastings Center, which publishes a very significant journal, *The Hastings Center Report.* Georgetown University, which is a Catholic institution, houses and sponsors the Kennedy Institute of Ethics, which is ecumenical in its membership and approach. However, other institutes have been set up primarily as Catholic centers as such. The best example of such institutes is the "Pope John XXIII Medical-Moral Research and Education Center" originally founded in 1973. This center publishes a newsletter and occasional books, sponsors workshops, including an annual workshop for bishops, and arranges meetings for various groups. The center tends to adopt a more conservative position on the issues of medical ethics.

In general in the last twenty years the academic aspect of Catholic theology has been stressed with a resulting strengthening of the position that the Catholic theologian cannot be seen merely as an extension of the hierarchical teaching office in the church.

II. CONTENT OF MORAL THEOLOGY

This second section will briefly discuss Catholic moral theology in the United States from the perspective of the content of moral theology itself. In the light of the very nature of the discipline as well as the context discussed above, moral theology will be involved in discussing the major problems faced by both the church and the society.

The areas of sexual and medical ethics have already been briefly mentioned. Here the majority of moralists contributing have adopted a revisionist methodology that argues against some, but by no means all, of the positions maintained in older Catholic approaches. According to revisionists the primary problem of the older methodology is a biologism that identifies the human moral aspects with merely the biological. The revisionist approach appeals to historical mindedness and personalism to argue against absolute moral norms, in which what is always forbidden is described in physical or biological terms, for example, contraception or direct killing. Many maintain that such physical or premoral evil can be done for a proportionate reason. Especially in the areas of sexual and medical morality much tension has arisen because here the revisionists propose that one can dissent from the authoritative noninfallible teaching of the hierarchical magisterium. Proponents of the older positions often modify the older natural law arguments but accuse the revisionists of gnosticism in failing to give enough importance to the physical aspects of embodied humanity.

Within the area of social ethics there again exists what is usually called a "conservative-liberal" dispute, but this difference is not exactly the same and does not necessarily involve the same people as the discussion in sexual and medical ethics. In the area of social ethics the American bishops with their earlier statements and especially with their recent pastoral letters on peace and the economy are generally judged to belong to the liberal approach. The more conservative position, as exemplified in a lay letter on the economy as an alternative to the bishops' approach, is much more supportive of the American economic system and more ready to defend the need for a strong nuclear defense policy than are the American bishops.[31] Michael Novak, who is the most prominent and prolific author in this area, proposes a realism which accepts human limitations and sinfulness, rejects utopian solutions, and faults the Catholic tradition for its insistence on distribution rather than on the call to creatively produce more wealth.[32] In this area too there is an ecclesiological discussion, with many of the more conservative authors maintaining that the hierarchical church should not be so specific in its teaching on social issues and should not adopt its generally liberal approach.[33]

How is one to evaluate the consistency of the hierarchical teaching in these two different areas? The United States bishops themselves, under the leadership of Cardinal Bernardin, have been arguing for a consistent life ethic affecting all life issues such as abortion, war, and capital punishment.[34] In general I think there is great merit in such an approach, but there is a tendency to become too unnuanced and to forget the distinction between law and morality.

In my judgment a lack of consistency exists between the positions taken by the American Catholic bishops and the universal hierarchical teaching office in the sexual and medical areas and the approaches taken in social ethics, for two different methodologies appear to be at work in official hierarchical teaching. In the social area official church documents strongly recognize the importance of historical consciousness, and they turn to the subject with an emphasis on the person. These emphases with all their logical conclusions are missing in contemporary hierarchical approaches in the areas of sexual and medical ethics.

In the general area of methodology and fundamental moral theology much work remains to be done. Most attention up to now has been given to the question of norms in moral theology, with Richard A. McCormick doing the most work to develop a theory of proportionalism, while Germain Grisez has strongly defended universal norms with his theory based on an understanding of the modes of responsibility and basic human goods. Speaking as a revisionist, I recognize the need to develop exactly what is meant by proportionate reason and to study all the ramifications of the theory in all aspects and areas of moral theology. Other methodological issues such as the use of scripture in moral theology, the distinctiveness of Christian ethics, and, to a lesser extent, the role of the sciences in moral theology have been discussed.

One fascinating aspect of the ecumenical dialogue has been the recent Protestant emphasis on virtue, character, and the importance of narrative and story, shown especially in the writings of Stanley Hauerwas.[35] As a result Roman Catholics are now much more conscious of what has been such a fundamental aspect of Catholic moral theology but has been generally overlooked in the last few years. However, sustained and systematic studies of the Christian person as agent and subject are needed. Moral development has received quite a bit of attention, especially in dialogue with Kohlberg, Gilligan, and other psychologists. Many articles and even some books have been written on conscience, but much remains to be done. In all these ares of fundamental moral theology one is conscious of the need for interdisciplinary approaches in order to do justice to the anthropological realities involved.

With all the significant changes in the discipline and the manifold specific questions that have emerged, it is natural that there have been few attempts to construct a systematic moral theology. Timothy O'Connell's *Principles for a Catholic Morality*, with its heavy dependence on the work of Joseph Fuchs, deals from a contemporary viewpoint with the issues raised by the older manuals in fundamental moral theology.[36] Daniel Maguire's *The Moral Choice* presents a lively and innovative approach to the specific issue of moral choice.[37] As helpful as these books are, especially for use with students, they are not intended to be systematic studies of all moral theology.

' Bernard Häring's three-volume *Free and Faithful in Christ* is really the first attempt at a systematic discussion of contemporary moral theology in a manual-type approach.[38] It is fitting that Häring's book, which was written in English, should be the first attempt at a systematic contemporary moral theology on the American scene. Häring has lectured widely and taught in many different Catholic, Protestant, and state institutions in this country in the past twenty years. It is safe to say that Häring has had a greater influence on the totality of the American Catholic Church than any other moral theologian. Recently Germain Grisez has published *The Way of the Lord Jesus,* vol. 1: *Christian Moral Principles,* a thousand-page treatise that is the first of a projected four-volume systematic moral theology.[39] Grisez here develops again his basic theory of moral responsibility and norms, but he tries to incorporate this within a larger and systematic moral theology.

Notes

1. Donald E. Pelotte, *John Courtney Murray: Theologian in Conflict* (New York: Paulist Press, 1976).

2. For a recent study by a well-informed journalist on the debate over contraception with heavy emphasis on the papal commission and the American context see Robert Blair Kaiser, *The Politics of Sex and Religion* (Kansas City, MO: Leaven Press, 1985). For a discussion of the contraception debate before 1970 with emphasis on the reactions in the United States see William H. Shannon, *The Lively Debate: Responses to Humanae Vitae* (New York: Sheed and Ward, 1970).

3. Germain G. Grisez, *Contraception and the Natural Law* (Milwaukee: Bruce, 1964).

4. Ibid., p. 20.

5. Ibid., p. 41.

6. John C. Ford and Germain Grisez, "Contraception and Infallibility," *Theological Studies* 39 (1978): 258–312. For a revisionist position see Joseph A. Komonchak, *"Humanae Vitae* and Its Reception: Ecclesiological Reflections," *Theological Studies* 39 (1978): 221–257.

7. Rosemary Rodgers, *A History of the College Theology Society* (Villanova, PA: College Theology Society, 1983). *Horizons* is the journal of the College Theology Society.

8. Anthony Kosnik *et al., Human Sexuality: New Dimensions in American Catholic Thought* (New York: Paulist Press, 1977). For what can accurately be called a conservative response to the above see Ronald Lawler, Joseph Boyle, Jr., and William E. May, *Catholic Sexual Ethics: A Summary, Explanation, and Defense* (Huntington, IN: Our Sunday Visitor, 1985).

9. Raymond E. Brown, "Bishops and Theologians: 'Dispute' Surrounded by Fiction," *Origins* 7 (1978): 673–682.

10. Richard A. McCormick has developed this theory in greater depth than any other ethicist. For the development of his thought see Richard A. McCormick, *Notes on Moral Theology 1965 through 1980* (Washington, DC: University Press of America, 1981); *Notes on Moral Theology 1981 through 1984* (Washington, DC: University Press of America, 1984).

11. President's Commission for the Study of Ethical Problems in Medicine and Biomedical and Behavioral Research, *Summing Up: Final Report on Studies of the Ethical and Legal Problems in Medicine and Biomedical and Behavioral Research* (Washington, DC: U.S. Government Printing Office, 1983).

12. For many different viewpoints on this question see Charles E. Curran and Richard A. McCormick, eds., *Readings in Moral Theology No 2: The Distinctiveness of Christian Ethics* (New York: Paulist Press, 1980). Other volumes edited by Curran and McCormick in this series are *Readings in Moral Theology No 1: Moral Norms and Catholic Tradition; Readings in Moral Theology No 3: The Magisterium and Morality; Readings in Moral Theology No 4: The Use of Scripture in Moral Theology* (New York: Paulist Press, 1979, 1982, 1984).

13. "The Pastoral Letter on War and Peace: The Challenge of Peace: God's Promise and Our Response," *Origins* 13 (1983): 3, 4.

14. Thomas A. Shannon, ed., *War or Peace? The Search for New Answers* (Maryknoll, NY: Orbis Books, 1980). This volume is in a sense a *festschrift* for Gordon C. Zahn, who has written most extensively on Christian pacifism from the Catholic perspective.

15. David Hollenbach, *Claims in Conflict: Retrieving and Renewing the*

Catholic Human Rights Tradition (New York: Paulist Press, 1979); Alfred Hennelly and John Langan, eds., *Human Rights in the Americas: The Struggle for Consensus* (Washington, DC: Georgetown University Press, 1982); Margaret E. Crahan, ed., *Human Rights and Basic Needs in the Americas* (Washington, DC: Georgetown University Press, 1982). All three volumes were written in connection with the Woodstock Theological Center in Washington.

16. Margaret A. Farley, "Feminist Ethics in the Christian Ethics Curriculum," *Horizons* 11 (1984): 361–372; June O'Connor, "How to Mainstream Feminist Studies by Raising Questions: The Case of the Introductory Course," *Horizons* 11 (1984): 373–392.

17. Edward LeRoy Long, Jr., *Academic Bonding and Social Concern: The Society of Christian Ethics 1959–1983* (no place given: Religious Ethics, 1984).

18. James M. Gustafson, *Protestant and Roman Catholic Ethics: Prospects for Rapprochement* (Chicago: University of Chicago Press, 1978).

19. "Presentation of the Linacre Quarterly Award to Dr. Paul Ramsey by John P. Mullooly, M.D.," *The Linacre Quarterly* 46 (1979): 7, 8.

20. Gustafson, *Protestant and Roman Catholic Ethics,* p. 151. For a fuller development of my analysis see Curran, *Politics, Medicine, and Christian Ethics: A Dialogue with Paul Ramsey* (Philadelphia: Fortress Press, 1973).

21. James M. Gustafson, *Ethics from a Theocentric Perspective,* vol 1: *Theology and Ethics;* vol. 2: *Ethics and Theology* (Chicago: University of Chicago Press, 1981, 1984).

22. "A Call to Concern," *Christianity and Crisis* 37 (1977): 222–224.

23. Long, *Academic Bonding and Social Concern,* p. 136.

24. Richard Hofstadter and Walter P. Metzger, *Academic Freedom in the United States* (New York: Columbia University Press, 1955).

25. Neil G. McCluskey, ed., *The Catholic University: A Modern Appraisal* (Notre Dame, IN: University of Notre Dame Press, 1970).

26. "Land O' Lakes Statement," in McCluskey, *The Catholic University,* pp. 336ff.

27. Frederick Walter Gunti, "Academic Freedom as an Operative Principle for the Catholic Theologian" (S.T.D. dissertation, The Catholic University of America, 1969).

28. Aldo J. Tos, "A Critical Study of American Views on Academic Freedom" (Ph.D. dissertation, The Catholic University of America, 1958).

29. James John Annarelli, "Academic Freedom and the American Roman Catholic University" (Ph.D. dissertation, Drew University, 1984).

30. Archbishop Rembert G. Weakland, O.S.B., "A Catholic University: Some Clarifications," *Catholic Herald* (March 21, 1985): 3.

31. Lay Commission on Catholic Social Teaching and the U.S. Economy,

Toward the Future: Catholic Social Thought and the U.S. Economy: A Lay Letter (North Tarrytown, NY: Lay Commission, 1984).

32. For Novak's latest work on the subject see Michael Novak, *Freedom with Justice: Catholic Social Thought and Liberal Institutions* (San Francisco: Harper and Row, 1984).

33. J. Brian Benestad, *The Pursuit of a Just Social Order: Policy Statements of the U.S. Catholic Bishops, 1966–1980* (Washington, DC: Ethics and Public Policy Center, 1982).

34. Joseph Cardinal Bernardin, "Fordham University Address on the Need for a Consistent Ethic of Life," *Origins* 13 (1984): 491–494; "Enlarging the Dialogue on a Consistent Ethic of Life," *Origins* 13 (1984): 705–709.

35. For the most systematic treatment of his position see Stanley Hauerwas, *The Peaceable Kingdom* (Notre Dame, IN: University of Notre Dame Press, 1983).

36. Timothy E. O'Connell, *Principles for a Catholic Morality* (New York: Seabury Press, 1978).

37. Daniel C. Maguire, *The Moral Choice* (Garden City, NY: Doubleday, 1978).

38. Bernard Häring, *Free and Faithful in Christ: Moral Theology for Clergy and Laity,* 3 vols. (New York: Seabury Press, 1978, 1979, 1981).

39. Germain Grisez, *The Way of the Lord Jesus,* vol. 1: *Christian Moral Principles* (Chicago: Franciscan Herald Press, 1983).

3. Moral Theology 1940–1989: An Overview

Richard A. McCormick

This chapter first appeared in *Theological Studies* 50 (1989).

In 1940 the first volume of Theological Studies carried a section entitled "Recent Canon Law and Moral Theology: Some Important Items."[1] These 31 pages were unsigned but research reveals that they were actually authored by editor William McGarry, S.J. John C. Ford, S.J., beginning with Volume 2, continued these critical surveys through Volume 6 (1945). Gerald Kelly, S.J., began his contribution with Volume 8 (1947) and produced an annual "Notes on Moral Theology" through Volume 14 (1953). Volume 15 (1954) saw the beginning of the rich and rewarding collaborative authorship of Ford and Kelly, as well as the first appearance in *TS* of John R. Connery, S.J. Connery and John J. Lynch, S.J. (along with three surveys by Joseph Farraher, S.J., one by Kelly, one by Ford-Kelly, and several by Robert Springer) carried the "Moral Notes" into the mid-sixties. The present author began his contributions in 1965 and concluded them in 1987.

I mention this bit of history because, by perusing the "Notes on Moral Theology" from the beginning, once gets a fairly clear picture of moral theology then and now, its strengths and weaknesses, as well as its methods and priorities. I say this with confidence because from the very outset these surveys ranged over moral studies in Latin, French, German, Spanish, Italian, and English, from *Angelicum* and *AAS*, through *Nouvelle revue théologique, Periodica,* and *Studia moralia,* to *Razón y fe* and *Stimmen der Zeit.* However, an overview of moral theology during these five decades would be incomplete without mention of theologians such as Francis Connell, C.SS.R.; Joseph Duhamel, S.J.;

Paul McKeever; Franciscus Hürth, S.J.; Edwin Healy, S.J.; and a host of others.

It is easy to caricature, and no serious scholar with an ounce of self-knowledge and a sense of history will do so. With that caveat in mind, it can be pointed out that in the 40s and 50s Catholic moral theology was the stepchild of the *Institutiones theologiae moralis* of Genicot, Noldin, Prümmer, Aertnys-Damen, et al. Concretely, it was all too often one-sidedly confession-oriented, magisterium-dominated, canon law-related, sin-centered, and seminary-controlled. In many books and articles Bernard Häring has excoriated this as "legalism." Yet, when reading the Ford-Kelly review of this literature, one must immediately add qualifiers that provide perspective to each of these sweeping indictments. Thus: very pastoral and prudent, critically respectful, realistic, compassionate, open and charitable, well-informed. Indeed, the two dominant American moral theologians of the 40s and 50s (Ford and Kelly) had such towering and well-deserved reputations that most of us regarded their agreement on a practical matter as constituting a "solidly probably opinion." It is easy to understand why their experience, wisdom, and prudence were treasured by everyone from bishops, college presidents, moral theologians, physicians, priests, and students to penitents and counselors.

All of us, however, bear the restricting marks of the cultural contexts in which we work. So, along with truly prophetic and pathbreaking studies that are still urgently relevant,[2] one finds during these earlier years discussions that strike us now as downright quaint. For instance, there is debate about knitting as servile work,[3] of organ-playing at non-Catholic services,[4] of calling non-Catholic ministers for dying non-Catholic patients,[5] of steady dating among adolescents,[6] of the gravity of using "rhythm" without a proportionate reason.[7] It is to the everlasting credit of theologians like Ford, Kelly, Connery, and Lynch that they brought an uncommon common sense to such "problems" that dissipated them before they could seriously quiver the ganglia of the Catholic conscience.

A few samples are needed to jar the unexposed and possibly incredulous postconciliar Catholic. In 1946, *TS*—under the editorship of the renowned John Courtney Murray, S.J.—carried an article on fasting. It concluded as follows:

In conclusion, then, just how much is allowed at breakfast and at collation for a person who is fasting but needs something extra? Some authors say sixteen ounces in all; one or two authors seem to suggest even more. As things stand at present, if one should be asked how much over the two-ounce/eight-ounce limit is permitted nowadays, it appears that one should reply: First, if a person can conveniently fast on that amount, absolutely nothing extra; otherwise, whatever is really necessary, up to around sixteen ounces; these sixteen ounces can be divided as the person requires—into four for breakfast and twelve for collation, into six and ten, into eight and eight, and so on. However, if the person needs much more than sixteen ounces, or if the mathematical juggling would make him scrupulous, he should be dispensed completely.[8]

If this citation seems extreme, one has only to recall that at the 14th Annual Convention (1959) of the Catholic Theological Society of America the moral seminar spent the better part of an hour wrangling over whether chewing gum broke the eucharistic fast. Another example is a paper delivered at the same meeting by Anthony F. Zimmerman, S.V.D. He concluded:

These and other documents of the Holy See have convinced me that "rhythm" cannot be recommended as a Christian solution for overpopulation. In my opinion Rome has spoken and the case is settled. For we are not allowed to promote the ideal of a small family in a nation, in opposition against the church's ideal of the large family. But "rhythm" could not be promoted as a means of solving a national overpopulation problem without setting up the small family as a new ideal for that nation.[9]

That conclusion was recognized even then as quite preposterous and I remember distinctly John C. Ford's immediate and magisterial refutation of it. It began: "Rome has not spoken." Today, of course, the refutation would remain vigorous, though it might well take a different analytic form.

My final example of how moral theology was pursued by the manuals that constituted the inherited *Weltanschauung* for the 40s and 50s is taken from a standard manual of moral theology. Antonius Lanza and Petrus Palazzini, Roman theologians of indisputable stature, discussed the morality of dancing, and specifically of "masked balls." I cite it partly in the original to forestall questions about authenticity.

> Likewise, masked balls offer a fairly facile opportunity for disaster; for there are some who hide their faces so that, no longer restrained by the bridle of shame, they may do incognito what they would not dare to do if recognized. Today, however, the situation has degenerated badly with more recent dances: one stoep (sic), paso doble, turquey-trot, pas de l'ours, spiru, charleston, fox-trot, rumba, carioca, boogie-woogie, samba, etc.[10]

Elsewhere I have summarized the perspectives and cultural context of pre-Vatican II moral theology as follows:

> For many decades, even centuries, prior to Vatican II Catholic moral theology conceived its chief task as being the training of priests to hear confessions. Within the sacramental perspectives of the times the confessor was viewed as exercising a fourfold office: father, teacher, judge, physician. Specially necessary to effective ministry were charity (of a father), knowledge (of a teacher and judge), prudence (of a physician)....
>
> The knowledge required of a confessor included many things, but above all knowledge of God's law *as proposed by the church,* i.e., the church's magisterium. At this period of time, for many understandable sociological reasons, the church's magisterium was understood in a highly authoritarian and paternalistic way. One did not question ordinary noninfallible teaching. Dissent was virtually unknown and would certainly have been extremely risky.[11]

In the remainder of this overview I will touch on three points: (1) Significant developments in moral theology over the past 50 years.

"Significant" refers in general to factors that affected moral theology, and especially to those that altered the cultural variables that framed the moral agenda of the first 20 years of *TS*'s existence and led to the types of moral concerns and judgments I have cited above. (2) Where we are now. (3) Some suggestions for the future. These last two points can be developed briefly, because they are implicit in the developments I list as significant.

SIGNIFICANT DEVELOPMENTS

Symptoms abound that there were deep stirrings of dissatisfaction with the brand of theology contained in the *Institutiones theologiae moralis*. One was the growing popularity of Bernard Häring's *The Law of Christ*. Another was the appearance in 1952 of G. Gilleman's *Le primat de la charité en théologie morale: Essai méthodologique*.[12] Or again, I shall never forget the shock waves produced by Daniel Callahan in 1964. Ford and Kelly had just published their volume *Contemporary Moral Theology* 2: *Marriage Questions*. It was a haven of moderation against those we called *strictiores*. Callahan described the revered authors as "loyal civil servants" and "faithful party workers," and their work as "years behind the [theological] revolution now in progress."[13] Gerald Kelly, I am told by reliable sources, was at his typewriter about to respond, but experienced chest pains in his agitation.

In retrospect, I think Callahan was correct. I do not believe that "revolution" is too strong a word for the developments that have occurred in moral theology in the last 30 years. Different authors might well produce different litanies of the revolutionary phases or ingredients. However, I am reasonably confident that the following ten items would appear in one way or another on many lists.

1) *Vatican II and ecclesiology.* The Council said very little directly about moral theology. Yet what it said about other aspects of Catholic belief and practice had an enormous influence on moral theology. These "other aspects of Catholic belief and life" are largely, though not exclusively, ecclesiological. For Vatican II was, above all, an ecclesiological council. There are many ways of wording this, I am sure. Once could, e.g., speak of it as the Council of the Holy Spirit to highlight the pervasiveness of the Spirit in its formulations. Richard McBrien, in a talk to

moral theologians at Notre Dame (June, 1988), neatly summarized in six points Vatican II's major ecclesiological themes.

a. The church as mystery or sacrament. The church is a sign as well as an instrument of salvation. As a sacrament, it causes by signifying. As McBrien notes, this powerfully suggests the need to be attentive to justice issues within the church as well as outside. It is this principle of sacramentality that undergirds the statement of the U.S. Catholic Bishops' pastoral letter *Economic Justice for All:* "All the moral principles that govern the just operation of any economic endeavor apply to the church and its agencies and institutions; indeed the church should be exemplary" (no. 347).

b. The church as people of God. All the faithful (not just the hierarchy and specialists) constitute the church. This has immediate implications for the elaboration and development of moral doctrine, for consultative processes, for the free flow of ideas in the church.

c. The church as servant. Besides preaching of the word and celebration of the sacraments, the church's mission includes service to human needs in the social, political, and economic orders. This suggests that these orders are also ecclesiological problems and that moralists and ecclesiologists must be closely cooperative. It also suggests that moral theology, following John Courtney Murray, must continue to probe the relationship between civic unity and religious integrity.

d. The church as collegial. The church is realized and expressed at the local (parish/diocese/region/nation) level as well as the universal. The collegial nature of the church helps to raise and rephrase the question of the use and limits of authority in the moral sphere, and the meaning of subsidiarity and freedom in the application of moral principles and the formation of conscience.

e. The church as ecumenical. Being the whole Body of Christ, the church includes more than Roman Catholics. The obvious implication is that Catholic officials and theologians must consult and take account of the experience, reflection, and wisdom resident in other Christian churches.

f. The church as eschatological. The church is a tentative and unfinished reality. It is *in via*. A fortiori, its moral and ethical judgments are always *in via* and share the messy, unfinished, and perfectible character of the church itself.

I believe McBrien is absolutely correct when he asserts that these ecclesial metaphors affect both the substance and method of moral inquiry in very profound and practical ways.

2) *Karl Rahner and fundmental freedom.* When I began theological studies toward the priesthood in 1950, Rahner was a "corollary" at the end of our theses on grace, creation, the sacraments, Christology. Not for long, however. During the next 35 years he became the most prolific and greatest theologian of the century, and arguably of several centuries.

One of Rahner's key contributions to moral theology was his anthropology, and specifically his recovery of the notion of the depth of the moral act.[14] He argued that the human person is, as it were, constructed of various layers of freedom. At the center is the area of core or fundamental freedom, which enables a person to dispose totally of her/himself. Other layers are more or less peripheral. The use of core freedom is the area of grave morality—of total self-disposition, or radical conversion, of truly mortal sin. Actuations of this intensity of freedom may be called "fundamental options" precisely because of their depth, stability, and permanence. The notion of *fundamental option* pervades Rahner's writings on grace, sin, conversion, the moral life in general, and, above all, his presentation of the Spiritual Exercises of St. Ignatius.

Such an anthropology has enormous repercussions on some very basic concepts of moral theology: sin, conversion, virtue, serious matter, priorities in the moral life, confession, temptation, laws of the church, spiritual discernment – to mention but a few. Systematic theologians began to use this anthropology in their presentations of Catholic teachings,[15] but it was domesticated in moral theology largely through the writings of Joseph Fuchs, S.J., and his disciple Bruno Schüller, S.J.[16]

Unfortunately, the notion of fundamental freedom can be and has been misunderstood, misrepresented, and abused.[17] Perhaps that is the unavoidable fate of the attempt to rethink the depth and complexity of the human person. Be that as it may, I believe that moral theology, largely through the pioneering work of Rahner, has been forever altered. We can no longer think of the moral-spiritual life in terms of the clear and distinct categories that were generated by an anthropology that conceived of freedom exhaustively as freedom of choice. Things are just not that simple.

3) *Moral norms and revision of method.* In 1965 Peter Knauer, S.J., published his seminal essay on the principle of double effect.[18] When I drove Joseph Fuchs, S.J., from O'Hare Airport that year, I asked him about the article. His reply: "Very interesting." Very interesting indeed! It proved to be the opening shot in a 25-year discussion of the proper understanding of the moral norms within the community of Catholic moral theologians. Specifically, it concerned the method for determining the morally right and wrong in concrete human conduct. At the risk of oversimplificiation, Knauer's basic thesis could be worded as follows: the causing or permitting of evils in our conduct is morally right or wrong depending on the presence or absence of a commensurate reason. When such a reason is present, the intention bears on it, not on the evil—and therefore the evil remains indirect. Knauer was on to something, yet he filtered it through traditional categories. The result was provocative, yet a bit untidy and unsettling. That is the way it is with many beginnings.

In 1970 Germain Grisez wrote of Knauer that he "is carrying through a revolution in principle while pretending only a clarification of traditional ideas."[19] Grisez was, I believe, right. That "revolution in principle" gradually led to a vast literature that huddles under the umbrella-term "proportionalism."

Unless I am mistaken, I can detect the general shape of this *Denkform* as early as 1951 in the work of Gerald Kelly. In commenting on a piece by William Conway in the *Irish Theological Quarterly* (wherein Conway considered some procedures involving mutilation as not evils), Kelly wrote:

> For my part, I prefer to say that there are some physical evils that are naturally subordinated to higher ends, and we have a right to cause these evils in order to obtain these ends. Thus, the bodily member is subordinated to the good of the whole body, and one has a right to remove this member where this is necessary for the good of the whole. The principle of the double effect is not required to justify this act; but the reason for this is not that the amputation is not an evil, but rather that it is an evil that one has a right to cause.
>
> In summary, let me suggest that the principle, evil is not to be done in order to obtain good, is not an absolutely uni-

versal principle. It refers absolutely to moral evil. As for physical evils, it refers only to those which lie outside the scope of the agent's direct rights (e.g., death of an innocent person); it does not refer to evils that one has a right to cause (e.g., self-mutilation to preserve life or health; the death of an enemy soldier or an unjust aggressor).[20]

Kelly was not at that time what is now known as a proportionalist. But those paragraphs indicate that with a few minor analytic moves he would be.

So-called proportionalists include some of the best-known names in moral theology throughout the world, though some are less explicit about their method: Joseph Fuchs, S.J.; Bruno Schüller, S.J.; Franz Böckle; Louis Janssens; Bernard Häring; Franz Scholz; Franz Furger; Walter Kerber, S.J.; Charles Curran; Lisa Cahill; Philip Keane; Joseph Selling; Edward Vacek, S.J.; David Hollenbach, S.J.; Maruice de Wachter; Margaret Farley; James Walter; Rudolf Ginters; Helmut Weber; Klaus Demmer; Garth Hallett, S.J.; and on and on. The leading published opponents of this methodological move are Germain Grisez, John Finnis, Joseph Boyle, William May, and the late John R. Connery, S.J.[21]

It is impossible in a brief space to give a fair summary of this development or an adequate account of the differences that individual theologians bring to their analyses, or of the objections lodged against them. However, common to all so-called proportionalists is the insistence that causing certain disvalues (ontic, nonmoral, premoral evils) in our conduct does not *ipso facto* make the action morally wrong, as certain traditional formulations supposed. The action becomes morally wrong when, all things considered, there is no proportionate reason. Thus, just as not every killing is murder, not every falsehood a lie, so not every artificial intervention preventing (or promoting) conception is necessarily un unchaste act. Not every termination of a pregnancy is necessarily an abortion in the moral sense.

This approach to moral norms has two interesting characteristics: (1) It contrasts markedly with earlier official understanding (e.g., *Humanae vitae*) which regarded some of the actions in question as intrinsic moral evils (i.e., under no circumstances could they be justified). (2) It touches the lives of people in very concrete ways. One may, and I do, suspect that this is why it is so strongly resisted. The 25-year discussion has been well summarized recently by Bernard Hoose, himself a proportionalist.[22]

4) *The Birth Control Commission and Humanae vitae.* I put these two together because only when *Humanae vitae* is seen in light of the previous consultations does it yield the full dimensions of the problem. The Commission for the Study of Population, Family, and Birth (widely referred to as the Birth Control Commission) voted by a heavy majority for a change in church teaching on contraception. So did the subsequently added (1966) cardinals and bishops. On Sunday, June 26, 1966, after the Commission had completed its work, Canon Pierre de Locht of Brussels, a member of the Commission, wrote in his diary:

> It will not be possible any longer to reaffirm the general condemnations of contraception. I do not understand what excuse he [the pope] can use to impose on the church his own personal option. The research he set in motion does not make sense if he does not take it into account. Why, then, would he have asked for it? Will he accept our conclusions only if they lean toward a reaffirmation?[23]

De Locht's statement summarizes the authority problem that *Humanae vitae* raised in 1968.[24] Paul VI had enlarged the Birth Control Commission and supported its work. Indeed, in 1966, under mounting pressure to issue a statement, he had intervened, almost agonizingly, with a kind of delaying plea. He said he was not ready to make his final statement. "The magisterium of the church," he said, "cannot propose moral norms until it is certain of interpreting the will of God. And to reach this certainty the church is not dispensed from research and from examining the many questions proposed for her consideration from every part of the world. This is at times a long and not an easy task.[25]

Yet *Humanae vitae* appeared in 1968. The problem is obvious. I wrote at that time: "If in February, 1966, the pope needed the studies of the commission to achieve (*raggiungere*) the certainty necessary to propose moral norms, and if having received the majority report of the commission he achieved or maintained a certainty contrary to it, then perhaps we need a long, long discussion about the nature of the magisterium."[26] This is exactly what de Locht meant when he wrote that "the research he set in motion does not make sense if he does not take it into account."

The firestorm that greeted *Humanae vitae* over 20 years ago is familiar to readers of *TS* and many others; no need for repetition here. What needs to be emphasized, however, is the enormous influence of this event on subsequent moral theology. Theologians became freshly aware of the inadequacy of a heavily juridical notion of the moral teaching office, and correspondingly they became more sensitive to their own responsibilities, especially their occasional duty to dissent in light of their own experience with the faithful and reflection on it. Nonreception became overnight a live theological issue. Questions were raised about the formation of conscience, about the response due to the ordinary magisterium, about the exercise of authority in the church, about consultative processes and collegiality, about the meaning of the guidance of the Holy Spirit to the pastors of the church. Contraception, as a moral issue, was virtually smothered in the ecclesiological tumult. The pope had been convinced by a minority of advisors from the Commission that any qualification of the condemnation of *Casti connubii* would compromise papal teaching authority. The fact is, authority has actually suffered in the process.

I can think of no moral issue or event in this century that impacted so profoundly on the discipline of moral theology. The reason was not only or primarily the sheer day-to-day practicality of the problem, but the fact that *Humanae vitae* was perceived by many to be the symbol of a takeback of important things that had happened in Vatican II. Bernard Häring once remarked to me that he thought we had learned more from *Humanae vitae* than we (as church) had suffered. He was referring, of course, to the place and exercise of authority in Christian morality. The lesson we learned had chiefly to do with limits. In a sense Paul VI, without really wanting to, or realizing that he was doing so, put Vatican II on the scales by testing it on a single burning issue.

5) *The emergence of feminism.* This is surely one of the "signs of the times" of which John XXIII and Vatican II spoke. Its full effect on moral theology is probably still ahead of us. Prior to Vatican II, the Catholic Theological Society of America was an all-male club and, even earlier, an all-seminary club. Now women are in positions of leadership in the C.T.S.A. It was not until 1971 that a woman (J. Massingberd Ford) first authored an article for *TS*.[27] Now it is common to see such

fine scholars as Lisa Cahill, Catherine LaCugna, Leslie Griffin, Elizabeth Johnson, Marjorie O'Rourke Boyle, Anne Carr, Sandra Schneiders, and Carol Tauer in these pages. In the field of moral theology the work of Griffin, Cahill, Tauer, Anne Patrick, Sidney Callahan, Christine Gudorf, Margaret Farley, Judith Dwyer, Eileen Flynn, Diana Bader, Corrine Bayley, Barbara Andelson, Elizabeth McMillan—to mention but a few—has been very effective and deeply appreciated.

The presence of women in the moral theological enterprise should have an obvious impact in several key areas of moral concern. Two that stand out are the place of women in the church and in society, and the theology of marriage and sexuality. But even beyond such issue areas, the theological contributions of women will be a constant reminder that Catholic Chrisitianity is still male-dominated and bears its own share of the blame for what the draft (as I write) pastoral *Partners in the Mystery of Redemption* calls a pervasive sin of sexism in the church.[28]

6) *The maturation of bioethics.* Within the Catholic community there had been for some years standard texts in medical ethics. One thinks of those authored by Charles J. McFadden, O.S.A.; Gerald Kelly, S.J.; Thomas O'Donnell, S.J.; and Edwin Healy, S.J.[29] As LeRoy Walters has noted of these texts, "the general approach to medical ethics was based on the standard textbooks of moral theology."[30]

The years 1969 and 1971 represented something of a turning point. In 1969 Daniel Callahan and Willard Gaylin founded the Institute of Society, Ethics and the Life Sciences, now more economically referred to as the Hastings Center. In 1971 André Hellegers founded the Joseph and Rose Kennedy Institute for the Study of Human Reproduction and Bioethics, now known as the Kennedy Institute of Ethics, at Georgetown University. These sister institutes brought physicians, scientists, philosophers, theologians, and lawyers together for the systematic and interdisciplinary study of the emerging problems in bioethics. The result was not only a fresh awareness of the breadth and complexity of the problems created by technology, but a huge outpouring of literature that attempted to wrestle with them. Bioethics had been born as a large and loosely but well-enough defined subspeciality of ethics. Since then centers for bioethics have sprung up all over the country and the world.

The significance of this for moral theology should not be lost. I will note three aspects. First, it became clear that it is impossible for any one theologian to be a truly reputable expert in all fields of moral theology in our day. Many of us are asked to teach, write, or lecture "on the moral aspects of" virtually anything; naively we used to think we could do that. To persist in such thoughts merely proliferates banality and incompetence, and threatens our theological credibility in the process. The present lacuna of moral-theological competence in certain areas of applied ethics should not tempt us to fill it with instant ethical energy but long-run incompetence. It should rather function as a challenge.

That leads directly to my second point. If bioethics establishes any kind of paradigm, it tells us that we need in law, business, and politics—to mention but three areas—truly well-trained and experienced persons who are ready to specialize in the ethical dimensions of the professions, i.e., limit themselves to such areas in a way that allows them to emerge as nationally recognized experts.

Finally, what is increasingly obvious in medicine—and I would guess, therefore, in the areas of law, business, and politics—is that an ethics of medicine can degenerate into a lifeless and detached body of knowledge that one dusts off now and then when faced with a nasty dilemma. That is the result of identifying ethics with "dilemma ethics." What we have come to see as essential to a genuine ethic is a formational dimension and therefore a spirituality of and for the professional person. When that is in place, decisional ethics will have a nourishing and supportive context and it will certainly flourish. Otherwise it remains spare-time aerobics. By "spirituality" I do not mean, e.g., a parallel-track, off-time retreat each year or two. I mean an approach to the profession developed from within its institutional ambience that views and lives the practice of medicine as a truly Christian vocation.

7) *The influence of liberation theology.* Liberation theology has the Vatican worried. In 1970 Gustavo Gutiérrez published in *TS* what he called "Notes for a Theology of Liberation."[31] With that article the Peruvian theologian alerted North America, as well as the world, that something terribly exciting was afoot in Latin America. In introducing the article, editor Walter J. Burghardt, S.J., referred to it as "*theological* dynamite." For a world sadly anesthetized to exploding automobiles and body counts on an almost daily basis, theological dynamite would seem to be a relatively cozy and comfortable threat.

Try again. Burghardt was prescient. Liberation theology is here— or, more accurately, there—to stay. I am not interested here in reviewing its salient features and its vast literature, or critiquing its sometimes overreaching claims. Others (theologians such as Roger Haight, S.J., and Alfred Hennelly, S.J.) are more competent to do so and indeed have done it. I simply point to it as a significant development. The term "significant" cries out for specification. Exactly how has liberation theology affected moral theology? I will list three ways.

First, there is the demolition of the separatist mentality. This refers to the approach that conceives of basic Christian realities such as faith, hope, and love—i.e., salvation—as exclusively or at least one-sidedly other-worldly realities. In other words, there is a radical continuity (even partial identification) between the eschatological promises and hope (the kingdom) and human liberation from systemic oppression. This entails a profound readjustment of our assessment of political and economic activity. These can no longer be viewed simply as "worldly" or secular pursuits. As Gutiérrez words it, "There are not, then, two histories, one profane and one sacred, juxtaposed or interrelated, but a single human progress, irreversibly exalted by Christ, the Lord of history. His redemptive work embraces every dimension of human existence."[32]

Second, as Gutiérrez and others such as Segundo and Sobrino make clear, the church's mission of charitable action is not merely that of social critique; it provokes all Christians to participate actively in construction of a just order. Only so will the people of Latin America (and elsewhere) believe the message of love at the center of the Christian idea. Paul VI put it this way in 1971: "It is to all Christians that we address a fresh and insistent call to action....It is not enough to recall principles, state intentions, point to crying injustices and utter prophetic denunciations; these words will lack real weight unless they are accompanied for each individual by the livelier awareness of personal responsibility and by effective action."[33]

Third, the theology of liberation is a constant reminder of the primacy of social concerns in our conception and presentation of the moral-spiritual life, and therefore of moral theology. This is a necessary corrective to the individualism of the West, since one form of that individualism is overemphasis on the personal (especially sexual) dimensions of the moral life. Paul VI in *Octogesima adveniens* emphasized this: "These are questions that because of their urgency, extent and complexity must, in the years to come, take first place among the preoccupations of Christians...."[34] Moral theology, in other words, cannot be equated with the problems and priorities of the Western industrialized democracies. We need other cultures to give us critical perspective on our own cultural and theological "locked-in syndrome."

8) *The person as criterion of the morally right and wrong.* Readers of *TS* will be familiar with this. But that does not diminish its importance. Vatican II (*Gaudium et spes,* no. 51) asserted that "the moral aspect of any procedure...must be determined by objective standards which are based on the nature of the person and the person's acts."[35] The official commentary on this wording noted two things: (1) In the expression there is formulated a general principle that applies to all human actions, not just to marriage and sexuality (where the passage occurred). (2) The choice of this expression means that "human activity must be judged insofar as it refers to the human person integrally and adequately considered."[36]

The importance of this can hardly be exaggerated. If "the person integrally and adequately considered" is the criterion of moral rightness and wrongness, it means that a different (from traditional) type of evidence is required for our assessment of human actions. For instance, in the past the criteriological significance of sexual conduct was found in its procreativity (*actus per se aptus ad procreationem*). Deviations from this finality and significance were viewed as morally wrong and the decisive factor in judging conduct. In my judgment, these perspectives continued to appear in *Humanae vitae* and "The Declaration on Certain Questions concerning Sexual Ethics."

However, Vatican II adopted the broader personalist criterion. As Louis Janssens words it, "From a personalist standpoint what must be examined is what the intervention as a whole means for the promotion of the human persons who are involved and for their relationships."[37] This commits us to an inductive method in moral deliberation about rightness and wrongness in which human experience and the sciences play an indispensable role.

9) *The Curran affair.* Prior to the removal of Charles Curran's canonical mission to teach on the pontifical faculty at the Catholic University of American, Bishop Matthew Clark (Curran's ordinary) wrote on March 12, 1986:

> If Father Curran's status as a Roman Catholic theologian is
> brought into question, I fear a serious setback to Catholic

education and pastoral life in this country. That could happen in two ways. Theologians may stop exploring the challenging questions of the day in a creative, healthy way because they fear actions which may prematurely end their teaching careers. Moreover, able theologians may abandon Catholic institutions altogether in order to avoid embarrassing confrontation with church authorities. Circumstances of this sort would seriously undermine the standing of Catholic scholarship in this nation, isolate our theological community and weaken our Catholic institutions of higher learning.[38]

Both possibilities have begun to happen and thus the Curran affair ranks as among the most significant developments in moral theology in the past 50 years. For instance, after the appearance of *Donum vitae* (the C.D.F.'s instruction on reproductive technology), I publicly but respectfully disagreed with a few of the instruction's conclusions. A young theologian told me that he agreed with me but added: "Will I get clobbered if I say so?" Such an attitude is understandable but profoundly saddening, especially in a church that rightly claims divine guidance. One would think that the promised guidance of the Holy Spirit would be the most solid basis for welcoming challenge and disagreement. It takes little imagination to see how the climate of fear may lead theologians to "stop exploring the challenging questions of the day" or to hedge their bets. This is especially the case if the individual has dependents. And sadly, these are the very people whose experience and reflection is so essential in approaching such questions.

As for abandonment of Catholic institutions, that has not happened yet. But what has begun to happen, I fear, is the gradual and impoverishing isolation of Catholic University. Over and over again I have heard theologians state that in the present circumstances they would recommend Catholic University to neither aspiring professors nor students. I emphasize that this is not a threat of mine; it is a report. But the report is threatening.[39]

There is a single theological issue in play in the Curran case, but one with many ramifications. That issue: public dissent from some authoritative but noninfallible teaching. The teaching in question, as Curran has repeatedly emphasized,[40] has these characteristics: (1) distant from the core of the faith; (2) based on natural law; (3) involved in such particularity and specificity that we should not realistically expect the same level of certitude enjoyed by more general norms.

The C.D.F. has denied the legitimacy of such dissent. This collides in principle with its acceptance by the American bishops in 1968. In this matter I stand by what I wrote in 1986:

> The implications of the Congregation's approach should not be overlooked. The first is that, to be regarded as a Catholic theologian, one may not dissent from any authoritatively proposed teaching. The second is that "authentic theological instruction" means presenting church teaching and never disagreeing with it, even with respect and reverence. Third, and correlatively, sound theological education means accepting, uncritically if necessary, official Catholic teaching. The impact of such assertions on the notion of a university, of Catholic higher education, of theology and of good teaching is mind-boggling. All too easily, answers replace questions and conformism replaces teaching as "theology" is reduced to Kohlberg's preconventional level of reasoning (obey or be punished).[41]

10) *The "restoration."* The description is that of Cardinal Joseph Ratzinger.[42] It refers in a very general way to the attempt to "tighten things up" in the church, especially by authoritative intervention into theological work considered suspect or dangerous. Cardinal Ratzinger has made no secret of the fact that moral theology heads his list. This restoration has taken two forms, one direct, the other indirect. The direct form involves the withholding of the canonical mission, the withdrawal of the imprimatur, dust-up actions, and letters to bishops and theologians. The indirect form is found above all in the appointment of bishops and the criteria of suitability for such appointment. Further symptoms of this restoration are seen in the failure of the synodal process and of the International Theological Commission. These were designed as vehicles for episcopal and theological collegiality, but have fallen a good deal short of these expectations and are widely dismissed as tokenisms.

The theological implications of this restoration are profound and far-reaching. I once listed them as ten "confusions" and have found no persuasive reasons for modifying this listing.[43] One can, of course, challenge the idea that we are involved in a restoration. Most would ridicule that challenge as unreal. What I think is beyond challenge is that, if we are, then these confusions will be exacerbated.

The above represent ten significant developments since 1940 that relate to moral theology.

WHERE WE ARE NOW

Once again I shall work in tens. Ten points can describe where we are now in moral theology, and I shall refer to them as "ages," as "we are in the age of...."

1) *The age of settling.* Charles Curran and this author have attempted, in our *Readings in Moral Theology,* to identify some of the areas of both importance and debate in contemporary moral theology. It is somewhat risky and difficult to assess the outcomes of these discussions, and for two reasons. First, they are still ongoing. Second, we are associated with an identifiable point of view. For instance, where dissent is concerned, we would both accept its legitimacy and even necessity in some cases. Or again, where moral norms are concerned, we would reject the notion of intrinsic evil as this was understood in manualist presentations and would accept some form of proportionalism.

My acquaintance with the literature leads me to believe that most theologians share similar perspectives.[44] Indeed, if this were not the case, one has to wonder why Cardinal Ratzinger (and even John Paul II) has aimed his guns in this direction. So the first thing that might be said about where we are is that there has been a quiet theological (even if not magisterial) settling, and a move to other issues in some of these matters. There are several possible readings of this. One is that a significant consensus has developed. Another is that a stand-off has been reached and further discussion appears nonproductive. Still another is that people are just bored with some of these concerns. I shall leave the decision to the judicious reader.

2) *The age of specialists.* I have already touched on this. Suffice it to note that the theologian should not aspire to be or expected to be *uomo universale.* It would be unrealistic to expect Daniel Callahan to be a hands-on expert in the field of international relations, or Bryan Hehir to be a standout bioethicist. These people have established reputations in the fields of their competence and have done outstanding work. Without specialization they would hardly have the influences they have.

3) *The age of justice.* There has been a sea-change of moral consciousness during the past 50 years. During that period we gradually began to speak of sin not simply as the isolated act of an individual, but as having societal structural dimensions. We began to see that the sins and selfishness of one generation became the inhibiting conditions of the next. The structures and institutions that oppress people, deprive them of rights, and alienate them are embodiments of our sinful condition. The notion of systemic violence and social sin entered our vocabulary and is so much a part of it now that John Paul II uses it freely. For instance, in *Sollicitudo rei socialis* he states:

> If the present situation can be attributed to difficulties of various kinds, it is not out of place to speak of "structures of sin," which as I stated in my Apostolic Exhortation *Reconciliatio et penitentia*, are rooted in personal sin, and thus always linked to the concrete acts of individuals who introduce these structures, consolidate them and make them difficult to remove.[45]

This is, I think where we are in much of contemporary moral theology. Many of the quite personal problems that so engaged the manualists are, obviously, still problems. Indeed, there is a pastoral wisdom there that remains somewhat undervalued, largely because it is unknown. Yet the focus has shifted. We are much more concerned about the rights of people that are denied by social structures. A symptom of this is the fact that the major problems in bioethics are perceived to be problems of access and distribution, problems of social organization and social responsibility. The same is true in other areas. For example, the women's issue is seen to be a structural problem. Similarly, life issues (abortion, war, capital punishment, etc.) are increasingly approached as a whole in terms of a "consistent ethic of life."

4) *The age of experience.* Through many initiatives of Vatican II (and the theology that led to and formed it) we now are more aware than ever that one of the richest and most indispensable sources of moral knowledge is human experience and reflection. To be ignorant of it or to neglect it is to doom moral theology to irrelevance and triviality.

I am deeply aware of the traps of overcontrast. But that being acknowledged, there is a residue of truth in the general assertion that for some decades Catholic moral theology proceeded as if its responsibility was to form and shape experience, but hardly ever be shaped by it. The overcontrast in that generalization refers to the work of theologians mentioned at the beginning of this overview. Anyone who reads "Notes on Moral Theology" from 1940 forward will see immediately that Ford, Kelly, Lynch, and Connery were intimately associated with psychiatrists, social ethicists, physicians, business persons, and laypeople. My generalization does not refer to these eminent authors.

Rather it refers to official formulations. On the one hand, we honor key ideas in Vatican II. For instance.

> She [the church] must rely on those who live in the world, are versed in different institutions and specialties, and grasp their innermost significance in the eyes of both believers and unbelievers. With the help of the Holy Spirit, it is the task of the entire People of God, especially pastors and theologians, to hear, distinguish, and interpret the many voices of our age, and to judge them in the light of the divine Word.[46]

For this reason the Council warned:

> Let the layperson not imagine that his/her pastors are always such experts that to every problem which arises, however complicated, they can readily give him/her a concrete solution, or even that such is their mission....Let the layperson take on his/her own distinctive role.[47]

On the other hand, we seem not to know how to deal with this "take on his/her own distinctive role." There are repeated attempts by some *immobilisti* to marginalize it as "mere polls." And they have a point. But not the only point. When I include the "age of experience" as a dimension of where we are, I mean to underline the fact that both authoritative statements and current theology admit experience as a *locus theologicus* in principle. There remain tensions about how to use and interpret it in systematic moral reflection. This is particularly true of some "authentic" utterances of the Holy See.

5) *The age of cultural diversity.* In 1979 Karl Rahner published in these pages "A Basic Interpretation of Vatican II."[48] Rahner saw Vatican II as the inauguration of the church as a world church. He saw three epochs in the history of Christianity: (1) the period of Jewish Christianity, (2) the period of Hellenism and European culture, (3) the period of the church as a world church.

Up to Vatican II, Christianity was basically a Western export that attempted to proselytize by imposing the Latin language and rites, Roman law and the bourgeois morality of the West on various cultures. Our challenge now—and one with profound implications for moral theology—is to recognize essential cultural differences and with a Pauline boldness to draw the necessary consequences. For instance, Rahner asks: "Must the marital morality of the Masais in East Africa simply reproduce the morality of Western Christianity, or could a chieftain there, even if he is a Christian, live in the style of the patriarch Abraham?"[49] Simply to suppose that we have answers to questions like these is to fail to de-Europeanize Christianity and to "betray the meaning of Vatican II."

6) *The age of technology.* Nearly every aspect of modern life in the Western world has been deeply affected by technology. The changes continue on an almost daily basis: travel, information flow, education, construction, cooking, business, medicine, and so on. I have no precise idea how this relates to moral theology. But one cannot avoid the nagging suspicion that it may reinforce some deeply embedded Western and American value priorities: efficiency and comfort. If these are indeed the values that shape the perspectives of many Americans, it should be fairly clear that we are knee-deep in danger that they will corrosively affect our judgments of the morally right and wrong, and more generally of the priority of values.

7) *The age of holiness and witness.* The past 50 years have led us to the point where we recognize the value but limits of rational argument and analysis. The very meaning of "in the Lord" is best gathered

from the lives of the saints. Johannes Metz notes that "Christological knowledge is formed and handed on not primarily in the form of concepts but in accounts of following Christ."[50] That is why the history of Christian theological ethics is the history of the practice of following Christ and must assume a primarily narrative form. We make Christ present in our world by embodying in our lives what Joseph Sittler used to refer to as "the shape of the engendering deed."[51] The saints do that best.

What I am suggesting by inference is that moral theology today, in its self-concept, is much more sensitive to the central importance of witness, imagination, liturgy, and emotions. There are many loose ends and incomplete agenda, of course. But it is where we are.

8) *The age of theological anthropology.* The *Institutiones theologiae moralis,* notwithstanding their compassion and practical pastoral wisdom, contained an image of the human person and of moral agency: the agent as solitary decision-maker. That may be an overstatement, but I think not by much. It is the result of presenting the moral life largely in terms of obligations and sins—itself the precipitate of a confession-oriented moral theology.

Moral theologians today are much more aware of the need of a sound theological anthropology. By theological anthropology I mean a doctrine of the human person that views him/her in terms of the great Christian mysteries: creation-fall-redemption. It is a doctrine that would yield an appropriate emphasis on vision, perspectives, and character, and the stories, metaphors, and images that generate and nourish these elements.[52] Vatican II summarized this very cryptically: "Faith throws a new light on everything, manifests God's design for man's total vocation, and thus directs the mind to solutions which are fully human."[53] The terms "God's design" and "total vocation" are shorthand for theological anthropology.

9) *The age of ecumenism.* Because of the ecclesiological moves of Vatican II (e.g., acknowledgment of the presence of the Spirit to non-Catholic Christians and the reality of church in many of their communions), it is simply accepted in contemporary moral theology that our non-Catholic Christian colleagues are an important locus theologicus in moral deliberations. This is in rather stark contrast to canon 1399, 4 of the old Code that forbade the reading of books of any non-Catholics who "*ex professo* treated of religion" unless it was absolutely clear (*constet*) that such treatments contained nothing against the Catholic faith.

In other words, the very separation of a Christian from Catholicism contained a presumption that that person was not a source of religious and moral wisdom and knowledge.

A symbol of where we are now is the fact that not a few of our Catholic moral theologians have studied under fine theologians such as James Gustafson, Paul Ramsey, Harmon Smith, et al. Once again I must advert to the fact that the discipline of moral theology has moved in this direction, yet it is far from clear that the sources of official statements have.

10) *The age of women.* I have already mentioned this above. Further comment, especially by a male, might be interpreted as a move in the reassertion of male dominance.

SUGGESTIONS FOR THE FUTURE

The detailing of significant developments and descriptions of where we are now implies directions for the future. The agenda seems fairly clear. We must develop these directions in a more profound, systematic, and pastoral way. Here I will simply list the qualities our continuing theological search should have if it is to respond to the needs of our time. Once again, in tens, I take these qualities from the preface of my recent volume *The Critical Calling: Reflection on Moral Dilemmas since Vatican II.*[54]

1) *Open.* The church is a world church. I add only that "open" does not mean unstructured, unsystematic, or dispassionate. In the American church, openness means a willingness to listen to what Hispanic Catholics have to say to us. In a real sense, but one I cannot specify, the future of the American Catholic Church belongs to Hispanics, much as its past and present were shaped by immigrant Catholics, especially the Irish.

2) *Ecumenical.* It must take seriously the activity of the spirit in other Christian and non-Christian churches.

3) *Insight-oriented.* This references an approach that views deeper understanding and corrective vision as the primary challenge of moral theology, not first of all conclusions or rules of conduct.

4) *Collegial.* Moral theology must be informed by the experience and reflection of all those with a true competence.

5) *Honest.* A "theology" rigged to justify pretaken authoritative positions merits the quotation marks I have given the term.

6) *Scientifically informed.* This speaks for itself.

7) *Adult.* The moral theology of the future must take personal responsibility seriously, both in developing moral convictions and in applying them. The older paternalism is dead.

8) *Realistic.* Past experience has taught us to beware of systems, and authors, that claim to have all the answers. A realistic theology will readily admit the limits of human concepts and verbal tools and not be upset with zones of ambiguity and uncertainty.

9) *Catholic and catholic.* The moral theology of the future must be proud enough of and loyal enough to its heritage to be critical of it in ways that make it more challenging to and meaningful for the non-Catholic world and prevent it from becoming comfortably and/or defensively sectarian.

10) *Centered on Christ.* A Catholic moral theology that is not centered on Christ had better change its name. By "centered on Christ" I do not mean repetitious and cosmetic overlays of biblical parenesis. I mean rather that the fundamental concepts of such a theology (e.g., vocation, *telos,* conversion, virtue, sin, obligation, etc.) should be shaped by the fact—and implications thereof—that Jesus is God's incarnate self-gift. The very gift of God in Jesus shapes our response—which means that the central and organizing vitality of the Christian moral life and moral theology is the self-gift we call charity. This must function, far more than it has, in the very notion of the moral life, in the discernment of moral rightfulness and wrongfulness of conduct, and in the pastoral education of the community of believers.

Notes

1. *TS* 1 (1940) 412–43.

2. One thinks immediately of John C. Ford's "The Morality of Obliteration Bombing," *TS* 5 (1944) 261–309. Interestingly, one finds reference in *TS* 5 (1944) 511–13 to an article by John Rock and Miriam F. Menkin entitled "In Vitro Fertilization and Cleavage of Human Ovarian Eggs," *Sciences,* August 4, 1944, 105–107.

3. *TS* 9 (1948) 105.

4. *TS* 10 (1949) 70.

5. *TS* 10 (1949) 71–74.

6. John R. Connery, S.J., "Steady Dating among Adolescents," *TS* 19 (1958) 73–80.

7. *TS* 11 (1950) 76, and 15 (1954) 101.

8. Francis V. Courneen, S.J., "Recent Trends with Regard to Fasting," *TS* 7 (1946) 464–70.

9. Anthony F. Zimmerman, S.V.D., "Morality and the Problems of Overpopulation," *Proceedings of the CTSA 14th Annual Convention* (1959) 5–27.

10. Antonius Lanza and Petrus Palazzini, *Theologia moralis*, Appendix: *De castitate et luxuria* (Rome: Marietti, 1953) 225.

11. Richard A. McCormick, S.J., "Self-Assessment and Self-Indictment," *Religious Studies Review* 13 (1987) 37.

12. Gérard Gilleman, S.J., *Le primat de la charité en théologie morale* (Paris: Desclée de Brouwer, 1952).

13. Daniel Callahan, "Authority and the Theologian," *Commonweal* 80 (1964) 319–23.

14. For a discussion cf. Ronald Modras, "The Implications of Rahner's Anthropology for Fundamental Moral Theology," *Horizons* 12 (1985) 70–90.

15. E.g., cf. M. Flick, S.J., and Z. Alszeghy, S.J., "L'Opzione fondamentale della vita morale et la grazia," *Gregorianum* 41 (1960) 593–619; P. Fransen, S.J., "Pour une psychologie de la grâce divine," *Lumen vitae* 12 (1957) 209–440.

16. Joseph Fuchs, S.J., *General Moral Theology* (Rome: Gregorian University, 1963). This is my translation of Fuch's *Theologia moralis generalis*. Fuchs has also discussed the matter elsewhere, e.g. in "Basic Freedom and Morality," in *Human Values and Christian Morality* (Dublin: Gill and Macmillan, 1970) 91–111. B. Schüller, S.J., "Zur Analogie sittlicher Grundbegriffe," *Theologie und Philosophie* 41 (1966) 3–19.

17. I believe the C.D.F.'s *Person humana* (*The Pope Speaks* 21 [1976] 60–73) presents the notion inaccurately. Cf. Charles E. Curran, "Sexual Ethics: Reaction and Critique," *Linacre Quarterly* 43 (1976) 147–64.

18. Peter Knauer, S.J., "La détermination du bien et du mal moral par le principe du double effet," *Nouvelle revue théologique* 87 (1965) 356–76.

19. Germain Grisez, *Abortion: The Myths, the Realities, and the Arguments* (Washington: Corpus Books, 1970) 331.

20. *TS* 13 (1952) 60.

21. There are others such as Benedict Ashley, O.P., and Kevin O'Rourke, O.P., in *Health Care Ethics* (St. Louis: Catholic Hospital Association, 1977). Their treatment on this point is rather sketchy.

22. Bernard Hoose, *Proportionalism: The American Debate and Its European Roots* (Washington: Georgetown Univ., 1987).

23. As in Rober Blair Kaiser, *The Politics of Sex and Religion* (Kansas City: Leaven, 1985) 177.

24. André Hellegers said much the same thing as de Locht. Cf. LeRoy Walters, "Religion and the Renaissance of Medical Ethics in the United States: 1965–1975," in *Theology and Bioethics,* ed. Earl E. Shelp (Dordrecht: Reidel, 1985) 9–10.

25. *AAS* 58 (1966) 218–29, at 219.

26. *Notes on Moral Theology 1965–1980* (Lanham, Md.: University Press of America, 1981) 212.

27. J. Massingberd Ford, "Toward a Theology of Speaking in Tongues," *TS* 32 (1971) 3–29.

28. "Partners in the Mystery of Redemption," *Origins* 17 (1988) 757, 759–88.

29. C. J. McFadden, *Medical Ethics* (Philadelphia: F. A. Davis, 1967); Gerald Kelly, S.J., *Medico-Moral Problems* (St. Louis: Catholic Hospital Association, 1949–54); T. J. O'Donnell, S.J., *Morals in Medicine* (Westminster, Md.: Newman, 1956); Edwin F. Healy, S.J., *Medical Ethics* (Chicago: Loyola Univ., 1956).

30. Walters, "Religion" 4.

31. Gustavo Gutiérrez M., "Notes for a Theology of Liberation," *TS* 31 (1970) 243–61.

32. Ibid., 255.

33. *Catholic Mind* 69 (1971) 37–58.

34. *Octogesima adveniens* (cf. n. 33 above) 7.

35. *The Documents of Vatican II,* ed. Walter M. Abbott, S.J. (New York: America, 1966) 256.

36. *Schema constitutionis pastoralis de ecclesia in mundo huius temporis: Expensio modorum partis secundae* (Vatican Press, 1965) 37–38.

37. Louis Janssens, "Artificial Insemination: Ethical Considerations," *Louvain Studies* 8 (1980) 3–29, at 24.

38. Found in R. A. McCormick, S.J., "L'Affaire Curran," *America* 154 (1986) 267.

39. I go out of my way here to point out that this in no way impugns the quality or integrity of professors presently at Catholic University. It seems to me to be a judgment about institutional policy.

40. Charles E. Curran, "Public Dissent in the Church," *Origins* 16 (1986) 178–84. Cf. also Curran, *Faithful Dissent* (Kansas City: Sheed and Ward, 1986) 61.

41. "L'Affaire Curran" 266.

42. Cf. Giancarlo Zizola, *La restaurazione di papa Wojtyla* (Rome: Laterza e Figli, 1985) 3.

43. Richard A. McCormick, S.J., "The Chill Factor: Recent Roman Interventions," *America* 150 (1984) 475–81. I cannot avoid the conclusion that the C.D.F. has somehow been isolated from contemporary discussions and therefore in significant respects misunderstands them.

44. As an example cf. Walter Kerber, S.J., ed., *Sittliche Normen* (Düsseldorf: Patmos, 1982).

45. "*Sollicitudo rei socialis*," *Origins* 17 (1988) 642–60, at 653.

46. *Documents of Vatican II* 246.

47. Ibid., 244.

48. Karl Rahner, S.J., "A Basic Interpretation of Vatican II," *TS* 40 (1979) 716–27.

49. Ibid., 718.

50. Johannes Metz, *Followers of Christ* (Mahwah, N.J.: Paulist, 1978) 40.

51. Joseph Sittler, *The Structure of Christian Ethics* (Baton Rouge: Louisiana State Univ., 1958), unfortunately out of print.

52. Such an emphasis may help to recognize obligation, but it does not justify it. Cf. James Childress, "Scripture and Christian Ethics," *Interpretation* 34 (1980)371–80.

53. *Documents of Vatican II* 209.

54. Georgetown Univ., 1989.

Part Two

PRE-VATICAN II

4. Moral Theology

August Lehmkuhl

This chapter first appeared in the *Catholic Encyclopedia.*

Moral theology is a branch of theology, the science of God and divine things. The distinction between natural and supernatural theology rests on a solid foundation. Natural theology is the science of God himself, in as far as the human mind can by its own efforts reach a definite conclusion about God and his nature; it is always designated by the adjective natural. Theology, without any further modification, is invariably understood to mean supernatural theology, that is, the science of God and divine things, in as far as it is based on supernatural revelation. Its subject matter embraces not only God and his essence, but also his actions and his works of salvation and the guidance by which we are led to God, our supernatural end. Consequently, it extends much farther than natural theology; for, though the latter informs us of God's essence and attributes, yet it can tell us nothing about his free works of salvation. The knowledge of all these truths is necessary for every man, at least in its broad outlines, and is acquired by Christian faith. But this is not yet a science. The science of theology demands that the knowledge won through faith be deepened, expanded, and strengthened, so that the articles of faith can be understood and defended by their reasons and be, together with their conclusions, arranged systematically.

The entire field of the theology proper is divided into dogmatic and moral theology, which differ in subject matter and in method. Dogmatic theology has as its end the scientific discussion and establishment of the doctrines of faith, moral theology of the moral precepts. The precepts of Christian morals are also part of the doctrines of faith, for they were announced or confirmed by divine revelation. The subject matter of dogmatic theology is those doctrines which serve to enrich the knowledge necessary or convenient for man, whose destination is supernatural. Moral theology, on the other hand, is limited to those doctrines which discuss the relations of man and his free actions to God and his supernatural end, and propose the means instituted by God for the attainment of that end. Consequently, dogmatic and moral theology are two closely related parts of universal theology. Inasmuch as a considerable number of individual doctrines may be claimed by either discipline, no sharp line of demarcation can be drawn between the subject matter of dogma and morals. In actual practice, however, a division and limitation must be made in accordance with practical needs. Of a similar nature is the relation between moral theology and ethics. The subject matter of natural morals or ethics, as contained in the Decalogue, has been included in positive divine revelation, and hence has passed into moral theology. Nevertheless, the argumentative processes differ in the two sciences, and for this reason a large portion of the matter is disregarded in moral theology and referred to ethics. For instance, the refutation of the false systems of the modern ethicists is generally treated under ethics, especially because these systems are refuted by arguments drawn not so much from faith as from reason. Only in as far as moral theology requires a defense of revealed doctrines does it concern itself with false systems. However, it must discuss the various requirements of the natural law, not only because this law has been confirmed and defined by positive revelation, but also because every violation of it entails a disturbance of the supernatural moral order, the treatment of which is an essential part of moral theology.

The field of moral theology, its contents, and the boundaries which separate it from kindred subjects, may be briefly indicated as follows: moral theology includes everything relating to man's free actions and the last, or supreme, end to be attained through them, as far as we know the same by divine revelation; in other words, among the things it includes are the supernatural end, the rule, or norm, of the moral order, human actions as such, their harmony or disharmony with the laws of the moral order, their consequences, and the divine aids for their right performance.

The contents of a modern work on moral theology, as for instance that of Slater (London, 1909), are: human acts, conscience, law, sin, the virtues of faith, hope, charity; the precepts of the Decalogue, including a special treatise on justice; the commandments of the church; duties attached to particular states or offices; the sacraments, insofar as their administration and reception are a means of moral reform and rectitude; ecclesiastical laws and penalties, only insofar as they affect conscience; these laws forming properly the subject-matter of canon law, insofar as they govern and regulate the church as an organization – its membership, ministry, the relations between hierarchy, clergy, religious orders, laity – or of its spiritual and temporal authority.

One circumstance must not be overlooked. Moral theology considers free human actions only in their highest end, not in their relation to the proximate ends which man may and must pursue, as for instance political, social, economical. Economics, politics, social science are separate fields of science, not subdivisions of moral science. Nevertheless, these special sciences must also be guided by morals, and must subordinate their specific principles to those of moral theology, at least so far as not to clash with the latter. Man is one being, and all his actions must finally lead him to his last and highest end. Therefore, various proximate ends must not turn him from this end, but must be made subservient to it and its attainment. Hence moral theology surveys all the individual relations of man and passes judgment on political, economical, and social questions, not with regard to their bearings on politics and economy, but with regard to their influence upon a moral life. This is also the reason why there is hardly another science that touches other spheres so closely as does moral theology, and why its sphere is more extensive than that of any other. This is true inasmuch as moral theology has the eminently practical scope of instructing and forming spiritual directors and confessors, who must be familiar with human conditions in their relation to the moral law and advise persons in every state and situation.

The manner in which moral theology treats its subject matter must be, as in theology generally, chiefly positive, that is, drawing from revelation and theological sources. Starting from this positive foundation, reason also comes into play quite extensively, especially since the whole subject matter of natural ethics has been raised to the level of supernatural morals. It is true that reason must be illumined by supernatural faith, but when illumined, its duty is to explain, prove, and defend most of the principles of moral theology.

Moral theology, in more than one respect, is essentially a practical science. Its instructions must extend to moral character, moral behavior, and the completion and issue of moral aspirations, so that it can offer a definite norm for the complex situations of human life. For this purpose, it must examine the individual cases which arise and determine the limits and the gravity of the obligation in each. Particularly those whose office and position in the church demand the cultivation of theological science, and who are called to be teachers and counsellors, must find in it a practical guide. As jurisprudence must enable the future judge and lawyer to administer justice in individual cases, so must moral theology enable the spiritual director or confessor to decide matters of conscience in varied cases of everyday life; to weigh the violations of the natural law in the balance of divine justice; it must enable the spiritual guide to distinguish correctly and to advise others as to what is sin and what is not, what is counselled and what is not, what is good and what is better; it must provide a scientific training for the shepherd of the flock so that he can direct all to a life of duty and virtue, warn them against sin and danger, lead from good to better those who are endowed with necessary light and moral power, raise up and strengthen those who have fallen from the moral level. Many of these tasks are assigned to the collateral science of pastoral theology; but this also treats a special part of the duties of moral theology and falls, therefore, within the scope of moral theology in its widest sense. The purely theoretical and speculative treatment of the moral questions must be supplemented by casuistry. Whether this should be done separately, that is, whether the subject matter should be taken casuistically before or after its theoretical treatment, or whether the method should be at the same time both theoretical and casuistical, is unimportant for the matter itself; the practical feasibility will decide this point, while for written works on moral theology the special aim of the author will determine it. However, he who teaches or writes moral theology for the training of Catholic priests would not do full justice to the end at which he must aim if he did not unite the casuistical with the theoretical and speculative element.

There can be no doubt that in judging the heinousness of sin, and in distinguishing between mortal and venial sins, the subjective element must be taken into consideration. However, every compendium of moral theology, no matter how casuistical, meets this requirement. Every manual distinguishes sins which arise from ignorance, weakness, malice without, however, labeling all sins of weakness as venial sins, or all sins of malice as mortal sins, for there are surely minor acts of malice which cannot be said to cause the death of the soul. Every manual also takes cognizance of sins which are committed without sufficient deliberation, knowledge, or freedom: all these, even though the matter be grave, are counted as venial sins. On the other hand, every manual recognizes venial and grievous sins which are such by the gravity of the matter alone. Or who would, abstracting from everything else, put a jocose lie on a par with the denial of faith? But even in these sins, mortal or venial according to their object, the casuists lay stress on the personal dispositions in which the sin was actually committed. Hence, their universal principle – the result of a subjectively erroneous conscience – may be that an action which is in itself only venial becomes a mortal sin, and vice versa; that an action which is in itself mortally sinful, that is, constitutes a grave violation of the moral law, may be only a venial sin. Nevertheless, all theologians, also casuists, consider a correct conscience a great boon and hence endeavor, by their casuistic discussions, to contribute towards the formation of correct consciences so that the subjective estimate of the morality of certain actions may coincide, as far as possible, the with objective norm of morality.

When, lastly, various opponents of the casuistical method object that the moralist occupies himself exclusively with sins and their analysis, with the "dark side" of human life, let them remember that it is physically impossible to say everything in one breath, that just as in many other arts and sciences a division of labor may also be advantageous for the science of moral theology, that the particular purpose of manuals and lectures may be limited to the education of skilled confessors, and that this purpose may very well be fulfilled by centering attention on the dark side of human life. Nevertheless, it must be granted that this cannot be the only purpose of moral theology: a thorough discussion of all Christian virtues and the means of acquiring them is indispensable. If at any time this part of moral theology should be pushed to the background, moral theology would become one-sided and would need a revision, not by cutting down casuistry, but by devoting more time and energy to the doctrine of virtues in their scientific, parenetical, and ascetical aspect.

Lately attempts have been made to develop moral theology along other lines. The reformers assert that the casuistical method has choked every other and that it must give place to a more scientific, systematic treatment. It is evident that a merely casuistical treatment does not come up to the demands of moral theology, and as a matter of fact, during the last decades the speculative element was more and more insisted on even in works chiefly casuistic. Whether the one or the other element should prevail must be determined according to the proximate aim which the work intends to satisfy. If there is question of a purely scientific explanation of moral theology which does not intend to exceed the limits of speculation, then the casuistical element is without doubt speculative, systematic discussion of the questions belonging to moral theology; casuistry then serves only to illustrate the theoretical explanations. But if there is question of a manual which is intended for the practical needs of a pastor and confessor and for their education, then the solid, scientific portion of general moral-theological questions must be supplemented by an extensive casuistry. Nay, when time and leisure are wanting to add ample theoretical explanations to an extensive casuistical drill, we should not criticize him who would under these circumstances insist on the latter at the expense of the former; it is the more necessary in actual practice.

5. Moral Theology:
Its Limitations

John B. Hogan

This chapter first appeared in *American Ecclesiastical Review* 10 (1884).

One of the most striking differences between the moral teachings of the Catholic Church and those of Protestantism or philosophy is found in the fullness and assurance of the former as compared with the habitual vagueness and hesitancy of the latter. The guidance of the Catholic Church is preeminently practical; it covers the whole ground of human conduct, and traces out a course easy to most, accessible to all, yet offering perfect security to those who follow it. At first sight nothing seems wanting to its completeness; but a closer examination reveals the fact that it remains unfinished on every side; that, in each one of its aspects, much remains which still may be discovered, much also which of its nature is hidden from human knowledge, to be seen only when the veil is withdrawn, and the narrow present vanishes into the boundless future. To consider the limits within which, as a necessity or as a fact, Moral Theology is thus confined, will, it seems to us, be a considerable help to a proper understanding of the science.

Moral Theology embraces in theory the whole field of human action, and has for its object to determine the existence—the extent—the gravity—the underlying principles—of all human obligations, and of the responsibilities consequent on them. We have to see how far these various objects have been or may be reached, and in what the efforts of theology fall short of them.

I.

As regards the question of their existence.

1. There are primordial duties which have been held as indubitable at all times by all races of men. Such are the duties of justice, benevolence, gratitude, religious reverence, a certain restraint of the lower appetites, and the like. They are always taken for granted, appealed to as self-evident, and never demonstrated because of their very evidence.

2. The number of these unquestioned obligations has been increasing in the course of ages, under the influence of divinely revealed truth, or as the outcome of progressive civilization. The Jewish code of morals was far in advance of that of the pagans; the Christian law corrected and completed in many particulars that of the Jews. Stoicism awakened the Roman empire to the consciousness of many duties unheeded in earlier times. A steady growth of ascertained moral truths is noticeable even in the church, the law of development having its application fully as much and for the same reasons in moral as in dogmatic theology. In many cases where the Fathers hesitated, we today are certain. To determine moral duty they turned mainly to scripture. "What scripture forbids we may not do," says S. Basil,[1] "and what it commands we should not fail to accomplish. But as regards those things on which it is silent, we have the rule of the Apostle: *All things are lawful for me, but all do not edify.*" The difficulty was to gather anything like a definite rule, either from the Old Testament, amid maxims and examples often perplexing, to say the least, and remote from the spirit of the Gospel; or from the Gospel itself, admirably clear as a direction and an impulse, but vague and indefinite as an obligatory law. It was reserved to the schoolmen to work out the problem systematically and in all its details, with the result of gifting us at the present day with a more definite and better ascertained rule of life than the world possessed at any previous period.

3. Yet the work is far from having reached its end. Our books of Moral Theology are still full of varying conceptions of duty. True, there is a happy tendency to agreement on many points long controverted. But agreement on such matters, recent, or ancient, does not necessarily imply the final settlement of them. All know the varying fortunes of certain opinions; how some spring up suddenly into life and rapidly win

favor; how others, long universally believed in, gradually lose their hold on men's minds, and finally disappear. Thus, to confine ourselves to a few more obvious instances, it was the disposition of the Fathers to erect into positive commands some of the evangelical counsels in regard to such subjects as chastity, matrimony, worldly pursuits, alms-giving, forbearance under injury, self-defense, and the like. But what was extreme in their views gradually gave way to a more correct esti-mate of human nature, still weak even when regenerated, and of the practical requirements of society. In the opposite direction several objectionable practices, such as judiciary combats and duelling, intro-duced by the barbarians, were long tolerated, invested even with reli-gious sanctions in many places, and yielded but slowly to the prohibi-tions of the church. Theologians themselves clung for many centuries to the ancient tradition forbidding "usury," understood as the practice of making money by lending money. They were long unanimous in maintaining the so-called "principle of equality" in contracts, to which modern society has substituted the much more intelligible principle of mutual freedom.

Again, oaths were long considered as binding, even when extorted by fraud or by fear, if only they could be kept without sin. Paternal authority was upheld by the earlier theologians to an extent and with consequences to which nobody could give countenance at the present day. Slavery was as universally and as readily admitted in past times as it is condemned in ours. Changes of a similar kind might be pointed out in various other directions, all going to show the fluctuating and uncer-tain character of moral rules long unanimously acquiesced in, and sug-gesting the possibility of more than one point, upon which there is pres-ent agreement, being reopened and discussed afresh, just as is happen-ing today in regard to so many social and scientific problems. Happily, the reflex principles which play so important a part in human conduct are ever at hand to direct our course, or to reassure us, despite our spec-ulative uncertainties.

II.

The existence of each duty once ascertained, a second question naturally arises: How far does it extend? to what exactly does it bind us?

Here again we have the same combination of certainties and uncertainties. In the case of negative duties, "Thou shalt not kill, thou shalt not steal," etc., the general law is clear enough, as also in the case of positive duties, when they are of a definite kind, such as paying one's debts, obedience to parents, and the like. But almost all such laws are subject to limitations, some again evident, but many others determined only with much difficulty, and leaving to the end a considerable margin of vagueness and uncertainty. Thus, for example, we are bound to pay our debts, but only when physically and morally able to do so. Physical impossibilities are easily ascertained; moral possibilities and impossibilities, on the contrary, as all theologians know, are extremely difficult to determine with any precision. Again, we are bound to avoid causing injury to others. Yet, directly or indirectly, remotely or proximately, we are doing it, in some measure, or sharing in it, almost every day, without scruple, doubtless because we consider that there is a sufficient reason for our doing so. But when is the reason sufficient?

The character of indefiniteness is still more sensible in certain positive duties. Who, for instance, can tell the man of wealth just what he is bound to do for the needy hundreds who appeal to him, or for the thousands whom he knows to be in deep distress? The sinner is subject to the natural and divine law of atonement, but strictly obliged to what? The Christian acknowledges the obligation of prayer. Christ tells us to pray always. When is the precept fulfilled in its integrity? Again, He describes the giving of scandal as a terrible evil, and the misfortune of being exposed to it as a thing to avoid at the cost of what is most necessary and most dear to us. How are we to interpret all this practically? Questions of this kind arise on all sides, especially in connection with duties of a general nature, forming, as it were, a deep fringe of penumbra around the central light of clearly defined obligations. To narrow this shadow more and more is the constant effort of Moral Theology, indeed, we may say, of the human conscience; and, considering the imperfection of the data, the results arrived at are truly remarkable.

1. The individual man, were he compelled to face such problems alone, could only feel his utter inability to grapple with them. But he knows that he is not alone, and as soon as perplexity arises as to the extent of any one of his duties, he instinctively looks around him to see how it is measured by his fellow-men, especially by those who are

deemed upright and good, and he feels safe provided he does just as they do.

2. If he is a Catholic, he looks to the church or to his confessor speaking in her name, considering that it is part of their mission to warn him if he unconsciously fails in the performance of any important duty. The church, in turn, and the confessor gather light from what is found and from what is absent from the traditions, the laws, the accepted customs of Christian ages, from the teachings of the Fathers and the mind of the saints, more likely, because of their nearness to God, to know the full extent of His will.

3. But, underlying it all—behind the appreciations of the Saints, of the Fathers, of theologians, confessors, and the public at large—there is a certain fundamental conception or philosophy of human life, individual and collective, of its practical possibilities and of its ultimate purposes, upon which all is unconsciously yet really built. To put it in a few words, the supreme law of man is that of the homage of his whole being to God. The will of God—necessary as regards what is due to himself—free in all else—is the complete rule of human action. What God means man to do and to be, that and that alone is his duty. Now, without entering into particulars, the object of the divine will would seem to be substantially *the conservation and progress of the individual and of society.* All man's moral impulses lead in that direction, and converge toward that end. It is the standard to which we instinctively compare human actions, and declare them good or evil. Whatever perfects man, singly or collectively, we believe to be pleasing to God; whatever weakens or lessens him, especially in the moral order which is felt to be supreme, we unhesitatingly declare to be wrong.

4. Besides this general direction, there are certain other more special lines of development along which man is led by his moral sense, and which are determined by the peculiar manner in which he is made. For man is not merely a rational being in general; he is a rational and moral being of a definite kind, offering a combination of special elements—sensations, emotions, thoughts, fancies, principles, etc., acting and reacting under special laws and limitations. It is just these that give human duty, not only its individual character, but also its true limits. And this is why that unconscious philosophy to which we refer, built on an obscure, yet real and concrete sense of things, feels itself able to determine the extent of obligations when abstract reason is unequal to

the task. Where the philosopher hesitates because he sees only the general features of the case, the practical man intuitively grasps all the elements, and reaches a decision.

In this way, then, much of the vagueness of duty has been removed. The process continues, and is bound to continue, with the result of making man's obligations ever clearer and more definite. Yet something of indeterminateness clings to several of them fatally, and will remain to the end. Besides, the constant change of surroundings, adaptation to which is as much a law of the moral as of the physical life, will even continue to raise new doubts according as the older ones are dispelled, thus leaving the science incomplete in this as in its other aspects.

III.

A full knowledge of our duties would imply not only our recognizing clearly their existence, and seeing distinctly how far they extend, but also the possibility of our determining accurately their degree of urgency. For each one of them has its definite measure of importance; each fault has its exact degree of guilt. Between the slightest obligation and the weightiest, between the faintest beginnings of evil and its lowest depths, there are degrees without number. It is with them as with colors, few in their original simplicity, yet so varied in nature that art is powerless to reproduce them with perfect accuracy. In the Gobelins' tapestry-work each color reckons tones by the hundred, from the darkest to the brightest, passing from one to the other so imperceptibly that only the trained eye of the artist can detect a difference between those which follow in close succession; yet their fifteen thousand different dyes are found inadequate – a true picture of the countless shades of moral obligation, and of the corresponding degrees of moral evil consequent on its violation.

Theology can offer no means of measuring them. It easily recognizes, of course, some evils as greater than others; it has also its distinction of imperfections, venial and mortal sins. But such a classification is at most a rough and rudimentary one, much like that of dividing all men into the good and the wicked, or the rich and the poor. It includes under the same denomination cases extremely unlike one another, an act of deep deliberate villainy and a transient weakness, being both called mortal sins, though a single case of the former may be worse than a hundred of the latter.

The theological distinction itself is not devoid of difficulty. If imperfection is displeasing to God, as implying a voluntary departure from his will, it is not easy to see how it is not sinful; nor is it easier to understand how the worst of venial and the lightest of mortal sins, with scarce a shadow of perceptible difference between them, should nevertheless be separated, in themselves and in their consequences, by an almost incalcuable distance.

But, accepting it such as it is, its application is often one of extreme difficulty. Thus, we know that the worst passions are only the abnormal development of what are originally blameless impulses. When do they become simply objectionable, when positively sinful, when grievously so? Waste of time is reprehensible; when is it properly a sin? What amount of money may a man squander in the indulgence of his fancies or his follies, without incurring a grave responsibility? We object to the habit of betting or gambling, yet very few scruple to indulge in a solitary act of either; and who can say just when the gambler may be stopped in his course by the threat of eternal perdition? To injure a man in his possessions is wrong; but when is it a grievous wrong? How much does it take to constitute a mortal sin? Here is a case of every-day occurrence, and theologians in trying to solve it tell us many true and helpful things. They remark that it takes more when one has only shared in the injustice than if he alone were to cause it; that much depends on the position of the injured party, on the view he is likely to take, or should if reasonable take, of the harm done him; on the way the wrong was done—stealthily or violently, deliberately or by carelessness or neglect; on the very title by which he held that of which he has been deprived; for, although the civil law places all cases of ownership on the same level, natural right admits many shades of difference between them. But all this helps more to show the complexity of the problem than to solve it, and in the end our theologians themselves can only form conjectures.

Much more, perhaps, is conjectural in such distinctions (between mortal and venial) than is generally thought. There are, of course, crimes which all civilized nations have looked upon with horror; there are practices which, if viewed leniently, would soon prove subversive of the providential order to which we visibly belong; there are deeds so frequently and so strongly denounced in Holy Writ that we have to consider them as capable of separating the soul from God, even though their intrinsic evil may not be apparent to us. But even here exaggeration is possible, still more in the region of positive law, where the fear of hell has been made to play more, perhaps, than its due part in order to secure a more prompt and more thorough obedience.

However that may be, it is always a grave and solemn act to trace a line of separation leading to such terrible issues. The Fathers were slow to do it. They confined themselves to what was most obvious, as do those good people of the present day whose sole concern is to know the will of God and to accomplish it. To ascertain just how far they may be unfaithful without incurring eternal damnation, has nothing more practical in it for them than for a dutiful son to consider what faults would lead to his expulsion from his father's home. The distinction is serviceable only to coarse, weak, or ungenerous souls, or to the priests who strive to preserve them or to rescue them from what is worst. It is to help the latter, principally, in the ministry of the confessional, that theologians have carried their distinction of what is mortal and venial into every branch of human duty. Their rulings are naturally of unequal and varying value, a fact which perplexed confessors are sometimes glad to remember, and which might induce them, in turn (besides other reasons), to dwell less on such sharp divisions than some do in their instructions to the faithful.

IV.

But even though it were possible to trace a distinct, clear-cut line of division between mortal and venial sin in every sphere of duty, it could, after all, respond only to the objective side of the question. Yet the subjective side is, in all its particulars, a no less essential element. Indeed, the moral value of human action is principally determined by the mental and moral condition of the agent, and that condition can be ascertained only in a very imperfect way.

Here lies what may be considered, perhaps, the principal weakness of moral science, its inability to measure with anything like accuracy, the moral value, positive or negative, of individual actions.

The positive value of an action, as all know, is in the motive. But what gives its moral value to the motive? Three things: its elevation, its purity, and its intensity. As regards the first, even in the order of virtues, there are motives higher than others; and it may not be difficult to establish the hierarchical position of each, or to ascertain its presence and moving power in a given action. But to measure its purity is out of the question. Motives scarce ever act alone. In our most generous deeds there is always something of self; and as for our daily life, we are borne along by countless impulses, good, bad, and indifferent, of whose presence we are for the most part very imperfectly conscious, and whose real power and relative share in our actions are to us a still greater mystery. As regards the intensity of the virtuous motive considered in itself, it cannot be measured at all, if for no other reason, because there is no standard to measure it by.

Still less can we attempt to determine the measure of moral evil. The man who sins is guilty in proportion to his general moral enlightenment; to the special knowledge he has of the evil contained in or consequent on his action; to his advertence or present consciousness of the same; in proportion also to the freedom of his action, which, in turn is determined by his antecedent habits, by the actual power of his evil impulses, by his natural strength of will and consequent ability to resist them, by the amount of help which comes to him from without, that is, from his surroundings, or from the grace of God. Now what is all this but a series of varying quantities, of which we cannot expect ever to reach even the approximate value?

All human responsibility is limited. It varies from one to another, and in the same individual it varies with times, conditions, and objects. The case, in particular, of a man who sins with his eyes open is clear enough in one respect. But how judge that of the man who does wrong through ignorance? It is easy speculatively to draw a distinction between vincible and invincible ignorance; but there are numberless degrees in both, and it is almost impossible to say where they meet in the concrete. Between two men who do evil, one consciously and the other through ignorance or inadvertence, there seems to be the widest difference; and yet the guilt of the latter may be very great, though he never at any time fully opened his eyes to the fact that he was unfaithful to duty. Similar responsibilities arising from thoughtlessness, neglect, or the unconscious or vaguely conscious working of unworthy inclinations in the soul, form one of the deepest and most unfathomable mysteries of the moral life. The very freedom of the will is in all its aspects one of the greatest of mysteries. All attempts to analyze or explain seem only to destroy it; and if the world continues to believe in it still, it is in spite of argument and as an intuitive, indestructible condition of the human mind. But the more we watch its action, the more we are convinced of its manifold practical limitations, making man less, on the whole, of a free agent than he gives himself credit for.

The consequence of all this is that we can know but very imperfectly the real moral value of other men, and that even of our own worth we never can be sure. On the subjective still more than on the objective side of morals our knowledge is variously limited, some things being seen distinctly, others vaguely, while many are hidden out of sight, and, it may be, beyond our reach. Such being our natural condition, as Aristotle observes, just in this connection,[2] "it is the part of an educated man to require exactness in each class of subjects only as far as the nature of the subject admits." If, after all, moral science has succeeded in ascertaining the chief component elements of the moral world and its principal laws, has it not done as much for it as physics and chemistry have done for the physical universe? Both worlds offer an endless variety and complexity of forms, combinations ever new of their primordial elements, now hiding, now revealing their secrets, and equally attractive in what they tell and in what they conceal. And as in natural, so in moral science there is constant growth. Through a deeper and more accurate knowledge of the soul, of human nature, of life, the older problems are coming to be more accurately solved, while new questions and new views are ever widening the moral horizon. On the other hand, by the steady expansion of the political, juridical, and social sciences, Moral Theology is ever stirred up to fresh efforts; and thus a new life flows in, as it were, upon it from all sides, and perennial youth is unceasingly brought back to the most ancient form of human knowledge.

Notes

1. Regul. breviev. I.
2. Moral., I.3.

6. Moral Theology at the End of the Nineteenth Century

Thomas J. Bouquillon

This article first appeared in *Catholic University Bulletin* 5 (1899).

In writing under this broad title, we do not propose to treat all the questions which might naturally suggest themselves to the reader. Such a work would take us far beyond the limits of a simple article, for it would necessitate a review of systems, principles and methods now in vogue; detailed examination of the condition of the science in seminaries and universities, and of its relation to the problems of modern life. That in turn would imply a critical review of the history of some centuries for the purpose of tracing out with accuracy the thousand converging lines of cause and condition which have produced the actual status of Moral Theology.

Inviting as is that field of investigation, we confine ourselves to narrower limits. We wish merely to call attention to the place which the science actually holds in the group of sciences to which it belongs, to indicate the faults therein, to explain the causes and conditions which have produced them, and to hint at the methods to be employed in order to reinstate Moral Theology in the place to which its dignity and character entitle it.[1]

I. Present Condition of Moral Theology

In order to fix the reader's attention at once, we may begin with the statement that the present condition of Moral Theology is in strange contradiction with its intrinsic character and with the spirit of the day.

When we consider the time and talent devoted to the study of the moral sciences in our day, the efforts made to improve methods and to awaken the public to a sense of their importance, we must regretfully admit that Moral Theology has failed to keep pace with the times.

Ten years ago Cardinal D'Annibale wrote: "Eloquar? Sensim sine sensu prope consenescimus; nam...quasi viribus deficientes, compendiariis lucubrationibus contenti sumus, et ea quae veteres Theologi longe lateque versarunt, attingimus vix summis digitis, et praesertim ea quae ad justitiam pertinent. Aliud hujus aetatis incommodum esse videtur, quod, indulgentiores facti, quasi assentari humanae imbecillitati videmur."[2] Soon after that, a writer in the *Civiltà Cattolica* commented on the Cardinal's words as follows: "It is a fact, deplorable but too true and evident to anyone who has carefully followed the development of the study of Moral Theology for the past forty years. With few exceptions, we have a mass of compendiums made and fashioned with a somnolency almost senile, without a trace of profound study or exact criticism. If one happens to find some proof of diligence, it has been used merely in collecting and copying the sayings of others. That is the view which greets one. In speaking thus, we do not by any means disapprove of compendiums; on the contrary, we recognize their necessity for the student. What we do condemn, however, is the carelessness with which they are made; the habit of representing as different, opinions which are identical; of citing authorities which have little or no bearing on a question, without having read them; of repeating with unparalleled *naïveté,* sophisms and arguments which have been examined, discussed, refuted countless times. In a word, we condemn the lack of precision, of erudition, of a critical habit in moral science. This reprinting, or more exactly, this collecting of different opinions is well described by the *consenescimus* and *vix attingimus summis digitis* of Cardinal d'Annibale."[3] Much in the same spirit Father Berthier, O.P., said recently, in speaking of manuals of Dogmatic and Moral Theology, "The literature of modern manuals must be considered as one of the plagues of theological science."[4]

Such being the case, it is not strange that Moral Theology has lost its place among the sciences of life. Instead of reigning among them as a queen, it is hardly recognized as an equal; instead of being consulted by those who direct human activity in its different spheres, its very existence is all but ignored. Though this condition is due in a measure to the decadence of the Christian spirit, still that does not explain all. The science has failed to put itself in touch with new currents of thought; failed to anticipate problems of life and to win consideration for the solutions which it offers. Modern civilization has forced to the foreground serious problems which properly belong to the domain of Moral Theology, but the world has not asked that science for guidance in meeting them. Even the clergy seem to be satisfied with the narrow professional side, for when important questions arise, such as those of wages, property in land, education, they as a rule seek solutions not in a profound study of the principles of Moral Theology, but elsewhere.

Still more, the very method followed in the teaching of Moral Theology is sometimes a source of doubt and difficulty to many. Though we might enumerate instances taken from the average seminary life, we prefer to mention but one case, striking and typical. It is that of the celebrated Ausonio Franchi, whose conversion was such a source of joy to the Church. His biographer says of him: "The comparison of doctrines learned from seminary manuals with those taught by other authors, the divergence of opinion among moralists on a majority of questions and the practice of the confessional, awakened grave doubts in the conscience of the young priest and caused a serious unrest in his mind. To instruct himself and bring peace to his soul, he undertook the study of theological principles whence opinions on moral questions are derived, and though he was dealing with controversies legitimately discussed in the Church and differently settled by theologians, he came to the conclusion (wrongly as he later admitted) that his seminary studies had not been directed in a spirit of truth, but rather with a sectarian bias, and that, when he thought he had finished he found it necessary to commence again."[5]

Nor is that the worst feature of the case. The nature and object of Moral Theology are being entirely forgotten or misrepresented. Proof is seen in a recent book which has been widely read and much praised for its stimulating character and suggestive views: "Our Seminaries," by Rev. J. Talbot Smith. We find there stated the following: "Moral Theology may have the *fifth* place without dispute (after holy scripture, philosophy, dogmatic theology, literature) but it should never be higher in the most limited and starved curriculum. Of its very nature it must rank second to the preceding studies. It is in one sense simply a *method of applying certain principles* to human conditions, and whatever the genius employed in its development and expression, it ranks only with the science of law. It must shift its interpretations with the shifting circumstances of races and nations....It is a noble science, and the writer has no disposition to speak of it with indifference, or to diminish its claims to respect. But it must keep its place, and avoid pretensions. It cannot rank with the study of the Scriptures, which is the study of Christ; nor with the study of philosophy, which is the study of man; nor with dogma, which is the mind of the Church; nor yet with literature, which is the mind of the people, expressed in all ages and under innumerable conditions. It is next to these, because it is the immediate instrument of the priest in his ministry to the people; without which his service would lack efficiency, and might easily lapse into raggedness. It can hold the fifth place with ease, for it is a facile science in its elements, practical and therefore dear to the hard-headed student with more vocation than brains, indispensable forevermore, and attractive to geniuses whose talents have legal bent, a twist toward the work of making statutes and renewing them to fit the uneasy nature of man."[6] When one reads that page for the first time, one thinks of an Aristotle, a St. Augustine, a St. Thomas, a Suarez, whose transcendent genius never appeared to better advantage than in their writings on the principles of moral science; one recalls the great Franciscus Victoria, who called theology the first of sciences, to which nothing was foreign, and who believed that this explained why there were so few really great theologians; or again, one understands how, in the seventeenth century, a subtle and original writer could have bitterly complained about those who tried to write on Moral Theology without sufficient preparation in metaphysics, logic, and the sciences, unaided save by a dose of common sense.[7] One is forced, in a word, to the melancholy conclusion that Moral Theology, the science of those principles which should direct man towards the supreme end of his existence, is in our day fallen exceedingly low, since even its friends scarcely recognize it and then manage to make room for it below philosophy and after literature!

Such is the situation. Moral Theology is all but an outcast. It is no longer recognized as possessing the dignity and rank it once had when genius loved to spend itself in elucidating its principles. Dwarfed beyond recognition, it is an adjunct, a mere technical necessity for the priest. Before attempting to examine the condition in detail and explain the causes which have led to it, we wish to sketch out ever so briefly the essential conditions of all theology, in particular of moral; to show its place in that order which alone corresponds to reality.[8]

II. THE PLACE AND THE CHARACTER OF MORAL THEOLOGY

I. As in the objective order all things are related to one another, forming a vast system whose crowning point is the Supreme Being to whom all is subject, so all sciences are related, and they form a system whose climax is the science of the Supreme Being.[9] Though it is beyond the powers of any individual to master all sciences, no matter how remarkable his genius or patient his industry, yet the ensemble of the sciences has been a favorite subject of study from time immemorial. The wish to construct the hierarchy of sciences has given rise to much interesting speculation. The efforts of Aristotle and St. Thomas, collective encyclopedias, classifications of sciences now much more numerous than ever,[10] universities wherein all sciences are taught or are supposed to be taught—all such are results of man's insatiable longing to reach final unity in knowledge. If the sciences, then, are closely related to one another, the understanding of those relations is essential if one wishes to master a science. Hence it is that man's ability to master any science is in direct proportion to the breadth of his knowledge beyond its field. It is strange that a truth so trite as this should be so often ignored. The separation of Theology from the other sciences does violence to it and to them. No university center can be complete without it. True enough, some have denied that Theology is a science; they have refused to accord it a place among the sciences and its chairs have been excluded from scientific centers. Those who maintain this position justify it by appealing to the *autonomy of human reason* and the need of *unity in the positive method.* Others, to justify its admission to a place among the sciences, have thought fit to mutilate it or circumscribe its limits.[11] But such errors are mere accidents, quite contrary to the deeper tendencies of the human mind; a natural reaction will in time deliver us from them.[12]

II. The truths of religion, which form the object of theology, combine, in turn, into one system whose parts are intimately related.[13] The genius of the theologian is shown by his power to bring out this unity; to analyze, subordinate and coordinate the whole field of religious truth that the nature of the parts and their relations to one another and to the whole may be clearly seen. It is a task reserved for genius of the highest order. Such a genius was St. Thomas; such a work is admirably done in his Summa. Therein theology is represented as it should be, as a harmonious whole, a living organism. The attempt to study one portion of the field of theology, therefore, to the neglect or exclusion of any other, must be fatal. The separation of the practical truths, which are the subject matter of moral science, from the theoretical and social, can be fraught only with evil consequences. Father Kleutgen, S.J., who has done so much to revive interest in scholasticism, has expressed the thought in this manner: "Moralis doctrina cum dogmatica multis in locis, ita cognata et concreta est ut divelli nisi violenter non possit; ut in quaestionibus de sacramentis, de gratia, justificatione et merito, de fine hominis etc. Sed ea quoque quae separari non incommode queunt, altera ab alteris illustrantur; quare praestat secundum veterum morem, utramque in unum doctrinae corpus redigere."[14] It is no surprise, consequently, to find that those who have attained eminence in one field of Theology should have been authorities also in others, as Palavicini remarked in speaking of Lugo: "Neque fuit in contemplatrici theologia subtilior quam in morali prudentior; quamvis ego hujus postremae conjunctionis decus non tanquam singulare aliquid suspexerim. Rarum hoc esse atque insociabile dictitant homunciones nonnnulli, quibus expediret, ipsam unius doctrinae vacuitatem alterius esse probabilem conjecturam; perinde ac si vera omnia, atque adeo scientiae omnes, cognato foedere, non coirent; perinde ac si quaecumque rata conclusio in rerum agendarum quaestionibus, ex meditantis philosophiae initiis, non emergeret; perinde ac si metaphysica non esset disciplinarum omnium praeceptrix ac parens. Quid enim? Annon, quem modo laudavi, Aristoteles inter ethnicos, Aristotelique proximus Aquinas inter Christianos, denique inter sodales nostros Toletus, Vasquius, Suarius, Molina, in utroque dicendi genere praecipui sunt? ita ut potius admirabile sit, quempiam in solis moralibus praestare?"[15]

III. Coming to the field of Moral Theology alone, we find it made up of one system of truths, capable of division and subdivision indefinitely. Naturally, one may study the ensemble of the science or any portion of it. If one takes the latter course, one must keep well in mind the relations of the part to the whole, and vice versa, just as the physiologist would do in studying the eye, ear or lungs. Whichever method be followed, the subject of study must be viewed as a whole and in all its relations.

1. We have first of all the *positive* side; the study of the sources of religious truth or its demonstration by suitable arguments drawn from revelation or reason. This process is of fundamental importance to the practical truths of revelation as well as to the theoretical. Yet what a difference! The literature of the latter is varied, abundant, and able (see for instance Petavius and Thomassinus), while that of the former is meager and insignificant. Everything remains to be done. Some writers now seem to favor the habit of treating moral principles along the lines of special sources instead of studying them in all their sources at once. Thus we have Rational, Biblical, Symbolic, Conciliar, Liturgical, Patristic Theology. While this method has its advantages, it must be admitted that there is danger of incomplete and inexact views, probability of error and superficiality. In fact, works published by Protestant writers under such titles as "Ethics of the Old or the New Testament," "Ethics of St. Paul," etc., show considerable defects, due in part to the methods employed.

2. Next, we have the *strictly dogmatic* point of view from which truths are examined in their relation to the definitions of the Church, their degree of certainty and the latitude consistent therewith. Here again we find the literature of the theoretical truths of revelation far in advance of that of the practical, though of equal importance for the latter.[16]

3. The *speculative* side is next in order. It includes explanation, exposition, consequences, comparisons of truths. The condition is more encouraging here. The chef d'oeuvre of St. Thomas is probably the Secunda of the Summa, and Suarez is certainly at his best in his treatise De Legibus—both works being largely devoted to the speculative side of moral truths.

4. Finally, we have the point of view which may be called polemic, apologetic, irenic. Error is exposed, truth defended, conditions of reconciliation stated. In polemics and apologetics, much more has been done by the great controversial works for the theoretical truths of revelation than for truths of a practical and moral nature.

Any study of theological truth which aims to be complete must include those points of view. Of course it is natural, even necessary, that one at times confine one's study to a particular aspect; we have real masterpieces of this kind in the literature of theology. We merely insist on the fact that the point of view is incomplete. The great scholastics of the middle ages, and those who came after the Council of Trent, realized this thoroughly. This alone explains how it is that the study of their works is so valuable in giving a broad and solid theological training. Those who are acquainted with the Summa of St. Thomas, De Legibus and De Religione of Suarez, De Justitia of Molina, De Poenitentia of Lugo, De Matrimonio of Sanchez, will readily appreciate the force of this observation.

IV. Theology is a science which must be applied. This is done in teaching and directing the Christian people. Thus we have, in teaching, catechetics and homiletics; in direction, casuistry and pastoral theology. Under these forms theology has always been carefully studied, even from the days in which St. Paul gave us true models in his letters. Probably casuistry has fared best. Requiring, as it does, a profound grasp of principles, exact knowledge of conditions, and of the human heart, and so much tact, it is not strange that it should have received great attention. The literature of casuistry is one of the glories of Catholic Theology. It excels by far, in dignity, character and sobriety, every other form of casuistry, whether that of the Talmud, the Stoics, or the Pandects.[17]

V. Moral Theology is clearly distinguished from the other moral (or normative) sciences by its object, sources and method. There are five such sciences—viz., Ethics, Sociology, Politics, Economics, Law. It is, however, so closely allied with them that they may not for a moment be neglected. All concern man's free activity and the laws which should govern it. But Moral Theology has to do with all human activity, which it directs to man's supreme destiny—the absolute good. The other moral sciences, however, are confined to particular spheres of human action and its direction to a proximate contingent good. Their relations to Moral Theology are intimate, for its laws are also laws for them, and they in turn furnish valuable data for the investigation of the truths of the moral order. A word as to each:

1. Ethics is to Moral Theology about what the natural law is to the supernatural law; natural religion to supernatural religion; in a word, what the whole natural order is to the supernatural order. It is not strange then that ethics should have entered so largely into Moral

Theology, where, in reality, it reached its highest stage of development. To find the best exposition of its bearings on Moral Theology we must again recur to the Summa. There is scarcely a question in all ethics that is not treated in the Secunda, yet its true theological character is never lost for a moment. Only the passions of schools could deny that the Summa is a theological work, moral as well as speculative, and only the superficial character of our own time could claim to see in it a half pagan ethics, a compromise between religion and the world, because Aristotle and Cicero are used by St. Thomas as auxiliaries in his work.

2. Sociology has not yet succeeded in clearly delimiting its field. It found many of its elements in other sciences, notably in Moral Theology, from which it has taken the conception of the social organism. If its various conflicting schools do not hinder its normal development, it will become a valuable ally of Moral Theology. There is in fact a supernatural as well as a natural sociology. The Catholic religion is essentially social, fitting admirably the social nature of man. Faith, worship, sacrifice, sacraments have a distinctly social character. In the communion of saints, in the sharing of indulgences, prayers, satisfaction and merit we have a perfect and beautiful supernatural solidarity. The instinct of association asserts itself in the varied forms found in the Church, from simple conference to religious order, from parish to universal Church.

3. Economics, for so many centuries a part of Moral Theology and the object of much careful discussion,[18] became a separate science a century ago. During the first period of its existence its writers, with some noble exceptions, represented it as not only distinct but even separated from ethics. They professed merely to aim to discover the laws of production and exchange. Such were the so-called orthodox or liberal economists of the Manchester school. Soon, however, writers began to study the relations of economics and moral science. A reaction then set in, becoming much stronger during the second half of this century. Today most economists not only recognize that men must obey moral law in the production, distribution and consumption of wealth, but they also hold that moral science must penetrate economics, permeate it, and that the science must be constructed in the spirit of moral principles; in a word that economics must be ethical.[19] It is not unreasonable to hope that the day is not far distant when even theological data will be accepted in the study of economics. The services that each may render

the other are admirably sketched in the Encyclical *Rerum Novarum* of Leo XIII.

4. Natural and civil law are so intimately connected with moral science that they really seem like subdivisions of it. This is particularly the case with justice. Theologians have shown great depth of thought and breadth of view in their writings on law. The sixty-three questions of St. Thomas, the Septipertitum Opus of Conrad de Sumenhart, the ten books of Dominicus Soto, the works of Lessius, Peter of Arragon, Malderus, de Lugo, and the six folio volumes of Molina—remain the pride of the literature of theology and the wonder and admiration of the jurisconsult.

5. In the relations of Canon Law to Moral Theology, we find still closer union. In fact, we can hardly indicate the lines of separation. Cardinal d'Annibale repeats what Melchior Cano said when he condemned as folly the study of Moral Theology without the assistance of canon law. The practical summas of the fourteenth and fifteenth centuries, whether methodical or alphabetical, have a decided canonico-moral character. In fact, it is this very feature which constitutes the chief merit of such works as the Enchiridion of Navarrus, the De Matrimonio of Sanchez, the Theology of Layman.

6. Finally, the field of national and international politics must be considered as not foreign to Moral Theology. Works of splendid merit, viewed merely as studies in political science, have come from the pens of theologians; St. Thomas de Regimine principum; Suarez, de Legibus and de Bello; Francis of Victoria, de Indis. As to the last named, a recent writer, unsuspected of any theological bias, says there is nothing else in the history of law to compare with it.[20]

III. GRADUAL DEVIATION

The brief description which we have given of the character of Moral Theology, of its relations to the other religious, moral and social sciences, and the partial enumeration of the masterpieces in theological literature, in which this character and the relations of our science appear, will serve to show that, at one time, Moral Theology held a place which comported in every way with its true nature and dignity. We have now to trace the successive steps in the process which led up to present conditions.

I. With the movement toward political secularization, there has existed a parallel movement of secularization in the world of science. Commencing about the end of the thirteenth century, the double movement developed in strength rapidly during Reformation times, reaching its greatest proportions during the Revolution and the period since then. At first, church and state separate; in the Reformation the church herself is divided; in the Revolution it is Christianity against Rationalism. When theology was expelled from the political world it began to lose contact with the other sciences. Finally it was driven from the universities and relegated to the seminaries and sacristies. In a country as solidly Catholic as Belgium, the too exact application of the principle of separation of church and state excludes theology from every one of the state universities. Louvain alone—supported by the Catholics—can lay claim to the honor of fully representing the entire field of human knowledge. The same condition is found in France, with this anomaly added, however, that, having no faculty of Catholic theology, two or three universities have Protestant faculties.[21] Italy and Spain are in like condition, with the one difference, that there is no freedom of teaching, and hence no free Catholic university. It is hard to see how the sciences gained anything by this. Certain it is that theology has suffered. The Holy Father has frequently reverted to these conditions in the encyclicals, *Aeterni Patris, Sapientiae Christianae;* in his discourse of March 7, 1880, to the pilgrimage of savants in Rome, and in the encyclical to the Bishops of Spain, October 25, 1893. In the last named he says: "In iis rerum publicarum fluctibus, qui superiore atque hoc ipso volvente saeculo, totam perturbarunt Europam; quasi procelloso impetu dejecta atque stirpitus divulsa sunt instituta quibus ad fidei doctrinaeque incrementa condendis, regia simul et ecclesiastica potestas curas opesque contulerant. *Sublatis ita catholicis studiorum universitatibus earumque collegiis, ipsamet seminaria clericorum exaruere, sensim ea deficiente doctrinae copia quae ex magnis gymnasiis effluebat.*" As to Italy itself, theological schools are not lacking, particularly in Rome. But they are deprived of much of their power by the conditions which surround them. An eminent Catholic, Godefroid Kurth, uttered the following remarkable words at the Freiburg Congress: "Where is the Catholic science of Italy, where its higher schools, its institutes, its publications? Is Italy at the head of the Catholic scientific movement? Instead of teaching others, is she not obliged to learn from other nations how to defend the civil and social rights of Catholicity?"[22]

II. While theology in general was thus cut off from the other sciences, Moral Theology suffered further by being separated from theoretical or dogmatic theology. This stroke destroyed the organic unity between them, which is shown so admirably by St. Thomas. Solid grasp of the fundamental relations between the theoretical and the practical truths of revelation became difficult to obtain. The latter, detached from their real source and foundation, lost energy; the former, robbed of their legitimate fruit, lost vitality and influence. It is universally true that the progress of both sciences is in direct relation. The social and moral power of the priesthood is never greater than when the clergy has a solid dogmatic formation.[23] Logic and history clearly show that moral separated from dogma quickly becomes moral independent of dogma, and that this paves the way for moral without dogma and a religion purely ethical. It is a little surprising that some Catholics seem to ignore the dangers of separation, not alone for the sciences themselves, but as well for the formation of the clergy.[24]

III. Deprived of the influences which close association with dogma should exert, Moral Theology next saw inroads made into its own peculiar field. The laws of Christian perfection were taken over by ascetical theology; those of the religious life, largely by liturgical science; moral laws governing public life were given over to the science of law. The result was that certain modern errors were less clearly understood and hence less effectively opposed. We have an example in the error—I might almost say heresy—that political life is not to be regulated by Christian moral law, as is the life of the individual.[25]

IV. Moral Theology was consequently forced to confine itself to the laws of *private* life alone. Still the encroachments continued. Writers began to pass lightly over *principles;* they cared chiefly for *conclusions* and *applications,* or even opinions. The speculative and apologetical points of view had been forgotten. On the positive side many moralists of the last century attempted to study the tradition and evolution of the revealed truths underlying moral life, but the taint of Jansenism, which was discerned in their writings, materially injured them. The test of scholarship today seems to be the ability to collect opinions of the theologians of the last three centuries. Equal zeal is not shown, even for the decisions of synods or councils. The result is that while Moral Theology furnishes to the priest sufficient knowledge to administer the sacrament of penance, it is of little assistance to him in preaching.[26]

V. One might think that the end had been reached. Not yet, however. The development of pastoral theology and casuistry forced Moral Theology to a point where it is possible to present it in a handy volume of five hundred pages. Pastoral Theology has a respectable literature, especially in German, though by no means any abler than that of former times. Casuistry has become a lifeless form, intended principally for teaching; by no means as living and actual as are the Responses of Diana, de Lugo and so many others.

VI. This process has so far affected the teaching of Theology that the different points of view of a question are treated in different courses and even by different professors. Thus the essential unity of science is destroyed, comprehensive views of questions are not obtained, a grasp of the whole field simply unthought of. Useless repetitions and unpardonable omissions occur. Not unfrequently, a professor will fail to treat a question which he wishes to avoid, referring his students to a colleague who is supposed to discuss it.[27] The writer of these pages studied the Sacraments in Dogmatic and Moral Theology, in Canon Law, Liturgy and Archaeology. A course in Pastoral Theology was lacking to complete the list. He had previously studied them according to the method of St. Thomas and Suarez in one course and under one professor. Though abler men conducted the divided courses, much more profit was obtained in the latter.

VII. We referred above to the intimate relations between Moral Theology and the other social or normative sciences. These latter, originally contained in the former, have been differentiated from it gradually since the Reformation, and they have practically lost contact with the Gospel. Ethics was the first to be separated; natural law, economics and sociology followed in rapid succession.[28] Moralists soon lost the habit of studying questions belonging to those sciences, seeing no need of so doing or fearing to encroach. At any rate, Moral Theology lost much of its influence and practical value by the process.

VIII. It may now serve our purpose to cast a glance over the recent literature of Moral Theology, and ascertain how far facts bear us out.

Taking the logical order, we have, first, the general or fundamental part, corresponding to the Prima Secundae of St. Thomas.

The treatise on the destiny of man, which is the foundation of the science, is met only in exceptional cases. Yet, the pagan Cicero was keen-sighted enough to have seen the place of such a treatise in any system of morals. "Fine in moralibus constituto, constituta sunt omnia." The study of human acts, despoiled of its ontological, psychological and supernatural portion, is so incomplete that many moral questions remain in perpetual obscurity. Hence the welcome we gave the work of Father Frins, S.J., in which he seeks to remedy some of the evils of this condition.[29] The treatise on the passions, to which St. Thomas gives twenty-seven questions in the Summa, never appears. Reference is made to them in the article on Concupiscence. Nothing is written on habits. In the treatise on Laws, the essential theological portion regarding the Law of God is very often neglected. The external canonical character is most insisted upon, while the obligation of civil law is studied in a superficial manner. The study of conscience is reduced to a minimum and then literally absorbed into the question of probabilism or aequiprobabilism. Finally the virtues, vices and sin are incompletely studied. As far as studied, they are superficially treated or reduced to pure casuistry. It is to be hoped that the recent letter of the Holy Father will call attention to this neglect of the study of the virtues, and bring about a more thorough manner of treating them.

That portion of our literature which corresponds to the Secunda Secundae of St. Thomas is not any more satisfactory. The treatise on the theological virtues is without doubt the most difficult and important in the science. They are the alpha and omega of Christian life. Only in their exercise does man strike his true attitude to God, who is his destiny, and to Christ, who is the way. Intellectual perfection is reached in faith, moral perfection attained in hope and charity. Thus the theological virtues give to Christian ethics its distinctive character and its mark of superiority over every other system of moral science. This has been recognized. The literature of the theological virtues is characterized by the abundance of masterly treatises which have appeared. And yet, in our manuals the whole field is covered in fifty pages; twenty given to Faith, two or three to Hope, and the rest to Charity. The more difficult questions, if not entirely omitted, are but indicated. It may be objected that those questions are treated elsewhere. Granted, they are not in their proper place and this is a serious error. But again, are they sufficiently studied? Where, for instance, do we find Faith discussed in its true character as the door to the whole edifice of Theology? Theology is, after all, but the science of Faith. We do not find it represented as the center of apologetics—its guiding star—as the bond uniting into one system of thought and demonstration, the Praeambula Fidei, the argument of Faith, the Church and its magisterium, tradition, Scripture, and inspiration. It seems that the utter failure of many attempts at so-called modern apologetics is due to the absence of a thorough and profound understanding of the role of Faith. The same may be observed with regard to Charity. Its real character as the source and queen of virtues, as the fulfilling of the law, as central in justification and reconciliation, merit and good works, is not by any means properly brought out.

A first glance seems to show that the cardinal virtues have fared better. Yet inspection reveals that Prudence and Fortitude have little place in our literature. We know of but one work wherein they are treated with any care. It is from the pen of the learned Bishop of Bruges.[30] Temperance is studied piecemeal. Justice has fared better. We have extensive treatises on it by Carriere and Crolly, and some special works of a high order by Marres, Waffelaert, Schwane. The sections devoted to Justice in our manuals is proportionately large—maybe three hundred pages. Yet, strange to say, it is about the treatise on justice that Cardinal d'Annibale complained in the citation made a moment ago. As to the higher virtues, and the evangelical counsels, while not entirely neglected, the studies made in them have been canonical rather than theological. None of them approach the last twenty questions of the Secunda Secundae. This may account for the indifference to religious life which we so frequently find.

Some of the sacraments have a rich and comprehensive literature, particularly the Eucharist, Penance, Matrimony. The other sacraments are neglected, in particular Baptism and Orders – both of which enter directly into the essential idea of the Church.

IV. CAUSES AND REMEDIES

The causes which have led to this condition are varied and complex. To state them adequately would require a summary of some centuries of history. They are political, social and religious, literary and academic, general and particular, universal and local. Nearly all, if not all, have been hinted at in the preceding pages. If we enumerate them here, it is merely to bring them out more clearly and to so grasp them that their character may be more correctly appreciated:

1. The vicissitudes to which the Church has been subjected to during the last two centuries; revolutions and uprisings in France, Spain, Portugal and Italy; persecutions in Switzerland, Germany and Russia; the suppression or secularization of universities, confiscation of ecclesiastical properties and benefices which had enabled so many priests to devote themselves to study, whereas nowadays they are forced into a busy ministry in order to obtain means of life; suppression and expulsion of religious orders; destruction and scattering of libraries. No one can measure the influence that such a course of events had on the development of Christian Catholic science.

2. The weakening, if not decadence, of certain nations which formerly stood at the front in Catholic science. In saying this, we think of Spain, which in the Middle Ages led nearly all nations in juridico-moral studies,[31] and in the sixteenth and early seventeenth centuries, certainly led the world in Catholic science. From the close of the Council of Trent to 1663 Spain produced nearly four hundred theologians, historians and canonists (mystic theologians not included), of whom fifty were of the highest order. During the succeeding century, 1663 to 1763, we find only two hundred and fifty, of whom but twelve are of the first class; from 1764 to 1869 we find but ninety, and only three or four are really eminent. The condition is equally striking in Portugal. The contributions of Ireland, England and Scotland to theology have been very limited, for reasons which everyone knows; Poland and Hungary are equally destitute of a theological literature. During the last century and the first half of this one, Belgium showed but little vitality. In the seventeenth century, the intellectual supremacy of Spain passed over to France. The remarkable fecundity of France, particularly in works of erudition and in eloquence, is well known. Yet she never produced a school of great thinkers in juridical or moral science. Italy showed some vigor up to a century ago, but since then she has done but little. Today Germany is in the lead, particularly in philological, exegetical, historical and critical studies, though probably less has been done there for Christian ethics

than in France. Spain's once proud place has not yet been filled. Resurgat.[32]

3. The Reformation, Jansenism and Rationalism caused the creation of forms of polemical literature which broke the unity and harmony of theological science. New treatises bearing on points of controversy appeared; older studies were recast to meet new issues; general questions were treated in part as the exigencies of the case required. Viewed in itself, this work was admirably done—superb treatises were produced. But the perspective of theological science was disturbed; secondary questions received undue prominence; parts replaced the whole. The synthesis had been destroyed and proportion, order and balance among the parts of theological science has not even yet been restored. Moral Theology was a victim of these circumstances. Attention was turned from it; it appeared to be merely a secondary division of theology, just as today dogmatic, speculative and moral theology are outranked by historical sciences and theological exegesis is being replaced by purely critical studies.

4. The gradual neglect of the Summa of St. Thomas has harmed Moral Theology. After the sixteenth century, two or three professors were occupied in expounding the Summa in the chief centers of learning. When there were three, each took a part of the Summa, to which four years were devoted; if there were but two, the Secunda Secundae was divided between them. By this arrangement, students had an incomparable textbook, and a careful complete exposition of the portion devoted to Moral Theology as well as of the other parts. At the same time, a practical course on cases of conscience was given, which lasted two years at least. When later, independent treatises were substituted for the text of St. Thomas, the second part of the Summa was replaced by the course on cases of conscience, excepting the questions of the Prima Secundae on grace and some questions of the Secunda Secundae regarding the rule of faith. Hence the manuals of Moral Theology, of which Busenbaum's Medulla is the type, differ so much in amplitude and erudition from the works of Franzelin and Palmieri, or of Sardagna and Perrone. The University of Louvain is probably the only university which has retained the Summa of St. Thomas as the textbook in Moral Theology.

5. The separation of Moral Theology from dogma, and the exodus of the various portions of our science which followed upon the surren-

der of the Summa of St. Thomas where all is unity, caused a further weakening. The French writer whom we have cited attributes this to Gallicanism and Jansenism. But an honest view of the teaching, literature and doctrines of Theology effectually disposes of that theory. The same movement is to be found in Spain and Italy, possibly more marked than in the countries where Gallicanism and Jansenism had their strongholds. Then again, the writer in question seems to be in error in his statements bearing on the French writers of the seventeenth century. He attributes to them the doctrinal separation of Moral from Dogma, no less than the pedagogic and academic separation. He finds in the works of Berulle, Condren, Olier, Tronson and Fénelon, and even in Bossuet, a vague, indefinite moral founded on *sentiment* rather than *dogma*. He even goes so far as to think one can find in many modern works the very formulas of the propositions of Molinos asserting the independence of moral and devotion from the principles of Theology and the direction of the Church.[33]

6. The tendency to separate principles from their application is well expressed in the familiar proverb, Praxis differt a speculatione. Taken to imply the need of prudence and tact in applying principles, the statement is perfectly correct. But when it is made to mean that correct theory may be inapplicable, that a practice may be lawful without regard to theory, that practice is opposed to theory, or that the study of principles is good for science and useless for practice, nothing could be more absurd in itself or more harmful to science. If practice differs from principle, the latter is false or the former is wrong—there is no escape. We merely wish to say, apropos of this point, that too many theologians have been so narrow in the exposition of principles that a reasonable application has often been out of the questions.[34] In a similar way many writers are broad in questions of faith and tendency in doctrine, yet extremely narrow, not in the first principles of moral science but in their secondary applications.

7. The intense controversies of the seventeenth and eighteenth centuries did incalculable harm to Moral Theology. There were two great tendencies which struggled for mastery; one broad or lax, the other narrow or more rigorous. We would call them minimist and maximist nowadays. They existed before Jansenism, which was in reality only a form of one of them. Naturally the two tendencies expressed themselves in the literature of Moral Theology and Devotion to which

they gave rise, and they called forth a double series of propositions condemned by the Holy See. The controversy caused more obscurity, gave birth to a lassitude and distaste for Moral Theology which have had an enduring effect.[35]

8. The principle of probabilism—perfectly true in itself when rightly understood—has been a source of injury to our science. Taking it for granted that it is licit to follow a solidly probable opinion, and that a law merely probable cannot be strictly enforced, theologians have seemed to busy themselves about the probability of opinions rather than about the search for truth. Hence the number of problems whose scientific solutions are not considered of much importance or sought with much zeal, since contradictory probable opinions are accepted. We could give an almost endless list of problems, in the solution of which there has been no advance for two centuries, and no attempt at anything new is being made. One would almost think that we had fallen into skepticism or that we are afraid of the truth. This is particularly the case where an opinion is recognized as probable by a high authority.[36]

9. The abuse of an essentially Catholic practice has caused damage to Moral Theology. It is that of recurring to the Roman Congregations for decisions when there is no necessity whatever for so doing. Fortunately enough, the Congregations seem to appreciate the situation justly when their replies are in the familiar form, "Consulat probatos auctores." But when the reply is "non sunt inquietandi," not only are the petitioners satisfied, but further research in the cause of truth is deemed unnecessary. We have not had a single new and profound study of usury in half a century, notwithstanding the prominence into which the socialists have drawn the question.[37]

It has been well said that a science may not be stationary. It must develop or suffer gradual extinction. Moral Theology must obey that law or undergo the penalty. Many think, with Cardinal d'Annibale, that it is in a state of stagnation or even torpidity. But it can be reestablished where it belongs. Many agencies must contribute, however, before that can be done. By the philosophy of St. Thomas the law of morals, as well as of faith, to use St. Augustine's words, gignitur, nutritur, defenditur, roboratur. A more intimate union with the theoretical truths of revelation is necessary, so that the laws of right living may be seen to spring from the very heart of dogma. Critical study and extended research into the development of the fundamental ideas and principles of moral life and their application, not alone in Christian times, but in Old Testament times as well and back to the beginning of humanity, must be made. The intelligent application of these principles to the problems of modern individual, social, religious and civil life is essential to the reestablishment which we seek, as is also a more constant contact with the other social sciences from which, rightly understood, only good can come. There is reason to hope that the coming century will see this done, for the impetus has already been given in the admirable encyclicals of Pope Leo XIII.

Notes

1. We have treated these matters in various publications. See especially *Theologia Moralis Fundamentalis*, pp. 1–139.

2. Summula Theol. Moralis III Ed., Vol. 1, p. 12, proemium. Regarding the excessive tendency to which the Cardinal's "indulgentiores" points; cf. Mgr. Isoard, bishop of Annecy: *Le système du moins possible et demain dans la société chrètienne,* Paris, 1896; C. 10–14, App. 6.

3. *Civiltà Cattolica,* ser XIV, Vol. 6, p. 443.

4. Maitre Thomas et St. Ignace Réplique au R. P. Brucker, S.J. Louvain, 1896, p. 31, note 3. Cf. Gayrand, Questions du jour, XI.

5. Ausonio Franchi, by Angelo Angelini, p. 16. Cf. Ultima Critica, p. 1, c. 2, ¶ 3, n. 116.

6. P. 270. Our purpose is not to refute the views here expressed. It is to call attention to a view of the nature and method of Moral Theology, which is unfortunately too widely shared. We make the citation with some embarrassment, for in the context from which the extract is taken, the author of the work pays an unmerited tribute to the writer of this article.

7. Caramuel. *Theol. Mor. Fund.* Francf. 1652, p. 27.

8. We speak of course of Catholic Moral Theology alone. Moral Theology was never seriously and methodically studied by non-Catholics. It scarcely finds place in their curricula of studies; possibly a couple of hours a week for a semester. President Harper of Chicago does not even mention it in his recent article in the *American Journal of Theology* where he reviews the entire theological curriculum and suggests some reforms. Phillip Schaff said that "English and American literature is very poor in works of Christian ethics." So dire, indeed, is this poverty that Hurst, in a painful effort to lengthen the list of *Christian* moralists, adds to it the names of Kant, Spencer, Spinoza, even of Marcus Aurelius and Seneca. *Literature of Theology,* p. 482.

9. Cf. M. Billia, L'unità dello scibile e la filosofia della morale. Turin, 1898.

10. One of the latest attempts in this line is *L'essai sur la classification des sciences,* Edmond Goblot, Paris, 1898.

11. It is a well-known fact that the French universities, as now organized, have no faculty of Catholic theology, though there are some faculties of Protestant theology. How this anomalous situation is to be explained, and especially how it harmonizes with "equal rights to all religions," is not at present our concern. We wish, however, to note that it is not the Catholics who begrudge Protestant theology its place in the university, but rather the free-thinkers and the secularizers. In answer to their objections, M. A. Sabatier has published, in the *Revue internationale de l'enseignement supérieur* (Nov., 1898), an article entitled: Les facultés de théologie protestantes et les études scientifiques dans les Universités. Some of its passages are suggestive. Here, for instance, is an objection as he presents it: "On pourrait d'abord soulever une sorte de question préalable. Ce qui constitue, l'unité de la science, et, par suite, une université moderne, c'est l'unité de méthode. Cette unité repose sur l'autonomie interne de la raison, c'est-à-dire sur l'inébranlable certitude qu'a l'esprit moderne de posséder en soi la norme souveraine de ses idées et de ses actes. L'evidence rationelle, l'expérience positive, la critique libre, – tels sont les principes ou les conditions premières de tout travail scientifique digne de ce nom; tel est le lien qui rattache en un faisceau puissant et homogène toutes les branches de la science. Une faculté de théologie peut-elle pratiquer cette méthode et entrer loyalment dans la solidarité intime de cet organisme?"

And here is M. Sabatier's reply: "On comprend à la rigueur qu'une telle objection soit élevée à propos des facultés de théologie Catholiques, qu'on suppose, à tort suivant moi, réglées par la méthode d'autorité. En fait, la méthode autoritative, c'est-à-dire, la méthode proprement scolastique, ne règne souverainement pour les Catholiques que dans une seule discipline, dans l'étude du dogme. Mais on ne voit pas que dans les autres, dans l'archéologie, dans la critique des textes par exemple, sauf quelques points réservés, un savant Catholique manque de liberté, au point de ne pouvoir rien faire de scientifique. La réalité dément ici une logique trop prompte. Il y a des facultés Catholiques nationales dans les universités allemandes, et elles y rendent d'incontestables services. Croit-on que des hommes tels que l'abbé Duchesne, le père Denifle, l'abbé Batifol, l'abbé Bouquet et d'autres encore, ne tiendraient pas bien leur place dans une université. Quoi qu'il en soit, il faut reconnaître que si l'objection a quelque chose de spécieux pour les catholiques, elle n'a aucune raison d'être à l'égard des facultés protestantes. Dans le protestantisme, il n'y a ni autorité fixe, ni tribunal dogmatique infallible, et, dès lors, le travail scientifique n'y saurait être arrêté on bridé par aucun pouvoir."...Details aside, we would simply observe that this answer, taken as a whole, involves a pitiable equivocation. If real university methods require the autonomy, the absolute independence of human reason, and if, on the other hand, Protestant theology takes divine revelation for its basis, then evidently there is no more room in a university for Protestant theology than for Catholic. Brought face to face with the Word of God, the Protestant must accept it; his scientific research is *arrêté, bridé.*

Under like pressure, Jean Réville, a colleague of M. Sabatier, chose as the subject of his opening discourse, in October, 1858: La théologie partie intégrante du cycle universitaire et fondement indispensable de la réformation. He endeavors to show that theological studies must have a strictly scientific character in order to hold a place in the university, and that university teaching cannot neglect the investigation of religious phenomena without self-mutilation. Now, let us see what his notion of theology is: "La théologie moderne n'est autre chose que la science de la religion. Elle a pour objet les faits et les phénomènes de la vie religieuse dans le passé et dans le présent, sans aucune restriction de race, de temps, de confession ecclésiastique....C'est d'abord une science historique, parce qu'elle se propose de connaître et de vérifier les faits et les textes religieux du passé au moyen de la méthode critique. C'est ensuite une science psychologique. En effet, après avoir étudié la religion dans ses inombrables manifestations du passé, elle étudie le phénomène religieux dans l'homme vivant de nos jours; elle observe, recueille, et analyse les sentiments religieux, la nature propre de la foi, les expériences religieuses, dout l'étude contemporaine jette le plus souvent un jour si précieux sur la vie du passé. Elle scrute les rapports de la religion avec la vie morale individuelle ou sociale; elle cherche les relations qui existent entre le développement religieux et le développement intellectual; bref elle fait une analyse aussi complete que possible des facultés religieuses de l'homme. Enfin c'est une science philosophique or dogmatique; car après avoir rénni tous les matériaux que l'histoire et la psychologie religieuse peuvent lui fournir, elle s'efforce de les co-ordonner en une construction d'ensemble." *Revue de l'histoire des religions.* November–December, 1898.

12. Signs of such a reaction are not wanting. Such, among others, are the letters on "Scientific Instruction among the Catholic Clergy," by Mgr. Baunard, Rector of the Catholic University of Lille, the "Report" on the same subject presented by Professor Senderens at the last national congress in Paris, and, from a non-Catholic source, President Harper's reflection on the curriculum (*American Journal of Theology, III,* 1).

13. They are naturally divided into three groups, *theoretical, practical, social or political.* The division is suggested by the Symbol, the Decalogue, and the Sacrament; it corresponds to the threefold character of Christ as Teacher, Priest and King; and to the threefold power of the Church, magisterium, minis-

terium, imperium. Euntes docete...baptizantes...servare quaecumque mandavi. Cfr. Franzelin, De Traditione, th. XII, sch. 1, pr. 2.

14. Inst. Theol., Tom. I, n.37.

15. Vita Lugonis–Beginning of *Responsa Moralia.*

16. We use the phrase *strictly dogmatic,* since the word dogmatic is ordinarily confined to theoretical truths. The practical or moral truths are also dogmatic.

17. Cfr. Catholic University Bulletin, Vol. II., p. 375. Also, Raymond Thamin *Un probléme moral dans l'antiquité,* étude sur la casuistique *stoicien.* Brunetière, *Revue des Deux Mondes,* Jan. 1, 1885.

18. Cf. Brants, Ashley, Cunningham.

19. Cf. Maurice Block, Les Progrès de la Science Economique depuis Adam Smith, Introd. 5.

20. Revue de droit international et de législation comparée. Tom XV., pp. 195–199.

21. There are, however, five free Catholic universities in France wherein Catholic faculties of theology exist.

22. Rivista Internazionale. Art. by M. A. Ratti, Dec., 1898; vol. xv., pp. 494–496. The Italian scholars present, hard as they found those words, admitted that there was some justification for them, that universities were needed, and that young men should be sought out and sent to study in foreign Catholic universities.

23. Non-Catholic writers do not seem to admit the close relation between ethics and dogma. In fact, the separation of the two is looked upon by some as a distinct advance. "The separation of theological ethics from theological dogmatics, made early in Reformation days, was one great step toward the constitution of our (moral) science; for a science of *agenda* is not a science of *credenda.*" Alfred Cave, *Introduction to Theology and its Literature,* p. 562.

24. Aubry, Les Grands Séminaires, C. XIII. Suggestive points of view are found in this work, though it is marked by some exaggeration and it shows a defective historico-literary knowledge.

25. Cf., Leo XIII, Enc. *Immortale Dei.*

26. Mgr. Isoard, in his recent publication, *Si vous connaissiez le don de Dieu,* cites these words of an eminent writer (probably Taine): "J'ai voulu me rendre compte de ce qu'est aujourd'hui la religion, avant de me décider à faire élever mes enfants dans le Catholicisme. Dans ce but, j'ai écouté attentivement une vingtaine des sermons dans telle église (une des principales églises paroissiales de Paris); j'ai assurément entendu de bonnes choses, de bons conseils, mais rien qui fasse connaître la religion. On donnait des observations morales empruntées un peu partout, et même à votre serviteur. Mais du fond de la religion, des grands dogmes de la Bible, rien, absolument rien."

Whereupon the Bishop declares: "Nous tenons pour bien fondé son jugement sur l'enseignement donné habituellement dans nos églises. Le dogme n'est pas exposé; les vérités primordiales de la religion n'apparaissent qu'à de rares époques; ce qui est ordinaire, c'est de donner les conséquences morales de principes que l'on parait supposer connus, mais qui, en fait, sont ou mal compris, ou méconnus ou tout à fait ignorés." pp. 47–49.

27. Suarez has remarked this. In writing on Faith, wishing to speak of the dona and gratiae intellectuales, he says: "Tractavit de hisce donis sanctus Thomas, secunda secundae variis in locis; sed operae pretium est de omnibus junctim agere, tum *brevitatis ac perspicuitatis* causa, tum quia dum ad alia loca remittuntur, prorsus omittuntur; adeo ut praeter Divum Thomam, nihil fere de his tractatum sit a Theologis, cum haec scribimus." De Fide. Disp. VIII. Intr.

28. Cf., Theod. Meyer, *Inst. Juris Nat. Proem.*

29. *De actibus humanis, ontologice, psychologice consideratis seu disquisitiones psychologicae theologicae de voluntate in ordine ad mores.*

30. De prudentia, fortitudine, temperantia.

31. Cf. E. Nys, *Les origines du droit international.* Bruxelles, 1894.

32. Comparative tables of greatest interest may be found in Hurter's Nomenclator.

33. Aubry, Les grands séminaires, Essai sur la methode des êtudes ecclésiastiques en France, pp. 357 ff. Another recent writer, whom no one will suspect of antigallican exaggeration, declares: "Je me charge de trouver, dans beaucoup d'ouvrages de piété modernes, des erreurs condannées par l'Eglise. Je dis cela même de ceux écrits par des prêtres, mais surtout de ceux (et ils abondent) écrits par des femmes. Et qui dire des entretiens spirituels de supérieurs de communautés, qui tirent toute leur théologie d'écrivains protestants." *Boussuet et le Jansénisme; notes historiques; publiées* par A. M. P. Ingold.

34. See the dissertation of the Bishop of Bruges, De dubio solvendo in re morali, p. 203.

35. Concina in his *Historia Probabilismi,* and Döllinger and Reusch in their *Geschichte der Moralstreitigkeiten,* give some account of these controversies; an impartial history of them has yet to be written.

36. Mgr. Isoard in *Le système du moins possible* ascribes the minimizing tendency of the day to the influence of Probabilism. This view we are unable to accept.

37. In his *Nouveau dire sur le système du moins possible* (Paris, 1898), Mgr. Isoard also, though from a different point of view, criticizes the practice of perpetual interrogation. See p. 60.

7. Cases of Conscience

John A. McHugh

This chapter first appeared in John A. McHugh, *The Casuist,* vol. 5 (New York: Joseph F. Wagner, 1925).

FORMAL AND MATERIAL COOPERATION

Case.—John, a public hack driver, declares, in confessing his sins, that he is in the habit of driving people to brothels. This he does at times on their simple request. At other times, in response to their demand if he knows of such places, he replies affirmatively, and drives them there. John argues that since such resorts are allowed to exist, it is not unlawful to drive his patrons to them, nor wrong to inform them of their existence and location; otherwise his business and income will suffer gravely, as others are prepared to do this work.

Questions:

1. What is formal, what is material cooperation?

2. What constitutes a grave cause sufficient to make material cooperation lawful?

3. What of the existence and the renting of houses to prostitutes?

4. Did John act rightly?

5. What is the confessor's duty?

Solution.—1. Formal cooperation is that by which we aid another in his sin, and consent to the malice of the sin. Material cooperation is the aid we give to the action of another, not as it is sinful, but precisely as it is a physical action. It is either: (1) immediate, if one takes part in the sinful deed; or (2) mediate, if one performs acts that lead up to or follow the sin.

Formal cooperation is never lawful. It includes the consent of the will to the sin of another. It contains a two-fold malice: against charity and against the particular virtue violated.

Material cooperation is lawful if the two following conditions are present: (1) The action of the one cooperating must be good, or at least indifferent; (2) there must exist for his action a just cause, proportioned to the gravity of the sin, and the proximity of the cooperation (Prümmer, Manuale Theol. Moral. I., No. 619).

2. What constitutes a grave cause in this matter depends on the opinion of prudent men. St. Alphonsus (Theol. Mor. Lib. II, No. 59) gives the following rules: The cause which permits material cooperation must be proportionately more serious and more weighty: (1) when the sin committed is graver; (2) when it is more probable that without your cooperation the other will not sin, or when the effect is more certain; (3) when your cooperation touches more proximately on the sin; (4) when you have less right to place the cooperating action; (5) when the sin is against justice, detrimental to a third party.

3. In large cities, in order to avoid greater evils, brothels are permitted by law, and according to a probable opinion it is morally lawful to rent houses for such purposes (Sabetti, No. 187). If, however, grave injury would thereby result to an otherwise respectable neighborhood, or if the location were such as to offer a greater opportunity for vice, such renting would not be permissible.

4. To answer the fourth question, we must determine the nature of John's cooperation. It does not appear that he cooperated formally, since he did not intend the evil involved. His cooperation, then, was only material. Further, it was not immediate, as it preceded the sins committed. But it does not seem that his action was indifferent. Rather it was evil, since John was driving his patrons to these places, not as to indifferent places, but precisely as to places of sin. Hence his act was seriously sinful.

5. The reason alleged by John that his livelihood depends on the good will of his patrons cannot excuse his action, since under the circumstances his act is morally wrong. He is giving information about the whereabouts of brothels and carrying patrons to them. The case would be different if he were merely directed to drive to a certain house, even though he knew the place was a bad resort, for then he would not be a cooperator in manifest evil. This is what the confessor should tell John.

UNLAWFUL MASS INTENTIONS

Case.—In a certain locality, the two priests, Fr. Philip and Fr. James, observed a totally different attitude in accepting stipends for Mass intentions. Fr. Philip would reject many intentions as not in accord with the rules of the Church, while Fr. James would accept them. The latter held that some of these intentions were lawful, and, in the case of others, he enlightened the stipend givers and induced them to agree to a modification of their intentions. Amongst the intentions rejected by Fr. Philip are the following:

1. For a child who died without Baptism.
2. For a deceased baptized Protestant.
3. For a deceased publicly excommunicated priest.
4. For the recovery of a sick Jewess, and for a good position for a Protestant girl.
5. For a Catholic suicide.

Question.—In how far does the acceptance and performance of theses intentions oppose the Church precepts?

Solution.—Above all it would be well to recommend to these two priests a uniform and harmonious procedure in this matter, for their present practice is calculated to cause, amongst Catholics and non-Catholics, scandal, misinterpretation, and gossip.

1. Regarding the Holy Mass asked for the child that died without Baptism, the principle applies: "*jure divino plane incapaces sunt cujuslibet missae fructus pro se recipiendi ii, qui jam sunt in ultimo termino suo, scilicet 1. damnati, 2. beati, qui Deum inseparabiliter possident; quod si pro his posterioribus missae sacrificum offertur, id fieri potest ad eorum laudem gratiasque Deo agendas pro beneficiis beatis illis collatis, 3. infantes sine baptismo defuncti*" (Lehmkuhl *Cas. Consc. II.* n. 192–194). Hence it follows: "*Cum igitur impossible sit pro iis cum effectu missam applicare, graviter peccaret sacerdos, qui id tentaret*" (*l. c.*). "For deceased baptized children the Holy Mass may be offered as a sacrifice of thanksgiving, or, indirectly, to obtain for them that which will bestow accidental glory" (Göpfert *III.* 6 *n.* 83 *p.* 120). If Fr. James made to the stipend-giver the following proposition: "Since Holy Mass can in no wise be of benefit to an unbaptized child that has died, let us

offer it as thanksgiving to God for the natural gifts He bestowed upon the child, for it was indeed a great blessing that God created it at all," and if the stipend-giver is satisfied with this intention, and no scandal or misunderstanding is to be feared, there would hardly be anything forbidden by Divine or ecclesiastical law in the acceptance or performance.

2. If the Protestant who died in heresy, was in good faith and therefore saved, he was *jure divino capax* of the fruits of the Mass. But would the Church's law permit the application of Mass to those who in life did not belong to her communion? If the departed had shown some signs of repentance before his death, Mass may be celebrated for him publicly, since in that case he enjoys the benefit of Canon 1240, Nos. 1, 10, according to which Church burial is allowed him, and it is a safe rule that those to whom this is granted are likewise granted public Mass. If no signs of repentance had been given by the deceased, it does not seem unlawful to say Mass for him privately, *i.e.,* without pomp or solemnity, provided no scandal is given; for there is no law that expressly forbids such an application (Cappello, De Sacramentis, Vol. I, No. 619).

3. If the deceased priest had given signs of repentance, he was entitled to ecclesiastical burial (Canon 1240), and hence to a public Mass. If no signs of repentance preceded his death, Mass could be applied for him privately, *remoto scandalo.*

This applies to deceased *excommunicati;* regarding those still living St. Alphonsus remarks (*L. 6. n.* 308): "*Pro excommunicato vitando tamen licite sacerdos potest offerre missam privatim, quatenus est opus proprium suae privatae personae, non autem nomine ecclesiae vel ut minister Christi.*" The reason is that the vitandi are deprived of the public and common suffrages of the Church, but not of such as are private. Hence the priest may offer for the *vitandus* such fruits as are *ex opere operantis* and perhaps even the *fructus specialissimus* that belongs to himself. Canon 2262, No. 2, allows the priest to apply Mass privately and *remoto scandalo* for a *vitandus* if the intention be to obtain his conversion. If the excommunicated person is a *toleratus,* the priest is allowed to say Mass for other good intentions requested by him and to accept a stipend for doing so. Of course the Mass is to be said *privatim et remoto scandalo.*

4. The fourth case concerns a Mass for a Jewess and for a Protestant, both still living.

(a) Regarding all unbaptized persons, St. Alphonsus writes (*L. VI.*

309): *"Probabilius potest offerri missa pro infidelibus: tum quia in lege veteri Judaei soliti fuerunt sacrificare pro gentibus, tum quia sic celebrans magis conformatur Christo, qui pro omnibus se obtulit."* This agrees with the response of the S. Office (July 12, 1865), which permits acceptance of stipends and intentions from Turks and unbelievers, provided that scandal, superstition, etc., are excluded.

(b) For heretics and schismatics the Church formerly allowed only the intention for the grace of conversion to the true faith, as the answer of the S. Office of April 19, 1837, set forth. But since Canon 2262, No. 212, makes such restriction only for the *excommunicati vitandi,* it appears that under the Code, Mass may be offered for heretics and schismatics just as for the unbaptized. A Mass may, therefore, be said for the recovery of the Jewess, and also for the Protestant girl's intention. For living non-Catholic executives of a nation even public and solemn celebration is allowed, as it concerns not merely their person but the welfare of the state.

5. For a Catholic suicide, if Christian burial was not denied him, Mass may be offered publicly if no scandal is to be feared; otherwise, *occulte* (Noldin *III* n. 176). The expression *occulte, privatim, etc.,* in opposition to public solemnization, means, according to Göpfert: a merely inner intention without announcing names or using such in the liturgy, also without special oration, etc. Ecclesiastical burial according to Canon 1240 is denied to those who killed themselves deliberately. Hence it is not disallowed to those who were irresponsible (Augustine, Commentary on Canon Law, VI, p. 155). The Canon also grants church burial to a suicide who gave signs of repentance before death. Those who die in the actual commission of sin may be buried with ecclesiastical rites, if the crime is not public and manifest (Cappello, De Sacramentis, I, n. 622).

8. Birth Control: The Perverted Faculty Argument

John A. Ryan and *Henry Davis*

This chapter first appeared in *American Ecclesiastical Review* 79 (1928) and 81 (1929).

THE IMMORALITY OF CONTRACEPTION

To the Editor, *The Ecclesiastical Review.*

With the first eight and one-half pages of Doctor Mahoney's argument in the August issue of the *Review,* I am in almost entire agreement. His statements concerning the ethical teaching of the Church, as compared with deductions from the natural law (p. 133), concerning the importance of showing (if possible) that birth prevention is intrinsically wrong (p. 134), concerning the practical weakness of the "perverted faculty" argument (p. 137), concerning the "ultimate reason" why the practice is immoral (p. 141), and concerning the difficulty of deriving an effective popular argument from the traditional ground upon which all sexual sins have been condemned by the moral theologians (p. 141)—all these I accept without qualification. But the argument presented in the last four pages of the article leaves me unconvinced.

All Catholic ethicians would, I assume, accept the proposition that contraception, like all other sins against chastity, is bad because it is "opposed to the good of a rational nature" (p. 141). How shall this phrase be interpreted? In the sense of consequences? Or in the sense of intrinsic badness? In the latter sense, answers Doctor Mahoney (p. 134), as do all the writers of treatises on moral theology. While I have consistently accepted and defended this view myself, I have never found it entirely free from difficulty. In the following paragraphs I shall note the most serious difficulty and suggest a provisional solution.

As Doctor Mahoney points out, contraception and all other sexual sins are pronounced "inordinate" and "disproportionate" because they aim at an end which nature intends to be only a means, that is, pleasure. He adds, however, that married persons can always find some reason or fact (for example, relief from concupiscence or promotion of mutual love) which frees the conjugal act from the imputation of being sought for pleasure alone. One or other of these reasons is held sufficient to justify intercourse during that portion of the intramenstrual period when conception is improbable, or during pregnancy, when it is impossible, or in the case one or both parties are sterile. Such intercourse remains morally blameless, even when avoidance of conception is deliberately desired.

The married couple that places positive obstacles in the way of nature, whether physiological, mechanical or chemical, can likewise correctly claim that they are not seeking pleasure alone. They may desire relief from concupiscence or the strengthening of mutual love. Why, then, is their conduct immoral, while that of the couples considered in the last paragraph is morally blameless? Because they "defeat the primary end of marriage," answers Doctor Mahoney (p. 144). But the couple that deliberately restricts intercourse to a certain time in the intramenstrual period also attempts to defeat the primary end; yet this aim is not condemned by the moralists. Nor is its attainment construed as a moral wrong.

The usual reply of the moral theologians to this difficulty is that the persons who employ birth-prevention devices accomplish the defeat of the primary end of marriage through positive acts which thwart the processes of nature, rather than through mere selection of times and circumstances. The obvious rejoinder is that this is the "perverted faculty" argument which, as Doctor Mahoney rightly points out, seems to be greatly weakened through the rejection by several theologians of the parallel argument against lying.

It seems to me, then, that the general argument for the intrinsic immorality of all sexual sin is quite as weak in theory as it is likely to prove in practice. And its theoretical defects apply, obviously, to every other violation of chastity as clearly as to contraception. Why is fornication wrong? I do not recall having ever seen a well sustained argument for its immorality on intrinsic grounds. In an article in the *New York Review* (vol. II, p. 423) more than twenty years ago, I tried to find the intrinsic immorality of that act in "the subjection of man's lower to his higher nature," in the assumption that the moral supremacy of man's higher faculties requires him to refrain from sexual satisfaction "until he has undertaken the burdens of self-control and self-denial involved in the marital union." As an "intrinsic" argument this consideration does not seem to me now to have as much cogency as I attached to it in 1907.

Nor is the argument for the universal immorality of sexual offences altogether satisfying when it is based upon considerations of consequences. So far as I have been able to observe, this is the argument commonly urged against fornication. When St. Thomas discusses the question, "*Utrum fornicatio simplex sit peccatum mortale,*" his affirmative answer is based upon the injury resulting to the offspring (2^a2^{ae}, Q. 154, a. 2). At the end of the article, he considers the objection that in some such cases the father might make sufficient provision for the welfare of the child; but his reply is scarcely conclusive: That which falls under the determination of law must be judged according to what ordinarily happens, not according to exceptional cases. While this consideration is to a considerable extent valid for positive law, it is far from convincing as applied to the natural law. Many actions are morally lawful, even though they fall under a general category of sins. They are given a special classification in conformity with their special nature or circumstances. It would seem that the same treatment should be accorded to the irregular sexual intercourse which involves no evil consequences to children, as in the case of sterility; and likewise to birth prevention in certain restricted cases, say, when the life or health of the wife would be endangered by pregnancy.

Nevertheless, I would raise the question whether an argument from consequences cannot be effectively drawn against birth prevention, as against every other recognized form of sexual sin, even in exceptional situations. And I would suggest an affirmative answer, provided that the argument takes into account not only direct but indirect consequences. In certain rarely occurring situations contraception can probably take place without any direct evil results to the individuals or to society. But the baneful indirect effects are manifest. No community which accepts this practice as morally lawful in exception conditions will long restrict it to those conditions, no matter how carefully the latter may be defined by persons assuming to speak authoritatively. If the definition of lawful use were so framed, as some physicians have suggested, as to cover only cases of ill health, it would receive wider extension from all persons who believed their situations to be equally urgent and "deserving"; for example, on account of domestic friction, poverty, the desire to improve the standard of living, the demands of "social" duties, the inconvenience of child-bearing and the disagreeable consequences when the parties are unmarried. Hence, there is no socially safe middle ground between complete prohibition of birth prevention and such general addiction to the practice as will inevitably bring about a declining population and a profound deterioration of social and individual character and competence.

Because of these indirect results the practice is forbidden by the moral law in every case. It is "utterly opposed to the good of a rational nature." The individual whose case is exceptional may plead that if birth prevention were restricted to situations such as his there would be no evil results, but he must recognize that he is supposing an impossibility. Therefore he must forego the practice in the interest of the human race. And this self-denial is reasonably imposed upon him as a moral obligation.

The moral principle underlying the foregoing argument is met with more than once in our manuals of moral theology. Actions not grave in themselves are forbidden, under pain of mortal sin, on the ground that acceptance of them as only venial would encourage such frequent commission as to bring about a grave amount of moral disorder. If consequences of this sort may make an otherwise venial sin mortal, may they not render an otherwise justifiable action morally unlawful?

Whatever may be the correct statement of the relation between birth prevention and the natural law, we Catholics should, as Doctor Mahoney points out, rejoice that we have the divinely inspired guidance of the Church. This is only one of many moral problems which reason is or ought to be capable of solving, but which have been more promptly and more authoritatively solved by the voice of Revelation.

John. A. Ryan

BIRTH CONTROL: THE PERVERTED FACULTY ARGUMENT

I. Statement of the Question

It is held by all moral theologians that the contraceptive act between husband and wife is mortally sinful, chiefly, it would seem because it is a grave abuse of a faculty, a gross perversion of a means – the act of marital intercourse—which is given by Nature, that is, God, to man for the immediate purpose of generation. The act may or may not have other secondary purposes in Nature, but we are not now concerned with these. By the contraceptive act we mean sexual intercourse so exercised that the act, as a means of generation, is positively frustrated by withdrawal, or by some chemical or mechanical method, which is calculated, in the physical sphere, and deliberately intended, to prevent the male element from penetrating into the uterus, lest there, or some-where further on, it should meet with, and fertilize an ovum. The explicit, direct, and antecedent intention in the contraceptive act, as such, is to exercise the conjugal act in such a way that conception can-not possibly issue. There may, indeed, be other intentions present, but the frustration of the act, i.e., the depriving the act of all possible rela-tion to conception, is absolutely a *conditio sine qua non* of intercourse. It is only on condition that the act shall not subserve its primary, essen-tial, and natural purpose that it is performed at all. This point is impor-tant, and we will not allow contraceptionists to obscure the issue by speaking of love, justice, economics, hardships, overburdened wives, and devitalized mothers. The two difficulties raised are:

1. Is the contraceptive act between man and wife a perversion of faculty?

2. If it is, is it a mortal sin?

II. The Controversy

Three contributions have appeared in *The Ecclesiastical Review* on the subject—"The Perverted Faculty Argument against Birth Control," by Dr. Mahoney, August, 1928, pp. 133 ff.; "The Immorality of Contraception," by Dr. Ryan, October, 1928, pp. 408 ff.; "Birth

Control, and the Perverted Faculty Argument," by Dr. Cooper, November, 1928, pp. 527 ff.

We propose to examine each of these contributions, in order to see what, if any, material help these writers offer to the solution of the problem, and incidentally, to reply, as we hope, to some difficulties which they raise.

We have endeavored, without prejudice, to get at the kernel of the matter, as each writer has presented it, and have stripped away everything that is irrelevant to the main contention. In order to make the case as clear as possible, we shall take the material points of each writer in succession, and venture to discuss any point that appears to call for criticism. These criticisms will be indicated by indented paragraphs. We shall venture to insist all through this contribution on what appears to us to be the one valid argument against contraception.

IV. The Contribution of Dr. Ryan

Dr. Ryan does not criticize the first part of Dr. Mahoney's article, but suggests as an argument against birth prevention the baneful indirect effects of it, namely, declining population, and a profound deterioration of social and individual character and competence. Because of these results, he says, the practice is forbidden by the moral law, and in every case it is utterly opposed to the good of a rational nature; people must therefore forego the practice of contraception in the interests of the human race. We could imagine a community living on an island, in whose case contraception would greatly improve the physique and the competence of the people. To limit families to four or five children who could be well reared would be most desirable, both economically and physically. The same might even be said of most European countries today, if it could not have been equally well said of them for centuries past. The suggested profound deterioration of individual character is not obvious, nor can it be proved. It is assumed *a priori*. It is not, by such an argument, impossible to substantiate that one can oppose contraception. One would get nearer to the root of the matter by examining the act itself. To urge, however, that contraception leads essentially to depopulation is to urge, and rightly urge, that in contraception the sexual faculty is perverted to a wrong use, or that the sexual act itself is frustrated. If its obliquity is in question, then we can look at its inevitable results, namely, depopulation, which is a very tangible result even if such a result were not, in the realm of effects from causes, as plain as the noonday sun.

Dr. Ryan further contends that actions, not grave in themselves, are forbidden under pain of mortal sin, on the ground that acceptance of them as venial would encourage such frequent commission as to bring about a grave amount of moral disorder.

But, seriously, how can actions, not grave in themselves, which are, *ex hypothesi,* only venial sins, be forbidden under pain of mortal sin? They cannot, unless some extrinsic element renders them grievously sinful. In the case of contraception we can certainly regard it in the light of its consequences, and then condemn it as gravely sinful. But can we not also antecedently look upon it as a human act, that is, in itself, inordinate in the highest degree? The reason here suggested is that man has the power of generation, which is the immense power of giving the greatest physical good, namely life. To use the faculty, and in the very use and act of the faculty to prevent so great a good positively and of set purpose, appears to us of all inordinations amongst the most inordinate.

Dr. Ryan writes that the couple who deliberately restrict intercourse to a certain time in the intramenstrual period also attempts to defeat the primary end of marriage, namely generation. Yet this aim is not condemned by the moralists. Dr. Ryan quotes the usual reply of moralists, namely, that the couple who use contraceptives defeat the primary end of marriage by positive acts which thwart the processes of nature, rather than through mere selection of times and circumstances. He does not appear to be satisfied with this answer, and says that the obvious rejoinder is that the perverted faculty argument seems to be greatly weakened through the rejection by several theologians of the parallel argument against lying.

We submit that the reply given by moralists is singularly apt and effective. To speak accurately, we should not say that the defeat of the primary purpose of the marital act is the same as the defeat of the primary purpose of marriage. People who lead a life of continence in the married state may be said to defeat the primary purpose of the married state, or of marriage considered as a state, for they never have children at all. But no one speaks of their action of refraining from marital intercourse as an abuse of a faculty. Married persons who use the intramenstrual period in the hope that they will not generate do not, in the act, attempt to defeat the primary purpose of the act, for they do nothing at all to defeat it. They are in all respects, so far as generation is concerned, in the same case as the continent. They do nothing that has the slightest effect on the issue. Whereas those who use contraceptive intercourse really do something in the act itself which the others do not do, they are doing something very positive indeed. They are defeating the primary purpose of the act itself. They are frustrating the act, though exercising the faculty. This distinction is extremely important, and the reader is begged to bear it in mind when he is asked to subscribe to the remark of Dr. Ryan, namely that "the couple that deliberately restricts intercourse to a certain time in the intramenstrual period, also attempts to defeat the primary end." The primary end of what? Of the marital act? The question has merely to be stated to make one realize the absurdity of the contention, unless Dr. Ryan wishes to imply that these people defeat the primary end of marriage in the very act of intramenstrual intercourse precisely because they do not have intercourse at other times! Can we therefore compare the two cases? We cannot, if we wish to think clearly. Is not the reply of moralists very apt and effective?

Dr. Ryan continues: The obvious rejoinder is that this, the perverted faculty argument, seems to be greatly weakened through the rejection by several theologians of the parallel argument against lying.

But as already stated, we shall leave those theologians to fight their own battles. We hold that lying is evil because the faculty of speech is abused in lying. Contraception is also an abuse of the sexual faculty, and a frustration of the sexual act, but indefinitely more serious than lying, as the withholding of life is more serious than the withholding of truth.

V. The Contribution of Dr. Cooper

1. It is not possible, says Dr. Cooper, on our own Catholic principles, to derive the mortal sinfulness of contraception from the secondary unnaturalness of it as a perversion of a faculty. Even granting that lying is the perversion of the faculty of speech, not every perversion, *in se,* constitutes mortal sin. On what ground, therefore, can it be maintained

that perversion of the faculty of reproduction, *in se,* constitutes mortal sin?

To this difficulty we have already suggested an answer which it is for the reader to examine. The answer is that every act of contraception, if it is true contraception—which is that which is always attempted—is an act that is designed to prevent the issue of life, the greatest physical good. This is not to judge of the act by its consequences. It is to judge it by what it actually does.

2. It will not help us, Dr. Cooper continues, to say that the gravity of the sin arises from the fact that the reproductive faculty is a gravely essential one, for the faculty of speech, and of eating, are likewise gravely essential ones, and yet no Catholic theologian holds that the perversion of either of these two faculties, and *in se,* mortally sinful We should not press the case of speech, for the race could get on if everyone was dumb. We do not admit the analogy with eating because the true analogy between the perversion of the faculty of eating and that of reproduction would be that, as in the perversion of reproduction, the act is the direct contrary of what Nature, i.e., God, intended so the direct contrary of what Nature intends in giving us the faculty of eating would be for us to cut out from the act of eating the purpose of eating, which is preservation of life. To do so we should have to eat that which is not nutritious, like sand, and enough of it to bring on death.

VI. Concluding Remarks

We do not establish the grave sinfulness in the misuse of the faculties of speech and eating by appealing to the individual and social effects of such misuse, but we do so by asking the question: What are the purposes of these faculties? The purposes are to reveal thought and to sustain life. But we cannot always say of a given act of misuse of these faculties whether or not it is a grievous perversion of the faculty. For that, we have to consider the good which the faculty achieves in a particular activity of it. When we ask what the purpose is of the reproductive faculty, we answer that it is to give life. The misuse of the faculty, or the frustration of the sexual act in contraception, is to prevent life ensuing. This is true of every act of contraception between persons who can generate, for we are not considering such an act between persons who cannot – they would hardly trouble to take any precautions against a result that cannot ensue. Since, therefore, life is the greatest physical good, every act that necessarily and positively prevents life when life would else ensue from the act that is intended by Nature to produce it, is a serious inordination against rational nature, and against the good of Nature, and against the purpose of Nature. It is comparable with eating in such a way as to cause death forthwith, or with speaking as to misuse speech so as to compass the death of oneself or another. The misuse in the reproductive act is, therefore, always a mortal sin, and essentially so. If a woman could have more healthy children by spacing their births through contraceptive methods, the effects, both individual and social, we can well believe, would be excellent. Nevertheless, each of her acts of contraception would be a grievous sin, for the reason assigned. No one would, it is to be hoped, maintain that the lives, even of sickly children, which by contraception could have been prevented, are not a great physical good.

It is not difficult, as Dr. Cooper seems to suggest, to say what precisely is the natural purpose or function of the faculty of reproduction. There is only one natural primary purpose of it. There is only one *proximus finis operis,* namely conception. But though there is only one proximate purpose of the faculty, there may be many purposes of the act itself intended by Nature. These purposes we know only from observation. For it is quite obvious that Nature intends intercourse during pregnancy, for it is, or may be, most healthful for husband and wife and can give the wife a certain psychological *elan* which she needs at that time. But that is not the only subsidiary purpose of it. It is admitted that the marital act can have a very beneficial effect on the health of the wife, apart altogether from its primary purpose. It would indeed be strange if this were not so, for Nature certainly prompts intercourse during pregnancy and, in cases of sterility, for the expression of love and for mutual comfort. In the absence of the possibility of conception from a given marital intercourse, other purposes of Nature are fulfilled and, as all the theologians admit, when the primary purpose cannot be realized, husband and wife may insure the other purposes of Nature. But it does not follow that the primary purpose of Nature may be cut out at will in order that by a contraceptive act some other purpose may be achieved, as for example the expression of love or the allaying of concupiscence.

It is impossible to follow Dr. Cooper in the contention which, he says, might be made for the sake of argument—that the purpose of speech is to make impressions on the minds of others—for we simply have to look on all human activities as having their proper proximate purpose in the act without reference to motive, or actual effect. No faculty can be defined by what it does accidentally, but should be defined by what it actually does, and this gives us the criterion whereby we judge what its natural purpose it. The proper and natural function of speech can be nothing else than to express thoughts. We think, therefore, that it is quite certain, and perfectly clear, that the natural function of speech is to reveal what is in the mind of the speaker, and it is legitimate to rest the case against lying on the argument based on the misuse of the faculty. Whether that misuse is always a grievous sin is another question, and has no bearing on the sin of contraception.

If, then, we can rest the case against lying on the misuse of faculty in the very act of speech, we can equally well rest the case against birth control on the misuse of faculty, function, or act. Dr. Cooper says that a more detailed formulation of the function of reproduction is imperative, in view of our Catholic moral teaching regarding the licitness of marital relations during pregnancy, and in cases of sterility. In reply to this, we think that the function of the reproductive faculty is manifold, not indeed *qua* reproductive, but *qua* faculty in the organs for sexual intercourse, and it is this fact that renders intercourse during pregnancy and in sterile cases legitimate and natural.

If, then, we admit, as we ought to admit, that the function of the reproductive faculty has other natural purposes besides those of conception and reproduction, it is true to say with Dr. Cooper that it is too general an expression to state: *Finis usus genitalium membrorum est generatio et educatio prolis.* This is, indeed, one purpose, and the primary one. But there are others, and to say so is to fall in line with all Catholic theologians who teach that the use of this faculty is permitted to husband and wife, not only for the purposes of reproduction, but also for expression of love and allaying of concupiscence. But we are very careful to say the use of the faculty, or in other words the sexual act, and not the faculty itself. It appears to the writer to be of the utmost importance to distinguish between the faculty and the use of it, or the act. In contraception, it is the act that is frustrated, but the faculty is used. The misuse of the faculty consists in the abuse or frustration of the act. Thus, Dr. Cooper asks: Just precisely how are we going to formulate such a definition of the natural function of the reproductive faculty as will permit relations in pregnancy and sterility, and yet bar contraceptive practices? There is, we believe, no need to find a new formulation. We need only define the natural sexual act itself, a definition that is hardly necessary since it is obvious in what the act consists. It is the act, not the function, nor yet the faculty, that is misused first of all in contraception; *per consequens,* the result of the functioning of the sexual organs is frustrated.

In intercourse during pregnancy, the sexual act is by no means misused or frustrated. The result of the act is left to Nature. In the sterile woman, the act is not misused or frustrated. The act is quite natural. To the perfectly natural act, Nature will give no issue. In contraception, on the other hand, the act itself is misused. The parties themselves do all they can to eliminate from their act its natural purpose, its *finis operis proximus,* and in that misuse lies the inordination of their act. These people use the functioning of the organs, they employ their reproductive faculty, in a way that robs the act of its character of means in respect of a common purpose of human life; they exercise the act contrary to Nature's purpose. We may, therefore, truly say that contraception is a misuse, an abuse, a perversion of a faculty, understood in the sense as explained.

But is it a grave misuse? There is no doubt about it; for, as already pointed out, this misuse positively thwarts the greatest good, namely potential life. We rightly say that certain sins of *luxuria,* a pollution that is voluntary and direct, are grave abuses or misuses of a functional act, because the act of the function has as its *finis operis* the giving of life. To thwart that appears to us to be one of the greatest inordinations.

It will not, we hope, be out of place to offer our readers two short extracts. The first is from the *Ethics* of Fr. Macksey, late professor at the Gregorian University. He says, "Intrinsic malice – moral evil – consists in frustrating the common end (purpose) of human life; that end, adequately viewed, which is intended by God to be achieved by human activity. In every natural means we find that the *finis proximus,* i.e., the *finis operis,* intended by God, is the purpose or achievement in act of that means. Therefore, if man uses that means so that the purpose of it in act is frustrated, he is acting against the purpose intended by God, and to that extent, he frustrates the common purpose of human life." This argument merely speaks of the misuse of a means, i.e., of an act.

It does not, of course, prove that the misuse is a grave inordination in every case. But the point is that the misuse is a perversion of a faculty. The *bonum* of every human activity is the *finis operis*. To insure this *bonum* is, for man a *bonum honestum*. To frustrate it is a *malum morale*. That is why contraception between man and wife is a *malum morale*, ethically wrong, precisely because it is the perversion of a faculty.

St. Thomas (*c. Gent.* III. C. 122) uses words that might have been expressly written against modern contraceptionists: *Inordinata vero seminis emissio repugnat bonum naturae, quod est conservatio speciei, unde post peccatum homicidii, quo natura humana jam in actu existens, destruitur, hujusmodi genus peccati videtur secundum locum tenere, quo impeditur generatio humanae naturae.* There appears to be no doubt but that, in the mind of St. Thomas, contraception—had he known modern methods—would have been condemned as an abuse of a faculty, in the sense explained, and that he does condemn it as a serious sin, precisely because it is an abuse of an act, which is a means of producing so great a good as life. Those were the two points which the present writer wished to stress. It remains for the reader to examine and criticize, in order that a very definite conclusion may be reached in so important a matter.

H. Davis, S.J.

COMMENT BY DR. RYAN

Father Davis has given us some very clear definitions and distinctions and has produced a comprehensive and valuable paper. But he has not solved the difficulty which Dr. Mahoney stressed; namely, the *practical* weakness of the perverted faculty argument. Inasmuch as this argument is rejected by some theologians, e.g., Tanquerey, as against lying, why may it not reasonably be rejected as against contraception? Father Davis makes no formal attempt to prove that it is valid in the former case. The fact that it is accepted by the majority of theologians does not constitute objective proof. If I reject the perverted faculty argument as applied to lying, why should I admit it in relation to contraception?

Father Davis does not remove this great practical difficulty by asserting and reiterating in varied phraseology the proposition that con-

traceptive intercourse is a "misuse of faculty," a "perversion of function," a "frustration of the sexual act," a "defeat of its primary end," etc.,
etc. Undoubtedly contraceptive practices are of this nature, but how
does this make them morally wrong? Father Davis does not solve this
problem.

Neither he nor anyone else can demonstrate that such "inordi-
nateness" is morally bad. The perverted faculty argument is intrinsic
and metaphysical. If its force is not immediately and intuitively perceived it cannot be made convincing through any process of argumentation. Thousands of persons (including many Catholics) do not accept
this argument against birth prevention and they can derive considerable
comfort from the fact that some authoritative theologians refuse to
admit its cogency against lying. This is the practical difficulty which
remains quite as formidable as it was before Father Davis' paper
appeared. Because of this practical difficulty I suggested that a more
effective argument might be drawn from consequences. Father Davis
seems to admit that the latter argument is valid, but contends that the
other is superior philosophically. Undoubtedly it is – for those who
accept it – but the question before us is whether it is superior pragmat-
ically.

At the request of the Editor, the following statement is added, in
order to set forth the mind of the Church on the problem.

Authoritative Catholic Teaching on Birth Control

Despite the general understanding of Catholic doctrine on this
subject, the question is occasionally asked: "When and where did or
does the Church prohibit this practice or pronounce it wrong?" Let us
try to answer this question as briefly as is consistent with thoroughness.

There are three general sources of Catholic teaching on conduct,
on the morality of human actions. The first is formal pronouncements
by the popes or by general councils on the Church. The second is
responses by certain Roman Congregations in answer to questions concerning the lawfulness or unlawfulness of certain actions. The third
source is the teaching of the moral theologians.

1. A formal papal pronouncement concerning birth control is
found in the Apostolic Constitution *Effraenatam* of Sixtus V (29

October, 1588), in which that pope decreed that the penalty to be inflicted upon persons guilty of procuring abortion should also be imposed upon those who used or provided women with the opportunity of using certain drugs for the purpose of inducing sterility. There is no doubt that this provision is an implicit condemnation of all methods of preventing conception.

2. The responses of the Roman Congregations, particularly that of the Holy Office and the Tribunal of the Poenitentiaria, impose the same moral obligation on the faithful as do the pronouncements of the pope himself. Several such responses or decisions have issued from these two authoritative bodies on the subject of contraception. The Holy Office issued responses on 21 May, 1851 and 19 April, 1853, declaring respectively that Onanism is contrary to the natural law and the use of instruments for preventing conception is intrinsically evil. On 10 March, 1886, 13 November, 1901, 3 April, 1916, and 3 June, 1916, the Poenitentiaria declared that a penitent who refuses to abstain from the practice of birth prevention may not be absolved and that one who is reasonably suspected of being addicted to the practice must be instructed and admonished by the confessor, etc., etc.

3. When the moral theologians unanimously teach that a certain moral principle is right, or a certain practice is wrong, their authority is complete. Refusal to accept such pronouncements is regarded as heretical or approximate heresy. Now the moral theologians are unanimous in declaring that all methods of birth control are morally wrong.

John A. Ryan

9. Human Acts

Francis J. Connell

This chapter first appeared in Francis J. Connell, *Outlines of Moral Theology,* 2nd ed. (Milwaukee: Bruce, 1958).

---

1. NATURE AND DIVISION OF HUMAN ACTS

The human act is one that is proper to a human being, an act that proceeds from the free will of man. It presupposes in the intellect some knowledge of the particular purpose of the act, and in the will freedom of choice to perform it or not to perform it. A human act (*actus humanus*) is different from an act of man (*actus hominis*). This latter is performed by a human being, but does not proceed from his free will. Thus, the beating of the heart, talking in one's sleep, the grasping of a toy by a baby, are acts of man, but not human acts. It can even happen that a person is so overcome by sudden passion that he does something that is objectively gravely sinful, yet it is not a human act. For example, a man enters his home and finds his wife murdered, the murderer being still in the room. The husband might be so overcome by grief and anger that he would kill the murderer, yet not be guilty in conscience of any sin, because his emotions deprived him temporarily of the use of intellect and free will. Theologians call such acts *first-primary* acts (*actus primo-primi*). When the use of intellect and free will is partially impeded, an act is called *second-primary* (*actus secundo-primus*). Such an act, even though objectively it were a mortal sin, would be subjectively only a venial sin.

Human acts are distinguished as follows:

1. *Elicited* and *commanded:* An elicited human act is one that proceeds immediately from the will, and is consummated in the will,

such as an act of love for God. A commanded act is one that proceeds immediately from another faculty, but at the command of the will, such as the act of walking down the street. Physically the act of the will is distinct from the act of the commanded faculty; but morally the two are regarded as a single act.

2. *Internal* and *external:* An internal act proceeds from an internal faculty, such as the intellect, the will, or the memory; while an external human act proceeds from an external faculty at the direction of the will, such as the hand or the tongue. An external human act is always a commanded act; but an internal act can be either elicited (if it proceeds immediately from the will) or commanded (such as an act of faith elicited by the intellect at the command of the will).

A human act is sometimes called a voluntary act (*voluntarium*). However, in theological terminology, a voluntary act is wider in scope. It includes even the necessary act of the will loving God as perceived through the beatific vision.

The omission of an act, to be voluntary and imputable, must proceed from a positive act of the will, deliberately choosing not to perform the act, or at least deliberately choosing not to will to perform the act, as takes place when a person chooses to perform an action incompatible with the act of obligation. For example, if a person decides to play golf all Sunday morning, knowing that thus he will be unable to hear mass, he is guilty of the sin of missing mass, even though he does not expressly will: "I will not go to mass."

An act may be *voluntary in cause.* This takes place when a person performs an action foreseeing that a certain effect will follow, even though he may not will this effect in itself. Thus, a man may realize that if he becomes intoxicated, he will blaspheme. He may not wish to blaspheme; nevertheless, if foreseeing this consequence, he gets drunk, he is guilty in cause of the blasphemy. However, it must not be inferred from this that a person is never allowed to perform an action when he foresees that some evil effect will flow from it. According to the principle of the double effect (to be explained later) a person may perform an action with the prevision that there will be a bad effect, as long as he does not will this effect (but merely permits it) and there will be a good effect also, following immediately from the action, sufficiently desirable to justify the permitting of the bad effect. Thus a man would be allowed to take ether to undergo an operation, even though he foresees that under the influence of the anesthetic he will blaspheme, for that would be only a material sin.

When a person does something to which his will is positively opposed (e.g., not realizing what he is actually doing) the act is *involuntary*, as in the case of the hunter who shoots his friend, thinking he is aiming at an animal. When he does something to which his will is not opposed, though in this instance he did not will it, the act is *nonvoluntary,* as in the case of the hunter who inadvertently kills an enemy whom he would gladly kill anyway.

2. Impediments to Freedom of Human Acts

Four factors may prevent or diminish the freedom of a human act. Two of these—violence and fear—come from extrinsic causes; two come from the person himself—ignorance and passion.

Violence is physical force brought to bear on a person to compel him to do something which he does not will. For example, a man might be compelled by violence to drink an excessive amount of intoxicating liquor, a girl might be physically forced to submit to a sexual attack.

When violence is complete – that is, when the victim resists physically as much as he can – any action performed by force of the violence is *involuntary*. At times, however, there is no obligation to use as much physical resistance as one can – that is, when there is question of merely submitting to another's evil act, not of performing a bad act oneself. Thus, if an attacker threatens a girl that he will kill her if she attempts resistance, she may submit passively, as long as her will is opposed to the deed, and there is no proximate danger that she will give consent to the resultant sensual pleasure. In such a case her part in the attack is *nonvoluntary*. If the victim resists less than he should, because he really wishes the evil deed to take place, there is strictly no question of violence, and the bad act is really voluntary on his part, though it can be said to be partially involuntary (*voluntarium simpliciter, involuntarium secundum quid*). This would be the case if the man being forced to drink too much liquor resists halfheartedly, because he really wishes to get drunk.

The "confessions" which are extorted from the victims of Communist aggression behind the Iron Curtain today are examples of violence. The tortures and drugs employed on these poor persons evidently retain their power for some time after they have been inflicted, so that the statements made by these accused persons are often involuntary. Consequently, they are not responsible utterances.

Fear, or mental anxiety because of an impending or future evil, may at times be so overwhelming that it deprives a person temporarily of the use of reason; and in that event an action by the instigation of that fear is not a human act, and consequently not imputable. However, ordinarily fear, however great, does not take away the use of reason and hence does not justify a person in performing an action which is *intrinsically* wrong, such as denying the faith or committing murder (e.g., abortion), though it might diminish the culpability to some extent. Fear could at times excuse one from the observance of a *positive* law, such as the observance of the Sunday obligation. Thus, if a person had good reason to fear that his enemy would shoot him if he set out for mass on Sunday, he would be excused from the positive (ecclesiastical) observance of hearing mass. Moreover, by special legislation of the church, certain acts performed under the influence of fear are null and void. For example, grave fear inducing a novice to make profession renders the vows invalid.[1] Similarly, a marriage is invalid if it is entered into through grave, unjust fear exerted by another person, in such wise that a person is forced to choose marriage in order to rid himself of the fear.[2]

Ignorance is lack of knowledge in a person who should possess such knowledge. Thus, in a physician lack of medical knowledge is ignorance, but not lack of knowledge of astronomy. From the moral standpoint inadvertence, failure to apply one's habitual knowledge to present circumstances, is equivalent to ignorance.

Ignorance is *invincible* or *inculpable* when it is not due to one's own fault. Thus, if a person is sick on Sunday and cannot attend mass and in consequence does not learn that Wednesday is a day of abstinence, he is guilty of no sin if he eats meat on Wednesday, for his ignorance is inculpable, and consequently acts proceeding from it are involuntary or nonvoluntary as far as their morality is concerned. But if on Tuesday a person gets the idea that perhaps tomorrow is a day of abstinence and can easily settle the matter by calling up a neighbor or the priest, but neglects to do so, and then eats meat on Wednesday with the thought: "I'm not sure about this, so I'll consider myself free," he commits sin, for his ignorance is *vincible* or *culpable*. It should be noted that the neglect to acquire knowledge necessary to observe the law is sinful (even though one does not wish the ignorance in itself), since in that event the ignorance is voluntary in cause, as in the case of a doctor who neglects to study sufficiently about a rare disease afflicting one of his patients, because the study is too irksome. A person is still more guilty if he directly wills to remain in ignorance, so that he may have greater freedom of action, as in the case of a doctor who will not attend lectures on medical ethics, lest he learn that certain of his practices are condemned by the Catholic Church as opposed to the law of God.

Passion (sometimes called concupiscence) is a tendency of the sensitive appetite toward some pleasurable good—e.g., intoxication, impurity. Like fear, it can sometimes deprive a person temporarily of the use of reason and free will, and in that event an action performed under the influence of passion is not voluntary or culpable. When it does not go this far, it diminishes the imputability of the act and the gravity of sin, sometimes to the extent of rendering what is objectively a mortal sin only a venial sin (a *second-primary* act).

This applies to *antecedent passion* which precedes the use of free will. Passion can be *consequent* —that is, it can be deliberately brought on, and in that event it rather increases the guilt. Thus, a man may arouse his anger by dwelling on the insults he has received from his neighbor. Again, a person may deliberately frequent some occasion of impurity, knowing that his passions will thus be aroused; and in that case the subsequent sins are in nowise diminished by the fact that he committed them under the influence of strong passion.

If a person has contracted a bad habit, so that he frequently commits an evil act with very little or no advertence, but is now seriously trying to eradicate the habit, any acts which proceed from this habit without advertence are involuntary. But on the other hand, if he adverts to the habit and decides to do nothing about it, he sins, and acts which subsequently follow from the habit are voluntary in cause. Usually, however, even in this event there is sufficient actual advertence to render these actions voluntary in themselves, especially if they are gravely sinful, such as impure desires or blasphemy.

3. MORALITY OF HUMAN ACTS

Morality in the strict sense can be predicated only of human acts or of the persons who perform them. Thus, we say it is good to pray, it is bad to steal; and the man who does the former is a good man, the one who does the latter is a bad man. It is only by an extension of the term that we speak of bad books or bad pictures. What we mean is books or pictures calculated to arouse morally evil thoughts and desires in the minds of the spectators.

Nowadays, outside the Catholic Church the ultimate basis of morality is placed by many in custom or human legislation. This is the theory of positivism, according to which all actions are good or bad merely because human beings have decided to consider them such, or because civil laws have determined that it should be so. From this it logically follows that actions which are morally good at one time will become morally bad at another period, or vice versa. Two Americans who have done much to propagate this theory are Judge Oliver Wendell Holmes and John Dewey. In *Newsweek* for December 25, 1950, Raymond Moley says: "Despite the wide veneration accorded these two men, it is well to note the havoc they have created in the thinking of contemporary America and the perversions of their teaching."

Some actions are commanded or forbidden by positive legislation— divine, ecclesiastical, or civil. Consequently, as Catholic theologians express it, some actions are good because they are commanded or bad because they are forbidden. Thus, by divine positive law we are commanded to receive holy communion, and forbidden to receive confirmation a second time. By ecclesiastical law we are commanded to go to mass on Sunday and forbidden to eat meat on Friday. By civil law we are commanded to pay our taxes and forbidden to drive through a red light.

But there are other actions which are good or bad by their very nature; and these are commanded because they are good, forbidden because they are bad. It is the morality of these actions which we are now considering.

By morality we mean a transcendental relation of a human act, either of agreement or of disagreement, to a norm or rule of goodness and evil, based on man's nature considered in its entirety. A transcendental relation is one that is inherent in the act itself.

To understand this principle, we must bear in mind that a thing is called good or bad in as far as it acts in accordance with its nature or does not act in this way. An ax is a good ax if it cuts well, an automobile is a good automobile if it runs properly. On the contrary, an ax that is dull and cannot cut well is not a good ax, an automobile that is constantly stalling is not a good automobile.

So, too, a man is a good man and his actions are good when those actions are in accordance with human nature and the purposes for which that nature was made. On the other side, actions which are contrary to man's nature are bad. It should be noted that we must determine this rule or norm from the consideration of man's nature *in its entirety,* and not merely from the consideration of an individual faculty. Thus, sexual gratification is adapted to the sexual faculty considered in itself; but it is not always conformable to man's nature taken in its entirety.

When we analyze human nature, we find that it has three essential characteristics, in as far as man is a *social* being, a *rational* being, a *created* being. When man performs actions in accordance with his nature under these aspects, the actions are good, and he thus fulfills his obligations toward his neighbor, toward himself, and toward God.

Man by his nature is meant to live in the society of his fellow men; consequently, those actions whereby social life is promoted are morally good, those actions whereby society is injured are morally bad. Thus, it is good to be kind and just toward others, to obey the laws passed by legitimate human authority, to propagate the human race in the married state (in which alone the welfare of the offspring is assured). On the contrary, it is detrimental to society (and consequently morally evil) to be unkind, to lie, to steal, to disobey lawful authority, to use the sexual faculties outside of marriage.

Man is also a rational being, which means that a spiritual soul animates his material body, and is intended by nature to be the dominating element, and to exercise reasonable guidance over the body so that it may remain healthy and strong as long as nature permits. Consequently, man performs good actions when he eats and drinks in moderation, when he uses reasonable means to preserve his health and life, when he keeps his emotions in proper check. On the contrary, he performs bad actions when he risks his life immoderately, when he mutilates himself or commits suicide, when he eats immoderately, and especially when he drinks excessively and thus subjects the soul to the cravings of the body.

Man is also a created being, and as such he has obligations toward his creator. Hence, he performs good actions when he worships and loves and thanks God; he performs bad actions when he blasphemes or neglects to worship God.

Thus, an analysis of man's very nature furnishes the basic norm of what is right and wrong. This is what we mean when we say that human nature is the *constitutive* norm of morality. This norm is within the capacity of human reason, which is the *manifestative* norm of morality. This does not mean that every individual by his own intellectual efforts can discover all the rules of morality. There are certain questions on which men would disagree if left to their own reasoning powers – for example, whether divorce, by public authority, is ever lawful. But every human being endowed with the use of intelligence is able to realize that certain actions are in accordance with human nature while other actions are at variance with human nature. In other words, every human being can know at least the basic norms of the moral law.

Father Slater, S.J., expresses this doctrine of the constitutive norm of morality in these words: "The teaching of St. Thomas and many others seem to be that the fundamental norm of morality is rational human nature as such. Good, in general is that which is conformable to the rational nature of man considered in itself and in all its relations.... The fundamental norm of right conduct is man's moral nature; morally right conduct is conduct in conformity with man's nature in itself and in all its relations."[3]

While human nature is the *proximate* constitutive norm of morality, the *remote* norm is the divine nature, which is the efficient cause and the prototype of human nature, so that whatever is in accord with human nature is necessarily in accord with the divine nature, whatever is opposed to human nature is also opposed to the divine nature.

Supernatural good is never opposed to the natural good, but is superior to it. Accordingly, what is naturally good—e.g., marriage—may meritoriously be renounced for a higher supernatural good, such as a greater opportunity to love God and to practice works of divine charity.

Besides the *constitutive* and the *manifestative* norm of morality, there is also a *preceptive* norm. The remote preceptive norm is the eternal law of God, the proximate objective norm is the natural law; the proximate subjective norm is conscience.

4. The Factors of Morality

To determine whether an individual act is conformable to the norm of morality or opposed to it—in other words, whether it is good or bad—three factors (known technically as the *fonts* of morality) must be considered. These are called respectively the *object,* the *circumstances,* and the *end.*

By the object of an act we mean its primary moral aspect; by its circumstances we mean those moral aspects which are present as accessories or additions to the primary aspect; by the end we mean the purpose of the person performing the act (*finis operantis*). Actually, the end is one of the circumstances; but it is given a separate classification because it has a very important bearing on human actions.

For example: A man steals money belonging to the church, his purpose being to buy liquor in order to get drunk. The object of the act is a sin of injustice; an essential circumstance is the fact that the money belongs to the church; the end is a sin of intemperance. Again, a man is extraordinarily generous in taking care of his sick father, because in this way he hopes to atone for the sins of his past life. The object of his actions is charity; a circumstance is filial piety; the end is penance. Just as an evil act is made worse by additional bad circumstances or ends if they are foreseen, so a good act is rendered better by additional good circumstances or ends, if they are foreseen and intended.

To be truly good, an action must be good in object, circumstances and end. The theological axiom expressing this is *Bonum ex integra causa, malum ex quocumque defectu* (Good is from the entire cause, evil is from any defect"). The reason is that moral goodness consists n conformity to a certain measure or norm, and conformity demands that a thing meet the standards of the norm in all respects. E.g., a beam to be used in constructing a house is no good for the purpose if even one measurement is defective, even though the other measurements are correct. So, too, all the factors of a human act must be good if the act is to be accounted as morally good. This is the reason why a good end does not justify a bad means. Thus, a person would not be permitted to tell a lie, even though by means of it he could bring about many conversions to the faith. A man would not be allowed to deny his Catholic faith even though he could thereby gain a very desirable job in which he could effect much good for religion.

Under circumstances are included chiefly *place* (e.g., the commission of a sin *in church*); *time* (e.g., working three hours unnecessarily *on Sunday*); person's state (e.g., a sin against chastity *by a religious*); and *manner* (e.g., theft *by violence*).

There are two classes of circumstances—those which change the species of the act, and those which merely increase or diminish the moral goodness or evil of the act within the same species. When a circumstance of the first type is present, the act is endowed with two species of virtue or of sin. Thus, the religious who overcomes a temptation against chastity practices both chastity and (because of the vow) religion. When a sinful act is accompanied by a gravely evil circumstance changing the species of the sin, this circumstance must be told in confession.[4] Thus, a boy who has seriously injured his father by giving him a beating must confess not only that he gravely injured another (fifth commandment) but also that this other was his father (fourth commandment).

The other type of circumstance does not change the specific nature of the sin, but makes it more or less grave within the same species. Thus, if a person steals money from a blind beggar it is a more despicable act than if he stole from one in good health; but it would not add a new species of sin. Similarly, a person who assists at mass with great fervor performs a better act than one who assists with very little devotion, but there is no new *species* of goodness added.

The fact that a circumstance of this latter type was present in a sin does not have to be made a matter of confession. Thus, the thief described above would satisfy his obligation by confessing, "I committed a mortal sin of theft," without mentioning the fact that the victim was poor or blind. However, if a circumstance is such that it renders a sin mortal which otherwise would or could be venial, it must be confessed. Thus a person who steals $100 commits specifically the same sin as one who steals 5 cents, but the circumstance that a large sum was taken must be told. In such a case we say that the circumstance, though it is merely aggravating as far as the *moral* species of the sin is concerned, changes the *theological* species of the sin. In discussing the end of an action, theologians consider the case of one who performs an action in order to obtain pleasure from it. The church teaches that it is sinful to eat and drink and to exercise conjugal relations (even when these actions are objectively lawful) *merely* for the sake of pleasure.

However, there would be no *mortal* sin, as long as the acts themselves are lawful. Moreover, a person does not act merely for pleasure in performing an action within the bounds of temperance as long as he has at least implicitly the intention of procuring reasonable *recreation,* a morally good end. Such an act can be raised to the state of a supernaturally meritorious act by a good intention, even though the desire of pleasure is also present. These ideas are emphasized in order to offset any false ascetical notions, which might propose the seeking of natural pleasure in a moderate degree as something sinful.

It is the more common teaching of theologians that no human act can be morally indifferent in the concrete. In other words, every deliberate human act is either good or bad. The reason is that, even though an act may be morally indifferent as regards its object (in the abstract), such as the act of walking, there will always be an end on the part of the agent, which will be either good or bad, and this will render the act in the concrete either good or bad.

5. THE PRINCIPLE OF THE DOUBLE EFFECT

A principle that is often employed in moral theology is known as the principle of the double effect. It means that under certain conditions a person may perform an action even though he foresees that one of the effects will be evil, either physical or moral. Four conditions must be fulfilled in order to justify one in acting thus:

1. The action which is to be performed by the agent must be morally good, or at least morally indifferent by its nature.

2. The bad effect may be only permitted; it may not be willed in itself.

3. The good effect must be caused at least as directly as the bad effect. In other words, the bad effect may not be a means to produce the good effect. Sometimes this condition is expressed by the phrase that the good effect must be at least equally immediate with the bad effect. But this immediacy refers to the order of *causality,* not the order of time. In the order of time the bad effect may precede the good effect.

4. The good effect must be sufficiently beneficial to compensate for the permitting of the bad effect. Many factors must be considered in determining this condition. Thus, a greater good is *per se* required to

compensate for the permitting of a *morally* bad effect (the sin of another) than for the permitting of a *physically* bad effect; a greater good is required when the bad effect is sure to follow than when it will only *probably* follow; a greater reason is required only when the bad effect is injurious to the *common* good than when it is harmful only to an *individual*.

SOME PRACTICAL CASES

The bomber can attack an enemy ammunition base, even though he foresees that some innocent civilians will very likely be killed, as long as the military benefit to his country from the destruction of the base will be very great. On the other hand, if the number of civilians who will be killed is so great that the benefit anticipated from the attack will not compensate for the loss of many lives (and, of course, it is not easy to establish a proportion between these two terms), the attack is unlawful. (For this reason, the use of the A-bomb on the Japanese cities in 1945 was immoral. Too many civilians were killed in comparison with the military objectives gained. Some tried to argue that by killing so many civilians our armies terrorized the people and induced them to surrender, so that eventually more lives were spared than were destroyed by the bomb. But such an argument fails to take into consideration the third condition. It results in a bad means to a good end.)

Four men are on a raft, and after a while it is discovered that the raft will hold only three. With four it will sink. One may jump off the raft, even though he knows that he will soon perish. But if the crisis is insufficient food, one may not jump off, though he may voluntarily abstain from food, even though it will result in death from starvation. These cases revolve around the third condition, the difference being that in some instances the good effect flows directly from the act (or omission), in other instances only through the causality of the bad effect.

SOME PROBLEMS TO BE DISCUSSED

The hunger strike as a protest against governmental injustice.... The shooting of a gangster by a policeman when the gangster is trying to shoot the policeman and is holding a child in front of himself....The man who shoots himself when trapped in a burning building....The man who leaps from the twentieth story of a burning building to escape the flames....The aviator who dashes his plane into an enemy warship, knowing that he will be killed, but hoping at the same time to inflict great damage on the vessel....The priest who goes into a burning building to baptize a child, knowing that he will be unable to escape.

The principle of the double effect can be applied to the case of one who goes into the proximate occasion of sin, so that at times he will be justified in doing this, as long as there is a sufficiently grave reason for doing so. For example, a man may go into a saloon which is a proximate occasion of sin to him, in order to persuade his son to come home. But a person is not justified in doing this unless he also uses means for rendering remote the proximate occasion, especially prayer. Moreover, a person may never use this principle if he is sure to sin. But one may sometimes lawfully perform an action foreseeing that it will be an occasion of sin to another, as will be treated under the subject of scandal.

6. THE MERIT OF HUMAN ACTS

Merit in the concrete sense is an act deserving of reward. In the abstract, merit is that quality of a good work whereby it is rendered worthy of a reward, or it is the right of the person to receive a reward.

Since every human act is either good or bad, every human act is either meritorious or demeritorious in the sight of God. A work can be *naturally* meritorious or *supernaturally* meritorious, depending on whether its motive is natural or supernatural. We are concerned here only with supernatural merit.

Supernatural merit is either condign or congruous. It is condign when a reward is due in justice; it is congruous when a reward is due only out of fitness. Congruous merit is again subdivided into infallible and fallible, the former being present when God has promised a reward, the latter when no such promise has been made. For example, when a sinner makes an act of perfect contrition, he merits congruously but infallibly[5] the restoration of the state of grace. However, if a person offers even heroic acts to obtain the grace of a religious vocation, he can merit it only congruously and fallibly.

A person can merit condignly (supposing the fulfillment of the conditions enumerated below) an increase of sanctifying grace, heavenly glory, and an increase of glory corresponding to the measure of his sanctifying grace.[6] No one (except Christ, divinely established as the head of the human race) can merit condignly for others. Of the three values that can be in a good work—merit (condign), satisfaction, and the impetration—the second and the third can be transferred to others, but the first remains one's own.

CONDITIONS FOR CONDIGN MERIT

1. On the part of the person meriting. He must be (*a*) in the present life. No one can merit after death. Not even our Lord merited after His death on the cross.[7] (*b*) In the state of sanctifying grace, for merit always implies an increase of grace, and no one can increase in grace unless he already possesses it.

2. On the part of the work. (*a*) Morally good, at least by reason of the end of the agent. It stands to reason that no one can merit by an evil deed. (*b*) Free—that is, the agent must have the power of will to perform the work or not to perform it; for merit comes to us from our giving something to God, and the only acts we can give to God are those over which we have power by free will. It is not necessary that an act be morally free in order to be meritorious. In other words, we can merit by deeds of obligation. (*c*) Supernatural—that is, it must be directed toward God and aided by actual grace.

3. On the part of God. He must have promised a reward. That God has made such a promise in regard to our good deeds is abundantly evident from revelation.[8]

Theologians are not in agreement as to the nature of the direction to God (Condition 2, *c*) required for a meritorious work. Some think that this is fulfilled as long as the person is in the state of grace. The better and the safer view, however, is that an *act* of love of God must be made, directing the work to Him because He is all-good in Himself. However, even in this view it suffices that the influence of charity persevere *virtually* from the previous act. Thus, if a person directs all his acts to God several times in the course of the day by an act of divine charity, all his good acts—even those that in themselves are only naturally good—are raised to the rank of supernaturally meritorious actions.

Notes

1. Can. 572. (This refers to a particular canon, or law, in the *Codex Juris Canonici,* the official code of ecclesiastical law, which began to bind in 1918.)
2. Can. 1087.
3. *Manual of Moral Theology,* p. 156.
4. *DB,* 917.
5. Jn. 14:23.
6. *DB,* 842.
7. Jn. 9:4.
8. Mt. 20:1–16; 25–34 ff.

10. Natural Law

Edwin F. Healy

This chapter first appeared in Edwin F. Healy, *Medical Ethics* (Chicago: Loyola University Press, 1956).

Wherever there is to be order in things that manifest activity, there must exist uniform modes of acting. Unless things act in a manner that is constant and dependable, chaos, not harmony, will result. If, for example, a stone tossed into the air might on one occasion fall to the ground, and at another time rise higher and higher until it disappeared into the stratosphere, and on a third occasion travel perpetually in an easterly or westerly direction, the unpredictable irregularity in its activity would lead to confusion and would create untold problems.

God has established order in the physical universe by means of laws which we call the physical laws of nature. All nonliving things have certain qualities or properties because of which they consistently act in a given manner under a given set of conditions. A stone dropped into a lake will sink to the bottom; gunpowder to which a flame is applied will explode; water raised to a certain temperature is converted into steam. Night follows day and spring succeeds winter because of the physical laws of nature. As to living things without the power to feel, the plants, they too are governed by certain laws. The brute animals act without freedom in response to stimuli. Thus all nonrational beings are guided to their destiny by a necessary conformity to the physical laws of nature.

There is another class of beings, however, which are not directed to their end by means of physical necessity. The creatures in this class are rational; that is, they are gifted with understanding and free will. This second category as found upon earth is made up exclusively of human beings, who have the power to act freely, who are able deliberately to choose to do this action and to avoid that one. In keeping with their rational nature human beings are directed to their eternal destiny by moral precepts. God imposes on them the obligation to conduct themselves in a reasonable way, in a manner which befits their nature. He has given them certain commands and prohibitions, the observance of which will enable them to accomplish the purpose for which He brought them into being. These fundamental commands and prohibitions form what is called the moral law of nature and are commonly referred to as the natural law.

The principles of the natural law fall into two categories: (1) the primary principles and (2) the secondary principles. The *primary principles* are general rules of conduct which are so fundamental that there can be little disagreement about their existence. "Evil is to be avoided" and "Parents should be respected by their children" are examples of primary principles. The *secondary principles* are particular conclusions drawn from the primary principles. "Adultery is forbidden" and "Stealing is wrong" are examples of secondary principles. The science of ethics investigates the nature of these precepts, explains their origin, and enumerates the more important primary and secondary principles.

Many today defend the theory that the principles of moral conduct change from time to time, and that they are not the same throughout the world but vary according to local conditions and under the influence of changes in society. "It is a mistake to suppose that moral principles alone remain fixed and unchangeable while everything else around us grows and develops," contends Professor Hollingworth of Columbia University. "Traditional systems of ethical doctrine do not relate very closely to contemporary activities and ideals, and they are often based on antiquated descriptions of our minds and misguided accounts of human motives."[1]

In his criticism of "traditional systems of ethical doctrine" Professor Hollingworth presupposes that "everything else around us" changes. This supposition all but the intellectually blind will deny. Do the physical laws of nature—the law, for example, of gravitation or the law of combustion – vary from century to century? In order to solve his problems must the mathematician follow one set of principles today and completely different principles ten years from now? The moral law, like the laws of mathematics, is intrinsically unchangeable. If it is unthinkable that two and two should equal four today and five tomorrow, it is likewise inconceivable that the law which forbids lying should be true today and false tomorrow. Actually, the fundamental principles are recognized as such by savage and civilized alike. Barbarians, it is true, have had moral codes which differed somewhat from the code of civilized nations, but the few differences in the savages' codes stemmed from their having falsely applied the teaching of the universally accepted general principles.[2]

It is true that the moral code of all civilized peoples is not identical in every detail. Within our own century there have been places in North America where fishing on Sunday was forbidden by law, and there are groups today which consider such things as dancing, card playing, and gambling evil in themselves. Others do not consider any of these things necessarily evil. But the fact that there are differences of opinion in regard to details of the code does not prove that there is nothing in the code that is fixed and unchangeable. Behind all these prohibitions are such absolute and constant principles as these: that nothing should be permitted to interfere with the worship and service of God; that our time should be used for some good purpose; that recreational activities should be decent; that things leading us into moral wrongdoing must be avoided. The rigorist can be too strict in his application of these principles, and the laxist can grant too much freedom; but both rigorist and laxist accept the same fundamental principles, and both make the same applications of the principles in very many matters. It is a common thing today for men to build up from instances of these opposed applications of fundamental principles an argument to the effect that nothing in the moral code is absolute, that the natural law is a mere fiction. The very fact that codes continue to exist and that applications continue to be made is an argument to the contrary, for every application presupposes the existence of the principle from which it is thought to follow. It is to be expected that some differences of opinion in regard to details should be found, especially among those who do not accept the existence of any authority competent to pass upon the soundness of their personal conclusions.

All men, then, are called upon to obey the natural law. Hence it matters not whether one be a Roman Catholic, a Protestant, a Jew, a pagan, or a person who has no religious affiliations whatsoever; he is nevertheless obliged to become acquainted with and to observe the teachings of the law of nature. In the present volume all the obligations which are mentioned flow from the natural law, unless the contrary is evident from the context.

If an action is evil in itself and so prohibited by the law of nature (for example, lying, stealing, or murder), no authority on earth, be it civil or ecclesiastical, can under any conceivable circumstances legitimately grant permission to perform that action. Nor can any authority on earth legitimately forbid an individual to perform an action that is clearly and under the circumstances required by the natural law. It follows that a work on medical ethics written by a Catholic is not merely a collection of rulings of an arbitrary nature made by his church. It is rather an application to the practice of medicine of the principles of the natural law. The Catholic looks to his church for guidance in his interpretation of the natural law, for in her role of teacher she has the right to explain and interpret difficult principles of the natural law and to pass judgment on applications of these principles. Because of confused notions which have at times arisen with regard to certain prescriptions of the natural law, the church has issued clarifying and authoritative pronouncements which serve to protect her subjects from error.

An example of such an official interpretation of one point of the law of nature is the decision of the Sacred Congregation of the Holy Office which condemned the direct killing of persons who had committed no crime worthy of death, though because of mental and physical defects some judged them to be useless to the nation.[3] This pronouncement contained nothing not already found in the natural law, nor was the principle on which it was based unknown to men in general. The church, however, knowing that dictators were unjustly condemning to death allegedly useless members of society and that some scholars of standing were defending the action on philosophical grounds, felt obliged to speak out in defense of the rights of humanity. To have remained silent might have created the impression that she tolerated or even approved the action. The church, as a matter of fact, has issued only a limited number of pronouncements on the subject of medical ethics, and these in general were either inspired by conditions such as that described or were issued in response to requests for a decision on difficult and doubtful points.

Notes

1. Harry L. Hollingworth, *Psychology and Ethics,* p. v (New York: The Ronald Press Company, 1949). Professor Hollingworth seems to classify under "principles" the Ten Commandments. See p. 130.

2. For a detailed study of this question see Michael Cronin, *The Science of Ethics,* vol. I, chap. 5, "The Moral Criteria," pp. 124–74 (New York: Benziger Brothers, 1949).

3. See *Acta Apostolicae Sedis* 32:553–54, January 22, 1940.

11. The Good Confessor

Gerald Kelly

This chapter first appeared in Gerald Kelly, *The Good Confessor* (New York: Sentinel, 1951).

HIS KNOWLEDGE

The good confessor must have *knowledge,* says the Ritual. But how much knowledge? What should he know? The Ritual does not give a set rule in this matter. But it does mention in particular that the confessor must be able to distinguish the various leprosies of the soul and to prescribe appropriate remedies for each of them. Also, he should know the cases reserved to the Holy See, as well as those reserved to his own Ordinary; and he should be thoroughly acquainted with the doctrine concerning the sacrament of penance and with everything that pertains to its correct administration.

It is my purpose in the present chapter to go beyond the words of the Ritual and to outline rather completely the various kinds of knowledge that are necessary or especially helpful for a confessor. At the outset I should emphasize the fact that this is merely an *outline,* and for that reason it may not be extremely readable. But I hope that it will prove useful.

Moral Theology and Canon Law

As regards the confessor's knowledge of moral theology and canon law, a general rule often given is that he should be able to solve the ordinary cases likely to be presented to him and "to doubt prudently" about the more difficult cases. This ability "to doubt prudently" would usually manifest itself in a hesitancy to give a definite decision until the case is checked in appropriate books or through necessary consultation.

In greater detail, the ability "to solve the ordinary cases," seems to call for knowledge of the following points:

(1) The requisite for the valid and licit administration of the sacrament of penance, and for the valid, licit, and fruitful reception of the sacrament.

(2) The differences between mortal and venial sin in general, and with regard to individual commandments and precepts; also, the practical signs for determining when *subjective* mortal sin is or is not committed.

(3) The various specific differences of sins on which moralists agree, and especially those that penitents would be expected to know. To get the "mind of the penitent" in this regard it helps very much to read the popular catechisms occasionally, for it is from these catechisms that the ordinary faithful learn their moral theology.

(4) The ways of estimating the number of sins committed.

(5) The principles for determining when restitution of goods or reputation is called for.

(6) The principles governing reserved sins and censures, and the reservations most likely to occur. In this matter in particular, one must know local legislation. If there is local legislation it will be found in the diocesan statute book or the *pagellum facultatum.* (Incidentally, I might mention here that statute books and *pagella* often contain many valuable practical suggestions.)

(7) The matrimonial impediments and the powers of dispensing in urgent cases.

(8) The principles governing occasions of sin, habits of sin, and recidivism; and the more common suggestions that can be made to help penitents who face these difficulties.

(9) The laws governing the reception of Holy Communion.

(10) The meaning and extent of one's special faculties (in case one has such faculties, e.g., because he is an army chaplain, a missionary, etc.), and the rules for the valid and prudent use of such faculties.

The points included in the foregoing outline (except in n. 10) represent the standard equipment in moral theology and canon law for every confessor. Circumstances might call for more extensive knowledge: for example, if one must be the regular confessor of priests, or seminarians, or religious, one should know the special obligations of such people and the special problems they are likely to have.

Ascetical Theology

Instructions for seminaries make it quite clear that the Holy See expects confessors to know at least the fundamentals of ascetical theology. A brief outline of these essentials (adapted from *The Spiritual Life,* by Tanquerey) may be stated as follows:

The confessor should understand the *objective* of the spiritual life. This objective is *perfection;* and perfection, in turn, is the love of God with one's whole heart, not only in affection, but also in deed, by trying to keep all the precepts and counsels. In directing penitents the confessor should never lose sight of this goal.

The means of attaining perfection are *interior* and *exterior.* The principal interior means are desire for perfection (without which there will never be sincere and constant effort), knowledge of God and of oneself, prayer, and conformity to the divine will. Exterior means are spiritual direction, a rule of life, spiritual reading and conferences, and the sanctification of social relationships. The confessor who understands these various means will be able to guide his penitents intelligently and to stress one or the other according to the needs of individuals.

It helps also to be familiar with the traditional "three ways," and to be able to catalogue, at least in a rough manner, each of those who seek direction.

The principal function of the *purgative* way is to do away with sin and its effects. It is marked by discursive mental prayer; by penance, to make up for past faults; by mortification, to secure self-control; and by struggle against the capital sins and temptations.

The special function of the *illuminative* way is to develop the virtues, theological and moral. Prayer at this stage should usually be affective and rather simple.

The unitive way, as the name implies, perfects one's union with God and one's docility to the Holy Spirit. The Gifts of the Holy Ghost play a large part in this stage of perfection.

All the points in the foregoing outline are well explained by Tanquerey. I might add here that, besides being able to direct souls in the way of perfection by the application of the principles of ascetical theology, confessors should also know something about infused contemplation so that they can at least suspect its presence in certain penitents.

Preserving Knowledge

The knowledge of moral theology, canon law, ascetical (and mystical) theology, is a part of the priest's profession. Ignorance concerning ordinary and fundamental things is lamentable. As a word of consolation, I might add that, generally speaking, a man who has gone through his course of theology with ordinary diligence knows at least these fundamentals, and perhaps much more. This does not mean that he has everything at his fingertips. It is easy to forget things or to become confused.

Knowledge once acquired is not retained without continued repetition. And broader knowledge is not acquired without further study. And this brings us to the question: what practicable resolve should the young priest make with regard to keeping fresh his knowledge of the fundamentals I have outlined and to the appropriate extending of his knowledge? There is no set answer to this question. My own suggestion as to the *minimum* program of reading would be this: keep repeating the texts of canon law and of moral and ascetical theology you had in the seminary; and read faithfully at least one ecclesiastical periodical that presents and solves practical cases and that makes it a point to keep its readers well-informed on new decisions of the Holy See and on recent developments in theology.

Some might object to my suggestion about continued repetition of the texts used in the seminary. They might say that this makes a confessor a man of "one book," and that being a man of one book makes him narrow-minded and unmindful of the opinions of other authors. I realize that this criticism has merit; yet I think that if most priests were to try to keep up on several texts they would become masters of none. The broadening influence of other opinions can be gained through conversations with other priests and through the faithful reading of a good ecclesiastical periodical, not to mention the *mentally active* attendance at the diocesan conferences.

My suggestion concerns the *minimum*; the priest who does less than that is not doing enough to keep up on his canon law and moral and ascetical theology. I prefer to keep it to the minimum and to allow the more elaborate schemes of keeping up – which are certainly possible for many priests – to be planned by the individuals themselves after consultation with experienced priests.

Other Knowledge

The young priest should take it as a standard rule that his power in the confessional will be greatly increased by any study or any experience that gives him a more profound and sympathetic knowledge of the human personality. For instance, he can learn much that is helpful from modern treatises on psychology, mental hygiene, and psychiatry. But it is very important that reading done in these fields should be, at least in some sense, supervised. By supervised, I mean that it should be done only through consultation with men who know these fields and who know something of the use that priests might make of such knowledge. A great part of the literature in these fields could be more interesting than useful; in fact, it might even be very harmful to the uninitiated.

It is advisable for a confessor to take advantage of every legitimate opportunity to know the practical problems of certain classes of people: for example, business men, laboring men, lawyers, doctors, religious, and so forth, because in directing such people, these practical difficulties must be taken into account. Moreover, it is helpful to know something of the theory and terminology of certain professions. For example, if a priest knows some civil law, he is better able to look up a point for himself, and is a more intelligent listener in case he must consult the expert. The same holds true for medicine: a little knowledge (of ordinary medicine, of psychic disorders, and so forth) is helpful.

However, for the most part, the priest's use of knowledge of other professional fields should be largely "negative"—that is, it should help the priest to suspect cases that ought to be referred to specialists. It is not wise for the priest to assume the specialist's role, for example, by trying to treat the mentally ill.

I would close this section with one warning for young priests. They will meet others, perhaps other priests, who will say that all one needs to be a good confessor is "common sense and experience." Both qualities are helpful; but neither of them will inform one about the requirements of positive law or tell one what are the common opinions of approved authors.

The priest who neglects his studies, with the rationalization about common sense and experience, is quite likely to make the same mistakes year after year and thus do great harm to souls because he guides them according to a code of morality that exists solely in his own mind. The Second Council of Baltimore had some very strong words for the preacher who gives his own views instead of the common teaching of approved authors. The words apply with at least equal force to the confessor.

HIS PRUDENCE

The third quality of the good confessor is *prudence*. A full treatment of this virtue would cover the whole range of confessional practice, for there is nothing that does not come under the rule of prudence. However, I shall limit my present treatment to certain general notions and rules, reserving many specific suggestions for the discussion of particular topics.

The exercise of prudence includes personal reflection, prayer for light, and sometimes consultation. Explaining the function of personal reflection, Tanquerey uses this example: "We may illustrate all that has been said by applying it to a particular virtue, chastity. History will tell us what the saints did in order to remain pure in the midst of the world's dangers; our own experience will recall our past temptations, the means used to resist them and our success or failure. From this we can conclude with a high degree of probability what will be the future result of such or such proceeding, of this or that reading, of such or such association" (*The Spiritual Life,* n. 1021).

This is a good example of how an individual prudently reflects on his own problem. And it is easy to make the transference from this to the manner in which the confessor ought to reflect on his penitent's problem. Before even entering the confessional, the priest is equipped with a general knowledge of human nature and human experience and with general principles built upon this knowledge. During the confession he tries to get a working knowledge of the penitent's character and experience. And from the combination of his general and particular knowledge, he is able to estimate that certain kinds of reading, occupation, or companionship would be harmful to *this* penitent; that certain devotional practices or acts of self-denial are necessary, or would be helpful; and so forth. Acting in this way, he helps the penitent to plan a course of action that is for his spiritual good.

Meaning of Prudence

The prudence practiced by an individual with regard to his own spiritual affairs is a virtue which "helps one in all circumstances to form a right judgment as to what one should seek or avoid for the sake of eternal life." When we apply this notion to a confessor, we are thinking in terms of the direction of others; hence the "eternal life" we have principally in mind is not the good of the confessor himself, but the spiritual good of the penitent. The word "principally" should be carefully noted; for it is wrong to think that the sole object of confessional prudence is the spiritual good of the penitent. An adequate description of the prudent confessor goes beyond that, and it might be stated somewhat as follows: A prudent confessor is one who is able to handle the various situations that arise in his confessional practice in such a way as to conduce to the greater spiritual good of his penitents, without at the same time harming his own soul or defeating a greater good, such as the good of the church. If the full meaning of these words is not immediately obvious, I trust that it will clarify as we proceed.

When I say that prudence covers the whole range of confessional practice, I am not inferring that every confession heard calls for carefully pondered advice. That would be quite unrealistic. There are some confessions, even many of them, in which all that a good confessor needs to do is to give a penance, absolution, and perhaps a very general word of advice or encouragement.

Nevertheless, it is evident that a confessor worthy of his name must often do more than this. He must, as occasions arise, give suggestions concerning the overcoming of bad habits and the practice of virtue, instruct people whose consciences are erroneous, warn of obligations to be fulfilled and perhaps indicate ways of fulfilling them, and so forth. Such cases call for the careful sizing up of a situation and for a clear practical judgment of what to say and what not to say. Before giving any final advice to a penitent with one of these delicate problems, the confessor must first answer clearly in his own mind such questions as these: what does this penitent need? how can I help him? what effect might my advice have on others with whom the penitent is associated?

Erroneous Conscience

For example, there is the case of the penitent with an *erroneous conscience that needlessly multiplies mortal sins*. Instances of this might be found in married people who erroneously think that perfectly legitimate incomplete mutual acts are mortally sinful, and in the unmarried who may think that involuntary thoughts or slight negligences with regard to impure thoughts are mortally sinful. It is certainly for the spiritual good of the penitent to have such a conscience corrected.

Yet, in attempting to give needed help, the confessor should beware lest he increase, rather than remove, the problem. One rule that may help a young confessor to steer a safe course in such matters is this: confine your advice to your penitent's precise problem; do not try to give him the "whole theology" of the subject. By this I mean that, if the penitent's error consists in thinking that involuntary thoughts are sinful, the confessor should confine his advice to that one point; in other words, he should simply impress on the penitent the fact that thoughts cannot be sinful when they are not wilful. Again, should the penitent happen to be a good person who occasionally has impure thoughts that he "tries to get rid of, but doesn't try quite hard enough," and who apparently thinks this conduct is seriously sinful, the confessor ought to handle this one problem directly by showing the penitent that he is negligent and that he ought to try harder, but he is not fully guilty and does not commit a mortal sin on such occasions.

I think this point needs emphasis. A student of theology may finish the treatise on impure thoughts (or any other treatise) and may be able to catalog his knowledge very handily by means of a few rules: such and such things are mortal sins; such and such are venial sins; and such and such are no sins. He rejoices over these wonderfully simple rules, and he wants to give them to his penitents who have problems regarding impure thoughts. After all, he can give the rules in two minutes! That kind of reasoning is fallacious, and the zeal, though laudable in itself, is misapplied. The student forgets that it took him several hours of class, plus many hours of study and discussion, before he formulated and understood these illuminating rules. The penitent can hardly do the same in two minutes! Hence, I would repeat: follow the rule of brevity and give them only what they need and can use. I believe that is sound advice for all young confessors; as they grow in experience they will become better able to judge for themselves just how much more might be given to certain penitents.

What I have just said applies to occasions when the penitent's false conscience concerns one particular point. There are times, of course, when the penitents ask for, or show they need, instruction on a somewhat wider scale. For instance, they may ask how far engaged persons may go in showing their affection, or what is allowed to married people, or when it is permissible to follow the rhythm. I know a very experienced confessor who always advises young priests to have thought out a clear, simple way of imparting such instruction when it is called for. No doubt, this is excellent advice. But I believe I would add that it might often be worth while to suggest to such people that they talk the matter over, outside confession, with some priest whom they know, or read something helpful on the subject. Even though one has the little talk well thought out, he wants to be sure the penitent grasps it; and this would often be more securely accomplished outside the confessional.

Another point. Though we want to remove the harmful false conscience whenever possible, we must realize that in some cases our efforts will be wasted. Some penitents, even after competent instruction, will continue to confess in the same old way, mentioning things as sins which really are not sins. They seem to like it that way. One comes to recognize such penitents after a time; and it seems that, once a reasonable effort has been made to instruct, it is best to let them do it their own way.

It might also be noted briefly that many good people merely *seem* to have a seriously erroneous conscience. For instance, a devout man may miss mass because of illness, and he may confess this in such a way that he seems to think he sinned. It is not unlikely, however, that down in his heart he knows he did not sin, yet he "feels better" when he confesses it. Perhaps some of the penitents mentioned in the previous paragraph belong in this category.

Good Faith

Just as difficult— though hardly as common in confessional practice—is the problem of the opposite kind of erroneous conscience. I refer to the case of the penitent who is doing things that are materially sinful without adverting to their malice. It is possible that a priest might notice this in the course of a confession, and if he does he must answer the question: "Should I instruct, or should I leave the penitent in good faith?" Correctly to answer the question calls for great prudence, for the answer can change with almost every added circumstance.

Let me make the possible shifting circumstances more concrete by means of a few examples. Suppose the confessor should discover that the penitent has a serious obligation to pay a debt but is not conscious of this duty. The ordinary rule is to remind him of this obligation. Yet, before imparting the reminder, the confessor ought to ask himself: "Is it likely that he will refuse to fulfil this duty, and thus his present good faith will be converted into bad faith?" If there is good reason to believe that this latter would be the case, then the ordinary rule would be: say nothing about the obligation. However, before a final decision is made, one more factor must be taken into account: the effect of the penitent's conduct on others.

For instance, suppose the creditor knows that the penitent is allowed to frequent the sacraments, despite his injustice, and suppose that because of this knowledge the creditor is himself being alienated from the church and is indulging in harmful talk. Should the confessor discover points like this, he could hardly refrain from reminding the penitent of his duty to pay the debt. And this would be true even though the penitent might be unwilling to fulfil the obligation; in that event he must at least cease to frequent the sacraments and it would thus become clear the church was not condoning the injustice.

The illustration indicates the general principle to be followed in all such cases of "good faith." The principle, completely stated, is this: *Instruct, unless you judge that greater harm than good will result from the instruction.* It is easy to see that great prudence is required for properly estimating the many factors that must be weighed in determining which course is more harmful, especially in cases that affect others besides the penitent.

That some people are saved by ignorance from the subjective guilt, or at least from the complete guilt, of their objectively sinful actions seems to be unquestionable. Some boys and girls do not realize that masturbation is a serious sin; others think it is serious only when complete; others apparently think that immodest fondling is not a serious sin as long as they abstain from fornication. Some Catholics seem to be quite unconscious of the evil of even grossly unjust or uncharitable conduct towards their neighbor, especially where racial differences are concerned. A wife may unjustly, though in good faith, consistently deny marriage rights to her husband. And it seems that even today, after so much general instruction has been given concerning the sinfulness of contraception, some married people do not realize *they* are doing wrong when they practice contraception.

In all these cases the confessor could rarely, if ever, leave the penitents in ignorance of their real duties. The ignorance of the young people with regard to purity can hardly last long, and the longer one waits to correct the conscience, the more difficult is the uprooting of the habit, and the greater may be the harm done, not only to the penitents, but to others. Hence, the confessor should tell them the truth, even though he judges that the bad habits will not immediately cease and that thus formal sins will be multiplied. As for those who sin against justice, if, after having been warned by the confessor, they refuse to amend their ways, at least they must cease to frequent the sacraments, and those whom they mistreat will see that the church does not excuse their conduct. And the same is to be said of the unjust wife. It is hardly possible that she can consistently refuse marriage rights without being a source of very serious danger to her husband and without causing him to wonder how it is that she can receive absolution. Finally, as regards the practice of contraception "in good faith," it is almost inevitable that husband or wife or both will talk to friends and thus create the impression that it is not so bad after all, or that "some people can get away with it, but others can't," or that some confessors are too hard. Instruction, even though failing to reform the penitent, would at least remove the scandal.

In all honesty, let me say that I think it is rather rare that cases of complete and genuine good faith are noticed in confession. For people usually mention only what they know, or think, or suspect is wrong. Nevertheless, what authors write about these things is by no means mere theory. It can happen that this kind of ignorance is brought to the attention of the confessor. When he notices it he must be prepared to act prudently. And though it is generally true that it is better to say nothing than to convert material sin into formal sin, this is not always the case. The prudent confessor will think not only in terms of the spiritual good of his penitent, but of others, too, and especially of the good of the church.

12. Doctrinal Value and Interpretation of Papal Teaching

John C. Ford and *Gerald Kelly*

This chapter first appeared in John C. Ford and Gerald Kelly *Contemporary Moral Theology,* vol. 1: *Questions in Fundamental Moral Theology* (Westminster, Md.: Newman, 1958).

At the annual meeting of the Catholic Theological Society of America in 1949, a paper read by Eugene M. Burke, C.S.P.,[1] devoted considerable space to the methods of teaching used by the magisterium, especially by the Roman pontiff, and to the doctrinal value of these methods. At the meeting of the same society in 1951, the entire paper read by Edmond D. Benard concerned the doctrinal value of the ordinary teaching of the Holy Father.[2] The discussion evoked by both papers showed that the topics were of speculative interest and practical moment. This response was not surprising. Problems relative to the doctrinal value of ecclesiastical pronouncements have always been of special interest to theologians; and it is safe to say that this interest has never been more intense, nor of more immediate practicality, than during the reign of Pope Pius XII.

MORAL TEACHING OF PIUS XII

An earnest student of papal pronouncements, Vincent A. Yzermans, estimated that during the first fifteen years of his pontificate Pius XII gave almost one thousand public addresses and radio messages.[3] If we add to these the apostolic constitutions, the encyclicals, and so forth, during that same period of fifteen years, and add furthermore all the papal statements during the subsequent years, we have well over a thousand papal documents. It is true, of course, that many of these were not concerned with faith or morals; yet certainly a very large percentage, if not the vast majority, were concerned with either faith or morality. The moralist in particular has only to think of the stream of pronouncements on international peace, on labor relations, on family morality, on medicine and so forth, to realize that his own work is profoundly affected.

Merely from the point of view of volume, therefore, one can readily appreciate that it was not mere facetiousness that led a theologian to remark that, even if the Holy See were now to remain silent for ten years, the theologians would have plenty to do in classifying and evaluating the theological significance of Pius XII's public statements. And it may be added that the theologians' problem is created not merely by the number and variety of the papal statements, but also by the fact that many of them are in modern languages rather than in the traditional Latin, and that they were given in a more or less oratorical setting. We mention these as added problems because, whatever be the disadvantages of Latin, it has the theological advantage of an "established terminology"; and oratory, though perhaps more pleasing than the cut-and-dried theological statement, forces the theologian to dig for the theological core of a statement.

Among these numerous pronouncements of Pope Pius XII, one (*Munificentissimus Deus*[4]) is certainly an ex cathedra definition, and another (*Sacramentum ordinis*[5]) seems to be such. Of these, only the second pertains to moral theology, and that more or less indirectly. In general, the teaching of the Holy Father on moral matters has been given in encyclicals, radio messages, and allocutions – which are normally the media of his authentic, but not infallible, teaching. This is not to say that such media could not contain ex cathedra pronouncements; but usually they do not, and there seems to be no reason for saying that during the reign of Pius XII these media have contained any infallible definitions concerning morality. By this we do not mean, however, that none of the moral teaching of Pus XII could be characterized as infallible. It is hardly conceivable that the papal teaching on such things as divorce, contraception, the direct killing of the innocent, and the possibility of observing continence with the grace of God is anything short of infallible. However, aside from such cases, we may safely assume that the moral teaching of Pius XII need not be characterized as infallible but rather belongs to the authentic, though not infallible, magisterium of the Church. Regarding this noninfallible teaching, questions of special interest concern (1) its doctrinal value, and (2) the function of theologians in their use of such teaching.

DOCTRINAL VALUE

Since the noninfallible moral teaching of Pius XII has been given through the medium of encyclicals, radio messages, and allocutions (as well as through papally approved decrees and instructions of the Roman congregations), something should be said here about the doctrinal value of these various media. Obviously, lest we turn this chapter into a book, we must be carefully selective in this matter. On the basis of such selectivity, the principal place must be given to the pope's own statement in *Humani generis* which is concerned primarily, but not exclusively with encyclicals. After criticizing the exponents of "the new theology" for their lack of appreciation of the ordinary magisterium (perhaps this expression is an understatement), the pope adds the following now celebrated paragraph:

> Nor must it be thought that what is contained in encyclical letters does not of itself demand assent, on the pretext that the popes do not exercise in them the supreme power of their teaching authority. Rather, such teachings belong to the ordinary magisterium of which it is true to say: "He who heareth you, heareth me"; very often, too, what is expounded and inculcated in encyclical letters already appertains to Catholic doctrine for other reasons. But if the supreme pontiffs in their official documents purposely pass judgment on a matter debated until then, it is obvious to all that the matter, according to the mind and will of the same pontiffs, cannot be considered any longer a question open for discussion among theologians.[6]

There have been many excellent commentaries on the *Humani generis* in general and on this paragraph in particular. Typical among these and especially notable, we think, for its simplicity and clarity, is the explanation given by Father Cotter under the heading, "Authentic Teaching of the Magisterium." We quote this in full:

> The Pope has no doubt that those Catholic theologians whom he has in mind throughout the encyclical are willing to abide by the definitive decisions of the magisterium, those handed down, "*solemni iudicio.*" They are neither heretics nor schismatics. But he complains that they ignore papal pronouncements that come to them with less authority, such as encyclicals. If reputable theologians have disagreed in the past, they assume that nothing less than a solemn definition can settle the matter; and as long as none such is forthcoming, everyone is presumed free to construe papal documents according to his own interpretation of Tradition (27).
>
> In reply, the Pope reminds them that encyclicals, besides often containing matters of dogma, may intend to settle points hitherto disputed, and that such decisions demand of themselves a positive assent on the part of the faithful, theologians included. In issuing them the popes exercise what is technically known as the ordinary or authentic magisterium, of which it is true to say: "He who heareth you, heareth me." The reason for all this is that to the living magisterium alone has God entrusted the official interpretation of the deposit of faith (21, 23).
>
> According to theologians, the doctrinal decrees of the Holy Office and the responses of the Biblical Commission belong in the same category because of the close connection of these two Roman congregations with the Pope. Also their decisions demand per se the positive assent of the faithful (Denzinger 2113).
>
> This is technically known as "religious assent." It is a true internal assent, not a mere *silentium obsequiosum* such as the Jansenists were willing to give the papal decrees issued against them. Yet it is not the assent of either divine or ecclesiastical faith; its motive is not the authority of God speaking nor the infallibility of the magisterium, but the

official position of the living magisterium in the Church assigned to it by Christ.

Complaints have been raised against this doctrine as if it were putting shackles on the Catholic theologian (18). Yes and no. First of all, there are any number of problems in Catholic theology on which the magisterium has said nothing so far either definitely or authentically; witness the numerous probable theses or assertions in our manuals and the questions freely disputed in our reviews. Secondly, the authentic decisions of the magisterium, when examined closely, are generally seen to leave the door open for further study of the problem; witness especially the responses of the Biblical Commission. And if a reputable scholar should arrive at a different solution, theologians advise him to communicate his findings to the respective Roman congregation, but not to broadcast them, in defiance, as it were, of the magisterium. Thirdly, even when the decision is definitive, progress is still possible and desirable (21), and that means, partly at least, further research on the same matter by theologians.[7]

As Father Cotter notes, though the papal statement refers primarily to encyclicals, it is not restricted to these. Rather, it covers the whole range of what is called the "ordinary magisterium" of the Holy Father. Everything that has been said, therefore, could apply to the papal radio messages and allocutions; yet, since these have played such a prominent part in the moral teaching of Pope Pius XII, they merit some special attention.

On at least one occasion, the pope himself made it strikingly clear that his discourses, even when given to small groups, can contain authoritative teaching for the whole Church. Thus, in his radio message on the education of the Christian conscience, he said:

> Mindful, however, of the right and duty of the Apostolic See to intervene authoritatively, when need arises, in moral questions, in the address of 29th October last we set out to enlighten men's consciences on the problems of married life. With the self-same authority we declare today to educators

and to young people also that the divine commandment of purity of soul and body still holds without any lesser obligation for the youth of today.[8]

At the conclusion of a commentary on this radio message and the subsequent allocution on the "new morality" (situation ethics),[9] F. X. Hürth, S.J., made a brief analysis of the doctrinal value of such pronouncements.[10] His conclusion was that, in general, they have about the same doctrinal value as encyclicals: they are an integral part of the ordinary teaching of the pope; and as such, though noninfallible, they require both internal and external acceptance. An analysis of their content, said Father Hürth shows that they consist largely of matters of faith or morals or of natural truths in their relation to faith and morals. The audience varies from the whole world (as in some of the radio messages) to a small professional group (as in an allocution to doctors); but even in the latter case the message assumes a universal character when, by command of the supreme pontiff, it is published in the *Acta apostolicae sedis*. As for the *speaker,* though the pope may, if he wishes, speak as a private person, Father Hürth thinks it obvious that such is not his intention when he professedly speaks on matters pertaining to faith and morals in these various public messages.

Joseph Creusen, S.J., who, like Father Hürth, was a consultor of the Holy Office, offers the following observations to help determine when, and to what extent, papal discourses should be considered teaching:

> What is important to us here is the character of the allocution: has the pope the intention of teaching, and in what measure does he invoke his authority? Apart from an express declaration, his intention can be manifested by the quality and number of the persons to whom he speaks, and by the subject-matter of the discourse.
>
> If the Holy Father, in an audience granted to a sports association, praises the physical and moral effects of sport, everyone remains quite at liberty not to share this or that opinion of the Holy Father in the matter. His praise will often be the delicate expression of an invitation to seek in the use of sports, or of any other human activity, progress in moral values, in nobility of soul, in the duties of one's state

well done. But the more the number of members of a congress increases, the greater the importance of their professions, of their responsibilities, and of their influence, the more we see the Holy Father select the subject-matter of his discourse and inculcate the duty of conforming oneself to his teaching and directives.[11]

Furthermore, Father Creusen tells us in another place, it would not make sense to restrict the obligation of assent and obedience merely to those who are present at the papal discourse:

> In our case [the allocution on conjugal morality] there is no doubt that the obligation of internal submission cannot be restricted to those whom the pope addressed. An obligation of this kind cannot be defined by the distance one happens to be from the pope during his discourse. But perhaps someone will say: we are not obliged to read the allocutions of the pope! Certainly, but we are all obliged to know our duties, especially those of our profession.
>
> The "how" is not relevant, whether we come to know them by means of sermons, reading good books, lectures, or conversations with learned and reputable men.[12]

NORMS OF INTERPRETATION

The foregoing seems to be sufficient discussion of our first point: the doctrinal value of the various media of the ordinary teaching of the Holy Father. As for the second point – the function of the theologians in their use of this teaching – we must first observe that the theologians have the same duty as the faithful in general to give the religious assent required by the papal teaching, as stated by Pope Pius XII and explained by Father Cotter.

But the distinctive function of the theologian goes much beyond this acceptance of the papal teaching; as a theologian he must study the papal pronouncements and incorporate them into his teaching and his writing. One writer has deplored the tendency of theologians to "interpret" the papal statements; according to him the theologians' function is to explain the papal teaching, not to interpret it. In practice, this is a distinction without a difference. To fulfill his acknowledged duty of explaining the papal teaching, a theologian must in some measure interpret it; and all that can be reasonably demanded of him is that he follow sound theological norms of interpretation. Unfortunately, we do not have an official set of norms for interpreting pronouncements on the moral law such as we have, for example, regarding canon law; nevertheless, there seem to be at least three basic norms of interpretation that are in conformity with the mind and practice of the Holy See.

One such norm concerns the verbal formulas used in the moral pronouncements. These formulas are very important and should be carefully studied by theologians. Nevertheless, the words themselves are not the ultimate criterion of the true sense of the papal pronouncement; they can be obscure and admit of reformulation. This can be illustrated by the *acta* of both Pius XI and Pius XII relative to punitive sterilization, as well as by the tenor of canon law and by the reactions of eminent theologians to certain aspects of significant moral pronouncements.

In the originally published text of *Casti connubii,* the words of Pius XI at least strongly implied that he was condemning punitive sterilization; but a *notandum* in the next fascicle of the *Acta apostolicae sedis* contained a rewording of the passage which showed that the pope did not intend to commit himself on the controversy among theologians about the licitness of punitive sterilization.[13] Ten years later the Holy Office, with the approval of Pius XII, condemned direct sterilization, without qualification, as being contrary to the natural law.[14] That was in 1940. But in 1951, and again in 1953, Pope Pius XII, when referring to this condemnation, restricted it to the direct sterilization of the innocent.[15] In both these instances, the popes apparently realized that, though perfectly apt for condemning the errors at which they were aimed, the formulas were broader than their own intention.

The very fact that popes themselves have gone out of their way to clarify or restrict their moral pronouncements indicates that a theologian is not necessarily irreverent or disloyal in supposing that other such statements may need clarification or restriction or rephrasing. This is confirmed, it seems to us, by the rules for the interpretation of canon law, as well as by theologians' reactions to some recent and very important papal pronouncements on the social order. In canon law, the Church explicitly admits that the meaning of some laws may be dubious or obscure. The reason for this is surely not that the legislator wanted to be obscure but rather that he failed to make his own intention clear when framing the law. It is true, of course, that this concerns canon law, not pronouncements regarding moral law. But we do not think this affects the point we are stressing: namely, that the words themselves may fail to express the mind of the Holy See. That this has actually been the case concerning some important moral pronouncements seems evident from the controversies among eminent and unquestionably orthodox moralists regarding the meaning of social justice, the title to a family wage and so forth. In these cases, as in the framing of ecclesiastical laws, the popes were certainly not intentionally obscure. They must have had something definite in mind, but this was not expressed with sufficient clarity—otherwise, how explain the controversies among learned commentators?

From the foregoing it follows that the words alone do not always give us the sense, the true meaning, of a papal pronouncement. To get to the true sense, the theologian must study not only the words, but their context and the papal intention in making the pronouncement. By the context we mean not so much the verbal context as the historical setting, because it is there particularly that we are apt to find the true meaning of the statement. For example, if the pope is settling a controversy, his words should be taken in conjunction with the controversy; if he is condemning an error, the words should be interpreted with reference to the error and so forth.[16]

In the *Humani generis,* Pope Pius XII made it clear that even a noninfallible pronouncement can close a controversy among theologians. We feel sure, however, that the pope himself would agree that this decisive character of the pronouncement must be evident. That is in accord with canon 1323, § 3, which states that nothing is to be understood as dogmatically declared or defined unless this is clearly manifested. The canon refers to infallible teachings; yet the same norm seems to apply with at least equal force to the binding character of noninfallible teaching, especially when there is question of pronouncements that would close a controversy.

To summarize briefly the main points of this section: A theologian must study and use and, to some extent, interpret papal pronouncements. In interpreting them, he should have regard not only for verbal formulas but also – and, it seems to us, especially – for the papal intention as manifested in the historical context of the pronouncement. When there is a question of official teaching that would end legitimate controversy, this decisive character should be evident.

Notes

1. Cf. "The Scientific Teaching of Theology in the Seminary," *Proceedings of the Fourth Annual Convention* of The Catholic Theological Society of America, pp. 129–73.

2. "The Doctrinal Value of the Ordinary Teaching of the Holy Father in View of *Humani Generis*," *Proceedings of the Sixth Annual Convention*, CTSA, pp. 78–107. Father Benard (*ibid.*, pp. 84–85) gives the following explanation of the terms *ordinary* and *extraordinary magisterium*.

"(1) *The Pope employs his Extraordinary Magisterium when he speaks* ex cathedra. *This Extraordinary Magisterium is* de se *always, and necessarily infallible.*... (2) The Pope employs his Ordinary Magisterium when he speaks to the faithful, indeed as their supreme Pastor and Teacher, but in order to expound, explain, present Catholic teaching, or to admonish, persuade, enlighten, warn, and encourage the faithful; without calling upon the supreme exercise of his Apostolic Authority, and without, in the strict sense, defining a doctrine. *In this case he does not speak* ex cathedra *and the Ordinary Magisterium is hence not de se infallible.* (3) *However, the Pope may, if he chooses employ a usual organ or vehicle of the Ordinary Magisterium as the medium of an* ex cathedra *pronouncement.* In this case, an Encyclical Letter, for example – certainly a type of document usually associated with the Ordinary Magisterium – may be used as the vehicle of the Extraordinary Magisterium, and hence as the vehicle of an infallible pronouncement...."

3. Cf. *The Catholic Mind*, 53 (1955), 252. Father Yzermans wrote originally in *Columbia* for January, 1955. The complete quotation given in *The Catholic Mind* is interesting:

"Some five years ago I began to dream of an American work that would record all the addresses of His Holiness, Pope Pius XII. So I set to work in search of the sources. Little did I dream I would be so quickly disillusioned! To my utter dismay I discovered that our Holy Father has spoken so often that the mere recording of his words would be a super-human task. It would entail, first of all, the collection of all the addresses from an innumerable variety of sources. During the first fifteen years of his pontificate, from March 2, 1939 to March 2, 1954, the Supreme Pontiff delivered almost 1,000 public addresses, allocutions and radio messages. Over and above the mere recording of these addresses there would be the added task of translating them from the various languages in which they were delivered. Of the total number of addresses only a little more than a third have been translated into English."

A recent advertisement for *The Pope Speaks* carries this information: "In the course of a year, the Holy Father delivers 80 to 100 public messages – encyclicals, allocutions, radio messages, letters, addresses to audiences from all over the world." And the autumn, 1956, number of the same publication, begins with the following paragraph:

"The Holy Father has temporarily overwhelmed our hopes of printing translations of all his important and interesting messages in a given quarter. In the second three months of this year (the period covered in this issue), Pope Pius XII addressed over sixty messages to various groups or to the world at large. And this includes only those which appeared in the *Acta* or *Osservatore Romano*. These messages range in length from the booklet-sized encyclical on devotion to the Sacred Heart (printed in this issue) to several one-page letters (just mentioned in this issue)."

4. Nov. 1, 1950; *AAS,* 42 (1950), 753–71.

5. Nov. 30, 1947; *AAS,* 40 (1948), 5–7.

6. *AAS,* 42 (1950), 568; for translation, cf. Cotter, *op. cit.,* pp. 21–23.

7. *Ibid.,* pp. 75–77. The numbers Father Cotter has in parenthesis refer to the paragraph numbers of the encyclical as given in his book. The question of the "assensus religiosus" that must be given to noninfallible teaching is an intriguing one. Closely connected with this, of course, is the problem of divine assistance for the magisterium in this kind of teaching. Dogmatic theologians give different explanations. For more about this, see the paper given by Father Benard (*supra,* footnote 2); also Charles Journet, *The Church of the Word Incarnate: I. The Apostolic Hierarchy* (New York: Sheed and Ward, 1955), esp. pp. 351–53; and Wernz-Vidal, as cited *infra,* chapter 3, footnote 6. And for the replies of the Biblical Commission in particular, see the remarks of E. A. Sutcliffe, S.J., in *A Catholic Commentary on Holy Scripture* (New York: Thomas Nelson and Sons, 1953), pp. 67–68. Father Sutcliffe's explanation is very complete and it shows that in some questions the submission required of the Catholic exegete may consist only "in not opposing by word or writing the decisions of the Biblical Commission."

8. *AAS,* 44 (1952), 275; English translation based on *Catholic Documents,* 8 (July, 1952), 5. The address of October 29, 1951, to which the pope refers in this quotation, was given to the Italian Society of Obstetrical Nurses, and it was certainly one of the most important moral pronouncements of his reign. Cf. *AAS,* 43 (1951), 835–54. It is often referred to as the allocution to

the "midwives"; but it seems that the Italian is better translated by "obstetrical nurses," or perhaps "obstetrical social workers."

9. For a more detailed consideration of these papal statements, as well as the subsequent instruction of the Holy Office on situation ethics, cf. chapters 7 and 8.

10. Cf. *Periodica,* 41 (1952), 245–49. See also Father Hürth's brief remarks about the doctrinal value of decrees of the Holy Office, *ibid.,* 45 (1956), 141; cf. *supra,* footnote 7.

11. *Bulletin social des industriels,* 24 (1952), 153. P. DeLetter, S.J., summarizes the teaching of Father Creusen and Father Hürth, in *Clergy Monthly,* 17 (1953), 181–83.

12. Cf. *Problemi di vita coniugale* (Rome: S.A.L.E.S., 1955), p. 31. It should be noted that Father Creusen is referring to the duties discussed in the allocutions on conjugal morality. These duties are obviously of universal application. But in some cases the practical applications of papal directives are not universal. Thus, Father Creusen himself later notes that such applications "can be obligatory in one country and not in another; they are also subject to change in accordance with changing circumstances" *(ibid.,* p. 32).

13. Cf. *AAS,* 22 (1930), 565, 604.

14. Ibid., 32 (1940), 73.

15. Cf. Ibid., 43 (1951), 844; 45 (1953), 606.

16. What is said in this paragraph seems to be in keeping with the spirit of the Church as manifested in canon 18, which prescribes that words are to be taken according to their proper meaning as indicated by text and context, and that in case of doubt one should consider the purpose and circumstances of a law and the mind of the legislator. As for verbal formulas alone, one might note the following quotation from the *Quamquam pluries* of Leo XIII: "*Certe matris Dei tam in excelso dignitas est, ut nihil fieri maius queat.* Sed tamen quia intercessit Josepho cum Virgine beatissima maritale vinculum, ad illam praestantissimam dignitatem, qua *naturis creatis omnibus* longissime Deipara antecellit, non est dubium quin accesserit ipse, ut nemo magis." Cf. *ASS,* 22 (1889–90), 66. The pope's meaning is obvious; yet a stickler for the primacy of verbal formulas would have no little difficulty with the expressions we have italicized.

Part Three

POST-VATICAN II

13. Proportionalism: Clarification Through Dialogue

Richard A. McCormick

This chapter first appeared in *Theological Studies* 43 (1982) and 44 (1983).

John Connery, S.J., has recently addressed these problems at length.[1] A brief recall must suffice here.

He first compares "proportionalism" with the traditional understanding of moral norms. In traditional terms, if the object, end, and circumstances were in accord with right reason, the act was morally right. "Proportionalists," by contrast, he says, "weigh all the good in the act against all the evil."

Next, against Knauer and Janssens, Connery denies that such a comparison (*ratio proportionata*) is necessary according to Thomas. All that is required is that damage associated with our actions (e.g., self-defense) be *praeter intentionem*. Third, Connery argues that the change to a proportionalist understanding of norms would mean that "such things as adultery, stealing, killing an innocent person are in themselves only ontic evil." Hence we would have to add a condition to every concrete rule ("unless there is a proportionate reason").

Finally, the article concludes with several critiques. For instance, for a proportionalist "a means has no independent morality of its own." Furthermore, this is a process of "demoralization" of all the good and evil in our actions. We can no longer say that "adultery, killing an innocent person, stealing" are morally wrong in themselves. Or again, the weighing of all the goods and evils (probable, possible, remote, etc.) is just too much to ask, whereas for the traditionalist "the main concern...is that the evil in the act be *praeter intentionem*." Connery concludes that shifting to a comparative standard "makes moral decision-making more difficult than is healthy for moral life."

I cannot possibly comment here on all the points raised in Connery's article. But I do want to respond extensively to several of them in the interests of clarifying the state of the question, a thing I do not believe Connery's study satisfactorily achieves.

1) *The notion of proportionate reason.* Connery conceives the term "proportionate reason" as synonymous with end or motive in the traditional sense. Thus he writes: an act "can be morally wrong by reason of its object and apart from an ultimate good intention." Or again: "an act can be bad apart from a good intention, i.e., a proportionate reason." Thus he interprets so-called "proportionalists" as saying that proportionate reason is something *in addition* to a clearly definable action. For this reason he can give as his example Thomas' example of the person who steals to commit adultery. The "to commit adultery" is seen as the end or motive and is identified by Connery as the proportionate reason. This is not, in my judgment, what this literature is saying. The proportionate reason is not in addition to an act already defined; it constitutes its very object, but in the full sense of that term. Take amputation of a cancerous limb to save a patient's life as an example. Connery should see amputation as the object and "to save a patient's life" as a motive. But the literature he is critiquing sees "to save a patient's life" (the proportionate reason) as the object in the full sense of that term. In other words, proportionate reason enters into the very definition of what one is doing. If one conceives proportionate reason as *in addition to an act already definable by its object*, then one does indeed get into some mischievous results. For instance, it makes it possible for Connery to attribute to proportionalists the notion that a *ratio proportionata* can justify a *morally wrong* act.

Or again, what is the proportionate reason for forcefully resisting an attacker? It is clearly saving one's life. But that is what the action is, self-defense. It is not a motive superadded to an act with its own definition. By identifying proportionate reason with motive (in the traditional sense), Connery has inaccurately presented the literature and created a vulnerability that is not there.

2) *Value terms and descriptive terms.* Very close to the first point is the failure to distinguish these two. Connery repeatedly uses "adultery, killing an innocent person, stealing, etc." as examples of actions

the tradition would judge "morally evil in themselves" but which "proportionalists might occasionally permit." Furthermore, he says that rules covering these actions "deal with moral evil." So they do – certainly, at least stealing and adultery. But these are compound value terms. They contain their own negative moral value judgment. For instance, tradition defines stealing as "taking another's property *against his/her reasonable will.*" That is always wrong and so-called "proportionalists" always would and do condemn it. But it is not the issue.

The issue is: What *materia circa quam* (object in a very restricted sense) should count as stealing or murder or lying? This is the issue as I read it in the works of Schüller, Fuchs, Janssens, J.-M. Aubert, W. Molinski, Chirico, John Dedek, F. Böckle, Charles Curran, Pater Knauer, Scholz, Helmut Weber, K. Demmer, F. Furger, Dietmar Mieth, Daniel Maguire, Henrico Chiavacci, Marciano Vidal, Walter Kerber, Timothy O'Connell, and many others. While these theologians differ in significant ways, they do share a certain bottom line, so to speak: individual actions independent of their morally significant circumstances (e.g., killing, contraception, speaking falsehood, sterilization, masturbation) cannot be said to be intrinsically morally evil as this term is used by tradition and the recent magisterium. Why? Because such concepts describe an action too narrowly in terms of its *materia circa quam* without morally relevant circumstances. This issue is confused by using value terms to describe the actions and then attributing this to "proportionalists" as if they are trying to justify adultery, stealing, lying etc.

3) *The morality of means.* Connery asserts that "to the proportionalist a means has no independent morality of its own. Its morality comes from its relation to the end of the act." As just noted, that depends on how the means is described. If it is described as "murder," "stealing," "lying," it is already morally wrong by its very description. But if a means is described without all of its morally relevant circumstances, then clearly it has no morality of its own.

Connery admits that "there are means which receive their morality from the end of the act, e.g., violence, mutilations etc." But, he says, this is not true of all means. As suggested above, most authors of my acquaintance would not conceive mutilation as a means to the end (motive) of saving a life. They would say that the very meaning (object in the full sense) of the action includes the notion of "saving the patient's life." Furthermore, it is to be noted that Connery describes what is going on (violence, mutilation) merely in terms of its *materia circa quam*. Of course that yields no moral rightness or wrongness. But why is that not true of terms like "masturbation," "sterilization"? This matter was treated extensively in these "Notes" earlier.[2] At that time I noted of Joseph Fuchs: "He has tightened the relationship between the traditional object-end-circumstances and argued that it is only the combination of the three that yields the total object of choice. The good intended in one's choice specifies the object without smothering it out of existence, and thus, in a sense, becomes an integral part of the total object."

We are at the heart of the problem here. We can analyze it as follows. Connery's major objection is that certain actions are (and have been taught by the magisterium to be) morally evil *ex objecto*. But, he argues, the proportionalist does not and cannot say this. From this objection nearly everything else that he says follows.

What is to be said of this objection? I think it misses the point of what so-called "proportionalists" are saying. When contemporary theologians say that certain disvalues in our actions can be justified by a proportionate reason, they are not saying that *morally wrong* actions (*ex objecto*) can be justified by the end. They are saying that an action cannot be qualified morally simply by looking at its *materia circa quam*, or at its object in a very narrow and restricted sense. This is precisely what tradition has done in the categories exempted from teleological assessment (e.g, contraception, sterilization). It does this in no other area.

If we want to put this in traditional categories (object, end, circumstances), we can say that the tradition has defined certain actions as morally wrong *ex objecto* because it has included in the object not simply the *materia circa quam* (object in a very narrow sense) but also elements beyond it which clearly exclude any possible justification. Thus, a theft is not simply "taking another's property," but doing so "against the reasonable will of the owner." This latter addition has two characteristics in the tradition. (1) It is considered as essential to the object. (2) It excludes any possible exceptions. Fair enough. Yet, when the same tradition deals with, e.g., masturbation or sterilization, it adds little or nothing to the *materia circa quam* and regards such *materia* alone as constituting the object. If it were consistent, it would describe the object as "sterilization *against the good of marriage*" as the object. This all could accept.

This consideration leads to a much broader one. It concerns the very usefulness of the traditional object-end-circumstances terminology. The major confusing element is the usage of "object." What is to be included in this notion? Sometimes traditional usage has included what really are morally relevant circumstances. Sometimes it has not and it has defined the object in terms of the *materia circa quam* (object in a very narrow sense). If this is unavoidable, then the terminology were better abandoned. I would think it better to speak of two characteristics of actions: (1) *materia circa quam* and (2) all morally relevant circumstances. These would include side effects, possible consequences, intentions, etc.

4) *Demoralization of good and evil in human acts.* Connery sees as a very "basic objection to proportionalism" the fact that it "demoralizes" the goods and evils in our actions. They are "only ontic or premoral." "It is not enough," he notes, "to judge that what one does goes against right reason to conclude that it is immoral." One must go a step further and balance the goods and evils in the action. This objection is virtually the same as that noted in no. 3 above, but in different language. Hence it deserves the same response. Take Connery's phrase "what one does." Suppose we describe this "what" as "mutilation." What is its morality? Clearly, we do not know, because no adequate human action has been described, only its *materia circa quam.* An action so described is neither in accordance with nor contrary to right reason.

Of course we must look to the goods and evils in the action, but we do that to find out "what one does." Only then can we determine whether it is against right reason or not. So, far from "demoralizing" the good and evil in our actions, contemporary authors are insisting that one cannot adequately describe a human action simply by presenting the *materia circa quam.* If the action is described as "adultery, stealing" – as Connery repeatedly does – this point is missed. No one to my knowledge is trying to discover whether such acts (adultery, stealing) "would produce more evil than good." Contemporary writers are trying to discover what should count as adultery. For instance, is every couple in an irregular second marriage living in adultery? We cannot know whether something is contrary to reason unless we know what it is. To miss the point is, in my judgment, a fundamental misunderstanding of the literature.

5) *"Praeter intentionem" and the tradition.* Connery states that the "main concern of the traditionalist is that the evil in the act be

praeter intentionem." No weighing or calculus of good and evil is required. He attributes this position to St. Thomas. I shall leave it to Knauer and Janssens to deal with Connery's understanding of Thomas. One can get almost anything from Thomas if enough texts are adduced. Still, several brief remarks are called for. First, while Thomas may not speak of a calculus of values and disvalues, I would further contend that he does not provide a true justification for violent self-defense. As Connery notes, "Thomas is satisfied with the simple explanation that it is natural for a person to defend himself." I think Connery is correct here. But to say that something is natural is hardly an adequate defense. Or if it is, it is arguably unchristian.

Second, if the main concern of the traditionalist is that the evil be *praeter intentionem*, and if "the requirement that the good effect be proportionate to the evil effect is meant to guarantee the proper direction of the intention" only, as Connery argues, then this reveals an unconcern with the evil effect. It looks very much like a "keep-the-hands-clean" morality, as Daniel Callahan has repeatedly noted. Franz Scholz has pointed out that looking evil in the eye avoids an "exoneration mentality" so easily associated with phrases such as "merely permitted, only indirectly willed."[3] In his lectures Joseph Fuchs constantly refers to *praeter intentionem* as a "psychological drug."

Finally, if one "does not have to weigh it [evil] against the good to be achieved to make a moral judgment about the legitimacy of self-defense," then any defensive reason could justify killing. I could kill my neighbor who is spanking my child. This reveals the inadequacy of a notion of agency centered solely on *praeter intentionem*.

6) *The novelty of proportionalism.* Connery notes that there is a history of exception-making in the church. "One did not have to wait for proportionalism to provide for exceptions." Connery's presentation—as well as that of other discussants—makes it look as if we are talking about an entirely new system or method. Actually that is not the case. In nearly all areas of moral concern, whether prescriptions or prohibitions, whether of natural law or positive law, it was the notion of *ratio proportionata* that qualified the norm and established the possibility of exceptions.[4] One can see this at work in the restrictive interpretation of the prohibition against killing, in the exceptions established in the areas of taking another's property, in the area of deceitful speech, of promise- and secret-keeping, of the Sunday obligation, of the duty of integral

confession, of the obligation of the divine office, of the duty of fraternal correction, of the duty to procreate, and on and on. Of course, we did not have "to wait for proportionalism to provide for exceptions," because we always had it. That is why Schüller and Gustafson have noted that traditional Catholic moral theology in its understanding of norms is profoundly teleological.[5] As Schüller earlier put it, "The point of the above hypothesis...is that an ethical principle which in its more particular form has long been recognized and acknowledged is being widened out to include all the actions of persons except those that have as their immediate object the absolute value of salvation and the moral goodness of the neighbor."[6]

For instance, with regard to the duty to procreate, Pius XII referred to "serious reasons" (medical, eugenic, economic, social) that could exempt a married couple from this affirmative duty. Of these "serious reasons" Ford and Kelly write: "We believe that a careful analysis of all these phrases in the context would justify the interpretation that they are the equivalent of 'proportionate reasons.'"[7] Does this make Ford and Kelly purveyors of a new system called "proportionalism"? Hardly.

Indeed, even those norms which were regarded as exceptionless were analyzed within such a framework. Take the confessional secret as an example. Lugo defends the absoluteness of this obligation as follows:

> If it [revelation of sins] were allowed in some circumstances because of some extremely important need, this alone would be sufficient to make sacramental confession always difficult. Penitents would always fear that the confessor would reveal their sins because he would think this is an example of the exceptional instance. To avoid this evil, it was necessary to exclude any exception. That rare evil which would be obviated by revelation of sins is *in no proportionate relationship to the perpetual evil and continuing harm* which would be associated with the difficulty of confession if an exception were allowed.[8]

Similarly, Lucius Rodrigo, S.J., in his massive *Theoria de conscientia morali reflexa,* argues that where doubts occur, probabilism must be excluded in dealing with the confessional secret. He argues as follows:

> This *certain* obligation exists or continues as long as the basis of the prohibition against using confessional information continues—that is, the probable common repugnance toward the sacrament traceable to the use of information that is certainly or probably sacramental in character, with the danger of the aforementioned annoyance [of the faithful]. For this repugnance is rightly judged to be such a huge common harm that even the danger of it is to be excluded *regardless of the inconvenience, because such inconvenience is rightly judged as the lesser inconvenience.*[9]

Rodrigo is arguing, just as Lugo had, that there is no *ratio* truly *proportionata* to the harm that would ensue if exceptions were allowed.

Considerations like these make it clear that we are not dealing with some new system of establishing exceptions, as Connery implies, when we use the notion *ratio proportionata*. The notion is utterly traditional. The only question, in my judgment, is: Why, if we are to be consistent, does not such utterly traditional moral reasoning apply to all areas where moral norms attempt to state the rightness and wrongness of human action? Specifically, there are two areas where this *Denkform* has been excluded. They are: (1) actions considered wrong because *contra naturam* (e.g., contraception, masturbation); (2) actions considered wrong *ex defectu juris* (e.g., direct killing of an innocent person). These actions were said to be intrinsically evil in the manualist tradition. Applying a new *Denkform* to these excluded categories does not necessarily change the conclusions, as Benedict Ashley, O.P., has noted,[10] and as Connery concedes—though I think it does in some cases. In fact, it might open us to a much richer analysis of the actions in question, and to a sharper insight into the church's substantial concerns in these areas.

To call this fairly modest attempt "proportionalism" leaves the impression that one is abandoning a long tradition and introducing something entirely novel. That has apologetic advantages, for people are wary about "a whole new system." But it is historically inaccurate, as anyone familiar with Catholic moral tradition will realize.

7) *Proportionalism as dangerous.* Connery's final problem is that so-called "proportionalism" is dangerous. It calls for a continuous "calculus" and he sees this as unhealthy for the moral life "particularly in the area of sexuality."[11]

I disagree with that judgment and for several reasons. First, it supposes a notion of the moral-spiritual life as a succession of decisions about conforming (or not) to rules. Donald Evans rightly refers to the "sheer irrelevance of a formulated-rule morality in much of our moral life."[12] There just is not that much of it. We do not live amidst crises as a regular way of life. The shape of most of our days is determined by vocation, employment, habit, family, etc.

Second, even when we get embroiled in conflict situations, there is often no calculus to be made for the simple reason that it has often already been made by the community. Being a Christian means being a member of a body, a *communio,* a people with experience, reflection, and memory. Just as our knowledge of the *magnalia Dei* is shared knowledge, so is our grasp of its implications for behavior. In other words, we form our consciences in a community. And not infrequently this community has made over its history certain value judgments that ought to instruct the individual, even though they are capable of being nuanced or even changed. For instance, Stanley Hauerwas has noted of abortion that it is meaningful to say that "Christians just...do not do that kind of thing."[13] I think something similar can be said about other conduct (e.g., premarital intercourse). In a sense, the very values one desires to achieve in such conduct have been judged disproportionate by the community to the disvalues inhering in it. One need not struggle through this calculus on every date. Therefore the danger Connery sees in this *Denkform* can reflect a lurking individualism of outlook.

Third, it can easily reinforce a kind of brinkmanship in attitude that is rather immature. One who is constantly concerned with rules, who needs rules to control life (especially absolute rules), was recognized by St. Paul as spiritually immature.[14] The mature do the just, fair, chaste thing by a kind of enthusiastic connaturality, without the coercive force of the law. That is what we should be aiming at in moral education.

Fourth, to regard personal conscience judgment (here the judgment of proportion) as dangerous is to perpetuate a kind of paternalism (let someone else make the judgment) in the moral life, the dependency syndrome. If anything is unhealthy and dangerous in the long run, it is that.

Finally, the objection seems to imply that conduct will be more chaste and consistent if rules are stated as unquestionable absolutes. And conversely, that suggests that cultural permissiveness is due to the theoretical rethinking of the meaning of norms in certain areas. There is no evidence that the rethinking of norms that Connery calls "proportionalism" has led to the permissiveness of our time. Such permissiveness is due to a whole host of cultural factors and would have occurred had all Catholic moral theologians been on vacation throughout.

I have devoted this large space to Connery's article for several reasons. First, he is thoughtful and careful. Furthermore, it is necessary to unpackage the jargon that all too often infects this discussion ("consequentialism," "proportionalism"). But another very important reason is that phrases in his essay such as "Church moral teaching," "Church rules," etc. can leave the impression that the teleological tendencies of many contemporary moralists involve "going against the Church's teaching." Paul McKeever is correct, I believe, when he notes that "defending proportionalism is not directly contrary to the explicit teaching of the church. There is no such explicit teaching."[15] Indeed, there is the contrary practice, if not the full-blown theory. So, rather than "going against the tradition," recent efforts are much more a dialogue with certain aspects of that tradition by adherents of the tradition....

In a previous edition of these "Notes" I had dialogued with my friend and colleague John R. Connery, S.J., and made some criticism of his critiques of so-called "proportionalism."[16] One of his major criticisms was that Catholic tradition has taught that certain actions are morally evil *ex objecto*. He further contended that "proportionalists" cannot say this. I responded by saying that this misses the point of what this school of thought is saying. "When contemporary theologians say that certain disvalues in our actions can be justified by a proportionate reason, they are not saying that *morally wrong* actions (*ex objecto*) can be justified by the end. They are saying that an action cannot be qualified morally simply by looking at its *materia circa quam*, or at its object in a very narrow and restricted sense. This is precisely what tradition has done in the categories exempted from teleological assessment (e.g., contraception, sterilization). It does this in no other area.[17] I further argued that the term "object" was so inconsistently used (sometimes including circumstances, sometimes not) that it might be better to abandon the object-end-circumstances in favor of *materia circu quam* plus morally relevant circumstances.

Connery has graciously replied to these suggestions and made several points[18] Since his rejoinder appeared in this journal, I will synthesize the points quite briefly, but I hope his major concerns will be clear. He does not believe that this new terminology clarifies anything. Indeed, he argues that "proportionalists" collapse into *materia circa quam* whatever they do not wish to consider a value term ("e.g., masturbation, contraception, contraceptive sterilization, killing an innocent person, and even adultery"). Rather, some of these are morally definable "merely by consideration of the object of the act, e.g., in solitary sexual acts." Or again, "one can make a moral judgment of sterilization when one knows that it is contraceptive," and therefore "apart from the kind of calculus the proportionalists would demand." He further argues that the chief reason for the vulnerability of "proportionalism" is "the reduction to *materia circa quam* or premoral evil of acts that had previously been considered immoral." Connery believes that one must not "weigh all the good and evil in the act, including all the consequences," for that would make our decisions "more difficult." Moreover, tradition used *ratio proportionata* only for affirmative obligations and positive legislation, not for negative obligations, "e.g., killing an innocent person."

I cannot respond in detail to many of the peripheral statements in Connery's article. For instance, whether "proportionalists" consider adultery or killing an innocent person value terms (actually I do so consider them) is of secondary importance. What is of greater importance is that those who oppose this *Denkform* do consider such terms value terms and then go about saying that "proportionalists" justify what has already been defined to be morally wrong. No "proportionalist" does that.

Again, Connery argues that *ratio proportionata* traditionally did not apply to negative obligations such as direct killing of the innocent. What he fails to observe is that this restrictive interpretation ("direct," "innocent") of killing could only have been made by a teleological procedure. In other words, we gradually arrived at a *moral* definition of certain actions ("*direct* killing of the *innocent*") by weighing all the good and evil in certain actions and then concluding that, all things, considered, they could never be morally acceptable. Whenever a moral norm is inadequately formulated, this process of restrictive interpretation must occur. But that is not to make exceptions to accepted moral formulations. It is to critique the adequacy of the formulations themselves. If we get to a *moral* definition of an act (as morally wrong) by a teleological procedure, then clearly the act so defined is subject to teleological inspection if we are to be consistent.[19]

But there are several points in Connery's response that I want to lift out for further dialogue.

1) The term "*materia circa quam.*" I am surprised that Connery sees my usage as "new." It is adapted from St. Thomas, and indeed in this very area. For instance, Thomas writes: "The objects as related to the exterior act are the *materia circa quam,* but as related to the interior act of the will they are ends, and it is from their being ends that they give species to the action, but as *materia circa quam* of the exterior action they are also termini by which the movements are specified.[20] I had suggested some such usage because the term "object" is used so inconsistently. Sometimes it includes morally relevant circumstances (theft = "taking another's property against his reasonable will"), sometimes it does not (masturbation). For this reason the term "ex objecto" becomes ambiguous, and not terribly useful, because it is not clear whether the moral wrongness roots in the object or the circumstances, as Karl Hörmann has recently noted.[21]

There are two ways to avoid this problem. The first is to cease speaking of the object and speak of the *materia circa quam* with all morally relevant circumstances. The second is to continue to use the term "object" but to include in it all morally relevant circumstances, as Thomas did.[22] For all practical purposes the two are the same.

2) *The proportionalist calculus.* Closely connected with the above point is Connery's insistence that there are actions that are morally definable "apart from the kind of calculus the proportionalist would demand." I am not sure what that means. It looks very much like a misconception. It makes me wonder what Connery is thinking of when he says "proportionalists" would demand a calculus beyond an already morally defined act. If an act is *morally* defined, obviously no further calculus is needed. And every "proportionalist" would say that. But a calculus is often called for before the act can be so defined.

At several points Connery refers to and rejects "weighing all the good and evil in the act, including the consequences." Perhaps this is the "calculus" to which he refers. He says that this is unnecessary and only complicating because certain actions are morally definable without it. I would turn that around and say that certain actions are *morally* definable precisely because and only insofar as "all the morally relevant good and evil in the act" has been weighed. Sometimes that is very easy, as when Thomas says that *occisio innocentis* is always wrong. Sometimes it is not. But it can never be bypassed; otherwise we have given the act its moral character independently of morally relevant circumstances.[23]

That is exactly what tradition has done in some instances. Take Connery's example of the "solitary sex act." He says that a moral judgment can be made "merely by a consideration of the object of the act." That is, it is always wrong regardless of the circumstances. This is precisely the type of physicalism many theologians reject (I say "physicalism" because the entire moral meaning of the act is gathered in precision from morally relevant circumstances and based on its physical structure). Thus we find theologians like L. Janssens, M. Vidal, F. Scholz, B. Häring, E. Chiavacci, L. Rossi, A. Valsecchi, and many others rejecting such an analysis and approving masturbation in the procreative circumstances of artificial insemination by husband. They distinguish "moral" from "biological" masturbation, or masturbation from "ipsation." The terminology is irrelevant. Connery is defending a tradition many, perhaps even most, theologians reject. If one sticks with that tradition, then one must buy its methodological implications, which many theologians think indefensible.

At this point it would be helpful to introduce some remarks of Louis Janssens. In a recent study[24] he notes that Thomas gave four classifications for the objects of external action as they relate to reason. (1) External actions whose object is indifferent, e.g., to pick up a blade of straw from the soil. Such actions get their morality from the end. (2) Actions which because of their object are good *secundum se,* e.g., to give an alms. These can become evil by reason of an evil end. (3) Exterior actions that by reason of their object "involve an inseparable moral evil," e.g., adultery, fornication, perjury, killing of the innocent. Of these we may say *mox nominati sunt mali;* or, in Janssens' words, "Certain words are used to name an action not merely under its material aspect, *but precisely insofar as it is a morally evil act.*" Such actions are given value descriptions, and insofar as they are, no further calculus is needed to pronounce them immoral, even though some calculus may be needed to decide what should count as fitting those categories. (4) Actions which, when abstractly considered, contain some important deformity or disorder but are made morally right by circumstances, e.g., in Thomas' words, "The killing and beating of a man involve some deformity in their object. But if it is added to this that an evildoer is killed for the sake of justice or that a delinquent is beaten for punishment, then the action is not a sin; rather it is virtuous."[25]

At this point Janssens makes several important points. First, the deformity or disorder Thomas refers to in category 4 is not *moral* deformity. "Were he speaking of moral disorder or deformity, then it could never be counterbalanced." In other words, no calculus need be made if the action is already given moral definition. Therefore the deformity is ontic or premoral.[26] Second, while we have the duty to prevent such deformities to the best of our abilities, still, "as the examples given by Thomas show, there are situations in which ontic evil may be caused– killing or beating a man–and is made morally good by outweighing circumstances."[27] The service of justice and the reasonableness of punishment "can be proportionate reasons to justify the causation of ontic evil." That is utterly clear in Thomas' example, an example that shows how traditional is the notion of "proportionalism."

Reflection on these last two classes of objects leads to the conclusion that a balancing or calculus is called for in the analytic process only when elements of an action are considered abstractly, before giving them a moral definition. For example, if no calculus were required, every killing would be a murder. None would ever be justified. Or, as Janssens notes, "To understand the meaning of the term 'murder,' we have to know the proportionate reasons why some killing is not murder."[28] We have to know what Janssens calls the "outweighing circumstances." And this is precisely what official and traditional teaching has not done in certain cases (contraception, sterilization, masturbation). As Thomas noted, some circumstances become "the principal condition of the object."[29] Now if this is true of an abstractly considered act of killing, why is it not true of an abstractly considered act like masturbation? The only reason I can think of is that the biological reality has been allowed to exhaust the notion of the *objectum actus*, as it does for Connery.

So it is not morally defined acts that are susceptible of a weighing and balancing–as Connery and others often asset or imply–but the goods and evils in the single action prior to giving a moral description. To say anything else is to exclude morally relevant circumstances from the assessment of the act. That would be very untraditional.

3) *Permissiveness and proportionalism.* Connery continues to assert that "proportionalism" is vulnerable to abuse and "must bear part of the blame" for the permissiveness experienced in recent years. Furthermore, he claims that there is evidence that this *Denkform* "has given rise to relaxation in attitudes toward moral norms." So many documented factors have been noted for this cultural phenomenon that to attribute it in any significant way to an academic discussion in moral theology is unreal.

But the occasion of Connery's remarks stimulates me to two glosses on this matter. First, if—*dato non concesso* —the discussion of "proportionalism" has indeed influenced an abusive laxness in conduct, then one might more accurately place the blame at the desks of those who misrepresent what many contemporary theologians are saying. I have read repeatedly over the past ten years assertions that many theologians are proposing that a good end justifies a morally evil means. That is, of course, totally false.[30] I have read repeatedly other misrepresentations.[31] When priests hear such misrepresentations associated with the names of our outstanding theolgians (Häring, Fuchs, Böckle, Schüller, Auer, Janssens, Vidal, Furger, Scholz, Weber, Curran, and a host of others), perhaps it is understandable that they are bewildered. But it must be remembered that we are dealing with a misrepresentation. Let blame fall where it is due, on the misrepresentation.

Second and more importantly, there is solidly based evidence that Catholics have adopted certain permissive attitudes because (among many other cultural factors) of the Church's apparent intransigence and unwillingness to dialogue in any meaningful way on sexual matters. The *Humanae vitae* phenomenon revealed this. The phenomenon was repeated in *Persona humana,* as the literature reported in these "Notes" testifies.[32] Many people with whom I have spoken over the years are convinced that Roman theology, and to that extent the official Church, is incapable of dealing with sexuality honestly and openly. *For this reason* people begin to develop their own approach to things. This is also documentable.[33] But once again, let blame fall where it is due.

Notes

1. John R. Connery, S.J., "Catholic Ethics: Has the Norm for Rule-Making Changed?" *TS* 42 (1981) 232–50.

2. *TS* 36 (1975) 86–89.

3. Franz Scholz, "Objekt und Umstände, Wesenswirkungen und Nebeneffekte," in *Christlich glauben und handeln,* ed. Klaus Demmer and Bruno Schüller (Düsseldorf: Patmos, 1977) 243–60.

4. As Daniel Maguire notes, "In a sense it [the principle of proportionality by which 'we face the delicate challenge of balancing goods and bads'] may be said to be the master principle of ethics" (*The Moral Choice* [Garden City: Doubleday, 1978] 164).

5. James Gustafson, *Protestant and Roman Catholic Ethics* (Chicago: University of Chicago, 1978) 49.

6. Bruno Schüller, S.J., "Zur Problematik allgemein verbindlicher ethischer Grundsätze." *Theologie und Philosophie* 45 (1970) 1–23, at 7.

7. John C. Ford, S.J., and Gerald Kelly, S.J., *Contemporary Moral Theology 2: Marriage Questions* (Westminster, Md.: Newman, 1963) 425.

8. *Tractatus de fide,* disp. 4, sect. 4, n. 57.

9. Lucius Rodrigo, S.J., *Praelectiones theologico-morales Comillenses* 4/2: *Theoria de conscientia morali reflexa* (Santander: "Sal Terrae," 1956) 635–36, n. 1760.

10. Benedict M. Ashley, O.P., "The Use of Moral Theory by the Church," in *Human Sexuality and Personhood* (St. Louis: Pope John XXIII Medico-Moral Education and Research Center, 1981), 223–42, at 237.

11. Cf. *TS* 42 (1981) 501.

12. Donald Evans, "Paul Ramsey on Exceptionless Moral Rules," *American Journal of Jurisprudence* 16 (1971) 184–214, at 188.

13. Stanley Hauerwas, "Abortion: Why the Arguments Fail," *Hospital Progress* 61, no. 1 (1980) 38–49, at 42. To say that such a statement is meaningful is not to say that it is a moral argument. It is rather the announcement of a finished moral argument, one that has grappled with the conflicting values.

14. 1 Tim 1:9.

15. Paul McKeever, "Proportionalism as a Methodology in Catholic Moral Teaching," in *Human Sexuality and Personhood* (n. 10 above) 211–22.

16. For discussions of this matter in some recent books, cf. David Hollenbach, S.J., *Nuclear Ethics* (Ramsey: Paulist, 1983); Neil Brown, *The Worth of Persons* (Sydney: Catholic Institute of Sydney, 1983). Cf. also Felix Podimattam, "Conflict Morality: An Interpretation," *Jeevadhara* 12 (1982) 409–54; George Lobo, "Moral Absolutes: Toward a Solution," ibid. 455–69.

These latter two articles are in substantial agreement with the perspectives adopted in these "Notes" over the years.

17. *TS* 43 (1982) 85.

18. John R. Connery, S.J., "The Teleology of Proportionate Reason," *TS* 44 (1983) 489–96.

19. Cf. John F. Dedek, "Intrinsically Evil Acts: The Emergence of a Doctrine," *Recherches de théologie ancienne et médiévale* 50 (1983) 191–226.

20. 1–2, q. 72, ad 2; cf. also 1–2, q. 18, ad 2, 3.

21. Karl Hörmann, "Die Unveränderlichkeit sittlicher Normen im Anschluss an Thomas von Aquin," in *Sittliche Normen,* ed. Walter Kerber (Düsseldorf: Patmos, 1982) 33–45, at 42.

22. 1–2, q. 18, a. 10c: "principalis conditio objecti"; ad 2: "Circumstantia...in quantum mutatur in principalem conditionem objecti, secundum hoc dat speciem."

23. Sebastian MacDonald, C.P., sees this discussion in terms of a shift away from scholastic syllogistic reasoning to an argument from fittingness, "a resolution based on a harmonious relation of goods that evidences signs of fittingness and appropriateness." He concludes: "Catholic moral theology is on the verge of a new era in methods and procedures. It will gradually emerge from a transition period of wide diversity in methods, as it has done in the past, and move toward consensus, though of a different kind. It will depend on a newly gained ability to discover and weigh the goods and the values (and the evils and disvalues) associated with proposed courses of action, to the point where arguments, guidelines, principles and laws gain public warrant and legitimacy because of this fittingness and appropriateness in helping people to live out their Christian lives well in this complex world" ("Can Moral Theology Be Appropriate?" *Thomist* 47 [1983] 543–49, at 549).

24. Louis Janssens, "St Thomas and the Question of Proportionality," *Louvain Studies* 9 (1982) 26–46.

25. *Quaestiones quodlibetales* 9, q. 7, a. 15.

26. I do not understand G. E. M. Anscombe's problem with such terminology; cf. her "Medalist's Address: Action, Intention and 'Double Effect,'" *Proceedings of the American Catholic Philosophical Association* 56 (1982) 12–25. The concept behind the terminology is quite traditional; cf. *Quaestiones quodlibetales* 9, q. 7, a. 15; also Franz Scholz, "Sittliche Normen in teleologischer Sicht," *Stimmen der Zeit* 201 (1983) 700–710, at 705.

27. "St. Thomas and the Question of Proportionality" 40.

28. Ibid. 40.

29. 1–2, q. 18, a. 10.

30. Bruno Schüller, S. J., calls attention to this and suggests that the eighth commandment still does make demands. Those who neglect or forget this

seem not to realize that by inaccurately attributing to others the axiom "the end justifies (any) means," they themselves act objectively according to that axiom. Cf. "Die Reductio ad absurdum in philosophischer und theologischer Ethik: Zur Moral wissenschaftlicher Kontroversen über Moral," in *Die Wahrheit tun,* ed. B. Fraling and R. Hasenstab (Würzburg, 1983) 217–40, at 237.

31. The most recent is that of Ronald D. Lawler ("Critical Reflections on Current Bioethical Thinking," in *Perspectives in Bioethics* [New Britain, Conn.: Mariel, 1983] 9–27, at 21). He caricatures teleological tendencies in the understanding of moral norms as "one does a deed that is in itself simply a doing of evil...in the hope that something good may come of it." Or again: "It is a view that producing good effects, having fine things happen in the world, is better and more important than *doing* actions which are free deeds honoring God by their goodness." I know of no contemporary theologian who would tolerate such totally misleading statements as a fair presentation of contemporary discussions. Similarly, Paul Quay, S.J., a physicist, has stated with vigor, and certainly in inverse proportion (if I may) to his grasp of the issues, that "proportionalists" propose that "the alternatives proposed in moral deliberations are, with only a few rare exceptions, nonmoral." He regards this as a "serious error," sufficient "of itself to vitiate the revisionists' entire approach to morality" ("The Unity and Structure of the Human Act," *Listening* 18 [1983] 245–59). He attributes this position to Knauer, Schüller, Fuchs, Janssens, Curran, and this author. "Proportionalists," of course, say nothing of the kind. Obviously, every choice is of an action with a moral character. What "proportionalists" do say is that, before assigning or determining that *moral* character, one must evaluate relevant circumstances. St. Thomas obviously held this; otherwise he would never have been able to approve (as he did) an action that involved the killing of a human being. Janssens makes this very clear in the article cited above. Quay's wild assertions are a reminder that we have a duty to understand the terms of a discussion or exercise self-restraint in entering it. Quay, I am sorry to say, has done neither. – For an accurate representation of the views in question, cf. Walter Kerber, S.J., ed., *Sittliche Normen* (Düsseldorf: Patmos, 1982). Of this book Bernard Häring writes: "Very seldom have I read a collection with such full agreement as I have this rich book, to which proven and well-known moral theologians and the esteemed exegete Heinz Schürmann have contributed." Häring concludes his review as follows: "If all those with magisterial authority, if theologians and pastors of souls would study this little book carefully and discuss it with each other, many misunderstandings would be dissipated and the pastoral peace of the church would be well served.... It would be a pity were this worldwide consensus of established authors not sufficiently noted" (*Theologie der Gegenwart* 26 [1983] 66–67). Cf. also Franz Scholz as in n. 26 above.

32. It was no less than Joseph Ratzinger who wrote in 1971: "I should like

to emphasize once more that I fully agree with Küng's distinction between Roman [school] theology and [Catholic] faith. I am convinced that Catholicism's survival depends on our ability to break out of the prison of the Roman-school type" ("Widersprüche im Buch von Hans Küng," in K. Rahner, ed., *Zum problem Unfehlbarkeit* [Freiburg, 1971] 97–116, at 105).

33. For instance cf. the interesting replies to a questionnaire on "Secular Ethics and Nonbelief" circulated by the Secretariat for Nonbelievers (*Atheism and Dialogue* 18 [1983] 4–34).

14. A Sounder Theory of Morality

John Finnis, Joseph M. Boyle, Jr., Germain Grisez

This chapter first appeared in John Finnis, Joseph M. Boyle, Jr., Germain Grisez, *Nuclear Deterrence, Morality and Realism* (Oxford: Clarendon, 1987).

1. BEYOND "TELEOLOGY" AND "DEONTOLOGY"[1]

The theory we propose is quite different from consequentialist and Kantian ethics. Consequentialist theories are often called "teleological" (goal-directed); they seek to ground moral judgments in human well-being. Kantian theories can be called "deontological" (duty-oriented); they seek to ground moral judgments in the rational nature of the moral subject, whose inherent dignity they emphasize. Teleology appeals to many because it seems to integrate morality in a wider view of human flourishing, and so avoids any absolutizing of the moral domain itself. Such absolutizing is feared if moral rectitude must always prevail over other elements of human welfare and happiness. But deontology also has its appeal, for it seeks to defend the absolute dignity of human persons, especially against any attempt to justify using some as mere means to the goals of others.

Not only individuals but groups of persons can engage in morally significant actions. For simplicity's sake, we speak in what follows of the "moral agent," the "acting person," and so on. This language must be understood inclusively to refer both to individual persons and to groups of two or more persons cooperating together. Thus, when we distinguish different ways in which acting persons participate by their actions in human goods, what we say applies, for example, to the ways in which persons who truly love one another are fulfilled in their communion by their common life of morally good action.

The theory outlined in this chapter seeks to combine the strengths and avoid the weaknesses of teleology and deontology. Morality is indeed grounded in human goods—the goods of real people living in the world of experience. Still, each person's dignity is protected by absolute moral requirements, and it is never right to treat anyone as a mere means.

2. THE IDEA OF BASIC HUMAN GOODS[2]

"Good," in the widest sense in which it is applied to human actions and their principles, refers to anything a person can in any way desire. "Good is any object of any interest." But people desire many things—e.g., pleasure, wealth, and power—which when made principles of action seem to empty a person and to divide persons from one another.

There are, however, other goods – e.g., knowledge of truth, and living in friendship—pursuit of which seems of itself to promote persons and bring them together. Goods like these are intrinsic aspects— that is, real parts—of the integral fulfillment of persons. We call these intrinsic aspects of personal full-being "basic human goods": basic not to survival but to human full-being.

Some goods are definite objectives, desired states of affairs—e.g., getting an enemy to surrender unconditionally, fulfilling the goals of the current five-year plan, or successfully completing a research project. But the basic human goods, in themselves, are not definite objectives. Interest in peace and justice, for example, goes beyond any particular objective sought for their sake, for they transcend any particular state of affairs which can instantiate them. People dedicated to such goods never finish doing what can be done to serve them. Peace and justice are more than things one wants, or goals one hopes to reach. Acting alone and in various forms of community with other persons, one can contribute to the realization of such goods and share in them, but can never lay hold of them, appropriate them, exhaust them.

But if the basic human goods are thus not definite objectives, not goals to be achieved, how do they guide action? By providing the reasons to consider some possibilities as choiceworthy opportunities. Thus the enemy's unconditional surrender becomes an objective to be pursued in the belief that it will contribute to lasting peace; the fulfillment of the five-year plan's goals is sought as a step toward a dreamed-of just world order; particular projects of theoretical research are carried on in the hope that their results will add to knowledge. These reasons for choosing and acting, provided by basic human goods, require no prior reasons. The prospects of human fulfillment held out by peace, justice, knowledge, and so on, naturally arouse corresponding interests in human persons as potential agents.

Thus, human practical reflection and deliberation begin from the basic human goods. To identify them is to identify expanding fields of possibility which underlie all the reasons one has for choosing and carrying out one's choices. Considered in this way, the basic human goods explain both human life's constant and universal features, and its diversity and open-endedness.

And because the basic human goods are at once principles of practical reason and aspects of the full-being of persons, there is no necessary opposition between pursuit of these goods and absolute respect for persons. Indeed, the grounding of ethics in these goods is the first step towards providing both a defense of the absolute dignity of each person, and the reason for every person to be moral.

3. WHICH ARE THE BASIC HUMAN GOODS?[3]

Many goods, though important, are not basic, because not intrinsic to the fulfilment of persons. External goods—anything human persons make, or have, considered as distinct from persons—cannot be basic. It is always for ulterior reasons, reasons which culminate within persons, that individuals and communities are concerned with such goods. Even goods of a more personal and interpersonal character are not yet basic if they can be desired only as instrumental to some further good. Political liberty, for example, is a great good; but it is not itself basic, for by itself it does not fulfil persons but only enables them to pursue various forms of fulfilment. People want liberty in order to pursue the truth, to worship as they think right, to participate in the responsible play of political decision-making, to live in friendship, and so on.

"Enjoyment" refers to a variety of states of consciousness, which have in common only that they are preferred to many other states of consciousness. A preferred state of consciousness is at best *part* of a person's sharing in some good, *part* of the instantiation of a good in a certain state of affairs. Thus enjoyment is not a basic good. Still, in so far as "enjoy" refers to conscious participation in one or more of the basic goods, one needs no ulterior reason to enjoy oneself.

There are several basic human goods. This is clear from reflection on one's own deliberation, and from observation of the ways people organize their lives. Truth and friendship, for example, mark out fields of concern which plainly are distinct; neither is reducible to the other or to any more fundamental interest. This diversity of basic human goods is neither a mere contingent fact about human psychology nor an accident of history. Rather, being aspects of the integral fulfilment of human persons, these goods correspond to the inherent complexity of human nature, as it is found both in individuals and in various forms of association.

As *animate*, human persons are living organic substances. Life itself—its maintenance and transmission—health, and safety are one form of basic human good. Health professions are directed to this good; and to it most people devote a substantial part of their activities. (Still, some argue [and many more somehow presuppose] that human life is no more than an instrumental good, a mere pre-condition within the human being to other, more properly personal goods.)

As *rational,* human beings can know reality and appreciate beauty and whatever intensely engages their capacities to know and feel, and to integrate the two. Knowledge and aesthetic experience are another category of basic good.

As simultaneously *rational* and *animal*, human persons can transform the natural world by using realities, beginning with their own bodily selves, to express meanings and/or serve purposes within human cultures. Such bestowing of meaning and value can be realized in diverse degrees; its fullness is another category of basic good: excellence in work and play.

All these are goods in which everyone to some extent shares prior to any deliberate pursuit of them. Life, knowledge, and the various skills are first received as gifts of nature, and as parts of a cultural heritage. But children quickly come to see these goods as fields in which they can care for, expand, and improve upon what they have received. Life, knowledge, and excellence in performance are basic human goods and principles of practical reasoning in so far as they can be understood and, being understood, can be cherished, enhanced, and handed on to others. But there is another dimension of human persons. As *agents through deliberation and choice,* they can strive to avoid or overcome various forms of conflict and alienation, and can seek after various forms of harmony, integration, and community (fellowship). Choices themselves are essential constituents of this relational dimension of persons. The already given ("natural") aspects of personal unity and interpersonal relationship provide grounds for this dimension, yet it goes beyond what is naturally given.

Most obvious among the basic human goods of this relational dimension are various forms of harmony between and among persons and groups of persons: friendship, peace, fraternity, and so on. Within individuals and their personal lives, similar goods can be realized: inner peace, self-integration (above all, the integration of feelings with one's practical intelligence and judgment), and authenticity. And beyond merely human relationships, there can be harmony between humans and the wider reaches of reality, especially reality's sources, principles, and ground(s). Concern for this last good underlies such diverse activities as a believer's worship and environmentalists' work to save an endangered species.

The relational goods are instantiated in appropriate syntheses of many elements—feelings, experiences, beliefs, choices, performances, persons, and groups of persons, and wider realities. Ideally, the harmonies achieved in these syntheses enhance their diverse elements, but in fact conflict is seldom overcome without some loss to the elements synthesized. Defective forms of harmony often are built on a significant level of conflict. Established working relationships between exploiters and exploited, for example, are a sort of peace, though radically defective. Such defective harmonies, as harmonies, are intelligible goods; they can serve as principles of practical reasoning and action. But they are mutilated forms of basic human goods.

4. THE FIRST MORAL PRINCIPLE[4]

To understand right and wrong, one must bear two things in mind. First, the possibilities of fulfilment are always unfolding, for there are several basic human goods, and endless ways of serving and sharing in them. Second, human beings, even when they work together, can only do so much. No one can undertake every project, or serve in every possible way. Nor can any community. Choices must be made.

Irresistibly compulsive behavior, bad luck, ineptitude, and the unwelcome results of honest human error are not wrongs. Only by choosing badly can individuals and groups go wrong morally. On any ethical theory, moral norms are standards for choosing well.

But how can there be bad choosing, if human goods are as we have said? Without reasons for choosing grounded in basic human goods, there could be no options; yet, we have also said, the choice of an option is never rationally necessary—otherwise there would not be two or more real options. Every choice is grounded in some intelligible good, and to that extent is rational, yet no choice has a monopoly on rationality. Moreover, virtually every choice has some negative impact on some good or other; no possibility can be chosen without setting aside at least some reason against choosing it.

Partly in response to this complexity, the consequentialist tries to distinguish good from bad choices by their effectiveness in maximizing good or minimizing evil. But consequentialism cannot serve as a coherent method of moral judgment. For although one may in various ways and for various purposes commensurate the measurable value and disvalue promised by different instantiations of goods, one cannot commensurate the goods and bads which make diverse possibilities choiceworthy opportunities: such goods and bads go beyond what is definite at any moment of choice.

But if consequentialism is unworkable, how can basic human goods mark the moral distinction between choosing well and choosing badly?

The basic principle of the distinction between right and wrong is not easy to discern reflectively and articulate. Before attempting to formulate it, we shall sketch, but only sketch, the outline of morality's foundation, as we see it.

All moral theorists, including consequentialists, recognize that the foundation of morality is broader and deeper than the prospective results of the options between which one must choose. Common morality suggested an ultimate foundation in "the blessings of the covenant," "the Kingdom," "beatitude," "the order of charity," and so forth. Secular moral theories pointed towards realities such as "the kingdom of ends," "the realm of freedom," "the greatest good of the greatest number," and so forth.

Like consequentialists, we think it clear that morality's foundation is to be located in the goods of human persons, as individuals and in community. Unlike consequentialists, we believe that an adequate description of morality's foundation will take into account aspects of these goods irreducible to even the widest and most long-run prospective consequences of eligible options. Among the important aspects of human goods are possibilities still unknown, for example the answers to questions no one today is in a position to ask, and forms of human community to which present aspirations for a better world do not even reach out. Other aspects of human goods, of the first importance for morality, come to be in the personalities and communities of those who cherish and serve them, and so act rightly in respect of their instantiations. For example, authenticity, neighborliness, and just social order come to be in good persons and communities, in and through their morally right choices, yet are not among the pre-moral values and disvalues upon which the consequentialist tries to ground moral judgment.

Plainly, the basic human goods, conceived so inclusively, cannot ground morality by differentiating possible choices with respect to the potential effectiveness of those choices in realizing instances of the goods. Rather, the moral foundation determines the rightness and wrongness of choices by differentiating attitudes toward basic goods. Underlying the willingness to make one choice or another, there can be entirely different dispositions of the moral agent toward the basic human goods.

Right choices are those which can be made by moral agents whose attitude towards the moral foundation is one for which there is no single adequate word. Certainly, it involves respect for all of the basic human goods in all their aspects, yet "respect" has too passive a connotation. The right attitude is one of concern and interest, but all connotations of partiality must be excluded from these words. The right attitude is perhaps best called "appreciation," provided that this word is used with its connotation of readiness to serve and to cherish what one appreciates. Morally right choices are those choices which can be made by one whose will is disposed toward the entire moral foundation with this attitude of appreciation.

Having completed a sketch of the outline of morality's foundation, we shall now articulate as best we can the moral truths which are at and very near the beginning of the process of moral judgment. First, we propose a formulation of the first principle of morality, and then, in the next sections, we unfold some of its most immediate specifications. The very abstract language in which the first principle has to be articulated renders it, we realize, quite opaque; but the somewhat less abstract language in which its specifications will be discussed will help make the first principle itself more understandable.

The first principle of morality can, perhaps, best be formulated: In voluntarily acting for human goods and avoiding what is opposed to them, *one ought to choose and otherwise will those and only those possibilities whose willing is compatible with integral human fulfilment.*

This formulation can be misunderstood. "Integral human fulfilment" does not refer to individualistic self-fulfilment, but to the good of all persons and communities. All the goods in which any person can share can also fulfil others, and individuals can share in goods such as friendship only with others.

Nor is integral human fulfilment some gigantic synthesis of all the instantiations of goods in a vast state of affairs, such as might be projected as the goal of a world-wide billion-year plan. Ethics cannot be an architectonic art in that way; there can be no plan to bring about integral human fulfilment. It is a guiding ideal rather than a realizable idea, for the basic goods are open ended.

And integral human fulfilment is not a supreme human good, beyond basic human goods such as truth and friendship. It does not provide reasons for acting as the basic goods do. It only moderates the interplay of such reasons, so that deliberation will be thoroughly reasonable.

Common morality's fundamental principles were formulated in theistic terms, while the ideal of integral human fulfilment is not. The primary principles of biblical morality were: Love God above all things; Love your neighbor as yourself. The first principle of morality as we formulate it captures much, if not all, the moral content of those love commands. For Jews and Christians, God is the supreme good and source of all goods; loving him therefore requires the cherishing of all goods. Among these are the basic human goods, which the ideal of integral human fulfilment, too, requires to be cherished. And loving one's neighbor as oneself at least excludes egoism and means accepting the fulfilment of others as part of one's own responsibility; the same demand is made by the first principle of morality as we formulate it.

5. Specifications of the First Moral Principle[5]

But this principle may at first seem too abstruse to be of service. How can any specific moral norms be derived from it?

No specific moral norm can be derived *immediately* from the first principle. But it does imply intermediate principles from which specific norms can be deduced. Among these intermediate principles is the Golden Rule, or the related principle of universalizability—for a will marked by egoism or partiality cannot be open to integral human fulfilment. And this intermediate principle in turns leads to some specific moral judgments—e.g., Jane who wants her husband Jack to be faithful plainly violates it by sleeping with Sam.

Thus there is a route from the first moral principle to specific moral norms. By reflection on the case we have just identified, we try in the next four paragraphs to clarify the intuitively obvious relationship between the first principle and the Golden Rule, and between the Golden Rule and specific norms of fairness.

Human choices are limited in many ways; some limits are inevitable but others are not. Among inevitable limits are those on people's insight into the basic goods, ideas of how to serve them, and available resources. In so far as such limits are outside one's control, morality cannot demand that they be transcended.

Some limits on moral choice, however, are avoidable. For one can voluntarily narrow the range of people and goods one cares about. Sometimes this voluntary narrowing has an intelligible basis, as when a person of many gifts chooses a profession and allows other talents to lie fallow. But sometimes avoidable limitations are voluntarily set or accepted without any such reason.

Sources of limitations of this last kind thus meet two conditions: (i) they are effective only by one's own choices; and (ii) they are non-rational motives, not grounded in intelligible requirements of the basic goods. Normally, the acting person either can allow these non-rational limiting factors to operate, or can transcend them. For they are one's own feelings and emotions, in so far as these are not integrated with the rational appeal of the basic goods and of communal fulfilment in those goods. Such non-integrated feelings offer motives for behavior, yet are *not* in themselves reasons for action. (However, one who gives in to them, whether through malice or weakness of will, always can find some reason for choosing in line with them.)

The first and master principle of morality rationally prescribes that non-integrated feelings be transcended. The Golden Rule requires one not to narrow one's interests and concerns by a certain set of such feelings—one's preference for oneself and those who are near and dear. It does not forbid one to treat different persons differently, when that is required by inevitable limits, or by intelligible requirements of shared goods themselves.

The first principle has other specifications besides the Golden Rule, because non-rational preferences among persons are not the only feelings which incline one to prefer limited to integral human fulfilment. Hostile feelings such as anger and hatred towards oneself or others leads intelligent, sane, adult persons to actions which are often called "stupid," "irrational," and "childish." Self-destructive and spiteful actions destroy, damage, or block some instantiations of basic human goods; willing such actions is plainly not in line with a will to integral human fulfilment. Yet behavior motivated by hostility need not violate the Golden Rule. People sometimes act self-destructively without being unfair to others. Moreover, revenge can be fair: an eye for an eye. But fairness does not eliminate the unreasonableness of acting on hostile feelings in ways that intelligibly benefit no one. Thus the Golden Rule is not the only intermediate principle which specifies the first principle of morality and generates specific moral norms.

So an ethics of Kantian type is mistaken if it claims that universalizability is the only principle of morality. Respect for persons—treating them always as ends in themselves, and never as mere means—must mean more than treating others fairly. The dignity of persons, as bearers of and sharers in human goods, sets at least one other moral demand: Do not answer injury with injury, even when one can do so fairly.

Not only feelings of hostility, but positive feelings can motivate one to do evil—i.e., to destroy, damage, or impede an instantiation of some basic human good. One can choose to bring about evil as a means. One does evil to avoid some other evil, or to attain some ulterior good.

In such cases, the choice can seem entirely rational, and consequentialists might commend it. But, as we have said, the appearance of rationality is based on a false assumption: that human goods do not matter except in so far as they are instantiated and can be commensurated. As we have argued, this way of trying to deal with human goods cannot be rational; the preceding sections of the present chapter indicate part of the reason why. What is morally important includes possible instantiations of goods diverse in kind from one another, and also includes not only those instantiations one now considers but the field of possibility opened up by the basic human goods. The indeterminacy of this aspect of the good utterly defies measurement.

Thus, it is unreasonable to choose to destroy, damage, or impede some instance of a basic good for the sake of an ulterior end. In doing this, one does not have the reason of maximizing good or minimizing evil—there is no such *reason*, for the goods at stake in choosable options are not rationally commensurable. Rather one is motivated by different feelings toward different instances of good involved. In this sort of case, one will-nilly plays favorites among instantiations of goods, just as in violating the Golden Rule one plays favorites among persons.

And so, in addition to the Golden Rule and the principle which excludes acting on hostile feelings, there is another intermediate principle: Do not do evil that good may come.

Because this principle generates moral absolutes, it is often considered a threat to people's vital concrete interests. But while it may be a threat to some interests, the moral absolutes it generates also protect real human goods which are parts of the fulfilment of actual persons, and it is reasonable to sacrifice important concrete interests to the integral fulfilment of persons.

Why? Because otherwise one plays favorites among the goods. Why not play favorites? Because doing so is incompatible with a will towards integral human fulfilment. Why worry about integral human fulfilment? That is like asking why man is man. Integral human fulfilment is not something alien to the moral agent, but is what the moral agent as a person is, and is together with others, and is most abundantly, and is still to be. And is, not only as moral *in distinction from* other human concerns, but as moral *including* most perfectly and harmoniously every truly human concern.

The Golden Rule and the other two principles enunciated in this section shape the rational prescriptions of the first principle of morality into definite responsibilities. Hence, we here call such intermediate principles "modes of responsibility." Besides the three modes we have discussed, there are others which moral reflection in the great cultures has uncovered: detachment, creative fidelity, purity of heart, and so on. Although we will not treat them here, the theory of moral principles we propose has a place for such fruits of previous moral reflection.

6. HUMAN ACTION[6]

Specific moral norms are deduced from the intermediate principles of morality. But one cannot explain this process without first saying something about human action.

Many people, including philosophers too, unreflectively assume a rather simple model of human action, with three elements: (i) a possible state of affairs which a potential agent wants to realize; (ii) a plan to realize it by causal factors in the agent's power; and (iii) the carrying out of the more or less complex set of performances to bring about the desired result.

This model of action is inadequate, yet it does refer to something: to what Aristotle called *making* as distinct from *doing*. Human goods are conceived as definite goals, and rightness of action as efficiency in obtaining results. Here we have the conception of action implicit in consequentialism.

The model fails to account for people's living their own lives as something more than a series of more or less well planned attempts to produce certain results. Reflection on one's own experience as an agent will verify a more complex model of action. (And one need not follow Kant, who saw the inadequacy of the simple model, but failed to challenge it at its own level, because he sought the moral subject in a noumenal realm outside experience.)

In human action, the acting person shares in and makes actual some part of what belongs to the full-being of persons. One's interest in the basic human goods—those broad fields of human possibility—

underlies the desire to realize any particular goal. For instance, beyond the specific objectives of a given course, dedicated teachers want their students to become more mature and cultured persons; beyond all strategic objectives, a statesmanlike military commander hopes to contribute to a more just and peaceful world.

Similarly with communal actions: when groups of two or more persons share fundamental interests, and conceive and decide to carry out joint projects, their communal choices and actions will be as real as those of individuals. These choices presuppose individuals' actions but are not reducible to them. When, for example, a team plays a game for the sake of playing well, there is a common action to which all team members contribute. The individual members of the team each do engage in their own proper actions, which include their individual performances. But one cannot make sense of the team's actions as such if one tries to reduce its play to nothing more than a collection of the distinct performances of the players, together with some sort of common plan. Such communal actions are morally significant, and are not created by legal fictions; law recognizes them as givens, and as models for whatever legal fictions of corporate action a sophisticated legal system may devise.

From a moral point of view, actions are significant primarily as the acting person's voluntary synthesis with, or participation in, human goods. There are at least three ways in which one's actions have this moral significance. These constitute three senses of "doing"; from the moral point of view, these are irreducibly diverse and must be carefully distinguished if acts are to be described adequately for moral evaluation.

First, one acts when one *chooses something for its intrinsic value,* intending it as an end, as something by which one immediately participates in a good. For example, when one gives a gift as an act of friendship, one chooses to realize a certain state of affairs—giving the gift— as a way of serving the good of friendship, the very fulfilment of self and other in this form of harmony, which is instantiated by giving and receiving the gift.

Second, one acts in a different way, when one *chooses something* not for itself but *as a means* to some ulterior end. What is chosen is not willed as an instantiation of a basic good, but as something through which one expects to bring about an instantiation of a good. For example, one consults a physician for the sake of health; one fights a war for the sake of peace; many people work only to get their pay, which they then use to pursue what they consider intrinsically good. The chosen means need not be such that it would never be chosen for its intrinsic value: for business purposes one sometimes makes a trip one might take as a vacation. The first two sorts of doing can be present together, as when one mixes business with pleasure.

Third, one acts in a still different way in so far as one *voluntarily accepts side effects* caused incidentally to acting in either of the two prior ways. Here one is aware that executing one's choice will affect, for good or ill, instances of goods other than the instances on which one's interest directly bears. Although one does not choose this impact on other goods, one foresees and accepts it—sometimes gladly (e.g., when one accepts the bonus of making new friends when one decides to go on a course of training), sometimes reluctantly (e.g., when one accepts the loss of a diseased organ to save one's life, or the leading of some listeners or readers into errors or confusions, when one tries to communicate something complicated).

"End," "means," "side effect" have legitimate uses other than those we define here. In fact, each of these expressions often is used to refer to the very realities to be distinguished from the realities referred to by that expression as we define it. "End" can, for example, refer to a result, even if it is not that for the sake of which one acts. "Means" often refers to the total complex of behavior with its results which one brings about in carrying out a choice. But this total complex always involves many side effects, which are no part of the proposal one adopted by choice. Moreover, that total complex sometimes includes the end for the sake of which one is acting. In ordinary language one hesitates to call something a "side effect" if it is foreseen as a certain or natural consequence of the behavior by which one carries out one's choice, even though it is no part of the proposal one adopts. For many, the hesitation becomes positive unwillingness when the foreseen consequence is something of substantial human importance. Thus, the technical meaning we give to "end," "means," and "side effect" must be borne in mind if one is to understand the analyses we propose.

Because willing something as an end, as a means, and as a side effect relate acting persons to goods in different ways, the meanings of "doing" which they ground are quite distinct, as we already noticed. A professional's playing a game only to make money is not playing the game in the same sense—it is not the same *doing*—as the amateur's playing of the game for the sake of the excellent performance itself. One who unwillingly benefits another by incidental effects of some action is not doing the other a favor.

The significance of these differences is clearest in negative cases. One may reveal shameful truths about another out of spite, or to arouse shame and provide an occasion for repentance, or as a side effect of preventing the conviction of an innocent person. In all three cases, one can be said to "destroy a reputation." But these are very different acts; only in very different senses do they destroy reputation. And corresponding to the ambiguity of "action" (and action-words) are diverse means of other words important in moral evaluation: "responsible," "deliberate," "intentional," and so on.

In formulating moral norms, it is especially important to distinguish the meanings of "intentional." One *intends* in different senses what one tries to bring about as an instantiation of a good and what one chooses as a means to something ulterior: one does not *intend* what one accepts as a side effect. But while, in common idiom, foreseen, accepted (and thus *voluntarily* caused) side effects are often called *un*intended if the question is whether they were part of the agent's plan, they often are said to be intended if the question is whether they were caused inadvertently or "accidentally."

7. DERIVING SPECIFC MORAL NORMS[7]

The derivation of specific moral norms from modes of responsibility can now be explained.

Its heart is a deduction which can be formulated in a categorical syllogism. In the simplest case, the normative premise is a mode of responsibility, which excludes a certain way of willing in respect to the relevant goods. The other premise is a description of a type of action, which is sufficient to make it clear that an action of this kind cannot be willed except in the excluded way. The conclusion is that doing an act of that kind is morally wrong.

Actions not excluded by any mode are morally permissible; those whose omission would violate some mode are morally required.

Many ways of describing actions, especially when interest is centered on their consequences, do not reveal what is necessary to derive a moral norm. For example, if killing is defined as "any behavior of a person which causes the death of a person," the description is insufficient for moral evaluation. Descriptions of actions adequate for moral evaluation must say or imply how the agent's will bears on relevant goods.

Not all the modes of responsibility apply to all the three sorts of doing, identified in the preceding section.

Universalizability does. Parents who show affection for a favorite child but are cold toward another violate the Golden Rule in a doing which immediately instantiates the good of familial friendship. Superiors who assign harder jobs to subordinates they dislike, and easier to subordinates they like, violate universalizability in choosing means. Commanders who tried to avoid killing non-combatants when liberating allied territory, but made no similar effort to avoid such incidental killing in their operations in the enemy homeland acted unfairly in accepting side effects.

Thus, accepting bad side effects of one's choices can be wrong if one does it unfairly. Similarly, even without unfairness to anyone, those excessively attached to some good can go wrong in accepting grave side effects—for example, the aging champion boxer who ruins his health in trying to retain his title.

Still, one cannot act at all without accepting some bad side effects. In any choice, one at least devotes part of one's limited time and other resources to the pursuit of a particular good, and leaves unserved other goods for which one might have acted. So there could not be a general moral principle entirely excluding the willing of every negative impact on a basic human good. One sometimes can accept bad side effects as inevitable concomitants of a fully reasonable response to the intelligible requirements of goods.

Thus, the principle that evil may not be done that good may come applies only to the choice of a means to an ulterior end, not to the acceptance of side effects. Whenever one chooses to destroy, damage, or impede one instantiation of a basic good for the sake of some other instantiation of that or another basic good, the second instantiation is preferred to the first. Since the goods immanent in possibilities available for choice cannot be commensurated, this preference must be arbitrary. Such a choice is at odds with openness to integral human fulfilment. But to accept a similar state of affairs as an unwanted side effect need not be. For it is not necessarily excluded by any mode of responsibility, and so it need not be at odds with integral human fulfilment. For example, the choice to kill a suffering person by a purposeful omission of treatment is morally excluded, as a case of doing evil that good may come. But a choice not to treat, when made to avoid the burdens of treating and with death accepted as a side effect, need not be wrong.

If an action's description, however limited, makes plain that such an action involves a choice to destroy, damage, or impede some instance of a basic human good, the wrongness of any action which meets the description is settled. Additional factors may affect the degree of wrongness, but further description of the act cannot reverse its basic moral quality. So, moral norms derived from this mode of responsibility can be called "moral absolutes." The norm, for instance, which forbids hanging one innocent person to satisfy a mob and protect any number of others is an absolute; no further information could make doing that right, though circumstances could mitigate its wickedness.

Different modes of responsibility work differently, so not all specific norms are absolute. Universalizability can exclude as unfair an action proposed under a limited description, yet allow as fair an action which includes all the elements of that description together with some other morally relevant features. For example: fairness demands keeping a promise, whenever there is no motive to break it except the sorts of motive whose operation promises are meant to exclude. But if one has another reason to break a promise – e.g., that keeping it would have such grave consequences that even those to whom it was made would agree it should be broken – one may break the promise without violating the Golden Rule.

In general, specific norms derived from the universalizability principle are not absolute. Ordinary language obscures this fact by often building the moral specification into the act-description—e.g., by limiting "stealing" to the wrongful taking of another's property. However, instances of justified taking can include all the elements which are present in unjustifiable taking; the addition rather than the subtraction of relevant features makes the taking justifiable.

Since universalizability usually does not yield moral absolutes, one who considers it the first principle of morality will not admit them, at least not in the sense of those absolute norms which are generated by the principle that evil may not be done that good may come. Thus a

Kantian ethics limited to universalizablility might approve the deterrent. But such an ethics is inadequate in many ways. It can condemn some things, but can justify nothing, inasmuch as it offers only a necessary and not a sufficient condition for moral rightness.

The theory we have outline in this chapter subordinates morality to human persons and their fulfilment, both as individuals and in communion. Yet the dignity of human persons is protected by moral absolutes. Among those absolutes, we believe, is one which forbids choices to destroy human lives. Killing people is not a permissible means to promote other goods or prevent other evils. Yet accepting death(s) as a side effect of one's chosen action is not the same thing as a choice to kill.

Notes

1. *Non-cognitivism and intuitionism in ethics...* For critical accounts of the efforts made by twentieth-century English and American philosophers to explain ethical statements as expressing (a) no proposition either true or false (non-congnitivism) or (b) intuitive judgments of right or wrong, or intuitions of specific moral norms, see e.g. Warnock, *Contemporary Moral Philosophy* (1967), 1–47; Brandt, *Ethical Theory* (1959), 225–31, 239–40; Rice, *Our Knowledge of Good and Evil* (1955); Mitchell, *Morality, Religious and Secular* (1980), 93–120; Finnis, *Fundamentals of Ethics,* chs. II, III.

2. "Good is any object of any interest"... On this widest sense of "good," see Perry, *General Theory of Value* (1954), 115–45. On this, and on the conception of good sketched in this section, see Grisez, *Christian Moral Principles,* 125, 139, 115–40 generally, and 180–3; Finnis, *Natural Law and Natural Rights,* 59-80.

3. *"Enjoyment is not a basic good"...* See Aristotle, *Nic. Eth.,* X, 4–5: 1174a12–1176a29; Finnis, *Natural Law and Natural Rights,* 95–7; Grisez, *Christian Moral Principles,* 119–20.

Classifications of basic human goods... For the classification set out here, see Grisez, *Christian Moral Principles,* 121–5, 130–2, 135–7. For other classifications, see Finnis, *Natural Law and Natural Rights,* 81–92, 97–8.

Classification of relational basic goods... The relational goods can be distinguished and classified in various ways. One way uses the language of virtue, but the realm of virtue is notoriously difficult to reduce to a system. And so, without challenging the main lines of our account of the basic goods, or our indications of which these are, other plausible candidates for the list of relational goods can easily be proposed.

4. *Integral human fulfilment as an ideal, not an end-state...* On the notion of "end-states" see Nozick, *Anarchy, State and Utopia* (1974), 153–64. On the relation between integral human fulfilment as an ideal and the Christian conception of the last end of man, see Grisez, *Christian Moral Principles,* 459–76, 807–30; Finnis, "Practical Reasoning, Human Goods and the End of Man," *Proc. Am. Cath. Phil. Assoc.* 58 (1984) 23–36.

5. *Intermediate principles, or modes of responsiblity...* For a more complete list, and a discussion of their relation to classic accounts of the virtues and the beatitudes, see Grisez, *Christian Moral Principles,* 189–94, 205–28, 627–55. See also the discussion of intermediate principles as basic requirements of practical reasonableness in Finnis, *Fundamentals of Ethics,* 68–76, and *Natural Law and Natural Rights,* 100–33.

6. *Aristotle's distinction between making and doing...* See *Nic. Eth.* II, 4: 1105 a 32; VI, 4: 114ob3–6; Cooper, *Reason and Human Good in Aristotle* (1975), 2, 78, 111.

Kant's model of action... Kant saw the inadequacy of modelling action on making. With his notion of an autonomous moral subject, he tried to take into account a dimension of moral life beyond the more or less successful pursuit of one goal after another. But he separated the noumenal realm from the world of experience. He thought the noumenal realm inaccessible to experience and theoretical reflection; consequently he could not give an account of human action appropriate to that realm. Yet since he considered that what is important for morality is in that inaccessible realm, he did not challenge at its own level the account of human action assumed by consequentialism, but considered it a sufficiently accurate description of the way acting persons *experience* themselves and others. For a more detailed account, with references to Kant's texts, see Boyle, Grisez, and Tollefsen, *Free Choice* (1076), 112–8.

7. *Act-description with built-in moral specifications...* Many moral norms contain act-descriptions which state or imply a presupposed moral specification. But it is gratuitous, and mistaken, to suppose that all the norms of common morality contain such terms.

Universality, Kantian ethics, and moral absolutes... Despite the apparent firmness of his pronouncements on specific moral norms, Kant himself, when he considers "casuistical questions," often seems to suggest that such norms (e.g., those excluding lying, or suicide) may well not apply in situations where individuals have special reasons for choosing to lie, kill themselves, etc. See Kant, *The Metaphysical Principles of Virtue: Part II of the Metaphysics of Morals* (Bobbs-Merrill, 1964) 84–5; and see xl–xli for Warner Wick's observations on Kant's casuistry.

15. The Moral Act in *Veritatis Splendor* and Aquinas's *Summa Theologiae:* A Comparative Analysis

Jean Porter

This chapter first appeared in *Veritatis Splendor: American Responses,* ed. Michael E. Allsopp and John J. O'Keefe (Kansas City, Mo.: Sheed and Ward, 1995).

Are there some kinds of actions which are never morally justifiable, whatever the circumstances or the foreseen consequences of acting otherwise? Traditionally, Catholic moral theologians have held that there are: for example, murder, theft, or adultery. Actions of these kinds are said to be intrinsically evil by virtue of the nature of the object of the act, and they can therefore never licitly be done, for any reason whatever. Over the past thirty years, however, this view has increasingly been questioned by moral theologians, variously described as proportionalists or revisionists, who argue, in the words of Richard McCormick, that "we must look at all dimensions (morally relevant circumstances) before we know what the action is and whether it should be said to be [morally wrong]."[1] These theologians, in turn, have been sharply criticized by Germain Grisez, John Finnis, and their followers, collectively known as deontologists or traditionalists, who insist that it is always morally wrong to act against certain basic goods such as life, knowledge, and the like.[2]

The encyclical *Veritatis Splendor* represents the long-anticipated official intervention in this debate. While the pope is careful not to condemn or to endorse the views of any particular theologian, and while he foreswears any attempt to "impose on the faithful any particular theological system, still less a philosophical one" (n. 29), nonetheless, his own position in the debate between revisionists and traditionalists is clear enough:

> One must therefore reject the thesis...which holds that it is impossible to qualify as morally evil according to its species—its "object"—the deliberate choice of certain kinds of behavior or specific acts apart from a consideration of the intention for which the choice is made or the totality of the foreseeable consequences of that act for all persons concerned (n. 79).

In the process of elaborating and defending this conclusion, the pope offers an encyclical that only a moral theologian could love. One commentator remarks that the second chapter of the encyclical "is very tough going, even for theologians, unless they specialize in moral thought or ethics,"[3] and another remarks on "their [i.e., moral theologians'] delight at its ponderously convoluted and technical second chapter, which will provide ample opportunity for scrutiny, exegesis, distinctions, comments and modifications of the papal animadversions...."[4] These commentators are quite right; the arguments of the encyclical *are* hard going. To some extent, the difficulties that the reader encounters are generated by its distinctive ecclesial style, but it is also the case that this encyclical is hard going because the issues that it addresses are difficult and complex.

Veritatis Splendor takes up other issues besides the question of intrinsically evil kinds of actions, including the grounding of moral norms (nn. 42–53 and nn. 71–75), the role of conscience in moral judgment (nn. 54–64) and the religious significance of persons' actions (nn. 65–70). Of course, all these issues are interconnected, but it is also the case that a short discussion must be focused, if it is to be of any use. Accordingly, in this essay I will limit myself to the task of identifying and clarifying the issues which underlie the discussion of intrinsically evil actions, beginning at number 79. I do not intend to offer a detailed commentary on the encyclical itself, or much less on the extensive and complicated debate between proportionalists and deontologists which forms its context. Rather, I hope to offer a brief guide to some of the relevant concepts and questions, which will enable the reader to make his or her own way through both the encyclical and the relevant theological literature more easily.

In what follows, I have structured my discussion around Thomas Aquinas's account of the moral act in the *Summa Theologiae.* In doing so, I do not mean to suggest that Aquinas's thought should be normative for the encyclical or for Catholic moral theology, nor do I hold that his account of morality is without limitations or errors. Nonetheless, Aquinas offers one of the most insightful accounts of moral judgment that is available to us, and his account, moreover, has set the framework for all subsequent moral theology. Both the current debate among moral theologians and the encyclical itself are cast in terms which Aquinas set. Thus, a review of Aquinas's exposition will provide a framework within which to sort out and to reflect upon the issues at hand, in terms of an idiom which is distinctively Catholic.

1. THE MORAL ACT: A PRELIMINARY CONSIDERATION

In his discussion of the moral act in the *Summa Theologiae,* Aquinas identifies three criteria in terms of which human acts are to be evaluated. That is, an act must be evaluated in terms of its object (I–II 18.2), the circumstances in which the act is done (I–II 18.3), and the agent's aim in acting (I–II 18.4).[5] In order for an act to be morally justifiable, it must be good in every respect; that is, good or at least neutral in its object, with due consideration of circumstances, and directed towards a good, or at least an innocent aim (I–II 18.4 *ad* 3). Thus, an action which is bad with respect to its object cannot be redeemed by a good aim, and yet an act which is generically good will be corrupted by a bad aim, or by the agent's failure to do what she should in the circumstances in which she acts.

The object of an act, as Aquinas understands it, is expressed in terms of that description which indicates its species, or as we would say, indicates the kind of act that it is, considered from a moral point of view (I–II 18.2); that is, it is an act of murder or theft or adultery, or alternatively, an act of capital punishment, or making use of what is one's own, or marital intercourse. Neither the agent's end in acting nor the circumstances of the act can be collapsed into the object for Aquinas. Thus, to take his own example, someone who steals in order to commit adultery is guilty of a twofold transgression in one act; that is, the object of his act of theft cannot be elided into his aim in that act, namely, to have the means to commit adultery (I–II 18.7). Similarly, the circumstances in which the agent acts do not change its object, unless they have some intrinsic relation to it. Thus, an act of theft is an act of theft, whether one steals from the rich or the poor, whether one walks off with a television set or appropriates funds by electronic transfer, whether one steals a valuable work of art or a painting on black velvet. These circumstances may well mitigate or exacerbate the wrongness of a given act of theft, but they do not alter its essential character or its wrongness (I–II 18.10, 11).

It might seem that on Aquinas's own terms, the aim for which an agent acts would always be a positive factor in the evaluation of the act, as he frequently reminds us, every agent necessarily acts in pursuit of something that is perceived to be good (for example, at I 5.4,5; 6.1; 60.3,4; I–II 1.2). However, it is also the case, according to Aquinas, that the aim of the agent is determined by what the agent knowingly does, and if what she does is wrong in itself, her aim is *ipso facto* bad (I–II 19.1, especially *ad* 1). Thus, for example, someone who aims to sleep with a woman whom he knows to be someone else's wife has the intention of committing adultery, even though what he wants is not the act of adultery *per se*, but the pleasure which he anticipates from the act. Thus, a morally bad intention cannot be redeemed simply by the fact that the agent acts with a view to securing some good.

So far, the terms of moral analysis which Aquinas sets forth would seem to correspond, more or less, to the teaching of *Veritatis Splendor.* According to the latter, "The primary and decisive object for moral judgment is the object of the human act, which establishes whether it is capable of being ordered to the good and to the ultimate end, which is God" (n. 79). For Aquinas, too, the object of an action provides a criterion for moral judgment that cannot be elided into a consideration of circumstances or the agent's aim. Moreover, if the object of the action is bad, the action cannot be redeemed morally by any other sort of consideration, although the evil of an action which is wrong by virtue of its object can be mitigated by the presence of a good aim or difficult circumstances. Thus, Aquinas would appear to agree with the encyclical that

> the opinion must be rejected as erroneous which maintains
> that it is impossible to qualify as morally evil according to

its species the deliberate choice of certain kinds of behavior or specific acts, without taking into account the intention for which the choice was made or the totality of the foreseeable consequences of that act for all persons concerned (n. 82).

Yet it would be misleading, at best, to say that Aquinas would agree without qualification with the encyclical at this point. The difficulty is this: *Veritatis Splendor* reflects a widely shared assumption that Aquinas's criteria for the evaluation of an action can be applied to specific acts prior to and independently of the process of determining the moral evaluation of a specific action. On this view, Aquinas's analysis of these criteria would provide us with a methodology for evaluating particular actions; we determine the object of the act, we take note of the agent's aim and the circumstances, and we then arrive at a moral evaluation, by means of an application of the formula, *quilibet singularis defectus causat malum, bonum autem causatur ex integra causa* (any single defect causes evil; good, however, is brought about through a complete and intact cause; I–II 18.4 *ad* 3).[6]

Yet matters are more complex than that. Aquinas does not in fact hold that the criteria for moral judgment set forth in I–II 18 jointly provide a methodology or a formula for the moral evaluation of specific actions. In order to draw out a methodology for moral decision-making from the criteria of object, circumstances, and aim, we would first need to be able to identify which component of a particular action is which, *prior to* forming a moral evaluation of the action. Yet as Aquinas recognizes, this is just what we cannot do. In order to determine the object of an action, distinguishing it in the process from circumstances and from the agent's aim in acting, it is *first* necessary to arrive at a correct description of the act from the moral point of view. That process, in turn, depends on prior evaluative judgments, in terms of which we determine what is morally relevant and what is not, and how the different components of the action should be interrelated to one another. Description is not prior to evaluation; to the contrary, to describe an action from the moral point of view is to form a moral evaluation of the action.

This point will be clearer once we have looked more closely at the relation between object and circumstances, on the one hand, and object and aim, on the other.

2. OBJECT AND CIRCUMSTANCES

The language of "the object of the act" is so familiar, at least in Catholic circles, that it is easy to assume that this language is clear and straightforward, forgetting just how puzzling it can be. *Veritatis Splendor* appears to reflect this assumption, since it does not offer any extended discussion of just what the object of an act is. We are told that:

> By the object of a given moral act, then, one cannot mean a process or an event of the purely physical order, to be assessed on the basis of its ability to bring about a given state of affairs in the outside world. Rather, the object is the proximate end of a deliberate decision which determines the act of willing on the part of the acting person. Consequently, as the *Catechism of the Catholic Church* teaches, "There are certain specific kinds of behavior that are always wrong to choose, because choosing them involves a disorder of the will, that is, a moral evil" (n. 78).

But surely this gets matters backwards. If the object of the act qualifies the will, surely that is *due to* the moral significance of that object.

Further on, we are told:

> The primary and decisive element for moral judgement is the object of the human act, which establishes whether it is capable of being ordered to the good and to the ultimate end, which is God....It is precisely these which are the contents of the natural law and hence that ordered complex of "personal goods" which serve the "good of the person": the good which is the person himself and his perfection. These are the goods safeguarded by the commandments, which, according to St. Thomas, contain the whole natural law.
>
> Reason attests that there are objects of the human act which are, by their nature, "incapable of being ordered" to God because they radically contradict the good of the person made in his image. These are the acts which, in the church's moral teaching, have been termed "intrinsically

evil" (*intrinsece malum*): they are such always and per se, in other words, on account of their very object and quite apart from the ulterior intentions of the one acting and the circumstances (nn. 79–80).

In other words, the objects of some actions, that is, those which are wrong by virtue of their object, are characterized by their intrinsic inconsistency with the good of the human person; moreover, such acts are contrary to the natural law.

This is more helpful. At least we now have some substantive criteria by which to determine which kinds of actions are intrinsically evil, and which are not. Yet questions remain. It is far from clear, for example, which specific kinds of actions are those which "radically contradict" the good of the human person, especially since the Catholic moral tradition has traditionally acknowledged that there are some kinds of actions which involve inflicting harm, and which are yet morally justified (for example, capital punishment). The difficulties involved in determining the content of the natural law are notorious and longstanding. Apart from these, however, there are additional problems associated with applying this language to the logic of the language. These problems are less frequently acknowledged, but they are, for that very reason, potentially more troublesome. These are the difficulties on which we will focus in this section and the next.

In the first place, it is not at all clear how we are to distinguish object from circumstances in the description of a particular action. Consider some examples: if one person kills another, it is surely circumstantial that the act takes place at dawn, or in the evening, in the city or in the countryside, quickly or slowly. The means that the killer uses are also circumstantial, as for example, whether the act is done with a knife or a gun or poison or a garrotte. But what about the personal characteristics of the killer and the victim? It is surely circumstantial that the killer is a woman and the victim is a man, that the killer is young and the victim is old, and so forth. But it is *not* a mere circumstance that the killer is an authorized executioner and the victim is a duly convicted criminal. Those details change the essential description of the act, from murder to legal execution; or to be more exact, they do, *if* we accept the traditional Catholic account of murder and justifiable homicide (cf. II–II 64.2).

Consider another example, this from Aquinas himself:

> The process of reason is not determined to any one thing, but when anything is given, it can proceed further. And therefore, that which is considered in one act as a circumstance added onto the object, which determines the species of the act, can be considered a second time by ordaining reason as a principle condition of the object that determines the species of the act. And so, to take what is another's has its species from the formal notion of "another" [*ratione alieni*], and by this fact [the act] is constituted in the species of theft, and if the notion of place or time should be considered beyond this, [such a notion] would fall under the formal description of a circumstance. But since reason can ordain also with respect to place or time, and other things of this sort, it happens that the condition of place is considered with respect to the object, as contrary to the order of reason; as for example, that reason ordains that no damage should be done to a sacred place (I–II 18.10).

In other words, it is not generally relevant to a description of a particular act of taking what is another's that the object is taken from a museum, or a private house, or from the street; in all these instances, the act is still an act of theft, and qualifications of place are circumstantial to that act. But for Aquinas, at least, it is not just a circumstantial detail that something is stolen from a church; that fact qualifies our essential understanding of the act itself, in such a way as to change its moral description, in this case, from an act of simple theft to an act of sacrilege.

As these examples suggest, the object of an action is not simply given perspicuously in the description of an act. It certainly cannot be equated with "what is done," described in a simple, nonmoral way. For one thing, any action allows for indefinitely many possible true descriptions of "what is done."[7] More to the point, whatever precisely is meant by the object of the action, as understood by Aquinas or by traditional moral theology, this is surely a *moral* concept. Thus, the object of an act is the generic moral concept in terms of which the act is correctly described from the standpoint of moral evaluation (or in Aquinas's terms, it determines the species of the act; I–II 18.2). Once the object of an act has been correctly determined, *then* it is possible to identify other components of the act as mere circumstances, which can mitigate the badness of the action (if it is objectively bad) but cannot alter its fundamental moral character.

Correlatively, it is not the case that the object of an action can serve as an independently given datum for moral evaluation. The determination of the object of an act presupposes that we have described the act correctly, from a moral point of view, and that process requires normative judgments about the significance of different aspects of the action. In other words, the determination of the object of an act, is the *outcome* of a process of moral evaluation, not its presupposition.

How, then, are we to determine the object of an act? Aquinas's response to this question, as given in the treatise on action in the *prima secundae*, is not immediately clear. We are told that the object is determined by reason, which determines whether what is done is appropriate (as, for example, to use what is one's own) or inappropriate (to take what is another's: I–II 18.5; cf. I–II 18.10). But what, specifically, does this mean?

In order to answer this question, it is necessary to turn from the programmatic analysis of I–II 18 to the *secunda secundae,* where we find Aquinas's discussion of the specific details of the moral life. It is here that he repeatedly raises and addresses questions of the form, "What kind of act is this?" or, in other words, what is the moral species of this or that kind of action? And since the species of the act determines its object (I–II 18.5), it follows that the generic descriptions which give the species of actions will also describe their objects.

When we turn to an examination of the relevant texts (especially, but not exclusively, found in the treatise on justice, II–II 57–122), it becomes apparent that the generic concepts in terms of which Aquinas identifies the objects of acts are taken from the same basic moral notions that serve as the starting points for moral reflection for nearly everyone else: for example, murder (II–II 64), injury (II–II 65), theft and robbery (II–II 66), fraud (II–II 77), usury (II–II 78), and lying (II–II 110). These basic concepts of kinds of actions are associated with widely accepted moral prohibitions (theft, murder, lying, adultery) or with stereotypical ideals of good behavior (almsgiving, restitution, prayer). Since the precepts of morality can all be traced to the natural law, which is contained (in diverse ways) in the precepts of the Decalogue (I–II 100.1,3), he would agree with the encyclical that the intrinsic wrongness of some kinds of actions is given by the natural law;

moreover, he would agree that these acts are such because they involve some kind of harm to another (I–II 100.5, II–II 72.1).

Thus, Aquinas takes his examples of objects of actions from those generic moral concepts which are the common currency of moral reflection, and which, in the case of morally bad kinds of actions, can be correlated with basic moral prohibitions. Yet how does this help him, or us, to distinguish the object from the circumstances in the description of particular actions? In order to answer this question, we must turn to those articles in which Aquinas considers whether some more specific kind of action, suspicious on its face, should be subsumed under the wider category of a prohibited kind of action; for example, does capital punishment, or killing in self-defense, count as murder (II–II 64.2,7)? In these and similar cases, Aquinas clarifies and extends the meaning of the basic moral concepts, such as murder or theft, through an extended reflection on the point of the prohibitions or injunctions connected with them. Thus, he distinguishes murder from legitimate forms of killing through an extended reflection on the point of the prohibition against killing, and the ways in which different sorts of killing do or do not fit within the rationale for the complex concept of murder (see especially II–II 64.2,3,5–7). This reflection, in turn, allows him to determine, in some detail, which aspects of an act of killing would be relevant to determining the object of the act; those, namely, which are relevant to the point of the prohibition against murder. Thus, it is determinative of the object of an act of killing that the victim is a duly convicted criminal, or conversely, is innocent (II–II 64.2,6), and it is similarly so determinative that the killer is a duly authorized executioner or soldier, or conversely, is a private citizen (II–II 64.3). Other features of the act, on the other hand, are circumstantial, for example, the gender and age of the killer and victim (cf. I–II 18.10 quoted above).

Of course, it follows that someone with a different understanding of the point of the prohibition against murder would draw the lines between murder and permissible forms of killing in a different way. For example, someone who does not accept the traditional arguments for capital punishment might well insist that an act of execution is a form of murder and, therefore, the officially sanctioned position of the executioner would be merely circumstantial in her view.

It is sometimes assumed that the object of an act can be equated with some form of behavior which can be described in terms that make no reference to cultural conventions or to particular institutional forms of life, and which is therefore natural in the sense of being comprehensible in nonconventional terms. This is the view of those moral theologians who defend a version of the traditional doctrine of intrinsically evil actions along the lines set out by Grisez and Finnis, and it appears to be the view of the encyclical as well (cf. n. 48). It is also Aquinas's view with respect to some kinds of actions, specifically lying and the so-called unnatural sexual sins (II–II 110.3; II–II 154.11). But Aquinas does not understand the object of every morally significant act in this way, as his discussion of murder, theft and robbery would suggest. To the contrary, in the majority of cases, he does not equate the object of an action with a form of behavior that is natural in the sense of being comprehensible in nonconventional terms (cf. I–II 1.3 *ad* 3, I–II 18.7 *ad* 1, I–II 20.6). Thus, every murder involves killing a human being, but not every act of killing as a murder. Every act of theft involves taking what is another's (which already builds in a reference to a convention), but not every form of taking what is another's counts as theft (to take a modern example, taxation does not). In most cases, the moral concept which gives the object of an action includes some essential reference to the institutional, or more broadly, the cultural context in which the act takes place, within which it takes on its distinctively rational and human meaning. Aquinas has specific arguments for not understanding lying and certain forms of sexual activity in this way, as an examination of the relevant questions makes clear. These arguments may or may not be convincing, but it would be a mistake to assume that all moral concepts must be analyzed in the same terms; Aquinas himself does not think so, and the view is in any case quite implausible.

There is one further point that must be made, before turning to an examination of the aim of an action and its relation to the object. We have already observed that the concepts of morally significant kinds of actions, in terms of which Aquinas identifies the objects of actions, are generic concepts. For that reason, they cannot be applied with absolute certainty in every case. While the correct description of an action in terms of its object will usually be straightforward, it will always be possible that we will find that we cannot arrive with certainty at the correct moral description of a particular act, even though we know all the morally relevant facts of the matter, and attempt in good faith to arrive at a correct evaluation of the act in question. This limitation to moral judgment is not a feature of positive injunctions only, as the encyclical suggests (see n. 67 in particular). Rather, it is a specific instance of the logical limitations in any kind of knowledge of singulars; that is, we cannot apply generic concepts to concrete individuals with certainty in every instance. That is why Aquinas holds that there will always be some uncertainty with respect to the application of the precepts of the natural law.

> As was said above, those things pertain to the law of nature, to which the human person is naturally inclined; among which, it is proper to the human person that he is inclined to act according to reason. However, it pertains to reason to proceed from what is general to what is specific....The speculative reason is constituted in one way with respect to this [procedure], however, and the practical reason, in another way. Since the speculative reason deals chiefly with necessary things, concerning which it is impossible that it should proceed otherwise [than it does], the truth is found without any defect in specific conclusions, as also [it is found] in general principles. But practical reason deals with contingent things, among which are human operations, and therefore, even though there is some necessity in [its] general principles, the more one descends to specifics, the more defect is found....With respect to things that are done, there is not the same truth or practical rectitude for all people with respect to specifics, but only with respect to general principles; and with respect to those things about which there is the same rectitude in specifics for all, it is not equally known to all (I–II 94.4).[8]

If Aquinas is right to insist on the indeterminacy of all moral concepts, as I believe him to be, then it follows that there are logical limits to the certainty and the degree of consensus that can be attained in moral judgment, even among those who share the same basic moral concepts and attempt to apply them in all good faith. The presence of moral uncertainty and disagreement in our society cannot be attributed without remainder to bad faith, or to moral pluralism, or to the effects of consequentialism (which in any case has not had all that much effect in the wider culture). There will always be some hard cases about which we, as individuals, just cannot judge, or about which we, collectively, cannot agree.[9]

3. OBJECT AND AIM

The philosopher Alan Donagan has divided the norms of common morality into what he calls first and second order precepts, which have to do with the evaluation of moral actions and the attribution of moral responsibility, respectively.[10] Intention, purpose, voluntariness and other such notions generally pertain to our second order evaluations, and thus, they normally presuppose that we have already evaluated the act that is in question.

In order for a person to be responsible for an action, the act must be hers in some fundamental way; that is to say, it must be voluntary. Almost everyone who has reflected on the moral life, from Aristotle to the present time, would agree on this much; Aquinas joins the general consensus at I–II 6. Moreover, the voluntary status, or otherwise, of a particular item of behavior would seem to be easy to determine. There is a basic difference between killing someone deliberately, and killing her inadvertently, say, by falling on her from a great height. In the latter case, an individual may be the material reason by which something occurs, which is nonetheless not her action in any sense.

Yet it is possible for an act to be voluntary in one respect, and yet to be involuntary in another sense. Medieval moral theologians were fond of the somewhat implausible example of someone who has sex with a woman whom he believes, wrongly, to be his wife; the act in question is not a *voluntary* act of adultery, and the man is not an adulterer, because in one respect, he does not know what he is doing (Aquinas uses this example at I–II 19.6; cf. I–II 6.8). Or consider the case of an actor who fires at her fellow performer in the course of a play. Unknown to her, a very nasty person has loaded the gun with live ammunition and so, to her horror, her fellow actor falls dead at her feet. Did she kill him? In one sense, she did, since he dies as the result of an action of hers. But in another sense, she did not, since she did not know that she was killing him, and did not intend to kill him. Her act is voluntary under some descriptions (in this case, acting a part, doing her job), but under the crucial description of killing a man, it is involuntary, that is, it is not *her* action.

On the other hand, there is a general presumption that a person *is* responsible for what she knowingly does. That is, if someone is aware that her act falls under a particular description, she is responsible for her action, so described, even if she does not particularly want to do *that*, but rather, chooses to do what she does under another description. We have already mentioned the example of the adulterer; what he wants is not to commit adultery, but to have a good time; yet his action is nonetheless adultery if he knows the relevant fact that his partner is someone else's wife. To turn to our second example, if the actor knew that her gun was loaded with live ammunition, her act would be an intentional act of murder, even if it were the case that she did not especially *want* to bring about the death of her unfortunate colleague. (She may just have said to herself, "Well, this is hard luck for Fred, but the show must go on.")

Aquinas's views on what we would describe as voluntariness, intention, and purpose, which he discusses in terms of voluntariness, the aim for which an act is done, and the object of the will, are quite complex. It would take us too far afield to attempt to sort them out in any detail; suffice it to say that for him, the goodness or evil of the will is determined by any morally relevant description of the act, which the agent herself knows, and which is therefore an appropriate description for her *voluntary* act (in general, see I–II 19.1,3 and I–II 20.1–3). Thus if it is the case than an action falls under one of the generic concepts of morally wrong kinds of actions, and the agent knows that it does, that fact corrupts her will, even if her purpose in acting is praiseworthy (I–II 20.4).[11] On the other hand, a bad aim corrupts an action that is generically good if, for example, someone gives alms to the poor out of vainglory (I–II 20.1).

The examples that we have been considering would suggest that the object of the action, considered as an external action, can be determined independently and prior to any consideration of the agent's aim in acting. This is indeed generally the case, for Aquinas, but it is not always so. In some cases, the agent's aim forms an essential component which must be taken into account, in order to determine the object of the action. Ordinarily, any act of killing another, carried out by a private citizen (as opposed to a soldier or public executioner) counts as murder.

But it is not murder to kill another in self-defense, because in such a case the agent's intention, to preserve her own life, determines the correct description of what is done (II–II 64.7). Similarly, it is ordinarily either theft or robbery to take what is another's (theft, if done secretly; robbery, if done by force). But if someone takes what is another's in order to sustain her own life, if this is indeed the only way in which she can do so, then the act in question does not count as either theft or robbery, because the point of the institution of property is to provide the necessities of life for all persons (II–II 66.7).[12] What is decisive in each case is the naturalness of the intention to preserve life, taken in conjunction with some consideration of what it is reasonable to expect someone to endure (II–II 64.7), or of what the point of a widespread human institution should be taken to be (II–II 66.7).

Thus, just as we cannot determine the object of an act, and distinguish it from its circumstances, prior to some normative evaluation of the different aspects of the action, so we cannot always determine the object of an act prior to some moral assessment of the agent's intention.

4. Moral Judgment and Consequentialism

Two points emerge from our assessment of Aquinas's account of the moral act. First, if Aquinas is correct, then we cannot derive a judgment about the moral value of an action from a determination of the object of the act because we cannot determine what the object of the act *is* without some prior consideration of the action, taken as a whole. Secondly, for Aquinas, there can be no formula which enables us to arrive with certainty at the correct moral assessment of individual acts. The difficulty of moral knowledge, as Aquinas understands the matter, should not be exaggerated. In most cases that he foresees, the correct assessment of a particular action will be obvious, or will follow with only a little reflection (cf. I–II 100.3). Nonetheless, it is always possible, on his terms, that we might encounter a particular action that is so difficult or complex that we cannot say with certainty whether it is right or wrong.

This latter point is worth underscoring, because it is easy to assume that Aquinas's analysis of the different components of an action is meant to provide a formula by which to determine whether a particular action is morally licit or not. In Aquinas's view, there can be no such formula, and his account of the moral act at I–II 18 is not meant to provide one. What he offers here, rather, is an analytic account of the different components of moral judgment, which is meant to indicate the different factors that must be considered in any assessment of a particular action.

If Aquinas holds that an action cannot be evaluated prior to some consideration of all its different aspects, and if, furthermore, he acknowledges that we cannot always arrive with certainty at the correct moral assessment of a particular action, then does it follow that his account of morality is a version of consequentialism? In answering this question, the first thing that must be noted is that Aquinas himself does not either endorse or reject consequentialism in so many words. He does consider the moral significance of consequences at I–II 20.5, but in my view, his remarks in this article do not settle the question of whether he should be considered to be a consequentialist as we understand the term.

At this point, we come to another question that must be addressed before we proceed. That is, how *do* we understand the term "consequentialism"? It is difficult to answer this question, because almost no one has denied that consequences have *some* moral relevance. Yet it is perhaps not too important to arrive at a definition of "consequentialism" that would satisfy everyone; it is enough, for our purposes, to arrive at some sense of the point of those theories of morality which are generally brought together under the rubric of consequentialism. In this way, we will be able to see more clearly what it would mean to describe Aquinas as a consequentialist, and more importantly, we will see what is at stake in affirming or rejecting a consequentialist account of morality.

Although consequentialism is a wider category than utilitarianism, the latter is the best known, the most influential, and probably also the earliest version of consequentialism. Thus, in order to arrive at a better understanding of consequentialism, we would do well to consider the thought of another moralist, the so-called father of utilitarianism, Jeremy Bentham.

As the title of Bentham's great work, *The Principles of Morals and Legislation,* suggests, utilitarianism began as a response to growing pressures for social and legal reform during the late 18th and early 19th centuries.[13] Bentham himself was trained as a jurist, and in the *Principles,* he attempts to place the laws of England on a rational and scientific basis by subjecting actual and proposed norms to the test of the utility principle. Thus, this book is as much a treatise on jurisprudence as it is a work of moral philosophy. The central idea of the utilitarian challenge to traditional mores, as Bentham developed it, is quite simple. The first task of the legislator, says Bentham, is to attempt to secure the well-being of every member of society; therefore, all norms should be evaluated by the test of what he calls the principle of utility, according to which an action is good if and only if it produces the greatest possible balance of happiness over unhappiness for all concerned.[14] But of course, so formulated, this criterion is *too* simple. It is one thing to assert in general terms that the first concern of the legislator should be the overall happiness of the community, but it is quite another thing to attempt to translate this ideal into a scientific method for evaluating moral and legal norms. Bentham attempts to do so by developing a formula for analysis whereby alternative courses of action in a given situation are to be assessed in terms of which one produces the greatest quantitative measure of pleasures over pains. As Henry Sidgwick would later make clear, this procedure implies that pleasures and pains are homogeneous, that is, that there are no qualitative differences among diverse pleasures or pains, and it furthermore implies that pleasures and pains can be quantified. And as Sidgwick also acknowledges, it is exceedingly difficult to carry out the latter task (although he himself attempted it), even if we grant this particular conception of mental states. Much of the subsequent debate over utilitarianism has focused on the cogency or the practicality of the "greatest happiness" principle.[15]

There is another aspect of the utilitarian account of morality that is more directly relevant to the subject of our inquiry. If particular actions are to be evaluated in terms of the overall balance of pleasures and pains that they produce, then clearly the basic moral concepts, which are correlated with generally accepted moral rules, cannot have *ultimate* validity for moral analysis. Some utilitarians have indeed attempted to argue that a utilitarian analysis can be applied to general rules, which, if so validated, should then be obeyed by individuals, but the cogency of this argument is questionable.[16] Others have admitted that there are advantages to sustaining an agreed-upon system of rules, and correspondingly, we are likely to bring about some pain through the infraction and weakening of a received norm, which should be factored into any utilitarian calculus. Nonetheless, as Sidgwick observes, this consideration does not, in itself, imply that the general norms of morality can never be broken, particularly by sophisticated and discreet persons who can appreciate the implications of what they are doing.[17] At any rate, whatever the details of particular versions of utilitarianism may be, it is clear that for the utilitarian, the norms of morality can never have ultimate and exceptionless validity.

This point is critical for understanding the significance of affirming or denying a consequentialist account of morality. We have already noted that almost no one denies that consequences have some moral significance. The critical difference between utilitarianism and other versions of consequentialism, on the one hand, and most other accounts of the moral life, on the other, lies in the kind of significance that is given to consequences. For the consequentialist, the moral evaluation of specific acts will always be determined by some assessment of consequences, as determined by one or more general criteria. The basic moral concepts, such as murder, theft, and the like, can never play anything other than a secondary and derivative role in such a system; at most, they might function as reminders of kinds of actions that generally turn out badly, on a consequentialist calculus.

For almost everyone else, on the other hand, there are at least some basic moral concepts (not necessarily the traditional ones) which are irreducibly significant for moral evaluation. Generic moral concepts of whatever kind stand in need of interpretation if they are to be applied to actual cases, and this process of interpretation and application will often include some assessment of consequences. But for most moralists, except for consequentialists, the considerations which govern the assessment of consequences, and which determine, more fundamentally, which consequences are morally relevant, will be derived from some reflection on the meaning and point of the basic moral concepts themselves. A Kantian will ask herself whether a particular dubious act does or does not involve some kind of failure to respect rational autonomy; a rights theorist will determine whether some action violates a right through a consideration of the forms of freedom that the right was meant to protect; and so on.[18]

It is at this point that we see the critical difference between Aquinas's account of morality and different versions of consequentialism. For Aquinas, like most other moralists, but unlike Bentham and his followers, the generally accepted concepts of morally significant kinds of actions (murder, theft, adultery and the like) are of basic and irreducible moral significance. Aquinas does not attempt to analyze these basic concepts in terms of more fundamental units of moral analysis, such as units of happiness, or values, or basic goods, in terms of which moral judgments can be given a more precise or certain formulation. Rather, for Aquinas, the basic moral concepts, which form the essential moral vocabulary for theologians and everyone else alike, are themselves basic units of moral analysis. Once it is determined that a particular action can be correctly described in terms of one of these generic concepts, then that fact alone may determine the moral value of the act (depending on which generic concept the act falls under).

Yet if it is the case that we cannot determine the object of the act prior to some consideration of the act as a whole, then perhaps there is no *practical* difference between Aquinas's view and some version of consequentialism. This would seem to be suggested by an interpretation of Aquinas's account of the object of the act offered by John Dedek in an influential essay published in 1979.[19] On Dedek's reading, the meaning of the basic moral concepts, as Aquinas understands them, is purely formal: so, for example, "murder" should be understood as "unjust or undue killing," "theft" as "unjust/undue taking," and so forth.

Dedek does not say that Aquinas is a consequentialist, and even if his interpretation were correct, it would not necessarily imply such a conclusion. Dedek's interpertation is based on Aquinas's discussion of the so-called sins of the patriarchs (for example, Abraham's intended killing of Isaac, discussed in the *Summa* at I-II 100.8 *ad* 3), and given this context, it would be more plausible, on Dedek's terms, to read Aquinas as an exponent of a radical version of a divine command theory of ethics.[20] Yet Dedek's interpretation would also be consistent with a reading of Aquinas as a consequentialist, on the further assumption that our human efforts to determine whether an act of killing (for example) is unjust could be made solely on the basis of an assessment of the overall balance of good and bad that would result from this particular killing. That is, on this reading, Aquinas would be a consequentialist, because the application of the basic moral notions to particular actions would be determined wholly on the grounds of considerations that could be formulated independently of any mention of those basic notions.

But in fact, this is not Aquinas's view. As we have already seen, the basic moral concepts do have a substantive meaning for him. He does not present these meanings in terms of formal definitions, but he does indicate his understanding of them by the terms in which he argues throughout the *secunda secundae*. That is, when Aquinas considers whether a specific kind of action should fall under the scope of a more general prohibition, he never argues in terms of the overall balance of good versus bad that is attained by the kind of act in question.[21] Rather, he couches his argument in terms of the *point* of the prohibition in question. Some kinds of acts, which look suspiciously like instances of (for example) murder or theft, are in fact justified, for reasons which are drawn from the point of the prohibitions in question themselves. Others, however, are not justified, because they *do* violate the point of the relevant prohibition. For example, Aquinas argues that it is not morally permissible to baptize the infant children of non-Christian parents against their (the parents') consent, because this would be a violation of natural justice, even though, on Aquinas's terms, the good that might thereby be secured, that is, the salvation of the children, would infinitely outweigh any misfortune whatever (II–II 10.12).

The point is this. Aquinas is not a consequentialist because he does not subject the basic moral concepts to any sort of reductive analysis, in terms of which moral judgments can be given a more precise meaning or a more certain foundation. This is significant for us, in turn, because it helps us to see what is at stake in either affirming or rejecting some version of consequentialism. It is not the case that Aquinas's analysis brings more certainty to individual moral judgments than does consequentialism; to the contrary, most consequentialists would assert what Aquinas more than once denies, namely, that we can arrive at a certain moral judgment about every specific moral act. Nor is it the case that Aquinas's account is more stringent than consequentialist alternatives. Again, it is at least arguable that the reverse is the case. Consequentialism is generally associated with perfectibilism, the moral doctrine that one is obliged to do the greatest and most perfect good that one can do. Aquinas not only does not claim this, he denies it (I–II 19.10).

The implication of affirming the independent significance of the object of an action, for Aquinas, is that moral judgment must be carried out in terms of the meanings of the basic moral concepts, such as murder and legitimate execution, for example, which form the framework for moral judgment and discourse for the whole society. Our understanding of these basic notions can be refined, and we can and do change our minds, individually and collectively, about the moral quality of some kinds of actions. Yet we cannot "get behind" the basic moral concepts to some simpler and more fundamental units of moral analysis. The wisdom and the commitments to the good that are embodied in these basic notions set the fundamental terms for moral judgement, whether that wisdom and those commitments are seen as coming from the human community and natural reason alone, or we trace them ultimately, as Aquinas himself would do, to the wisdom and love of God.

Notes

1. Richard A. McCormick, "*Veritatis Splendor* and Moral Theology," *America* 169:13 (Oct. 30, 1993), pp. 8–11, 10.

2. The literature generated by this debate is enormous. Bernard Hoose offers a helpful and sympathetic exposition of proportionalism in his *Proportionalism: The American Debate and Its European Roots* (Washington, D.C.: Georgetown University Press, 1987), and John Finnis discusses the same issues from the deontologists' perspective in *Moral Absolutes: Tradition, Revision and Truth* (Washington, D.C.: Catholic University of America Press, 1991). Germain Grisez has commented on the encyclical; see his "Revelation vs. Dissent," *The Tablet* 247 (Oct. 16, 1993), pp. 1329–31.

3. Richard P. McBrien, "Teaching the Truth," *Christian Century* (Oct. 20, 1993), pp. 1004–5.

4. Lawrence S. Cunningham, et al., "*Veritatis Splendor*," *Commonweal* (Oct. 22, 1993), pp. 11–18.

5. These and subsequent references to Aquinas's work are taken from *Summa Theologiae*; all translations are my own.

6. Aquinas is here quoting, approvingly, pseudo-Dionysius's *The Divine Names*.

7. This point is frequently made by philosophers who deal with action or the philosophy of language; the most influential of such treatments would include G.E.M. Anscombe, *Intention*, 2nd ed., (Ithaca: Cornell University Press, 1963) and the essays of Donald Davidson on action theory, many of which are collected in Donald Davidson, *Essays on Actions and Events* (Oxford: Clarendon University Press 1980/1982). Eric D'Arcy offers a very useful discussion of this point seen in the context of moral theology in his *Human Acts: An Essay in Their Moral Evaluation* (Oxford: Clarendon Press, 1963).

8. For a helpful discussion of Aquinas's views on the general logical

problem of knowledge of particulars, see Anthony Kenny, *Aquinas on Mind* (London: Routledge, 1993), pp. 111–18.

9. This point has been made by more than one contemporary moral philosopher; see, for example, J. M. Brennan, *The Open-Texture of Moral Concepts* (New York: Barnes and Noble, 1977), and Julius Kovesi, *Moral Notions* (London: Routledge, 1967). I have also defended this account of moral judgment, in considerably more detail, in *Moral Action and Christian Ethics* (Cambridge: Cambridge University Press, forthcoming).

10. Alan Donagan, *The Theory of Morality* (Chicago: The University of Chicago Press, 1977), pp. 112–42. Donagan's treatment of the issues discussed in this section is extremely helpful, and I am indebted to it at a number of points.

11. There is an ambiguity that should be noted here. It is one thing to know, or to reasonably believe, that an action falls under the description of an intrinsically evil kind of action. In such a case, the agent knows the relevant features of the action which bring it under the category in question, and furthermore, she has no reason to believe that there is any other aspect of the act which would alter its description. It is something else to draw the further conclusion that the act is, in fact, morally wrong; the agent may not believe that an act of kind X is wrong, or she may believe, wrongly, that some feature of the act changes its moral description. Aquinas does not, in fact, believe that a mistaken judgement of the latter sort excuses; see I-II 19.5,6. However, it seems to me that he is too quick to draw this conclusion.

12. This passage is often taken as an early statement of the principle of double effect, but in my view, that would be a mistake. Aquinas does not say that the causal relationship between what the agent aims at, and what she does, is morally determinative; rather, it is the nature of her intention, seen within a context of what we can reasonably expect of ourselves and one another, that is decisive.

13. Jeremy Bentham, *The Principles of Morals and Legislation,* with an introduction by Laurence J. LaFleur (New York: Hafner Press, 1948/1989).

14. Ibid., pp. 1–7.

15. Henry Sidgwick, *The Methods of Ethics*, 7th ed. (New York: Hackett Press, 1981), pp. 123–98 and pp. 460–95.

16. This position has often been traced to John Stuart Mill, but this seems not to have been Mill's view; see the discussion in Donagan, pp. 193–94.

17. On both points, i.e., the utility of generally respecting moral rules, and the legitimacy of breaking them, secretly or not, see Sidgwick, pp. 475–95.

18. There is no one contrast position to consequentialism, but in addition to Aquinas's own account (as I argue below), Kantianism, classical human rights theories, and most forms of intuitionism would all fit the description that I have just offered. On the other hand, it is not so clear to me that the so-called

deontological theories of Grisez and Finnis would answer to this description. For Grisez and Finnis and their followers, the fundamental units of moral analysis are basic goods, such as life and knowledge, which are self-evidently such to all mature persons. Generic moral concepts can by analyzed without remainder in terms of forms of behavior which either tend to, or absolutely do not respect these basic goods. Thus, the Grisez/Finnis theory of morality is closer to consequentialism than it is to Kant's classical deontological theory of morality; what saves it from being consequentialist without remainder is the stipulation that there are some kinds of consequences, namely, the destruction of basic goods, which are never morally permissible. In addition to Finnis's *Moral Absolutes,* cited above, see Germain Grisez, *The Way of the Lord Jesus,* Vol 1, *Christian Moral Principles* (Chicago: Franciscan Herald Press, 1983); John Finnis, *Natural Law and Natural Rights* (Oxford: Clarendon Press, 1980), *Fundamentals of Ethics* (Washington D.C.: Georgetown University Press, 1983); and Germain Grisez, Joseph Boyle, and John Finnis, "Practical Principles, Moral Truth and Ultimate Ends," *American Journal of Jurisprudence* 32 (1987), pp. 99–151.

19. John Dedek, "Intrinsically Evil Acts: An Historical Study of the Mind of St. Thomas," *The Thomist* 43 (July, 1979), pp. 385–413.

20. This does, in fact, appear to be Dedek's view, although he does not say so explicitly; see Dedek, pp. 401–06.

21. As an examination of I–II 100.8 *ad* 3 indicates, Aquinas attempts to justify even the so-called sins of the patriarchs in this way; that is, he does not just appeal to the power of God, as Supreme Legislator, to dispense from the natural law, but he argues, as far as possible, in terms of the point of the relevant prohibitions. Thus it would not have been murder had Abraham killed Isaac at God's command, because God has supreme authority over life and death, just as the leaders of a human community have authority over the life of malefactors. Ultimately we all die at God's command, and yet we cannot say that God is the murderer of us all. Dedek does recognize that Aquinas argues in this way, but he does not seem to me to appreciate the full significance of this fact; see Dedek, p. 404.

16. *Veritatis Splendor:*
A Revisionist Perspective

Charles E. Curran

This chapter first appeared in *Open Catholicism: The Tradition at Its Best: Essays in Honor of Gerard S. Sloyan,* ed. David Efroymson and John Raines (Collegeville, Minn.: Liturgical Press, 1997).

Pope John Paul II's encyclical, *Veritatis Splendor,* officially signed on August 6, 1993, has the "central theme" of the "reaffirmation of the universality and immutability of the moral commandments, particularly those which prohibit always and without exception intrinsically evil acts" (n. 115).[1]

The pope directs his remarks primarily to the state of Catholic moral theology today, but since the Catholic approach always saw its moral teaching affecting society as a whole the encyclical makes important remarks about life in the world today. The pope had publicly mentioned his intention of writing such an encyclical on August 1, 1987, the second centenary of the death of Alphonsus Liguori, the patron saint of moral theologians and confessors (n. 5). Rumors about the preparation, the primary authors, the central themes, and even the possible scrapping of the whole idea surfaced in the intervening years. The pope himself refers to the encyclical as "long awaited" and proposes as one reason for the delay that the *Catechism of the Catholic Church* should be published first (n. 5).

1. Overview of the Encyclical

The encyclical is addressed to "the venerable brothers in the episcopate who share with me the responsibility of safeguarding 'sound teaching'" (n. 5).

The occasion for the new encyclical is the "new situation" within the Catholic Church itself. "It is so longer a matter of limited and occasional dissent, but of an overall and systematic calling into question of traditional moral doctrines on the basis of certain anthropological and ethical presuppositions" (n. 4). These dissenting positions are heard even in seminaries and theological faculties with regard to questions of the greatest importance for the life of the church and souls (n. 4). This reality constitutes "a genuine crisis" for the church (n. 5).

At the root of these unacceptable presuppositions causing the present crisis are currents of thought which end by detaching human freedom from its essential and constitutive relationship to truth (n. 4). This explains the whole thrust of the encyclical, with its title of the "Splendor of Truth" and with the very first paragraph of the introduction citing 1 Pt 1:22 about the need for "obedience to the truth." The whole structure of the document with its three chapters follows logically and coherently from the understanding of the occasion for it and the root causes of the problem.

The first chapter involves an extended reflection on the story in Mt 19:16ff. of the rich young man who came to Jesus with the question, "What good must I do to have eternal life?" Jesus' response is to obey the commandments and to give up all his possessions and come follow Jesus. This comparatively long biblical reflection involves a somewhat new approach in papal teachings on moral matters. Catholic moral theology is traditionally based on human reason and natural law. However, similar but shorter reflections on biblical passages can be found in other encyclicals of the pope.[2] The pope uses this scriptural passage to point out that God's revelation includes moral commandments and the moral life is intimately connected with faith. However, in no way does the pope abandon the Catholic emphasis on natural law, as the second chapter makes abundantly clear.

The real import of the first chapter comes from its relationship to the purpose of the entire document. "Jesus' conversation with the rich young man continues in a sense in every period of history including our own" (n. 25). The church ('the pillar and bulwark of the truth' – 2 Tm 3:15) continues the teaching role of Jesus with the "task of authentically interpreting the word of God...entrusted only (sic) to those charged with the church's living magisterium, whose authority is exercised in the name of Jesus Christ" (n. 27).[3] These quotations come from the end of the first chapter and make the point that the pope today continues the work of Jesus in teaching the commandments to guide the moral life of all the followers of Jesus.

The way in which scripture is used depends on the purpose of the one using it. Here the pope's purpose has shaped and limited the use of the scripture. The moral life is understood primarily in terms of commandments (to the exclusion and underplaying of other elements, such as the change of heart, virtues, vision, attitudes, moral imagination, goals, etc.), and the role of Jesus and consequently of the church is reduced to teaching commandments. Jesus as exemplar or paradigm is left out. The risen Jesus through the Spirit as the enabler and empowerer of the Christian life is not mentioned. The moral life itself is understood in light of a legal model, with the pope following the role of Jesus proposing the commandments "with the reaffirmation of the universality and immutability of the moral commandments, particularly those prohibiting always and without exception intrinsically evil acts" (n. 115).

The second chapter has an entirely different feel and approach. The pope, carrying on the moral teaching function of Jesus, points out and condemns certain interpretations of Christian morality which are not consistent with sound teaching. The pope explicitly denies any intention "to impose upon the faithful any particular theological system, still less a philosophical one" (n. 29). However, in reality John Paul II strongly reasserts the nineteenth and twentieth century Neo-Scholasticism of the manuals of moral theology within his more personalistic framework.

The general error pointed out in this section is a failure to recognize the importance of truth in moral theology, which absolutizes freedom or conscience, cutting off their basic relationsip to truth. The pope specifically mentions and condemns the most important aspects of the so-called revisionist school of Catholic moral theology (he does not use that term) that has been evolving since the Second Vatican Council—an autonomous ethic, the charge of physicalism made against the accepted

Catholic teaching in sexual and medical ethics, the theory of fundamental option, and the ethical theory of proportionalism. All these in their own way have called into question the existence of some intrinsically evil acts. *Veriatis Splendor* in this chapter also strongly criticizes in the broader context the absolutization of freedom, false autonomy, subjectivism, individualism, and relativism.

Chapter three develops a number of related points. The first stresses the bond between freedom and truth. Commitment to the truth above all shows forth in the willingness of people to give their lives for the truth of the gospel of Jesus. Although martyrdom represents the high point of witness to moral truth, and one to which few people are called, all Christians must daily be ready to make a consistent witness at the cost of suffering and sacrifice (n. 93). Second, universal and unchangeable norms are at the service of persons and of the society, thus showing the necessary connection between freedom and truth. Only a morality which acknowledges certain norms and rights as valid always, everywhere, and without exception can guarantee an ethical foundation of social coexistence on both the national and international levels (nn. 95–101). Third, the chapter recalls that God's grace transforms and strengthens weak and sinful human beings to be able to obey God's law (nn. 102–105). A final section on morality and evangelization contains an important section dealing with the roles of the magisterium and of moral theologians who are called to be an example of loyal assent, both internal and external, to the magisterium's teaching (nn. 106–117).

Reaction to the encyclical has followed a somewhat predictable course.[4] Proponents of what has been called revisionism in Catholic moral theology have tended to be quite negative,[5] whereas more conservative moral theologians have been quite positive, although some want the pope to go even further to a definitive and infallible magisterial judgment on the received teaching on intrinsically evil acts, and to the same kind of judgment on certain understandings of faith and revelation which are even more fundamental.[6] Some more evangelically rooted scholars have lauded the pope's great emphasis on scripture and the gospel, but perhaps they do not give enough importance to how strongly the second chapter of the document holds on to Neo-Scholastic philosophy.[7] Feminists readily find fault with the methodology involved.[8] A good number have been appreciative of the pope's dealing with the broader societal issues.[9] All of us interpret and react to the document in the light of our own understandings and interests, but we all must be careful to try to understand precisely what the pope is saying before entering into dialogue with him. In this spirit I recognize that I am coming from a revisionist position and have disagreed over the years with papal teaching on intrinsically evil acts and dissent in the church. One commentator has pointed out that the encyclical is directed at my work.[10] However, I also find myself in agreement with many points made in the encyclical.

2. Positive Evaluation

I find myself in agreement with many of the pope's problems with some contemporary ethical thinking, with the positive points he makes against them, and with the applications especially in the area of social ethics. Moral truth is most important. Freedom and conscience can never be absolutized. There are many things one should not do (nn. 35–53). The Catholic tradition in the past often failed to give enough importance to freedom, as exemplified in its long-standing opposition to religious freedom and the continuing problems with academic freedom. However, as the twentieth century developed, the Catholic Church in reaction to the danger of totalitarianism began to give a greater role to human freedom. A very significant development occurred in Pope John XXIII's writings within two years. In *Mater et Magistra* in 1961 he claimed that the ideal social order was founded on the values of truth, justice, and love.[11] In *Pacem in Terris* in 1963 he added freedom to this triad.[12] Freedom is very significant, but it must be seen in its relationship to other values. The pope in *Veritatis Splendor* is concentrating on freedom's relationship to truth, but it is fair to say he is not denying the other important relationships of freedom with justice and charity. One is not free to deny fundamental human rights.

Just as freedom cannot be absolutized, so too conscience cannot be absolutized. Conscience cannot make something right or wrong (nn. 54–64). Adolph Eichmann claimed that he only followed his conscience, but he was rightly convicted of crimes against humanity. Conscience is called to recognize and respond to moral truth.

Intimately connected with the absolutization of freedom or conscience is the false autonomy of the individual. The individual is not autonomous in the sense that the individual makes something right or wrong on her own. Here too, however, the Catholic tradition has not given enough importance to the role of creativity and the initiative of the individual. But one cannot go to the other extreme and proclaim the absolute autonomy of the individual. Any theistic morality sees the individual in relationship to and dependent on God.

The challenge is to avoid both a one-sided autonomy or a one-sided heteronomy. *Veritatis Splendor* deals well with this aspect of autonomy in the first part of the second chapter (nn. 38–42). To its credit the Catholic tradition, with its emphasis on participation, has been able to provide a very satisfactory approach to this question. Too often the issue is proposed in terms of a competition between the divine and the human. If you have 100 points to assign to both, then you might assign eighty to God and twenty to the human. But maybe human beings should have more and God less. The traditional Catholic emphasis on participation and mediation as mentioned in the encyclical avoids such an either-or approach. The glory of God is the human person come alive. God wants us to attain our happiness and our perfection. The basic insight of Thomas Aquinas well illustrates this approach. In the Second part of the Summa, Aquinas treats of the human being. The human being is an image of God because, like God, she is endowed with intellect, free will, and the power of self-determination.[13] The human person imitates God by using her intellect, free will, and the power of self-determination. Traditional Catholic moral theology, following the teaching of Thomas Aquinas, sees the natural law as the participation of the eternal law in the rational creature. Human reason reflecting on God's created human nature can arrive at the plan of God for us which involves our own fulfillment.[14] All theists and even some nontheists would join the Catholic tradition in denying the absolute autonomy of the human being. But the Catholic tradition does not want to embrace a heteronomy which downplays the place of self-direction and human fulfillment.

Likewise, the pope properly points out the related danger of individualism in our society (n. 33). The absolutization of freedom, conscience, and autonomy logically lead to individualism. The individual becomes the center of all reality, and not enough importance is given to the community in general, the various communities to which we all belong, and the relationships that tie us to other human beings. In the past, again, the Catholic tradition has not given enough importance to the individual, and sometimes in the name of community restricted the role and rights of the individual. Think of the acceptance of torture in some cases and the failure to recognize the right of the defendant not to incriminate oneself. Until this century it was universally held that the state could and should use capital punishment to protect itself, but now many Catholics, recognizing more the dignity of the person, strongly oppose capital punishment. A greater emphasis is being given to the rights of the individual vis-à-vis the state, but contemporary Catholic thought, in keeping with the best of its own tradition, rightly rejects individualism. In the United States society today, many are criticizing American individualism in the name of a more communitarian understanding of human anthropology.[15] The Catholic tradition strongly supports such a communitarian critique of individualism.

Subjectivism logically follows from all the above-mentioned approaches. The pope correctly condemns the subjectivism that makes the subject the center of right and wrong and does not give enough significance to objective reality (n. 32). Here again the Catholic tradition in the past has not given enough importance to the subject, and many recent developments in Catholic theology and philosophy have embraced the turn to the subject, but this does not entail a radical moral subjectivism.

This radical subjectivism often appears in our society, but without much philosophical grounding. The morality accepted by many people today proclaims that you do your thing and I'll do my thing. Just don't interfere with each other. Such subjective individualism destroys any possibility of a community of shared truths and values. To have a community, one needs such shared moral values. The pope rightly points out there are rights that are always and everywhere to be acknowledged and protected. There are actions such as torture, arbitrary imprisonment, and treating workers as mere instruments of profit that should never be done (nn. 95–97). The dangers of individualism and subjectivism are present in our contemporary American society.

Finally, John Paul II points out the danger of relativism for human social living (nn. 96–101). The Catholic tradition by definition stands opposed to relativism. Catholic means "universal," and the pope insists on the existence of universal principles and norms. The danger in the Catholic tradition has been not to give enough importance to diversity in all its different forms. Think, for example, of the insistence on the universal language for liturgical prayer before Vatican II, so that almost no Catholic understood the language of the Eucharist. The Catholic emphasis on universality too easily claimed universality for what was a historically or culturally conditioned reality. Feminism reminds us how easy it was for those in power to impose patriarchy in the name of universality.

One of the most significant debates in contemporary ethics focuses on the possibility of universality in ethics, with many either theoretically or practically denying the possibility of such universality.[16] However, the Catholic tradition, with its emphasis on the one God who is Creator, Redeemer, and Sanctifier of all, can never accept a relativism. We are brothers and sisters of all other human beings and called to live together with them in peace and harmony. In the midst of the pluralism and diversity of our world, universalism is more chastened than in the past and more difficult to ground and explain. I think that the pope tends to gloss over too easily some of the objections to universalism, too readily grounds it in Thomistic natural law, and at times claims too much for it. However, the Catholic tradition has correctly insisted on universality.

The signs of the times also demand some universality. We experience the lack of unity in many countries in the world, including our own. Religious, ethnic, and tribal differences are the cause of war and disintegration in many nations. In our own United States' society, the divisions based on color and economic class are evident in every one of our cities. In our world with its growing interrelatedness, we badly need to be able to communicate with one another despite religious, linguistic, ethnic, and cultural differences. In many ways the challenge to our society today is how to achieve unity in the midst of the great diversity that exists on all levels.

3. Negative Evaluations

My strong disagreements with the papal letter center on his understanding of and approach to contemporary Catholic moral theology, and what might be described as the churchly aspect of moral theology as distinguished from Catholic social ethics. Having already identified myself as a revisionist Catholic moral theologian, one would expect such differences to be there. Naturally, I disagree with the position that condemns the revisionist developments in moral theology, but I am even more disturbed by other aspects of the papal document.

1. The Role and Understanding of Law. The first objection comes from the moral model which the pope proposes in *Veritatis Splendor.* Here John Paul II understands morality primarily on the basis of a legal model. Such an approach, which characterized the manuals of moral theology in vogue until very recent times, sees morality primarily in terms of obedience to the law or the commandments of God. No one can doubt that *Veritatis Splendor* employs such a model. The very first paragraph emphasizes the need for obedience to the truth, but recognizes that such obedience is not always easy. The pericope of the rich young man stresses Jesus as the teacher proposing the commandments that are to be obeyed. The first and longest of the four parts of chapter two deals with freedom and the law (nn. 35–53). Chapter two especially emphasizes the role of the natural law. Positive precepts of the natural law are "universally binding" and "unchanging." The negative precepts of the natural law oblige always and in every circumstance—*semper et pro semper* (n. 52). The third chapter continues this approach with its emphasis on laws and commands and the church's firmness in defending the universal and unchanging moral norms (n. 96).

In the judgment of many, the legal model is not the best and most adequate model for moral theology or any ethics. At the very minimum the legal model cannot adequately cover all the moral decisions that a person makes. In fact, the vast majority of moral decisions are not made on the basis of existing laws. Law directly enters into comparatively few of the moral decisions by which we live our lives. In addition, the legal model tends to restrict moral considerations only to acts and forgets about the more important realities of change of heart, vision, attitudes, dispositions, etc. Thomas Aquinas did not follow a legal model, but rather a teleological model, based on what is the ultimate end of human beings. For Aquinas, the ultimate end of human beings is happiness, and actions are good if they bring one to that end and evil if they prevent one's arriving at that end. Reality, of course, is quite complex so there exists not only the ultimate end but also other ends which are not ultimate and interrelated with one another. In addition, Thomas Aquinas developed the moral life primarily in terms of human powers and habits and only brings in law at the end of his discussion of what we call fundamental moral theology.[17] The manuals of moral theology, the textbooks in the field before Vatican II, did adopt a legal model. Much has been said about the legal model, but for our present purposes it suffices to point out the inadequacy of the model and the fact that Thomas Aquinas himself adopted a different approach.

One might defend the legal model in *Veritatis Splendor* precisely because the pope is dealing primarily with the existence of universal and immutable moral commandments, especially those which prohibit always and without exception intrinsically evil acts. However, at the very minimum the encyclical should have pointed out that the legal model is not the most adequate model for moral theology, and this document is dealing only with one aspect of moral theology. Neither explicitly nor implicitly does the pope make such an admission. *Veritatis Splendor* thus gives the impression that it is describing the model for moral theology in general.

Ironically, someone in the Catholic tradition using the legal model tends to weaken the basic assertion of the entire encyclical that there is no opposition between freedom and law. Historically, the manuals of moral theology, with their legal model ever since the seventeenth century, and later debates over probabilism tended to posit an opposition between law and freedom. This assertion needs further explanation.

The Catholic tradition as illustrated by Thomas Aquinas has always insisted on an intrinsic morality. Something is commanded because it is good. For Aquinas the ultimate end of human beings is happiness. Morality involves what is good for me as a person and ultimately makes me flourish. There is no opposition between freedom and moral obligation, because the moral obligation is based on what is good for the individual. This is the central point to which the pope so frequently returns in his document. However, in the manuals of moral theology ever since the probabilism controversy, a greater opposition rather than harmonious agreement exists between freedom and law. Probabilism maintains that one may follow a truly probable opinion going against the existence of law, even if the opinion favoring the existence of the law is more probable. The so-called reflex principle used to defend this position holds that a doubtful law does not oblige—an adage more attuned to human law than anything else. The individual starts out with freedom and this freedom can only be taken away by a certain law.[18] Ironically, the law model, as it was employed in the manuals of Catholic moral theology in the light of the probabilism controversy, emphasized the tension and apparent opposition between freedom and law, rather than the harmony which the pope wants to emphasize.

2. Laws which Always and Everywhere Oblige. The major thrust of the encyclical insists on universal, immutable moral commandments which prohibit always and without exception intrinsically evil acts. In this context note that the pope never cites the fifth commandment, "Thou shalt not kill." Everyone recognizes that killing is not always and everywhere wrong. We have justified killing in cases of self-defense and war. In fact, after much discussion and nuancing the manuals of moral theology came to the conclusion that the intrinsically evil act which is always forbidden is the following: direct killing of the innocent on one's own authority. Thus we allowed indirect killing, killing in self-defense or in war, and capital punishment.[19]

Notice the difference between the two. Killing is a physical act which in some circumstances can be permitted. The second rule tries to account for all the possible justifying circumstances and thus states the norm that admits of no exceptions. But one has to circumscribe quite severely the generic "no killing." The pope himself in this document does not cite this very specific absolute norm that was developed in Catholic moral theology.

What then is the papal example of the universal, immutable condemnation of an act that is always and everywhere wrong? The answer: murder. Thus in the passage about the rich young man in Matthew, Jesus begins the commandments with, "You shall not murder" (n. 13). All would agree that murder is always wrong because by definition murder is unjustified killing. Thus we have here three different types of norms dealing with killing. The pope cites only the very formal norm of no murder.

But there is a problem in *Veritatis Splendor* from the pope's own perspective because of a fourth formulation that is proposed. The pope wants to illustrate the point that there are intrinsically evil acts which are always and *per se* such on account of their very object and quite apart from the intention of the agent and circumstances. He quotes the *Pastoral Constitution on the Church in the Modern World,* paragraph

27, to illustrate this thesis (n. 80). The quote begins: "Whatever is hostile to life itself such as any kind of homicide...." However, homicide is not an intrinsically evil act. Homicide is the physical act of killing a human being. Our language recognizes that homicide can be justifiable in certain circumstances.

But the problem might not come primarily from the pope. The official Latin version of the encyclical, in its citation from the *Pastoral Constitution on the Church in the Modern World,* uses the world *homicidium.*[20] *Homicidium* in the Latin can refer either to murder or to homicide. As mentioned above, in this case the pope is citing a text from the *Pastoral Constitution of the Church in the Modern World* of the Second Vatican Council. Two unofficial English translations of the Vatican II documents translate *homicidium* as "murder"[21] However, the official translation of the papal encyclical that came from the Vatican uses the word "homicide." The error might rest with the translator and the approval of that translation by the Vatican. However, at the very minimum this goes to show how intricate and difficult it is to speak about norms that are always and everywhere obliging without any exception.

In fact, the list of actions found originally in the *Pastoral Constitution on the Church in the Modern World* and quoted in *Veritatis Splendor* contains some actions which are not always and everywhere wrong. Both documents include abortion under the category of "what is hostile to life itself." However, the Catholic tradition has always recognized the existence of some conflict situations and concluded that direct abortion is always wrong. Indirect abortion can be justified for a proportionate reason so that abortion is not always and everywhere wrong. One would have to be stretching the point beyond belief to claim that the original clause of "whatever is hostile to life itself" means that homicide is murder and abortion is direct murder. The reality is that any homicide or abortion is hostile to life itself, but in some circumstances might be justified.

The second category of those actions in both documents which are now claimed by the pope to be always and everywhere wrong concerns "whatever violates the integrity of the human person such as mutilation...." However, Catholic moral theology has consistently recognized justified mutilation. In fact, the primary precept in medical ethics justifies a mutilation of a part of the body for the sake of the whole.[22] Here again, one cannot appeal to the opening clause "whatever violates the integrity of the human person" to show that the mutilation in such a context excluded medical mutilation for the good of the whole person. If the heading were the dignity or total good of the human person then one could make such a claim. By definition all mutilation goes against the integrity of the person, but the Catholic tradition does not say that all mutilation is wrong. The pope's efforts to uphold laws that are intrinsically or always and without exception wrong by reason of the object is fraught with difficulties. There are such actions when the act is described in merely formal terms, such as murder. One could also make the case that there are such acts when the significant circumstances are included. In reality, *Veritatis Splendor* itself does not succeed in making a consistent case to prove its own position about acts that are always and intrinsically evil by reason of the object alone.

3. Evaluation of Contemporary Moral Theology. Veritatis Splendor strongly disagrees with and condemns many of the developments in Catholic moral theology since Vatican II and stands opposed to the revisionist moral theology in general.

However, *Veritatis Splendor* distorts and does not accurately describe the various positions attributed to so-called revisionist moral theologians. The first part of the second chapter disagrees with a school of autonomous ethics which first arose in Germany (nn. 36, 37). I have disagreed with the name autonomous but accept the reality proposed in the sense that the moral content for life in this world is the same for Christians as for non-Christians. In my judgment, this position is in keeping with the traditional assertion that the Christian life brings the human to its perfection and fulfillment. Like *Veritatis Splendor* I have also disagreed with the contention that the scripture provides only *parenesis,* or exhortation, as some hold.[23] However, the supporters of autonomous ethics in the Catholic tradition would strongly disagree with the following description of their position. "Such norms...would be the expression of a law which man (sic) in an autonomous manner lays down for himself and which has its source exclusively in human reason. In no way could God be considered the author of this law except in the sense that human reason exercises its autonomy in setting down laws by virtue of a primordial and total mandate given to man by God" (n. 36).

Veritatis Splendor, in the same first part of chapter two, points out that some Catholic moral theologians have disagreed with the teachings of the hierarchical magisterium in the area of sexual morality because of their "physicalism" and "naturalistic" argumentation (n. 47). Such a statement is correct. In my opinion physicalism is the *a priori* identification of the human or the moral aspect with the physical, natural, or biological process. So far, so good. But the pope goes on to explain this theory in this way. "A freedom which claims to be absolute ends up treating the human body as a raw datum devoid of any meaning and moral values until freedom has shaped it in accordance with its design. Consequently, human nature and the body appear as presuppositions or preambles, materially necessary for freedom to make its choice, yet extrinsic to the person, the subject, and the human act....The finalities of these inclinations would be merely 'physical' goods, called by some *premoral.* To refer to them, in order to find in them rational indications with regard to the order of morality, would be to expose oneself to the accusation of physicalism or biologism. In this way of thinking, the tension between freedom and a nature conceived of in a reductive way is resolved by a division within man (sic) himself" (n. 48).

Those who charge the hierarchical magisterium's teaching on sexuality with physicalism do not "treat the human body as a raw datum devoid of any meaning." The physical is one aspect of the moral or the fully human. The moral or the fully human must embrace all the aspects of the human – the physical and the spiritual, the sociological and the psychological, the eugenic and the hygienic, etc. In keeping with the Catholic tradition, one should never be guilty of a reductionism that reduces the fully human to just one aspect of the human, no matter what that aspect is. Yes, there are times when the physical is the same as the moral and the truly human, but this needs further justification to make the point.[24] In this very citation the pope contradicts his own assertion. *Veritatis Splendor* refers to this physical aspect as physical or premoral goods. Note the word "goods." They are not just "raw datum" or "extrinsic to the person." Those making the charge of physicalism take seriously the position of Pius XII that the physical and the bodily exist to serve the higher spiritual good of the person.[25] That one in theory can interfere with the physical or biological process because of the good of the total person as a whole seems to be very much in accord with any kind of personalism. But at the very least *Veritatis Splendor* distorts the position of those who characterize hierarchical Catholic sexual teaching as guilty of physicalism. We do not absolutize freedom and we do not deny any value or meaning to the physical. In our judgment, the hierarchical magisterium in this matter has absolutized the physical and the biological at the expense of the truly and fully human.

The second part of chapter two deals with the relationship between conscience and truth. However, John Paul II also dealt with that question earlier in the encyclical. The pope claims that those who invoke the criterion of conscience as "being at peace with oneself" (he puts the words in quotation marks) are guilty of absolutizing freedom, forgetting the claim of truth, and subjectivism (n. 32).

I have proposed a theory of conscience which "attempts to explain in a more systematic and reflective way the traditionally accepted notion that joy and peace mark the good conscience which is the adequate criterion of good moral judgment and decision."[26] I explicitly point out that my approach disagrees with the position of the manuals that the judgment of conscience is based on conformity with the truth "out there." I developed this theory in dialogue with the transcendental approaches of Karl Rahner and Bernard Lonergan. However, I insist that one's judgment has to attain the true and the real value. I do put great emphasis on the subject but insist that "thus we have established the radical identity between genuine objectivity and authentic subjectivity."[27] Such an approach is proposed as a theory, and others might readily disagree with it, but it does not "exalt freedom to such an extent that it becomes an absolute" nor "adopt a radically subjectivistic conception of moral judgment" (n. 32).

In the second part of chapter two on conscience, it seems that the pope's insistence on the relationship between conscience and truth has influenced him to take a position which at the very least is in opposition to the generally accepted position in Catholic moral theology. *Veritatis Splendor* states: "It is possible that the evil done as the result of invincible ignorance or a nonculpable error of judgment may not be imputable to the agent; but even in this case it does not cease to be an evil" (n. 63). Thomas Aquinas maintained that invincible ignorance renders the act involuntary and excuses from sin. In other words, the evil act done in invincible ignorance is never imputable to the agent. The encyclical does not go as far as Aquinas and simply says that it "may not be imputable to the agent." However, St. Alphonsus Liguori, the patron saint of moral theologians and confessors, goes even further than Aquinas. Alphonsus maintains that an act done out of invincible ignorance is not only not imputable but it is actually meritorious. This opinion of Alphonsus became the more common posiiton among Catholic theologians.[28] Louis Vereecke, now an emeritus professor of the history of moral theology at the Academia Alfonsiana in Rome and a consultor to the Holy Office, concludes his article on conscience in Alphonsus Liguori by claiming that Alphonsus' moral doctrine on conscience embraces three values – the importance of truth, the importance of reason and conscience, and the importance of freedom.[29] By so emphasizing and perhaps even absolutizing the relationship of conscience to truth, *Veritatis Splendor* not only does not accept the position of Alphonsus, but does not even accept the position of Thomas Aquinas that does not go as far as Alphonsus.

The third part of chapter three addresses the theory of the fundamental option. Here also the theory is distorted. For example, the encyclical speaks of the theory as separating "the fundamental option from concrete kinds of behavior" (n. 67, see also n. 70). The theory of fundamental option distinguishes the different levels of human freedom and of transcendental and categorical acts, but it does not separate them. As Joseph Fuchs, who has written much on the fundamental option, points out, the encyclical distorts the meaning of the theory by failing to recognize that the fundamental option and categorical acts happen on different levels, and thus the fundamental option does not occur in the area of reflex consciousness.[30]

The fourth part of chapter three deals with the moral act, insists on acts that are intrinsically evil by reason of their object, and condemns teleological and proportionalist theories which hold "that it is impossible to qualify as morally evil according to its species—its 'object'—the deliberate choice of certain kinds of behavior or specific acts apart from a consideration of the intention for which the choice is made or the totality of the foreseeable consequences of that act for all persons concerned" (n. 79). On a number of occasions the pope points out that a good intention is not sufficient to determine the morality of an act (nn. 67, 78). But no Catholic moral theologian I know has ever claimed that the intention alone suffices to determine the morality of an act.[31] Above, I pointed out that as a revisionist I accept some acts as always and everywhere wrong if the significant circumstances (not the totality of the foreseeable consequences) are included.

I have no doubt that the pope disagrees with all these recently developed theories in Catholic moral theology, but the encyclical tends to distort them and thus does not reflect their true meaning. In a certain sense, they are made into straw people which then are much easier to reject. However, this is not the worst distortion in the encyclical about the present state of Catholic moral theology.

The pope claims that the "root of these presuppositions [of the dissenting Catholic moral theologians] is the more or less obvious influence of currents of thought which end by detaching human freedom from its essential and constitutive relationship to truth" (n. 4). This sentence is found in the opening introduction to the entire document. The introduction to chapter two points out "these tendencies are at one in lessening or even denying the dependence of freedom on truth" (n. 34). Note some qualification in these statements, but the fundamental problem the pope has with revisionist Catholic moral theologians is their tendency to detach or lessen human freedom's relationship to truth. Such an assertion itself is not accurate. I know no Catholic moral theologian who absolutizes freedom or detaches conscience from truth. The real question remains the proverbial one: What is truth?

As a result of this misreading of the present state of Catholic moral theology, the pope apparently sees no difference between Catholic revisionist moral theologians and the proponents of absolute freedom, conscience separated from truth, individualism, subjectivism, and relativism. Non-Catholic colleagues or any fair-minded interpreter of the present state of Catholic moral theology would readily recognize that revisionist Catholic moral theologians are not absolutizing freedom or conscience and are not supporting individualism, subjectivism, and relativism. Catholic revisionist moral theologians strongly agree with the pope in opposing these positions. That is why I made it a point earlier in this essay to stress my strong agreement with the pope on these points.

All recognize that the pope strongly disagrees with and condemns revisionist Catholic moral positions, but the problem here is the understanding of revisionist moral theologians. Their theories are caricatured, but even worse, the pope falsely accuses them of absolutizing freedom and separating it from truth and wrongly identifies them with subjectivists, individualist, and relativists.

What is going on here? I do not know. Some have blamed the pope's advisors.[32] Such an approach is a familiar Catholic tactic. When

Catholics disagree with the pope it is always easier to blame it on the advisors than on the pope. On the other hand, I have never heard anyone who agreed with a papal statement say that they agreed with the pope's advisors! Popes obviously have advisors but the final document is the pope's and not the advisors. More worrisome is the fact that the pope's area of expertise is ethics. Does he really think that Catholic moral theologians who dissent on some church teachings (especially in the area of sexuality) are subjectivists, individualists, and relativists?

A realistic assessment of the contemporary state of Catholic moral theology differs considerably from the picture painted in *Veritatis Splendor.* The differences between the pope and revisionist moral theologians are by no means as great as *Veritatis Splendor* states. Yes, different methodologies are often at work, but revisionist moral theologians have generally agreed with the papal teaching in the area of social ethics. Likewise, revisionist moral theologians are willing to accept some intrinsically evil acts when the object of the act is described in formal terms (murder is always wrong, stealing is always wrong) or when the act is described in terms of its significant circumstances (not telling the truth when the neighbor has a right to the truth).

The primary area of disagreement concerns the understanding of the moral object. The encyclical claims that morality is determined by the three sources of morality—the object, the end, and the circumstances—and that some actions are intrinsically evil by reason of their object (nn. 71–83). The question is, how does one describe the object? As mentioned above, revisionist theologians would be willing to admit intrinsically evil acts by reason of the object if the object were described in a broad or formal way or with some significant circumstances. The earlier discussion about always obliging laws pointed out a very significant problem in the encyclical itself in describing the moral object.

Revisionists in general object to those cases in which the moral act is assumed to be identical with the physical structure of the act. These areas occur especially in the area of sexuality. As pointed out, not every killing, mutilation, taking something that belongs to another, and false speech are always wrong. Contraception, however, describes a physical act. The physical act described as depositing male semen in the vagina of the female can never be interfered with. Some people have mistakenly thought that the hierarchical teaching against contraception was based on a pronatalist position. Such is not the case. The hierarchical teaching also condemns artificial insemination with the husband's seed (AIH) even for the good end of having a child. The reason why both contraception and AIH are wrong is because the physical act must always be there and one can never interfere with it, no matter what the purpose.[33]

The charge of physicalism is intimately connected with the theory of proportionalism. Rather than describe the physical act or object as morally wrong, this theory speaks of premoral, ontic, or physical evil that can be justified for a proportionate reason. This challenges the hierarchical teaching on contraception, but also explains the existing hierarchical teaching on killing, mutilation, taking property, etc. There is no doubt that Catholic moral theologians are calling for a change in hierarchical teaching, especially in the area of sexuality, but they are precisely challenging these areas in which the moral aspect has been *a priori* identified with the physical aspect of the act. Thus the differences between these revisionist moral theologians and the pope are much less than the encyclical recognizes. The problem is not that dissenting moral theologians absolutize freedom and/or conscience or separate them from truth. The question remains: What is moral truth?

4. Hierarchical Magisterium and Theologians. The confrontation and differences within Catholic moral theology in the last few decades have centered not only on the moral issues themselves but on the ecclesiological question of the role and functioning both of the hierarchical magisterium and of theologians. *Veritatis Splendor* explicitly addresses these issues in the third chapter (nn. 106–117), although the role of the hierarchical magisterium is mentioned throughout the document.

The encyclical itself deals primarily with moral truth. The ultimate questions for both the hierarchical magisterium and for moral theology are "What is moral truth?" and "How do we arrive at moral truth?" *Veritatis Splendor* condemns many approaches in moral theology and in the broader ethical world, but it never really explicitly addresses the question about how the hierarchical magisterium itself arrives at moral truth. In fact, the encyclical gives the impression that the hierarchical magisterium just has the truth. However, the hierarchical magisterium like everyone else has to learn the moral truth. How is this done? The most frequently used phrase in this regard in the encyclical is the "assistance of the Holy Spirit." Mention is also made of the revelational aspect of morality and the hierarchical magisterium's role as the protector, guarantor, and interpreter of revelation.

The entire second chapter, with its discussion of very complex theories and positions, shows that the hierarchical magisterium also uses human reason in its attempt to know and explain moral truth. The Catholic insistence on mediation means that God works in and through the human and does not provide short circuits around the human. The assistance of the Holy Spirit does not exempt the hierarchical magisterium from using all the human reason necessary to arrive at moral truth. The tradition of Catholic natural law, once again affirmed and developed in this encyclical, maintains that its moral theology is based on human reason and is accessible to all human beings. Yes, the encyclical reminds us (correctly) that human sin affects all our reasoning processes, but sin does not take away human reason's ability to arrive at moral truth (nn. 86–87). In learning moral truth, the hierarchical magisterium must use human reason like everyone else.

In the last few decades, many theologians have also pointed out the experience of Christian people as a source of moral knowledge. Once again, sin affects human experience and a proper discernment is required. One cannot just work on the basis of a majority vote. However, the hierarchical magisterium itself, in its Declaration on Religious Freedom of the Second Vatican Council, recognized the experience of Christian people as a source of moral wisdom by saying that the fathers of the council take careful note of these desires for religious freedom in the minds of human beings and propose to declare them to be greatly in accord with truth and justice.[34] However, *Veritatis Splendor* never mentions even implicitly that the hierarchical magisterium can and should learn from the experience of Christian people. The pope explicitly says the fact that some believers do not follow the hierarchical magisterium or consider as morally correct behavior what their pastors have condemned cannot be a valid argument for rejecting moral norms taught by the hierarchical magisterium (n. 112).

The Thomistic moral tradition which the hierarchical magisterium claims to follow has insisted on an intrinsic morality: something is commanded because it is good, and not the other way around. The hierarchical magisterium does not make something right or wrong, but the hierarchical magisterium must conform itself to the moral truth. Thus the hierarchical magisterium must use all the means available to arrive at that truth.

In addition, the Thomistic tradition recognizes that one cannot have the same degree of certitude about practical truths as about speculative truths.[35] The hierarchical magisterium has a role in guaranteeing and protecting revelation under the inspiration of the Holy Spirit, but must also use all the human means available to arrive at moral truth and live with the reality that practical truths do not have the same degree of certitude as speculative truths. One cannot expect an encyclical to say everything on the subject, but a document dealing with the splendor of truth might have been expected to say something about the nature of moral truth, and how the hierarchical magisterium itself learns and knows this moral truth.

History points out that the teaching of the hierarchical magisterium in moral matters has been wrong in the past and has developed or changed. John Noonan has recently documented this change in the areas of usury, marriage, slavery, and religious freedom.[36] The fact that past teachings of the hierarchical magisterium in morality have been wrong must have some influence on how one understands the pronouncements of the hierarchical magisterium today.

The Catholic tradition itself has rightly recognized a hierarchy of truths,[37] and even the pre-Vatican II theology developed a system of theological notes to determine how core and central teachings are in Catholic faith.[38] All interpreters would admit that most of the papal teaching (I would say all, as would many others) on specific moral issues involves the noninfallible teaching office of the pope. The fact that something is noninfallible does not mean that it is necessarily wrong or that Catholics can disagree with it, but by definition it means that it is fallible. Catholic moral theologians, as well as the hierarchical magisterium, today must do more work to develop and talk about these different categories in the light of the general insistence on the hierarchy of truths and the older theological notes. At the very minimum, the hierarchical magisterium itself must also be willing to recognize the more tentative and peripheral nature of some of its pronouncements. In addition, the hierarchical magisterium has never come to grips with the fact that some of its teachings in the past have been wrong and subsequently changed.

Veritatis Splendor understands the role of the moral theologian in the light of its understanding of the hierarchical magisterium. The assumption is that the hierarchical magisterium, with the assistance of the Holy Spirit, has the moral truth and proclaims it. Therefore moral theologians are to give an example of loyal assent, both internal and external, to the hierarchical magisterium's teaching (n. 110).

Veritatis Splendor in an adversative clause acknowledges "the possible limitations of human arguments employed by the magisterium," but calls moral theologians to develop a deeper understanding of the reasons underlying the hierarchical magisterium's teaching and to expound the validity and obligatory nature of the precepts it proposes (n. 110). Thus there might be limitations in the arguments proposed by the hierarchical magisterium, but these in no way affect the validity of the precepts it proposes.

In condemning dissent, the present document follows the approach of *Donum Veritatis,* the 1990 document of the Congregation for the Doctrine of the Faith on the role of theologians.[39] Dissent, in the form of carefully orchestrated protests and polemics carried on in the media, is opposed to ecclesial communion and to a proper understanding of the hierarchical constitution of the people of God. Opposition to the teaching of the church's pastors cannot be seen as a legitimate expression either of Christian freedom or of the diversity of the Spirit's gifts (n. 113). I know no Catholic moral theologian who dissents from church teaching who would propose what she or he has done in those terms. One might argue that such a definition of dissent leaves the door open for a different type of dissent. However, the encyclical itself calls for moral theologians to give an example of loyal assent, both internal and external, to the magisterium's teaching (n. 110).

The consideration here of the hierarchical magisterium does not intend to be a thorough discussion of the role of the hierarchical magisterium or of the moral theologian. This discussion is sufficient to point out the differences that exist. Revisionist Catholic moral theologians recognize the role of the hierarchical magisterium, but insist that its teachings cannot claim an absolute certitude on specific moral issues, have been wrong in the past, and might in some circumstances be wrong today. In this light dissent is at times a legitimate and loyal function of the Catholic moral theologian. However, *Veritatis Splendor* at the very minimum does not admit any kind of tentativeness or lack of absolute certitude about the teachings of the hierarchical magisterium, and in no way explicitly recognizes a positive role for dissent.

Ever since the pope announced his intention in August 1987 of writing an encyclical dealing more fully with the issues regarding the foundations of moral theology in the light of certain present-day tendencies, any student of moral theology had a pretty good idea of what the encyclical would do. The pope was certainly not going to change any of the teachings that have recently been reinforced, nor was he going to abandon the reasoning process behind those teachings. As a result, then, no one should be surprised by those aspects found in *Veritatis Splendor*.

What is surprising is the fact that the pope caricatures the positions of Catholic revisionist moral theologians and refuses to recognize the great areas of agreement between them and himself. One can only wonder why *Veritatis Splendor* proposes such an either-or or all-or-nothing understanding of the positions taken by Catholic revisionist moral theologians. The fundamental question remains: What is moral truth?

Notes

1. Pope John Paul II, *Veritatis Splendor, Origins* 23 (1993), pp. 297–334. References will be given in the text to the paragraph numbers in the encyclical.

2. E.g., the parable of the prodigal son in *Dives in misericordia,* nn. 6–7. See Pope John Paul II, "*Dives in misericordia,*" in Michael Walsh and Brian Davies, eds., *Proclaiming Justice and Peace: Papal Documents from Rerum novarum through Centesimus annus* (Mystic, CT: Twenty-Third Publications, 1991), pp. 344–47.

3. This passage is a citation from *Dei Verbum, the Constitution on Divine Revelation* of the Second Vatican Council, n. 10.

4. Symposia on *Veritatis Splendor* have appeared in *Commonweal* 120 (October 22, 1993), pp. 11–18; *First Things*, 39 (January 1994): 14–29. *The Tablet* (London) devoted a series of eleven articles to the encyclical beginning with October 16, 1993 issue, pp. 1329ff.

5. E.g., Bernard Häring, "A Distress that Wounds," *The Tablet* 247 (October 23, 1993), pp. 1378–79; Richard A. McCormick, "Killing a Patient," *The Tablet* 247 (October 30, 1993), pp. 1410–11; Daniel C. Maguire, "The Splendor of Control," *Conscience* 14: 4 (Winter 1993/1994), pp. 26–29.

6. John Finnis, "Beyond the Encyclical," *The Tablet* 248 (January 8, 1994), pp. 9–10; Robert P. George, "The Splendor of Truth: A Symposium," *First Things,* 39 (January 1994), pp. 24–25; Germain Grisez, "Revelation vs. Dissent," *The Tablet* 247 (October 16, 1993), pp. 1329–31.

7. Stanley Hauerwas, *"Veritatis Splendor,"* *Commonweal* 120 (October 22, 1993), pp. 16–17; L. Gregory Jones, "The Splendor of Truth: A Symposium," *First Things,* 39 (January 1994), pp. 19–20; Oliver O'Donovan, "A Summons to Reality," *The Tablet* 247 (November 27, 1993), pp. 1550–52.

8. Lisa Sowle Cahill, "Accent on the Masculine," *The Tablet* 247 (December 11, 1993), pp. 1618–19.

9. E.g., Mary Tuck, "A Message in Season," *The Tablet* 247 (December 4, 1993), pp. 1583–85.

10. Maguire, p. 28.

11. Pope John XXIII, *Mater et Magistra,* n. 212, in David J. O'Brien and Thomas A. Shannon, eds., *Catholic Social Thought: The Documentary Heritage* (Maryknoll, NY: Orbis Books, 1992), p. 118.

12. Pope John XXIII, *Pacem in Terris,* n. 35, in O'Brien-Shannon, *Catholic Social Thought,* p. 136.

13. Thomas Aquinas, *Summa Theologiae* (Rome: Marietti, 1952), Iᵃ IIᵃᵉ, Prologue.

14. Ibid., q. 91, a. 2. John Paul II cites this passage in *Veritatis Splendor,* n. 43.

15. E. g., Robert Bellah et al., *The Good Society* (New York: Alfred A. Knopf, 1991); Amitai Etzioni, *The Spirit of Community* (New York: Crown Publishers, 1993).

16. For my response to this debate, see *The Church and Morality: An Ecumenical and Catholic Approach* (Minneapolis, MN: Fortress Press, 1993), pp. 96–109.

17. Thomas Aquinas, *Summa,* Iᵃ IIᵃᵉ.

18. See, for example, John Mahoney, *The Making of Moral Theology* (Oxford: Clarendon Press, 1987), pp. 224–45.

19. P. Marcellinus Zalba, *Theologiae Moralis Summa II: Tractatus de Mandatis Dei et Ecclesiae* (Madrid: Biblioteca de Autores Cristianos, 1953), nn. 243–66, pp. 255–86.

20. *Acta Aposolicae Sedis* 85, n. 12 (December 9, 1993), p. 1197.

21. Walter M. Abbott, ed., *The Documents of Vatican II* (New York: Guild Press, 1966), p. 226; Austin Flannery, ed., *Vatican Council II: The Conciliar and Post-Conciliar Documents* (Northport, NY: Costello Publishing, 1975), p. 928.

22. Zalba, nn. 251–52; pp. 263–68.

23. Charles E. Curran, *Toward an American Catholic Moral Theology* (Notre Dame, IN: University of Notre Dame Press, 1987), pp. 57–59.

24. Charles E. Curran, *Directions in Fundamental Moral Theology* (Notre Dame, IN: University of Notre Dame Press, 1985), pp. 127–37; 156–61.

25. Pope Pius XII, "The Prolongation of Life" (November 24, 1957), in Kevin D. O'Rourke and Philip Boyle, eds., *Medical Ethics: Sources of Catholic Teachings* (St. Louis, MO: Catholic Health Association, 1989), p. 207.

26. Curran, *Directions in Fundamental Moral Theology*, p. 244.

27. Ibid., p. 242.

28. Louis Vereecke, *De Guillaume d'Ockham à Saint Alphonse de Liguori* (Rome: Collegium S. Alfonsi de Urbe, 1986), pp. 555–60; James Keenan, "Can a Wrong Action Be Good? The Development of Theological Opinion on Erroneous Conscience," *Église et Théologie* 24 (1993), pp. 205–19. However, Aquinas, Alphonsus, and Pope John Paul II all recognize that the external act remains an objective disorder and is wrong.

29. Vereecke, *De Guillaume d'Ockham*, p. 566.

30. Joseph Fuchs, "Good Acts and Good Persons," *The Tablet* 247 (November 6, 1993), p. 1445.

31. McCormick, "Killing a Patient," pp. 1410–11.

32. Fuchs, p. 1445; McCormick, p. 1411.

33. See "Artifical Insemination" and "Contraception," in O'Rourke and Boyle, eds. *Medical Ethics*, pp. 62, 92–95.

34. *Declaration on Religious Freedom*, n. 1, in Abbott, *Documents of Vatican II*, p. 676.

35. Thomas Aquinas, Iᵃ IIᵃᵉ, q. 94, a. 4.

36. John T. Noonan, "Development in Moral Doctrine," *Theological Studies* 54 (1993), pp. 662–77.

37. *Decree on Ecumenism*, n. 11, in Abbott, *Documents of Vatican II*, p. 354.

38. Sixtus Cartechini, *De Valore notarum theologicarum* (Rome: Gregorian University Press, 1951).

39. Vatican Congregation for the Doctrine of the Faith, "Instruction on the Ecclesial Vocation of the Theologian," *Origins* 20 (1990), pp. 117–26.

17. The Duty and Right to Follow One's Judgment of Conscience

Germain Grisez

This chapter first appeared in *Linacre Quarterly* 56 (February 1989).

The duty to follow one's conscience is neither one specific responsibility among others nor a supreme responsibility which perhaps could conflict with and nullify others. For no matter what in particular one ought to do, one ought to follow one's conscience. That is so because the duty to follow conscience is reducible to the duty to do what is morally good. One's conscience simply is what one judges to be moral truth considered insofar as one has tried to know that truth, thinks one knows it, and compares one's prospective or past choices with it.

"One ought to do what is morally good" is true by definition. But although the duty to follow one's conscience is reducible to that tautology, we consider it interesting and informative to say: "One ought to follow one's judgment of conscience." Why do we consider that worth saying?

One says that one ought to follow one's judgment of conscience in the face of a temptation not to do so. A temptation to do what one believes to be wrong often is strengthened, especially if one is under pressure from others, by the thought that one's judgment of conscience could be mistaken. For example, a law-abiding citizen always hesitates to violate the law's requirements, and so if compliance with a law would be morally wrong, will reflect: "I know my access to moral truth is not infallible, but I am convinced that it would be wrong to comply with this legal requirement." In such a situation, "One's duty is to follow one's judgment of conscience" means: One ought not to do what one believes to be wrong, but, having tried to know the moral truth and thinking that one knows it, one should choose and act, *despite every contrary pressure,* in conformity with the moral truth insofar as one has access to it. Thus, the point of saying that one ought to follow one's judgment of conscience is that one ought to try to do what is morally good by choosing in conformity with what one thinks to be moral truth, although one is aware that one's judgement of conscience could be mistaken.

Since the duty to follow one's conscience is reducible to one's duty to do what is morally good, the specific duty pertaining to conscience is to "form" it—that is, to do beforehand what one can to avoid making mistakes when one judges prospective or past choices by the standard of what one thinks to be moral truth. If one does what one thinks is morally good, but has failed to form one's conscience, one does not really follow a judgment of conscience. Due to one's negligence, one's subjective opinion about what is morally good cannot be considered conscience, using "conscience" in an unqualified sense.

HIGHEST STANDARD OF MORALITY

Christians and others who acknowledge Abraham as their father in faith believe that God's loving wisdom is the highest standard of morality, and that he guides those who believe in him not only by the natural light of reason but by faith. Therefore, in forming their consciences, they conform their judgements to moral truth derived from this source.

Among people of faith, some hold that God makes his plans and it will be known immediately to each individual by an inner light. Others recognize various external means by which God guides his people. All Christians believe that the illumination of the Holy Spirit and the inspired scriptures should contribute to the formation of their conscience.

Catholics believe that divine revelation not only makes known specifically Christian moral norms which they could not know without faith, but also clarifies and confirms those moral truths which human persons can know even without hearing the gospel. Without diminishing the factors which all Christians recognize, Catholics believe that they receive divine revelation by believing what the Catholic Church believes and teaches, and that they can discern what the church believes and teaches by attending to the magisterium. By the authorization of her divine founder, the Catholic Church, speaking through her magisterium, teaches all her members what they must do to be saved. So, faithful and clearheaded Catholics consider the moral guidance offered by the pope and the bishops in communion with him to indicate moral truths by which they must form their conscience.

Therefore, for faithful and clearheaded Catholics, the duty to follow one's judgment of conscience *cannot* conflict with the duty to live according to the moral teaching which the magisterium proposes. For unless they fulfill the latter duty, they have only their own subjective opinion to follow, not an authentic judgment of conscience.

Insofar as the duty to follow conscience is reducible to the duty to do what is morally good, the right to follow conscience is reducible to the right to do what is morally good. Plainly, that is not one specific right among others. However, one does have certain specific and limited rights to follow one's judgment of conscience—rights which are entailed by the duties of others to take into account the fact that one is acting (or wishes to act) on a judgment of conscience, rather than on some other basis, and therefore to limit themselves in certain ways.

Those who have power to control the behavior of another person should do so only in accord with their own judgment of conscience. In making this judgment, they must take into account what the other person may rightly do. They may never require the other person to act (or not to act) in a way which they themselves believe conflicts with moral truth. But they sometimes may require the other person to act (or not to act) in a way which the other person thinks conflicts with moral truth—that is, contrary to his or her own judgment of conscience. For instance, public authorities may prevent a religious body from practicing human sacrifice even if members of that body sincerely believe they ought to practice it.

However, whenever those who have power to control the behavior of another person bring it about that the other person acts contrary to his or her conscience, serious harm is done in three ways to basic human goods. (1) If the other person freely chooses to act contrary to his or her conscience, he or she commits sin. (2) Solidarity is harmed insofar as submission to or determination by coercion replaces voluntary collaboration. (3) Some sorts of acts, such as religious acts, are valueless if done unwillingly. For these reasons, those who have power to control the behavior of another person sometimes ought not to use their power for the precise reason that if they did so, that person would act contrary to his or her conscience. For instance, within certain limits public authorities should not require anyone to act contrary to his or her conscience in matters religious.

Corresponding to such specific and limited duties of those who have power not to use it when doing so would cause another person to act contrary to conscience are specific and limited rights of that person to follow conscience. Therefore, one does have certain specific and limited rights to follow one's judgment of conscience, and *all such rights are immunities from coercion to act contrary to conscience.*

The magisterium of the Catholic Church is a teaching office, not a body with the power to control behavior. So, the magisterium cannot compel anyone to act contrary to his or her conscience. Moreover, as explained above, for faithful and clearheaded Catholics, the duty to follow one's judgment of conscience cannot possibly conflict with the duty to live according to the moral teaching which the magisterium proposes. Others do not consider the moral guidance offered by the pope and other bishops in communion with him to indicate moral truths by which to form their consciences. For them, the magisterium simply is irrelevant in questions of conscience, and so they need no right to follow their judgment of conscience contrary to the magisterium's teaching. Therefore, nobody can have a right to follow his or her judgment of conscience contrary to the magisterium's teaching.

Elsewhere I have argued that the Catholic Church's constant and most firm teaching concerning contraception and certain other moral questions not only is true, but has been proposed infallibly by the ordinary magisterium. From this thesis, a second one follows: Theological dissent from such teachings is not justifiable. Here I address my reflections to those who either accept these two theses as established or, at least, are willing to grant them for the sake of argument.

Between June, 1964 and the publication of *Humanae Vitae* in July, 1968 many Catholics came to believe that the Church's teaching concerning contraception was in doubt and that they might follow their own "conscience" in this matter. Three factors fostered this belief.

First, in June, 1964, Pope Paul VI announced the famous Commission for the Study of Population, Family, and Births, but he never made clear the scope of its mandate. At that time and subsequently he also made statements which were widely taken to mean that a change in the church's teaching concerning contraception was possible. In November, 1965, he proposed amendments to *Gaudium et spes* which would have clarified the matter, but then allowed the relevant conciliar commission to modify those amendments in such a way that Vatican II also seemed to leave an opening for the approval of contraception. Moreover, even after documents of the papal commission were leaked and published in April, 1967, and expectations that the teaching would change became more widespread and intense, Paul VI allowed fifteen more months to pass before he completed his evaluation of the commission's report and issued *Humanae Vitae.*

Second, during those four years, a growing number of theologians and a scattering of bishops expressed their opinion that the church herself was in doubt about the morality of contraception, and that faithful Catholics might rightly form judgments of conscience contrary to previous Catholic teaching on this matter. The arguments offered for this opinion were weak, but to those without theological sophistication they seemed strong, especially inasmuch as they were not authoritatively rejected. And so, some faithful and clearheaded Catholics became convinced that the church no longer had a firm teaching concerning contraception. Many such Catholics had to make choices about contraception. Without violating their responsibility to form their consciences, many of them reached the judgment of conscience that they might use (or formally cooperate in others' using) contraception and they acted on that judgment.

Third, during those four years, some theologians and others began to spread in the church a nontraditional conception of conscience.

ANALYSIS CLARIFIES

It is clear that for a faithful and clearheaded Catholic, there is no right to follow a judgment of conscience against the teaching of the magisterium. But in that analysis, "conscience" means what one judges to be moral truth considered insofar as one has tried to know that truth, thinks one knows it, and compares one's prospective or past choices with it.

However, dominant elements in the societies and cultures of all the affluent nations deny that there is any source of meaning and value beyond the human. Those who share that view give "conscience" an entirely different meaning, according to which conscience becomes merely subjective opinion. For the denial of any source of meaning and value beyond the human leads to relativism. According to this relativism, moral judgments cannot be objectively grounded, and moral norms are nothing more than the attempts of societies to control their members and of individuals to influence one another's behavior. In this relativistic context "conscience" refers to the individual's subjective judgment as to what is most authentic for himself or herself—what will best serve his or her interests in the face of pressures to conform to others' standards.

Thus, in all the affluent nations, the role in moral life which, according to the Christian tradition, rightfully belongs to conscience, all too often is played today by merely subjective opinion. In this subjectivist perspective, the moral truths handed on throughout the church's tradition seem to be no more than one body of opinion among others. To those who share this view, the magisterium seems authoritarian, for they think that it is trying to impose its opinion on the faithful in violation of their right to follow their autonomous conscience.

Catholics always are in danger of beginning to conform to the unbelieving world in which they live. By the time *Humanae Vitae* appeared in July, 1968, many Catholics in the affluent nations had become confused and more or less accepted the subjectivist perspective and its nontraditional conception of conscience. Such Catholics came to think that even if the Catholic Church were in no doubt they could rightly follow their subjective opinion against the moral guidance offered by the pope and the bishops in communion with him. This position often was expressed by saying that Catholics rightly follow their own judgment of conscience even if it conflicts with "official" church teaching.

EFFECTS OF THEOLOGICAL DISSENT

Much of the theological dissent after *Humanae Vitae* implicitly presupposed, applied, and so consolidated and spread the subjectivist conception of conscience which had begun to take hold in the church.

For example, one famous dissenting statement took for granted that the teaching reaffirmed in *Humanae Vitae* is not infallible, claimed that it "is common teaching in the church that Catholics may dissent from authoritative, non-infallible teachings of the *magisterium* when sufficient reasons for so doing exist," and concluded that "spouses may responsibly decide according to their conscience that artificial contraception in some circumstances is permissible and indeed necessary to preserve and foster the values and sacredness of marriage."

In this context, many episcopal conferences issued pastoral statements. Most discussed conscience, and several suggested that nonassent to or dissent from *Humanae Vitae* might be licit under conditions. While virtually everything said in these statements about conscience and dissent has some true sense, still many people were misled by them. Why this happened can be understood from the following observation.

Normally, conscience becomes a subject of reflection when one is thinking about someone else's action or one's own past action, or when one must resist a temptation to submit to pressure to do what one believes to be wrong. In forming one's conscience here and now, one pays attention to the relevant moral norms, not to conscience. It follows that when someone seeks pastoral guidance, he or she wants to know that the church believes is truly the morally good thing to do. If one responds by saying that a person who follows a sincere conscience is morally blameless, the remarks can be misleading. It is true, but the truth about conscience is not what is being asked for. The question is: What should I think I may do? The question is not: If I do what I think I should but happen to be mistaken, then how do I stand?

Thus, when an adviser in a pastoral situation talks simultaneously about conscience and about the moral norms proposed by the church, the talk about conscience is likely to be mistaken for talk about one's substantive moral responsibilities. The teaching on conscience does not form conscience (that is, help one to know the relevant moral truth); it merely says that if one blamelessly thinks doing X is morally good, then choosing to do X is blameless.

But this truism is likely to be taken as significant and to be misinterpreted to mean: "If you think that doing X is morally unobjectionable, and if you are blameless in having come to think so, then I, as your pastor, assure you that you may do X blamelessly." In other words: "If you think anything is morally good, then it is morally good for you."

Thus, inappropriate talk about conscience is likely to be understood by the faithful as an endorsement of subjectivism.

UNDERSTANDING OF BISHOPS' STATEMENTS

Several of the statements issued by bishops' conferences in response to *Humanae Vitae* were widely understood in this way. Two factors reinforced this understanding: first, some of the statements were poorly formulated and/or included approval of dissent; second, many dissenting theologians invoked the bishops' statements to support theological dissent and the subjectivism it fostered.

Bishops' statements which did not approve dissent and which spoke carefully of conscience were not misinterpreted. Dissenting theologians quietly ignored those statements which clearly taught that one's duty is to form one's conscience and that for Catholics that means conforming to the divine law, which is unfolded by the magisterium. But several of the collective bishops' statements were framed in such a way that they could be read as suggesting that a Catholic who had formed a judgment of conscience at odds with the teaching which *Humanae Vitae* reaffirmed could rightly continue to follow that judgment simply because it had been a judgment of conscience. The bishops who made these statements avoided dissenting openly from what Paul VI reaffirmed, but in doing so they unintentionally encouraged subjectivism.

Many dissenting theologians claimed that at least some of the bishops' statements amounted to an endorsement of their dissent, including that dissent's encouragement that Catholics consider their subjective opinion to be a judgment of conscience which they might rightly follow against the magisterium. This claim of the dissenting theologians gained credibility, because time passed and the confusion created by the bishops' statements never was cleared up—either by the episcopal conferences, by the synod of bishops, or by the Holy See.

With the magisterium of the church in this state, dissenting theologians were able to consolidate their position. Eventually, many theologians, including some of the best known in the world, argued that the magisterium's lack of unity and its toleration of theological dissent constituted consent by silence both to theological dissent and to the subjectivist conception of conscience dissent had fostered.

Once these positions were established, theological dissent quickly spread to many other received Catholic moral teachings related to sex, marriage, and innocent life. Eventually, many dissenting theologians claimed both that no specific moral norm can be taught infallibly and that every specific moral norm is open to exception.

Faithful and clearheaded Catholics will find no inconsistency between their duty to follow their judgment of conscience and their duty to live according to the teaching which the magisterium proposes. And neither for such Catholics nor for anyone else does it make sense to talk about an authentic right to follow conscience against the magisterium's teaching, since the magisterium cannot coerce anyone. Nevertheless, many Catholics today are uncertain or confused about their duty to follow the judgment of conscience formed by the teaching the magisterium proposes.

In the midst of dissent and the confusion to which it led, Popes Paul VI and John Paul II continued to propose received Catholic moral teaching firmly and clearly. The present pope also has worked hard to explain and clarify those moral norms which have been attacked most heavily. In doing so, he has made a powerful case that the norm concerning contraception pertains to the moral order revealed by God. Some bishops and groups of bishops also have taught clearly and firmly enough to leave no doubt that they believe that the church's moral teaching on contraception and on other disputed matters is true and that the faithful should conform their consciences to it.

However, the clarity and firmness of this substantive teaching does not help those many Catholics who have adopted a subjectivist notion of conscience. For them, the moral truth which the church teaches is merely a set of opinions from which they can pick and choose. Sometimes, perhaps, such subjectivism is a sign of bad faith and an expression of an apostate heart; nothing the magisterium can do is likely to help such Catholics to regain their moral balance. But sometimes subjectivism is a sign of poor catechesis and more or less innocent confusion, and in such cases the magisterium needs to do better than it has during the past twenty-five years.

Moreover, clear and firm moral teaching by the popes and some of the bishops, while essential and quite helpful, has not been adequate to the needs even of those Catholics who have avoided subjectivism and remained faithful and clearheaded. For they look to the magisterium both for guidance in forming their own consciences and for support in teaching and handing on the way of the Lord Jesus to others, especially to children. But they find the guidance and support they look for obscured and weakened by the lack of unity in the magisterium itself.

HERITAGE OF DIVISION AND CONFUSION

What bishops and conferences of bishops, theologians and groups of theologians said in 1968–69 has not gone away. It remains with us today as a heritage of division and confusion. The 1980 session of the Synod and the splendid apostolic exhortation, *Familiaris consortio,* superseded the inadequate or defective elements contained in some of the pastoral statements published soon after *Humanae Vitae.* Yet that splendid collegial effort failed to restore solidarity even to the magisterium itself, because the reality and depth of division never was frankly acknowledged, much less confronted and overcome.

But the division in the magisterium is real. Against the clear and firm moral teaching of the popes and some of the bishops, some other bishops quietly but clearly accept and foster dissenting opinions. They never straightforwardly and firmly assert Catholic teaching on the disputed questions, and if they do not openly reject that teaching, they do consult and follow the advice of dissenting theologians, invite such theologians to instruct their priests, appoint these theologians to teach their seminarians and direct their marriage preparation programs, and make it clear that they reject the "narrowness" and "rigidity" of "official teaching" in favor of a pluralism which admits dissenting opinions and encourages subjectivist consciences to follow them.

Somehow and sometime, the collegial magisterium, under the leadership of John Paul II or a later pope, must confront and overcome this division. The issues raised in 1968–69 must be clarified and resolved. Only then will a reunified magisterium be able to propose more credibly the true meaning of the duty to follow one's judgment of conscience and so help to save the faithful from the quicksand of subjectivism into which so many have been led by theological dissent and by the inadequacies of the magisterium's response to it.

Furthermore, pending reunification of the magisterium, that part of it which continues to hold and teach the church's constant and most firm moral teaching—and in what follows I shall be concerned only with those who make up that part of the magisterium—needs to avoid crossing the fine line which divides justifiably tolerating dissent from unjustifiably cooperating with it. Despite everything, some Catholics have resisted subjectivism and have remained faithful and clearheaded. The question is: Just how much can a bishop accept without failing in his duty to help such Catholics to form their own consciences and to meet their responsibility of handing on their Christian way of life to others?

First, one must recognize that many things are done in a diocese which simply are beyond the control of the bishop, and similarly many things are done in the Catholic world which simply are beyond the control of the pope. Whenever that is literally true, no question even of toleration arises, since one cannot tolerate that over which one has no control. In such cases, bishops must choose between denouncing error and not mentioning it but serenely, clearly, and firmly teaching and explaining the truth. The latter course has many advantages, but when it is chosen and the Church's constant and most firm moral teaching is reaffirmed, its authoritativeness and exclusive legitimacy ought to be emphasized. Otherwise, dissenting theologians will say—and even some faithful and clearheaded Catholics will be led to believe—that the error which is not expressly denounced is a licit theological opinion which may be followed in practice.

Second, many actions are carried on in a diocese or in the Catholic world which are in various ways subject to the bishop's or pope's authority but do not precisely participate in and exercise his authority. For example, in some parts of the world many Catholic media of communication and institutions of higher education are autonomous entities whose operations clearly are in no way operations of the bishops. In a different but analogous way, the acts of other bishops are not the acts of the pope. In such cases, pastoral leaders must choose between using the authority they have to try to prevent or put a stop to dissent and not using that authority and so tolerating dissent. Plainly, as long as division in the magisterium continues, the Holy See has little choice but to tolerate widespread dissent. Regarding the Holy See as their model of pastoral leadership, other bishops naturally tend not to use their authority against dissent, but rather try to contain it by exhortation and administrative maneuvers.

LEGITIMATE TEACHING

But third, no one legitimately teaches in the church except by sharing in the teaching authority of the popes and other bishops. Many priests and others who openly dissent from the church's constant and most firm moral teaching exercise teaching roles in the church by virtue of episcopal authorization. Can a bishop be acting consistently if he tolerates dissent by those who share by virtue of his authorization in his own teaching office?

Of course, he can remain consistent if he does not know that his authorization is being abused to teach dissent or if, knowing about the abuse, he simply cannot withdraw the authorization which he previously gave. But setting such cases aside, I do not see how a bishop can be acting consistently if he tolerates dissent by those who share in his teaching office with his own continuing authorization. For when a pastor continues to *authorize* others to teach and preach, knowing what they are doing, he is personally responsible for what they do with his authorization. Acting in and through those who teach and preach with his authorization, the pastor somehow cooperates with dissent when he continues to authorize the teaching and preaching of those whom he knows very well to be engaging in it.

Sensing this to be so, the faithful—and even the nonbelieving world—assume that bishops do not unconditionally exclude those positions which they knowingly allow others to teach with their authority. The inconsistency is especially plain when the theologians who openly dissent from the church's constant and most firm moral teaching are continued in their posts, year after year, in seminaries and ecclesiastical faculties. True, not every dissenting theologian has been allowed to continue teaching with the authorization of his bishop. But many have been. In this matter, too, other bishops who personally hold and teach what Rome does, tend to consider acceptable what they see being done in Rome.

My point is not that dissenters who exercise various offices in the church are abusing those offices and should be disciplined for doing so. That may be true, but it also may be true that most dissenters are in good faith and do not deserve punishment. My present point is not even that those who dissent from the church's teaching on sex, marriage, and innocent life are denying truths which pertain to faith and leading people into sins and other great evils. I believe that is so, but the point I am now making would hold even if the church's teaching were false and the opinions which dissent from it were based on a fresh divine revelation – as some who hold those opinions suggest by their talk of the Holy Spirit's work in the "sense of the faithful."

A PASTOR'S RESPONSIBILITY

My point, rather, is that a pastor who believes the church's teaching true and who faithfully teaches and preaches it also simultaneously himself undercuts that teaching when he does not withdraw his authorization to teach and preach from those whom he knows are using it to teach and preach dissenting opinions. Such a pastor is hardly acting consistently, and I can think of no justification for that inconsistency. Moreover, inconsistency in this matter is grave, for by it a pastor both personally calls the faithful to conform their lives to difficult norms which concern grave matters and allows his authority to be abused by others whose dissent encourages the same faithful to do what their pastor continues to teach to be a grave sin. (Of course, only God knows the state of a pastor's heart; like anyone else, he may be guilty of little or nothing due to lack of sufficient reflection.)

Consequently, I believe that the following is a true moral norm: Every one of the church's pastors should make it clear to all those who have his authorization to preach and teach that he cannot and will not tolerate their using that authorization to dissent from Catholic teachings which he himself accepts. Instead, as soon as it becomes evident that anyone having his authorization preaches or teaches dissenting opinions, he will withdraw the authorization, not to punish the dissenter, but to act consistently as a pastor. I respectfully ask only this of the pastors of the church: that they consider whether this norm is indeed true and binding on their consciences.

In a letter to Charles Curran, September 17, 1986 Cardinal Ratzinger, as Prefect of the Congregation for the Doctrine of the Faith, wrote: "It must be recognized that the authorities of the church cannot allow the present situation to continue in which the inherent contradiction is prolonged that one who is to teach in the name of the church in fact denies her teaching" (*Origins,* 15 [1986], 668). I believe Cardinal

Ratzinger's argument is entirely sound. Indeed, what I have been trying to show is that every one of the church's pastors should apply a similar argument in respect to every individual whom he in any way authorizes to share in his pastoral ministry of teaching and preaching. Inconsistency which Rome rightly finds intolerable in Washington can hardly be tolerable in any other part of the church, least of all in Rome itself.

Despite everything that has happened, faithful and clearheaded Catholics who have not been seduced by subjectivism still know that to fulfill their duty to follow their judgment of conscience, they must form their conscience by conforming to God's law, submissive to the magisterium which interprets that law in the light of the Gospel. Yet they find it nearly impossible to teach and hand on the way of Jesus to others, especially to children, when even the part of the magisterium which continues to proclaim it clearly and firmly also inconsistently continues to authorize those who teach dissenting opinions.

18. Proposing Cardinal Virtues

James F. Keenan

This chapter first appeared in *Theological Studies* 56 (1995).

Recent work in virtue ethics, particularly sustained reflection on specific virtues, makes it possible to argue that the classical list of cardinal virtues (prudence, justice, temperance, and fortitude) is inadequate, and that we need to articulate the cardinal virtues more correctly. With that end in view, the first section of this article describes the challenges of espousing cardinal virtues today, the second considers the inadequacy of the classical listing of cardinal virtues, and the third makes a proposal. Since virtues, no matter how general, should always relate to concrete living, the article is framed by a case.

CONTEMPORARY CHALLENGES

Fifteen years ago, while preparing for priestly studies, I took my first exam in moral theology. The question was simple: resolve the case of Mrs. Bergmeier. Like all good cases, Mrs. Bergmeier's has undergone several incarnations;[1] thus some may be surprised to find her in a Nazi camp as opposed to a Soviet Gulag. In any event, the case that I was given was the following: Mrs. Bergmeier is a married woman with several children and a husband who is ill. She has been arrested by the Nazis for assisting her Jewish neighbors and sentenced to six years without parole. After months in the camp, she learns that her husband's health is progressively declining due to his tending to the children, and that the children are not faring at all well due to their father's ailing state. She also learns something else: because of overcrowding, the camp releases pregnant women who are held for lesser crimes, like hers. Aware of one particular guard who regularly makes outrageous advances on her, Mrs. Bergmeier, for the sake of her family, submits herself to him. Three months later a pregnant Mrs. Bergmeier returns to her family to care for her husband and children.

When I took the exam, Catholic moral theologians responding to the case were grouped into two camps. The first simply reiterated a position held for several centuries that any act of sexual relations outside of marriage is always intrinsically wrong. These called themselves deontologists. For them the case was simple; Mrs. Bergmeier's action was wrong. The second group found the case difficult; but, rather than challenge the first group, they debated among themselves. They were called proportionalists or revisionists. They raise two types of concerns. The first type asked what the object of Mrs. Bergmeier's activity was. Was her action an extension of her marriage, or a contradiction of it? That is, did her activity compromise the institution of marriage? They second type concerned its effects—on the guard, the husband, the children, and the new child. Acknowledging the guard's own evident wickedness, did she further compromise the reprobate by engaging him in illicit activity? Did she betray her husband? How would her children understand this new child? What would life be like for this child born under such tragic circumstances?

Despite these considerations, nowhere did anyone ask how this action affected Mrs. Bergmeier. Instead, the entire case concerned how her action affected others. Reflection on this omission leads to the question: What should be at the center of any discussion involving the famous case of Mrs. Bergmeier? Should the acts of intercourse and the effects of those acts be at the center of ethical discussion, as they were for the deontologists and the proportionalists?[2] Or should Mrs. Bergmeier be at the center? Placing the moral agent and not moral action or its consequences at the center of moral reflection distinguishes a third school of moral reasoning called virtue ethics.

Long before William Bennett, theologians and philosophers were seeking a new method of ethics that would be agent based. In 1973, with its premiere issue, the *Journal of Religious Ethics* published a debate between those advocating an act-based ethics and those advocating a person-based or virtue ethics.[3] In 1981 Alasdair MacIntyre published *After Virtue,* probably the most influential book to date on the topic.[4]

Since that time, what was once a select interest has become a very productive enterprise. Thus we find in 1987 an already outdated 36-page "selected bibliography" of philosophical essays on virtue.[5] And in more recent years, a number of extensive review essays have made their appearance, in the *American Philosophical Quarterly,*[6] the *Religious Studies Review*[7] as well as in this journal.[8]

Certainly, some like William Frankena and Bruno Schüller find that virtue ethics cannot be an independent method of moral reasoning. For them, virtues merely augment an existing method; they do not supply specific directives for determining right or wrong conduct.[9] Frankena and Schüller claim that principles and rules direct, while virtues merely enable us to perform what the principles command. Thus virtues are auxiliary and derivative, recommended as the appropriate exercises necessary to accomplish the end to which specific principles and rules direct us. But Martha Nussbaum argues that the Greeks used virtues precisely to judge moral conduct: virtues can provide the standards of morally right conduct. Virtues, not principles, are the source for understanding normative conduct. In fact, principles and rules are derived from virtues: they are directives that obtain their content from the virtuous activity which humanity enjoins.[10] As opposed to the auxiliary use that they are assigned by others, in this schema the virtues are adequate life guides.

In order to understand virtue ethics as life-guides, we can turn to MacIntyre's *After Virtue,* where he proposed that the issue of morality is a three-fold question: Who am I? Who ought I to become? How ought I to get there? The answer to each question refers to the virtues. Applying the list of classical cardinal virtues, then, the first question is not simply "Who am I?" but "Am I just, temperate, brave and prudent?" The second question reflects on the first, and in asking, "Who do I need to become?" It presumably answers, "more just, temperate, brave, and prudent." The third question asks, "In which virtuous practices ought I to engage in order to attain that goal?" Paul Waddell sums up the answer to the threefold question in this way: "The project of the moral life is to become a certain kind of person."[11] That person is a virtuous one.

The task of virtue is defined, therefore, as the acquisition and development of practices that perfect the agent into becoming a moral person while acting morally well. Through these practices or virtues, one's character and one's actions are enhanced. Now the issue that emerges is: Precisely what are the virtues that make one a "moral person"?

The answer is extraordinarily complicated, especially for two reasons. The first concerns the claims of culture. MacIntryre warns that it belongs historically to local communities to determine the practices that shape the excellent person.[12] He notes that Homeric culture, for instance, held the warrior as the prototypically excellent person and therefore emphasized the virtue of bravery, while Aristotle presumed the Athenian gentleman as the excellent person and promoted the virtue of prudence. Likewise, in our own country the excellent person in 17th-century pioneering America was considerably different from the one in late 20th-century urban America.

MacIntryre's claim concerns differences not only in history, but also in geography. Consider the evident differences in the excellent person among the people of Zaire, Malaysia, France, or Brazil. Likewise, persons from New York, Biloxi, Miami, Kansas City, and Beverly Hills cannot easily propose their own ideal to others. Even within American Roman Catholic culture(s), there are no shared presuppositions about the ideal of the excellent person.[13]

Besides the claims of culture, the uniqueness of the individual makes its own claim. Owen Flanagan argues that any attempt to articulate a single anthropological portrait normative for moral conduct is pointless, because such a normative portrait would be a fiction. A realistic psychology teaches that the possibilities for moral excellence are as unlimited as the individual is complex and as human experience is itself original.[14]

A discussion of great saints and heroes helps illustrate that no single portrait of a moral saint or hero has ever provided a definitive expression of what a human person ought to be. Saint Elizabeth was not Mahatma Gandhi; St. John the Baptizer was not the Little Flower. Upholding the uniqueness of these morally excellent individuals, Flanagan takes an iconoclastic swing at any attempt to make these figures role models: their singularity prevents their being paradigms.[15] The Christian community supports this insight. The communion of the saints demonstrates the enormous variety of ways that the holy is incarnated; it demonstrates, as Flanagan beautifully puts it, "the deep truth that persons find their good in many different ways."[16]

In particular, Flanagan attacks the moral-developmental model of

Lawrence Kohlberg.[17] Kohlberg proposed that the morally right thinker must go through a series of six stages of growth to reach the final stage of moral development, which is to understand and articulate the universal claims of justice. The thinker at this final stage is Kohlberg's idea of the morally excellent person, an idea that is very influential today in our school systems. Flanagan complains that Kohlberg's six stages of moral development are reductive and demand an unreasonable conformity; in effect, people do not come out of Kohlberg's system as right thinkers but as Kohlberg clones. Kohlberg's theory suppresses that fact that "the heterogeneity of the moral is a deep and significant fact."[18]

Like MacIntrye's cultural claims, Flanagan's anthropological arguments are refreshing and important. He insists that people can only become morally excellent persons by being themselves. The saint has always been an original, never an imitation.

This insight strikes at the current American preoccupation to understand ourselves through prefabricated categories and to be able to predict behavior based on that understanding. For this end, we submit ourselves to tests that give us a code of letters or numbers. In particular, our religious communities form their members by inviting them to be tested and subsequently labelled. If we do Myers-Briggs, we walk around asking, "Are you a J, and E, or a P?" If we do enneagrams, we ask, "Are you a 1 or an 8?" These methods are fundamentally reductive and frustrate the self-understanding they propose to offer. Flanagan reminds us that when we settle for describing ourselves by such categories, we surrender the uniqueness of our identities.

So if we want to pursue the naming of cardinal virtues, we need to take the claims of culture and the uniqueness of individuals into account. First of all, Flanagan's concerns are not really about naming the cardinal virtues, but rather about whether we ought to preconceive a definitively excellent person, that is, a unique incarnation of the virtues. Our task is not to describe an ideal expression of the excellent person. We need simply to identify the minimal conditions that must be met to call any person virtuous.

Second, in *Whose Justice? Which Rationality?* MacIntyre contends that specific cultures shape through their practices the answers to the questions that his title raises. Despite his argument, he seems to presume that the virtues of justice and prudence exist universally and prior to any culture's particular determination of them. What we are investigating, then, is the possibility of naming certain minimal though universal expressions of virtue that are subsequently given content in diverse cultures. Our modest pursuit is not the very specific, culturally articulated morally excellent person, but rather the basic qualities of the minimally virtuous one.

Nussbaum, instead of beginning with the priority of distinctive cultures, recognizes that humans enjoy common spheres of experience and that each sphere is perfected by virtue. She lists from Aristotle eleven spheres and adds that they are so essential to human living, that "no matter where one lives one cannot escape these questions, so long as one is living a human life."[19] Nussbaum advocates an ethics based on an understanding of the human that crosses cultural boundaries and precedes the actual moral perfecting and informing of those eleven areas. Thus she finds some common ground to discuss with other cultures how they proceed to instruct their members about living and acting well in those spheres.

The proposal here is similar. Rather than being definitive expressions of character, the cardinal virtues perform a heuristic function to answer broadly the three questions of MacIntyre. These three questions are extraordinarily general; they do not fill in the claims of either culture or the individual.

Thus we pursue the cardinal virtues because they express what minimally constitutes a virtuous person. Philosophers and theologians have recognized that being virtuous is more than having a particular habit of acting, e.g. generosity. Rather, it means having a fundamental set of related virtues that enable a person to live and act morally well. The cardinal virtues have the task of making a person sufficiently rightly ordered to perform morally right action. Beyond the cardinal virtues, other virtues are certainly important, but the cardinal virtues perfect the fundamental anthropological dimensions of being human, that are needed for integrated virtuous behavior. Thus Thomas Aquinas describes the four virtues as principles of integration both in the person[20] and in the action itself.[21]

The cardinal virtues are based on modest claims. They do not purport to offer a picture of the ideal person nor to exhaust the entire domain of virtue. Rather than being the last word on virtue, they are among the first, providing the bare essentials for right human living and specific action. Thus, as the word cardinal derives from the word hinge, the cardinal virtues provide a skeleton both of what human persons should basically be and at what human action should basically aim. All other issues of virtue hang on the skeletal structures of both rightly integrated dispositions and right moral action.

This article makes an even more modest claim. Admittedly the days are gone (did they ever exist?) when a member of one culture could articulate the actual content and the actual application of specific virtues universally. Even more problematic is a definitive transcultural depiction of the four cardinal virtues. These admissions made, is it not legitimate to propose a highly formal description of the virtuous person for the sake of discussing transculturally and transgenerationally our understanding of right human living? Could we not make the description of the cardinal virtues formal enough so that each culture could fill each virtue with its specific material content and apply it practically? If we cannot, that is, if we believe that something even this formal is untenable, then we will have to acknowledge that cultural boundaries are absolute. That would contradict one of the functions of virtue: to provide understanding, not only about the practices that specific cultures recommend, but also about the humanity we share. Toward this end, the cardinal virtues that I propose—prudence, justice, fidelity and self-care—will be thinly described. There is no flesh on this skeleton. But they actually provide us with a way of talking across cultures.

To appreciate the importance of this project, by way of example, it is reasonable to assume that every society has a concept for what ought to be the internal disposition for waiting, and for the proper exterior way of acting as one waits. Every culture recommends what many cultures call "patience," but each articulates and applies the virtue in a different way. Nonetheless, "patience" itself becomes a reference point by which members from one culture can discuss with another the ways that persons learn to perceive, understand, and acquire the right stance for waiting. Similarly, we read cross-cultural studies of particular virtues like courage and honor.[22] These studies prompt an attempt to propose cardinal virtue, precisely to see whether we can exchange with one another across time and place what it means to be and to act in a minimally integrated virtuous way.

INADEQUACY OF THE CLASSICAL CARDINAL VIRTUES

Before scrutinizing the classical cardinal virtues, we need to set two basic parameters. First, though philosophers distinguish between a good act and a right act, arguing that the former conforms to virtue and the latter to rules, theologians distinguish goodness from rightness in a completely different way. They argue that goodness pertains to charity, and rightness describes an action or a way of living that conforms to the criteria of the method which they advance. Thus a deontologist calls people good if they have charity, but calls conduct right if it is neither intrinsically wrong nor disproportionate. Likewise, a proportionalist calls people good if they have charity, but calls conduct right if it has proportionate reason. Finally, a virtue ethicist also calls people good who have charity, but conduct right if it conforms to the virtues. Charity aside, the virtues are about our being rightly ordered in essential areas of life.[23] The virtues are about right actions coming from rightly ordered or virtuous persons.[24]

Contemporary Catholic moral theologians like Klaus Demmer,[25] Josef Fuchs,[26] Louis Janssens,[27] Richard McCormick,[28] and Schüller[29] advance the distinction and add that in order to call a person good the person's conduct does not need to be right; striving out of love for the right sufficiently describes a good person.[30] This is the response to the gift of charity: to strive for right living.[31] Thus these authors do not separate goodness and rightness: as goodness pursues the right, true charity pursues the cardinal virtues.

Second, the four cardinal virtues do not necessarily engage one's faith life. In scholastic language they are the acquired virtues and not the infused ones which, like charity, God gives through grace. Certainly these cardinal virtues can be "informed" by a community's faith life.[32] But the virtues can be pursued by anyone who intends and exercises them rightly. Thus we can urge each other to acquire them whether we are sitting in the same pew or on the same park bench.

To scrutinize the classical list of the cardinal virtues, we turn to Aquinas's writings because they fulfill these two conditions: virtues concern rightly ordered lives, and acquired virtues are accessible to all people.[33] In the question on the cardinal virtues in the *Prima Secundae* of the *Summa theologiae,* Thomas cited Ambrose, Gregory, Cicero, and Augustine, and with them named the four cardinal virtues as prudence, justice, fortitude, and temperance.[34] The virtues are called cardinal because they are "principal" that is they are *fundamental* to attaining the "rectitude of appetite" of virtuous living. That rectitude is central because "virtue not only confers the faculty of doing well, but also causes the good deed done.[35] This rectitude consists in ordering the appetitive and intellectual powers that enable us to act. Prudence orders our practical reason; justice orders the will or our intellectual appetite; temperance and fortitude perfect the passions, which are divided into the concupiscible or desiring power and the irascible or struggling power.[36] The four virtues are cardinal because they sufficiently order all those areas of our lives that are engaged in moral acting.[37] Moreover as principals they provide the basics for all right order in human action. They are necessary and sufficient conditions for describing an agent and an action as virtuous.

Despite its evident attractiveness, the classical list of the cardinal virtues fails to serve contemporary needs for three reasons. First, it is deceptively simple and inadequate. Second, a different anthropology has more recently emerged that insists on the relationality of the human. Finally, as if to prove this anthropological claim, philosophers and theologians have proposed virtues that are premised on our relationality.

First, Thomas's structure insists on a hierarchal uniformity that does not anticipate or admit conflict.[38] Since each virtue has domain both in the particular part of the subject in which it inheres and in the dimension of activity of which it is principal, there are no shared grounds among them by which the claims of one could appropriately challenge or contradict the claims of the other. Thus matters that pertain to the irascible powers concern courage, while those of the practical intellect concern prudence. Similarly, any discussion about the external operation of an activity is governed by justice, and the balance of desires is governed by temperance. The components of the human and the act are so distinctively divided that the claims of one do not overlap into the claims of another.

Even if they did overlap, so as to share similar subjects or similar matter, they could not conflict because Thomas argues that they are hierarchally distinguishable. The only intellectual virtue among the cardinal virtues, prudence, is not that tepid little virtue that warns against taking bold steps. It looks forward to the overall end of life and sets the agenda for attaining that end[39] and all intermediate ends. It discerns and sets the standards of moral action.[40] Moreover it enjoys nearly the same function and authority over the moral virtues that charity does with the infused virtues: as charity unites the infused virtues, prudence unites and connects the moral virtues.[41] In short, the "whole matter of moral virtues falls under the one rule of prudence."[42] With Aristotle, Thomas upholds the absolute priority of prudence; no acquired virtue is more important.[43]

But what does prudence govern? It governs the three moral virtues. Though the virtues of temperance and fortitude order ourselves interiorly,[44] justice orders all our operations or exterior actions.[45] For this reason, justice provides the real mean to human action.[46]

Sometimes, however, we need to establish the mean with regard to ourselves, that is, we need to attain the balance of our own concupiscible and irascible powers in order to become more rightly ordered. In these instances we pursue temperance and fortitude; yet we pursue them eventually in order to be more just.

Thomas's organizing principle is hierarchical: the overall end of the cardinal virtues is that practical reason can properly direct the agent to be just. Thus a virtue is greater wherein more rational good can shine forth.[47] Now justice expresses that greater good both by the fact that it is in the rational appetite and thus nearer reason, and because it alone orders not only the agent, but the agent in relationship to others. For this reason justice is the chief moral virtue.[48]

This classification illustrates three important points. First, justice is the only relational virtue. Second, since the virtues are distinguished by their matters and their subject, the virtues do not have competitive claims against each other. Moreover, because there is a hierarchy according to their relationship to reason, where temperance is subordinate to fortitude and then to justice, *if* there were some matter that concerned the claims of two virtues, the claims of justice would take simple priority. Finally, the virtues of the passions are auxiliary to justice. Justice in a manner of speaking, then, governs all our actions.[49]

If we return to Mrs. Bergmeier's case, we can see how Thomas would have assessed her situation, namely by asking whether what she does is just. Clearly, Mrs. Bergmeier's justice is evident both in her actions for her Jewish neighbors and in her roles as mother and wife. But the issue at hand is whether she can engage in an act of intercourse outside of her marriage, despite her legitimate concerns. Thomas would argue, I think, that justice is about giving each one their due and that the due in marriage is, among other goods, exclusive access to marital relations.[50] Thus justice in marriage is precisely founded on a marriage contract and that contract is absolutely exclusive: only the two partners may express themselves in sexual intercourse. Moreover, Mr. and Mrs. Bergmeier's marital rights are given them not by their choice but by the institution of marriage that they have entered; it is not their prerogative to suspend that contract. Justice requires, therefore, that Mrs. Bergmeier be a model wife and that she not engage in intercourse with the guard or with anyone other than her husband.

This assessment is not directly connected to the thinking of the deontologists mentioned earlier. Their objection was based on the notion of intrinsic evil, that any act of sexual intercourse outside of the context of marriage is intrinsically wrong. John Dedek has repeatedly demonstrated that the concept of intrinsic evil was foreign to Thomas. It was developed a century after Thomas's death by Durandus of Saint Pourçain, probably the most outspoken opponent of Thomism in the 14th century.[51] Thus Thomas's own argument is based not on some absolute moral quality intrinsic to the act, but on the singular claim of justice. Could there be any other claim made on Mrs. Bergmeier that could justify the violation of justice in marriage? Not in Thomas's thesis, for there is no other primary virtue that could compete with or supersede the claims that justice makes on Mrs. Bergmeier. Since the only question for Thomas here concerns the just way of acting, he has no way of counterbalancing the universal claim that out of justice all spouses must reserve their acts of intercourse for one another.

There is something deeply disturbing about the inadequacy of this answer. Other issues should have been raised. Isn't there something specific about Mrs. Bergmeier's case that merits further attention? Do we not want at least to introduce the specific context of her marriage: that this marriage is during a time of war, where one spouse is imprisoned, the health of the other is dramatically declining, and the welfare of the children is terribly endangered? Do we not also need to ask some questions about Mrs. Bergmeier's care for herself in the face of such an obvious act of compromise? There are many questions that we need to ask, and justice alone does not provide a sufficient context for analyzing the rightness of her activity.

The complaint, then, is that justice alone is insufficient. This insufficiency can be seen from another perspective. There are now newly coined virtues, that are often in part descriptive of justice, sometimes even hyphenating justice. Walter Burghardt in describing the characteristics of social justice spirituality refers to Fred Kammer's book *Doing Faithjustice*. Commenting on Kammer's title, Burghardt explains, "Not faith *and* justice; one word, a newly coined word... faithjustice. This is the faith that does justice. Each word is significant in itself, but it is the two in combination that shape a spirituality of justice."[52]

The most common coupling occurs between justice and love. Daniel Maguire writes, "In the Bible, justice and love are hyphenated in a way that is 'good news to the poor' (Luke 4:18)."[53] Likewise Margaret Farley holds that the norm for sexual ethics is "just love," that is, our love must be founded on justice, and correspondingly our justice must be loving.[54] Similarly, William Werpehowski argues for a professional ethics rooted in the vocations of love and justice.[55] These insights clearly depend on the important writings of Reinhold Niebuhr who argued that love and justice must define one another: alone each virtue is insufficient.[56]

Moreover, Pope John Paul II prefers the concept of solidarity, a concept that on the one hand seeks equality, but on the other hand expresses a loving bondedness among its members.[57] Again we find at least implicitly the two virtues of love and justice shaping and defining one another.

Paul Ricoeur studies these two virtues as dialectical. Rather than reducing one to the other, eliding the two together, or placing the two in a pure and simple dichotomy, Ricoeur places them in a "tension between two distinct and sometimes opposed claims."[58] Ricoeur's insight that the virtues are distinct and at times opposing stands in contrast with Thomas's strategy of the cardinal virtues where justice is supported by fortitude and temperance and none contradicts, opposes, or challenges the claims of the other. Thus only when one cardinal virtue stands on equal footing with another cardinal virtue can there be a dialectical tension in which the virtues challenge and define one another, and, as Ricoeur suggests, "may even be the occasion for the invention of responsible forms of behavior."[59]

The unity of the virtues that Thomas offers us, however, is one prompted not only by prudence interconnecting the other three, but also by the privileged place that justice holds. The virtues enjoy a unity in part because justice has no competition. That insight stands in sharp contrast to contemporary figures who find justice alone insufficient and who posit another competing virtue, like love.

Contemporary virtue ethics acknowledges, then, the possibility that cardinal virtues could be in competition with one another. Indeed, William Spohn contends that most virtue ethicists presume that the virtues conflict.[60] In that presupposition they admit a certain congruency with deontologists and proportionalists, that is, that conflict among key directing guidelines is inherent to all methods of moral reasoning.

For instance, the mixed deontologist Frankena, after presenting the two fundamental principles of beneficence and justice, raises "the problem of possible conflict" between the two principles and writes, "I see no way out of this. It does seem to me that the two principles may come into conflict, both at the level of individual action and at that of social policy, and I know of no formula that will always tell us how to solve such conflicts."[61] Likewise in an enormously influential work, Tom Beauchamp and James Childress argue that "there is no premier and overriding authority in either the patient or the physician and no preeminent principle in biomedical ethics – not even the admonition to act in the patient's best interest."[62]

If, as in other methods, the cardinal virtues conflict with one another, then the function of the virtue of prudence greatly expands. In the more harmonious classical list of cardinal virtues, prudence's primary task was to determine justice when dealing with our actions, temperance when dealing with our desires, and fortitude when dealing with our struggles. But in this new proposal, prudence would have to name not only what the claim of each particular virtue is, but also what priority that claim enjoys.

Stanley Hauerwas seems to see this point when he argues that we have the task of sorting out "conflicting loyalties" throughout our lives. That sorting out means that in the long run we are to live a life that ethically incorporates the variety of relational claims which are made on us. This we do through the narrative of the lives we live.[63] Thus the virtues are related to one another not in some inherent way, as they seem to be in the classical list of the cardinal virtues. Nor do they complement one another per se. Rather, they become integrated in the life of the prudent person who lives them. The unity of the virtues is found not in some theoretical apportioning of the cardinal virtues to specific powers or matters. It is found rather in the final living out of lives shaped by prudence anticipating and responding to virtuous claims.

So the insufficiency of the classical list of cardinal virtues prompts us to find virtues that satisfactorily encompass the basic and at times competitive claims to which a virtuous person must respond. That insight then prompts our second concern: to consider the anthropology that underlies the cardinal virtues.

The turn to the subject has prompted many to abandon a classicist anthropology that examined humanity by asking "*what* is it?" The contemporary ethicist does not examine humanity as something to be known, but reflects on humanity as knowing and asks "*who* are we?" In the older design, there was an investigation of what the human has and does. Thus, Thomas divided the human according to several powers and argued that the virtues perfect each of them. Like others,[64] I believe that to have a viable anthropology is to understand ourselves as agents and not as objects; moreover, as agents we are always relational.[65] Thus virtues do not perfect what we have or what we do; rather they perfect who we are in the mode of our being, what is as being in relationships. Virtues do not perfect powers or "things" inside of us, but rather ways that we are.[66]

A PROPOSAL

In this context, I propose my own list of cardinal virtues. It includes justice, fidelity, self-care, and prudence.

As persons, we are relational in three ways: generally, specifically, and uniquely.[67] And each of these relational ways of being demands a cardinal virtue. As a relational being in general, we are called to justice.[68] As a relational being specifically, we are called to fidelity.[69] As a relational being uniquely, we are called to self-care. These three virtues are cardinal. Unlike Thomas's structure, none is ethically prior to the other; they have equally urgent claims and they should be pursued as ends in themselves. Thus we are not called to be faithful and self-caring in order to be just, nor are we called to be self-caring and just in order to be faithful. None is auxiliary to the others. Each is a distinctive virtue, none being a subset or subcategory of the others. They are cardinal. The fourth cardinal virtue is prudence, which determines what constitutes the just, faithful, and self-caring way of life for an individual.

Justice

To consider each virtue I turn to the third task of demonstrating that many recent expressions of specific virtues point toward the relational configuration that I am offering. First, our relationality generally is always to be directed by an ordered appreciation for the common good in which we treat all people as equal. Apart from all specific relations, we belong to humanity and are expected to respond to all its members in general, equally and impartially. Paul Ricoeur notes that from Aristotle to Rawls *justice* is always associated with equality.[70]

I cannot recall where I read or heard the remark, but I remember John Rawls stating that a child's earliest moral insight occurs when the child witnesses an unequal distribution of food, drink, or some other object and remarks, "That's unfair." That the child can recognize that inequality is unfair does not mean, however, that the child knows what fairness is. But the child does know that in any human grouping equality governs in general the participation of the members. This insight can lead to the claim of Lawrence Kohlberg that the aim of the moral life is to become impartial and to recognize the universal claims of equality.

But while Rawls and Kohlberg argue for justice as a principle, in this article we understand justice as a virtue. As a virtue, justice is not simply concerned with external activity. Rather, as Bernard Williams notes, justice is about ordering all our interior dispositions so that the claim of equality originates from within.[71]

Fidelity

If justice urges us to treat all people equally, then *fidelity* makes different claims on us. Fidelity is the virtue that nurtures and sustains the bonds of those special relationships that we enjoy whether by blood, marriage, love, or sacrament. Fidelity requires that we treat with special care those who are closer to us. If justice rests on impartiality and universality, fidelity rests on partiality and particularity.[72]

Obviously naming fidelity as the second cardinal virtue is a development of the insights of Niebuhr, Ricoeur, and others who wrote about a love that challenges justice. I prefer to name this virtue fidelity, rather than love, because of a certain confusion in the use of the word "love."

Generally speaking, Roman Catholics tend to consider love as the basis of all virtues. For instance, Thomas distinguishes charity or Christian love from the four cardinal virtues. If we want to know what to do in the concrete, we must turn not to charity, which is about union with God, but to the cardinal virtues, which are about right living.[73] As Karl Rahner would say, charity or Christian love is transcendental.[74] But Protestant theologians, as we have seen, tend to use love much more concretely as being as categorical as justice. Thus, in a debate between the Protestant philosopher Frankena and Catholic theologians McCormick and Schüller,[75] Frankena argued that love was not inclusive of justice because love is particular and justice is universal. The Catholic theologians responded, equating love with charity and arguing that love seeks justice. With good Thomistic instincts, they saw justice without competition and love of God and neighbor as prior to all virtue, as universal, and as impartial.

Fidelity here is admittedly like Niebhur's love. It is also like the claim that Carol Gilligan made in an important work.[76] Gilligan criticized Kohlberg for arguing that full moral development was found in the person who could reason well about justice as impartial and universal. She countered that the human must aim for the impartiality of justice as well as for the development of particular bonds. In effect, I think, she would be quite comfortable with naming fidelity as articulating this different voice.

Fidelity also captures the concern of contemporary moral theologians and ethicists. Fidelity expresses, for instance, the covenant ethics of the late Paul Ramsey,[77] the friendship ethics of Gilbert Meilaender[78] and Paul Wadell,[79] the loyalty ethics of George Fletcher,[80] and the commitment ethics of Margaret Farley.[81]

Though it may be new to suggest these two virtues as distinct and at times competitive, the stuff of a good story has long been based on the tension between these two claims. For instance, the drama of Antigone is caught as she stands between supporting a universal peace for her whole city and obeying Creon's law, or else tending to her brother who remains unburied outside the city walls. But Greek culture is not the only setting for conflicts between justice and fidelity. The American movie industry regularly depicts justice calling us away from our special relationships. A lawyer abandons her father's defense and becomes his accuser of crimes against humanity in *The Music Box*. A wife rejects her husband's commands and participates in a civil rights demonstration in *A Long Walk Home,* and a mother campaigns against apartheid while a teenage daughter feels neglected in *A World Apart.* Curiously, contrary to Gilligan's arguments, these films depict women choosing the universal claims of justice over the particular claims of fidelity. As if in a gender reversal, two recent movies depict the opposite: a young male choosing fidelity over justice. In *Scent of a Woman* a prep school student decides not to report on his friends despite the harm that they have caused the entire school. And in *The Terminator* a boy is called to save the world, but decides instead to save his mother first, risking humanity's entire existence. From *Antigone* to *The Terminator,* from the heights to the depths of human drama, we watch in suspense as characters are caught between what Riccoeur calls "two distinct and at times opposed claims."

Self-Care

Neither of these virtues, however, addresses the unique relationship that I as a moral agent have with myself. Still love or *care for self* enjoys a considered role in our tradition.[82] For instance, Aquinas argued against suicide because it offends both justice by depriving the common good of one's life and charity by doing harm to oneself.[83] Thomas, through his order of charity,[84] developed the love of self that Stephen Pope describes in his latest work.[85] I prefer to avoid calling this virtue "self-love," however, because of the same confusion about the word love, though Edward Vacek calls it "self-love" in a new work in which he discusses the triple end of the love command: self, neighbor and God.[86]

I also prefer "self-care" to "self-esteem" or "self-respect."[87] Admittedly there is an extensive literature on self-esteem and considerable debate about what role it ought to play in our lives.[88] But the moral task is to take care of oneself and that includes, among other tasks, self-esteem.[89] Thus self-esteem is a subcategory of self-care.[90] In short, we each have a unique responsibility to care for ourselves, affectively, mentally, physically, and spiritually.

Some Christian activists may balk at self-care. Some could go so far as to note that if Jesus Christ let self-care be a cardinal virtue we would never have been redeemed by the blood of the cross. But we have every reason to believe that the historical Jesus took care of himself; we need only think of how often he is contrasted with John the Baptizer. Likewise we have no reason to suppose that Jesus suffered from lack of self-esteem. In fact, I think we can say that it was precisely because Jesus knew the virtues of fidelity, justice, and self-care that the agony in the Garden was so painful. He was a man who loved God, humanity, his friends, and himself: his conflict, like all true conflicts, was to determine which relationship made the greater claim on him.

Prudence

Finally, *prudence* has the task of integrating the other three virtues into our lives, just as it did when it was among the classical list of the cardinal virtues.[91] Thus prudence is always vigilant, looking to the future, not only trying to realize the claims of justice, fidelity, and self-care in the here and now, but also calling us to anticipate occasions when each of these virtues can be more fully acquired. In this way prudence is clearly a virtue that pursues ends and effectively establishes the moral agenda for the person growing in these virtues.[92] But these ends are not in opposition to nor in isolation from one another. Rather, prudence, in forming our narratives, helps each virtue to shape its end as more inclusive of the other two.

Conversely, by naming three other cardinal virtues, the prudential is now identified with justice, fidelity, and self-care. That is to say that any action or way of life that neglects the consideration of one of these virtues is itself wrong or imprudential. The prudent person now must consider the claims of all three.

CONCLUSION

On this note I conclude by finally giving the answer to the case of Mrs. Bergmeier that I should have given fifteen years ago. In evaluating the morality of her conduct, prudence advises us to ask questions about her triple self-understanding in having general, special, and unique relationships, each with a cardinal virtue. From the viewpoint of justice, she demonstrates an obvious concern for her neighbors and their equality;

we note too that in her society she has also been a caring wife and mother. Until the point when she violated the institutional claims of marriage, she was true to her culture's institution of marriage. But this violation is not pursued for its own sake. From the viewpoint of fidelity, she has special bonds with her husband and children that distinguish her situation. Her husband's and children's health are in jeopardy, and she alone is the primary caregiver. Her absence leaves those others neglected. She chooses to engage in an action whose consequences mean new life, a child with whom she will probably have a particularly faithful relationship precisely because the conception and birth of that child led to the rescue of her other children and husband. Finally, the claim of self-care is the real neuralgic point. We have no reason but to believe that Mrs. Bergmeier is a just and faithful person. But Mrs. Bergmeier decides to submit herself to the guard, and to carry, raise, and love a child who is the fruit of that loathful union. A person who lacks the virtue of self-care could not possibly endure the emotional burden of such a decision. Without that virtue, shame, self-loathing, and hatred would most likely materialize in her life and eventually become insurmountable. Only a person who can be as caring of herself as she is faithful to her husband and children and just in fighting for her fellow citizens could live with this decision. But knowing that is the task of prudence.

Inasmuch as this is all the information that the case provides, we conclude by simply acknowledging that practical wisdom will help Mrs. Bergmeier understand further, not only what these virtues mean in general, but what they mean specifically. Toward that end she will rely on her understanding both of herself and of her culture as it specifically determines and recommends the practices of these virtues. But whether she is in Nazi Germany, the Soviet Gulag, or anywhere else, she will deliberate better knowing that these cardinal virtues are being discussed elsewhere as well.

Notes

1. See the case debated over years in Richard McCormick, *Notes on Moral Theology: 1965 through 1980* (Washington: University Press of America, 1981) 356–57, 512, 536, 753–54.

2. Some might reject the suggestion that proportionalists are fundamen-

tally act-oriented ethicists and not agent-oriented. But proportionalists like Janssens, McCormick, and Schüller have always written about the premoral or ontic values of acts and have not invoked the anthropological standards of the virtues. See *Readings in Moral Theology No. 1: Moral Norms and Catholic Tradition,* ed. Charles E. Curran and Richard A. McCormick (New York: Paulist, 1979).

3. See Frederick Carney, "The Virtue-Obligation Controversy," *Journal of Religious Ethics* 1 (1973) 5–9; William Frankena, "The Ethics of Love Conceived as an Ethics of Virtue," ibid. 21–31. Carney, "On Frankena and Religious Ethics," *Journal of Religious Ethics* 3 (1975) 7–26; Frankena, "Conversations with Carney and Hauerwas," ibid. 45–62; Stanley Hauerwas, "Obligations and Virtue Once More," ibid. 27–44.

4. Alasdair MacIntyre, *After Virtue: A Study in Moral Theory* (Notre Dame: University of Notre Dame, 1981).

5. *The Virtues: Contemporary Skills on Moral Character,* ed. Robert Kruschwitz and Robert Roberts (Belmont, Calif.: Wadsworth, 1987) 237–62.

6. Gregory Trianosky, "What is Virtue Ethics All About?" *American Philosophical Quarterly* 27 (1990) 335–44); also Gregory Pence, "Recent Work on Virtues," *American Philosophical Quarterly* 21 (1984) 281–97.

7. Lee Yearley, "Recent Work on Virtue," *Religious Studies Review* 16 (1990) 1–9.

8. William Spohn, "The Return of Virtue Ethics," *TS* 53 (1992) 60–75.

9. William Frankena, "Conversations with Carney and Hauerwas"; "The Ethics of Love Conceived of as an Ethics of Virtue"; Bruno Schüller, *Die Begrundung sittlicher Urteile* (Düsseldorf: Patmos, 1980).

10. Martha Nussbaum, *The Fragility of Goodness: Luck and Ethics in Greek Tragedy and Philosophy* (New York: Cambridge University, 1986) 299; "Non-Relative Virtues: An Aristotelian Approach," in *Midwest Studies in Philosophy* 13, *Ethical Theory: Character and Virtue* ed. P. French, T. Uehling, and H. Wettstein (Notre Dame: University of Notre Dame, 1988) 32–53. Likewise, see John Kekes, *The Examined Life* (Lewisburg: Bucknell University, 1988).

11. Paul Waddell, *Friendship and the Moral Life* (Notre Dame: University of Notre Dame, 1989) 136.

12. A. MacIntyre, *After Virtue;* see also his *Whose Justice? Whose Rationality?* (Notre Dame: University of Notre Dame, 1988).

13. Anne Patrick reflects on how different Roman Catholic communities elevate a variety of icons of holiness; a young virgin like Maria Goretti who dies fighting off a rapist is not a Dorothy Day ("Narrative and the Social Dynamics of Virtue," *Changing Values and Virtues,* ed. Dietmar Mieth and Jacques Pohier [Edinburgh: T. & T. Clark, 1987] 69–80).

14. O. Flanagan, *Varieties of Moral Personality: Ethics and Psychological Realism* (Cambridge, Mass.: Harvard University, 1991).

15. Caroline Walker Bynum warns us against considering a saint as a model of virtue: "Medieval hagiographers pointed out repeatedly that saints are not even primarily 'models' for ordinary mortals; the saints are far too dangerous for that" (*Holy Feast and Holy Fast* [Berkeley; University of California, 1987] 7).

16. Flanagan, *Varieties,* 158.

17. L. Kohlberg, *The Philosophy of Moral Development* (New York: Harper and Row, 1981).

18. Flanagan, *Varieties* 195.

19. Martha Nussbaum, "Non-Relative Virtues" 36.

20. *Summa theologiae* 1–2, q. 61, a. 2.

21. Ibid. a. 3.

22. Lee Yearley, *Mencius and Aquinas: Theories of Virtue and Conceptions of Courage* (Albany: State University of New York, 1990); Frank Steward, *Honor* (Chicago: University of Chicago, 1994).

23. Besides Nussbaum, see John Kekes, *The Examined Life.*

24. See my "Die erworbenen Tugenden als richtige (nicht gute) Lebensführung: Ein genauerer Ausdruck ethischer Beschreibung," *Ethische Theorie praktisch,* ed. Franz Furger (Münster: Aschendorff, 1991) 19–35; "A New Distinction in Moral Theology: Being Good and Living Rightly," *Church* 5 (1989) 22–28.

25. Klaus Demmer, "La competenza normativa del magistero ecclesiatico in morale," in *Fede Cristiana e Agire Morale,* eds. K. Demmer and B. Schüller (Assisi: Cittadella Editrice, 1980) 144–69; *Deuten und Handeln* (Freiburg: Universitätsverlag, 1985); "Erwägungen zum intrinsece malum," *Gregorianum* 68 (1987) 613–37; *Leben in Menschenhand* (Freiburg: Universitätsverlag, 1987); "Sittlich handeln als Zeugnis geben," *Gregorianum* 4 (1983) 453–85; "Sittlich handeln aus Erfahrung," *Gregorianum* 59 (1978) 661–90.

26. J. Fuchs, *Christian Ethics in a Secular Arena* (Washington: Georgetown University, 1984); *Christian Morality: The Word Becomes Flesh* (Washington: Georgetown University, 1987); *Essere del Signore* (Rome: Gregorian University, 1981); *Personal Responsibility and Christian Morality* (Washington: Georgetown University, 1983).

27. L. Janssens, "Norms and Priorities in a Love Ethics," *Louvain Studies* 6 (1977) 207–38; "Ontic Good and Ontic Evil," *Louvain Studies* 12 (1987) 62–82.

28. R. McCormick, "Bishops as Teachers and Jesuits as Listeners," *Studies in the Spirituality of Jesuits* 28 (1986); *Notes on Moral Theology, 1981 through 1984* (Lanham, Md.: University Press of America, 1984).

29. B. Schüller, *Die Begrundung sittlicher Urteile*; "The Debate on the Specific Character of Christian Ethics," in *Readings in Moral theology 2: The Distinctiveness of Christian Ethics*, ed. C. Curran and R. McCormick (New York: Paulist, 1980) 207–33; "Direct Killing/Indirect Killing," in C. Curran and R. McCormick, eds., *Readings in Moral Theology* 1.138–57; "The Double Effect in Catholic Thought: A Reevaluation," in *Doing Evil to Achieve Good*, ed. R. McCormick and P. Ramsey (Chicago: Loyola University, 1978) 165–92; "Gewissen und Schuld," in *Das Gewissen*, ed. Josef Fuchs (Düsseldorf: Patmos, 1979) 34–55; "Neuere Beiträge zum Thema 'Begrundung sittlicher Normen'," in *Theologische Berichte* 4, ed. Franz Furger (Zürich: Benziger, 1974) 109–81; *Wholly Human* (Washington: Georgetown University, 1985).

30. See also Bernard Hoose, *Proportionalism: The American Debate and Its European Roots* (Washington: Georgetown University, 1987).

31. Schüller rightly argues that, regardless of one's method of moral reasoning, charity remains the descriptive category for goodness; see "The Double Effect" esp. 167–69.

32. Joseph Kotva, "An Appeal for a Christian Virtue Ethic," *Thought* 67 (1992) 158–80; "Christian Virtue Ethics and the 'Sectarian Temptation'," *Heythrop Journal* 35 (1994) 35– 52.

33. See my "Distinguishing Charity as Goodness and Prudence as Rightness: A Key to Thomas' *Pars Secunda*," *The Thomist* 56 (1992) 407–26; *Goodness and Rightness in Thomas Aquinas' Summa Theologiae* (Washington: Georgetown University, 1992); Conrad van Ouwerkerk, *Caritas et Ratio: Etude sur le double principe de la vie morale chrétienne d'après S. Thomas d'Aquin* (Nijmegen: Drukkerij Gebr. Janssen, 1956); Jean Porter, "The Subversion of Virtue: Acquired and Infused Virtues in the *Summa theologiae*," *Annual of the Society of Christian Ethics* 1992 (Washington: Georgetown University, 1992) 19–42. Aquinas departs from Augustine on these two points, as is evident in his definition of virtue in *ST* 1–2, q. 55, a. 4.

34. See Josef Pieper, *The Four Cardinal Virtues* (Notre Dame: University of Notre Dame, 1966); Jean Porter, "Perennial and Timely Virtues: Practical Wisdom, Courage, and Temperance," in *Changing Values and Virtues*, ed. Dietmar Mieth and Jacques Pohier (Edinburgh: T. & T. Clark, 1987) 60–68; *The Recovery of Virtue* (Louisville: Westminster, 1990). On the first proponents, see John Mahoney, *The Making of Moral Theology* (Oxford: Clarendon, 1987) 248–49.

35. *ST* 1–2, q. 61, a. 1 corp.

36. *ST* 1–2, q. 61, a. 2 and 3.

37. See Jean Porter, "The Unity of the Virtues and the Ambiguity of Goodness," *Journal of Religious Ethics* 21 (1993) 137–64.

38. Rarely does Thomas admit in the *Summa theologiae* the possibility of

conflict where two parties have legitimate claims; for an exception, see 1, q. 113, a. 8: "Whether there can be strife or discord among the angels?"

39. *ST* 1–2, q. 66, a. 3 ad 3.

40. *ST* 1–2.64.1 corp. ad 1, and 3 corp; 2–2.23.6 corp; 47.7 corp and ad 2. See Domenico Capone, *Intorno alla verità morale* (Rome: Gregorian University Press, 1951) 19ff., 46ff. Karl-Wilhelm Merks, *Theologische Grundlegung der sittlichen Autonomie* (Düsseldorf: Patmos, 1978) 125ff.

41. *ST* 1–2.66.2 corp; 68.5 corp.

42. *ST* 1–2.65.1 ad 3.

43. *ST* 1.79.12 corp; 2–2.47.6 and 7.

44. *ST* 2–2.58.3 corp and 8 corp.

45. *ST* 2–2.58.2 corp and ad 4; 58.3 corp.

46. *ST* 1–2.64.2.

47. *ST* 1–2.66.1.

48. *ST* 1–2.66.4.

49. *ST* 1–2.61.2–4; 66.4 corp; 2–2.58.1 corp.

50. See *ST* Supplement 41–68.

51. John Dedek, "Intrinsically Evil Acts: The Emergence of a Doctrine," *Recherches de théologie ancienne et médiévale* 50 (1983) 191–226; "Intrinsically Evil Acts: An Historical Study of the Mind of St. Thomas," *The Thomist* 43 (1979) 385–413; "Moral Absolutes in the Predecessors of St. Thomas," *TS* 38 (1977) 654–80.

52. Walter Burghardt, "Characteristics of Social Justice Spirituality," *Origins* 24.9 (1994) 157–64, at 159; Fred Kammer, *Doing Faithjustice* (New York: Paulist, 1991).

53. Daniel Maquire, "The Primacy of Justice in Moral Theology," *Horizons* 10 (1983) 72–85, at 74.

54. Margaret Farley, "An Ethic for Same Sex Relations," in *A Challenge To Love*, ed. Robert Nugent (New York: Crossroad, 1986) 93–106; *Personal Commitments: Beginning, Keeping, Changing* (San Francisco: Harper and Row, 1990).

55. William Werpehowski, "The Professions: Vocations to Justice and Love," in *The Professions in Ethical Context*, ed. Francis Eigo (Villanova: Villanova University, 1986) 1–24.

56. Reinhold Niebuhr, *Love and Justice: Selections from the Shorter Writings of Reinhold Niebuhr*, ed. D. B. Robertson (Louisville: Westminster, 1957); on a similar insight see Karen Lebacqz, *Justice in an Unjust World* (Minneapolis: Augsburg, 1987); José Miranda, *Marx and the Bible* (Maryknoll, N.Y.: Orbis, 1974).

57. See John Paul II, *Sollicitudo rei socialis*, (Vatican City: Libreria Editrice Vaticana, 1987); *The Logic of Solidarity: Commentaries on Pope John*

Paul II's Encyclical "On Social Concern," ed. Gregory Baum and Robert Ellsberg (Maryknoll, N.Y.: Orbis, 1989); Howard Gray, "Religious Life's Spirit of Solidarity," *Origins* 23.10 (1993) 173–76.

58. Paul Ricoeur, "Love and Justice," in *Radical Pluralism and Truth: David Tracy and the Hermeneutics of Religion,* ed. Werner G. Jeanrond and Jennifer L. Rike (New York: Crossroad, 1991) 187–202, at 196.

59. Ibid. 197.

60. Spohn, "The Return of Virtue Ethics."

61. William Frankena, *Ethics,* 2d ed. (Englewood Cliffs, N.J.: Prentice-Hall, 1973) 52.

62. Tom Beauchamp and James Childress, *Principles of Biomedical Ethics* (New York: Oxford University, 1989) 211.

63. Stanley Hauerwas, *A Community of Character* (Notre Dame: University of Notre Dame, 1981) 144.

64. For the turn to the subject, see Bernard Lonergan, *Collection* (New York: Herder, 1967); *A Second Collection* (Philadelphia: Westminster, 1974); *The Subject* (Milwaukee; Marquette University, 1968); Michael Himes, "The Human Person in Contemporary Theology. From Human Nature to Authentic Subjectivity," in *Introduction to Christian Ethics: A Reader,* ed. Ronald Hamel and Kenneth Himes (New York: Paulist, 1989) 49–62.

65. Interestingly, Augustine claims to support the philosophers in this, "that the life of the wise man should be social" (*City of God* 19.5, trans. Henry Bettenson [New York: Viking Penguin, 1984] 858). I am expanding Augustine's claim to all humanity as both descriptive and prescriptive. Stephen Pope develops this relational anthropology in "The Order of Love and Recent Catholic Ethics: A Constructive Proposal," *TS* 52 (1991) 255–88.

66. Paul Lauritzen has done an important synthesis of recent works on morality and the self in which he argues that the turn to narrative ethics enables us to see both that the self as fragmented becomes integrated by the narrative one lives and that, as he writes, "the narrative self is necessarily a social and relational self." A relational view of the self requires us to rethink our understanding, not only of the self, but of morality ("The Self and Its Discontents," *Journal of Religious Ethics* 22 [1994] 189–210, at 206).

67. I prescind here from charity, which concerns our relationship with God.

68. See my "Learning the Virtue of Justice," *Church* 9/3 (1993) 38–40.

69. See my "The Virtue of Fidelity," *Church* 9/2 (1993) 38–39.

70. Ricoeur, "Love and Justice" 195.

71. Bernard Williams, "Justice as a Virtue," in *Essays on Aristotle's Ethics,* ed. Amelia Oksenberg Rorty (Berkeley: University of California, 1980)

189–99. Besides Maguire, see Seamus Murphy, "The Many Ways of Justice," *Studies in the Spirituality of Jesuits* 26/2 (1994) 1–40.

72. See a similar insight in Spohn, "The Return" 72. In several questions dealing with charity, Aquinas argues that we have greater obligations to those with whom we enjoy specific relationships; see *ST* 2–2.31.3 and 32.9. See the tension between love in general and love in particular in William Werpehowski, "'Agape' and Special Relations," in *The Love Commandments*, ed. Edmund Santurri and William Werpehowski (Washington: Georgetown University, 1992) 138–56.

73. For the formality of charity, see Gerard Gilleman, *The Primacy of Charity in Moral Theology* (Westminster, Md.: Newman, 1959) 29–45, esp. 42–45.

74. Karl Rahner, "The Commandment of Love in Relation to the Other Commandments," *Theological Investigations* 5, trans. Karl-H. Kruger (Baltimore: Helicon, 1969) 439–539.

75. See McCormick, using Schüller against Frankena, in his "A Commentary on the Commentaries," in *Doing Evil to Achieve Good*, ed. Richard McCormick and Paul Ramsey (Chicago: Loyola University, 1978) 193–267, esp. 241–54.

76. Carol Gilligan, *In a Different Voice: Psychological Theory and Women's Development* (Cambridge, Mass.: Harvard University, 1982).

77. Paul Ramsey, *The Patient as Person: Explorations in Medical Ethics* (New Haven: Yale University, 1970); *The Essential Paul Ramsey: A Collection*, ed. William Werpehowski and Stephen Crocco (New Haven: Yale University, 1994).

78. Gilbert Meilaender, *Friendship: A Study in Theological Ethics* (Notre Dame: University of Notre Dame, 1981).

79. Paul Wadell, *Friendship and the Moral Life* (Notre Dame: University of Notre Dame, 1989).

80. George Fletcher, *Loyalty: An Essay on the Morality of Relationships* (New York: Oxford University, 1993).

81. See note 54 above.

82. Oliver O'Donovan, *The Problem of Self-Love in Saint Augustine* (New Haven: Yale, 1980).

83. *ST* 2–2.64.5 ad 1.

84. The concern for self-care runs throughout the *Summa,* from 1.5.1 corp and 48.1, which describes how all nature seeks its own perfection, to 1–2.27.3 that insists it is natural to prefer oneself over others, and 29.4 that states the impossibility of hating oneself. In 2–2, Aquinas argues that though inordinate self-love is the source of sin (25.4, 28.4 ad 1), self-love belongs to the order of charity and is prior to neighbor love (25.12, 26.4). He adds that charity is the

source of peace which aims at ending conflict not only with others but also within oneself (29.1). By introducing self-care into the constellation of the cardinal virtues I believe that I am developing Thomas's own thoughts.

85. Stephen Pope, *The Evolution of Altruism and the Ordering of Love* (Washington: Georgetown University, 1994); see also his "Expressive Individualism and True Self-Love: A Thomistic Perspective," *Journal of Religion* 71.3 (1991) 384–99.

86. Edward Vacek, *Love, Human and Divine: The Heart of Christian Ethics* (Washington: Georgetown University, 1994) 239–73.

87. Until recently I preferred self-esteem; see my "The Virtue of Self-esteem," *Church* 9/4 (1993) 37–39. See also Stephen Massey, "Is Self-Respect a Moral or a Psychological Concept?" *Ethics* 93 (1983) 246–61; David Sachs, "How to Distinguish Self-Respect from Self-Esteem," *Philosophy and Public Affairs* 10 (1981) 346–60.

88. See Christina Hoff Sommers, *"Who Stole Feminism? How Women Have Betrayed Women* (New York: Simon Schuster, 1994).

89. Therapists use the term self-care in professional ethics; e.g. L. S. Brown, "Ethical Issues in Feminist Therapy: Selected Topics," *Psychology of Women Quarterly* 15 (1991) 324–33; Katherine M. Clarke, "Lessons from Feminist Therapy for Ministerial Ethics," *Journal of Pastoral Care* 48 (1994) 233–42.

90. Marc Lappe, "Virtue and Public Health," in *Virtue and Medicine,* ed. Earl Shelp (Dordrecht: D. Reidel, 1985) 289–303.

91. Joseph Burroughs, *Prudence Integrating the Moral Virtues according to Saint Thomas Aquinas* (Washington: Catholic University, 1955).

92. See Daniel Mark Nelson, "Karl Rahner's Existential Ethics: A Critique Based on St. Thomas's Understanding of Prudence," *The Thomist* 51 (1987) 461–79; *The Priority of Prudence* (University Park: Pennsylvania State University, 1992).

19. How Shall We Love in a Postmodern World?

Margaret A. Farley

This chapter first appeared in *The Annual of the Society of Christian Ethics* (1994).

In the process of preparing this address I came to appreciate why Socrates and his friends told stories to one another after their banqueting. A leisurely dinner is not always conducive to abstract considerations or rigorous philosophical argument. I decided, therefore, to follow the example of some of the participants in Plato's *Symposium* and to begin with stories—or, more accurately, small pieces of stories. I do not propose to generate a theory from these tales, nor will I say a great deal about them as I move eventually to more theoretical issues. They are simply stories, bits of narratives, that were burned into my mind when I first encountered them at various times in the past, and that now intrude themselves periodically when I think about abstract questions such as my topic for tonight: How shall we love in a postmodern world?

An image from the first of these stories was inscribed in my memory some years ago when I saw the Brazilian film *Pixote*. This is a story of countless numbers of children and young adults who fend for themselves in the streets of great cities and little towns in Brazil. Not tied to families, these children struggle for life, alone and with each other. The film follows one small boy, Pixote, as he moves through his experiences in a reformatory, back into the streets, playing with others a deadly game (a child's game, nonetheless) of survival through stealing, prostitution, the sale of drugs, and murder. Pixote's is not a highly dramatic tale; indeed, his own emotions and those of all the other characters are thinned, flattened, almost nonexistent. That is, in part, the point. The children appear incapable of feeling much at all—not horror, not guilt, not fear, not compassion, not even desire. They show little reaction to the violence, the contempt, the squalor, of their outcast existence. Ordinary life is engaged only by the need for cunning, and even this is perfunctory most of the time. Yet in a final scene, Pixote accidentally shoots and kills one of his companions. At first, his response is the same as it always is to deaths he causes and death that threatens. Observing the results of his shooting, he simply sits on a bed with his usual impassive expression. A few moments pass. Then he vomits, into the camera. This is followed by what is for the film a most extraordinary but fleeting interaction, a small gesture of comfort. The film ends with Pixote walking down one more railroad track, heading once again for nowhere in particular.

The second story, or suggestion of a story, is more positive. It appears in a poem called "Aria," by Delmore Schwartz. I first saw this text placed on a page opposite a photograph of a magnificent glass sculpture of two figures: a woman and a man, as beautiful as a Greek goddess and god, glorious and shining in naked strength and splendor, standing in mutual embrace. The lines of the poem were not gender assigned, and it does not really matter which figure speaks which lines (or, for that matter, whether the figures were male or female):

"– Kiss me there where pride is glittering
Kiss me where I am ripened and round fruit
Kiss me wherever, however I am supple, bare and flare
(Let the bell be rung as long as I am young;
    let ring and fly like a great bronze wing!)
Until I am shaken from blossom to root."
"– I'll kiss you wherever you think you are poor,
Wherever you shudder, feeling striped or barred,
Because you think you are bloodless, skinny or marred;
    until, until
    your gaze has been stilled –
Until you are shamed again no more!
I'll kiss you until your body and soul
    the mind in the body being fulfilled –
Suspend their dread and civil war!"[1]

The third and final story is a factual account presented at a women's conference designed as an alternate to the Conference of Bishops of Latin

America in Puebla, Mexico, in 1979. Speaking of the experience of peasant women in Venezuela, Leonor Aida Concha reported the following dialogue between a Venezuelan Indian woman and a priest:

Father Gumille, scolding a woman who killed her daughter deliberately during birth, received the following answer: "God grant, Father, that when I was born, my mother had loved me well and would have had pity on me for all the trials we endure, poor Indian women among Indian men. They go with us to plant the fields, carrying their bow and arrow, no more; we go with a basket full of dishes on our backs, one child nursing and another in a basket. They go to kill a fish or a bird, and we dig and drop [give birth] in the fields. In the afternoon they return to the house carrying nothing, and some of us, besides the load of our children, bring roots to eat and corn for cold drink. When they arrive home, they go to talk with their friends, and we go to look for firewood. Then we spend the whole night grinding corn for *chichi* [cold corn drink], and what is the end of all this trouble? They drink, get drunk, and when they are beyond reason they beat us. They take us by the hair and stamp on us. If only, Father, my mother had buried me when I was born. You know well that we complain legitimately, because you can see what I am telling you every day; but our greatest affliction you cannot know. You know, Father, for the Indian woman death is serving her husband as a slave, sweating in the fields and at home without any sleep. After twenty years he gets another girl without sense; he loves her, and even if she beats our children, we can say nothing, because the husbands do not pay any attention to us. The young girl can command us and treat us as her maids, and if we speak, they silence us with a stick. How can we suffer like this, Father? The Indian woman cannot do her child a greater favor than to liberate her from these trials, to take her out of this slavery that is worse than death."[2]

I intend these stories, these images, to constitute a background as well as a central presence in relation to which my considerations of love in a postmodern world can be interpreted and assessed. At the very least, let them stand as a reminder that questions of love ought not be abstracted from real persons who love and are loved, who are not loved and do not love, whose love is shaped by the groups to which they belong, who cry out sometimes across the centuries against the expectations of duty and love.

My title, "How Shall We Love in a Postmodern World?" signals my intention to concentrate on a set of questions that have escalated in interest with the challenges to moral philosophy and theology by so-called postmodern thought. What is so interesting about these questions, and so urgent, is that they take us once again to the heart of our understandings of human freedom, moral agency, interpersonal and social connectedness, and love.

A POSTMODERN WORLD

The trouble with beginning with postmodernism as if it were an ordinary school of thought or social and political program is that it is amorphous, a massive mixture of heterogeneous theories—about art and architecture, literary criticism and linguistics, philosophy and religion.[3] It combines substantive proposals with skeptical method, and the sensibilities it evokes are varied though they bear a family resemblance of sorts. Postmoderns have been both iconoclastic and apocalyptic, both elitist and aligned with mass culture. They have been accused of being neoconservative, yet they are heatedly repudiated by most standard neoconservatives. Postmodernism largely despairs of the emancipatory potential of Enlightenment modernism, but sometimes it appears with at least a limited emancipatory agenda of its own. It challenges much of ethical theory, though from its perspective morality frequently modulates into aesthetics.

Postmoderns and their critics are, I think it is fair to say, generally agreed that what postmodernist philosophy is against includes the universalizing tendency of the Enlightenment, the philosophical project of establishing general moral norms, the search for a stable reality behind historical contingencies, the assumption of individual inwardness and self-possession, an ahistorical subject beyond the constituting influences of language, the notion of a transcendent entity underneath fluid appearances. Of course, postmodernism is not the first philosophical movement to be suspicious of universal theorizing, to challenge the unity of the human self, to object to the idea of transcendent reason or transcendent reality. Indeed, there is plausibility in the observation that Derrida, Lyotard, Foucault, Kristeva, and others continue the skeptical traditions of thinkers like Hume, Marx, Nietzsche, Freud, and Dewey. Yet the project of demythologization in the hands of postmoderns seems more focused, more total—more revolutionary, if you will. There is the claim on the part of at least some postmodern thinkers that all past theory is swept away; a radically new way of thinking is now at hand; the very possibility of theory is now gone.

It is not difficult to appreciate the salutary aspects of postmodern thought—to acknowledge the ongoing need for deconstruction of theoretical idols and illusions of isolated individuality. It has been a major contribution of postmodernism to lift up the importance of particularity and difference, of historical situatedness, of the dynamics of power, of false security in settled views of society and the world. The virtue of epistemic humility ought to develop more readily in a postmodern world.

It is less easy to follow with appreciation the movement of postmodern thought to the extremes of deconstruction and the borders of a new construction. Iris Murdoch may be justified in her judgment that what some self-proclaimed anti-metaphysical postmoderns are finally about is offering a new metaphysics.[4] It is not just that we are to question the existence of an ahistorical self or an unimpeachable self-identity, for example; it is that language is the ultimate structure of reality. Like traditional metaphysics, postmodern thinkers search for a hidden *a priori* that determines the form of everything. Reality is in the medium, not beyond it. As for human persons, it is not just that we are shaped, influenced, by social forces beyond ourselves, as every behaviorist would hold; it is not just that the individual is subordinate to the community, as Marxists or theorists of the social self might maintain; it is not just that the ideology of the subject as male, white, and middle class, must be challenged, as feminists would agree; it is that we seem to disappear altogether as centered selves. Individual experience is illusory; even our bodies, so important for our situatedness, appear boundaryless and hence disembodied. The whole of human activity emerges from a matrix of linguistic codes, but it is not our own activity. So pervasive is the reality of language in which we are submerged, and the hidden net-

works of power by which we are controlled, that individual consciousness may not really exist. Perhaps we do have here a new metaphysics,
what Murdoch is willing to call linguistic idealism, linguistic monism,
linguistic determinism.[5]

It is in a world so understood that we may ask: How shall we
love? What can it mean to love as a human individual? What sort of love
is called for by individuals who are "only" social constructions, whose
identity is "only" a protean self subject to impersonal dynamics of
power, nonpersonal linguistic codes? What kind of love can come from
persons whose agency is diffused? Is it finally meaningless to ask how
we should love as if there were guidelines and choices to be made
regarding our loves?

To answer these questions we have several alternatives. We can
address the questions in terms of the postmodern world as I have so far
described it, in which case most of the answers will lean toward the
negative and will almost certainly (and intentionally) come up empty of
an ethic of love. Or we can sidestep postmodern thought, either because
it mistakenly opposes the advances of modern theories or because modern theories, too, (upon which postmodernism is parasitic) have little to
say about how we should love. Hence, perspectives that are either anti-
modern or simply after-modern can hardly be expected to offer much
wisdom regarding our loves. We can, in this case, return to premodern
insights or try to forge something entirely new but more adequate than
postmodern efforts to date. Or, finally, we can take postmodern thought
more seriously. We can, like some postmoderns,[6] be eclectic (expecting
helpful insight from the old and the new, the premodern, the modern,
and the postmodern); and in so doing, we can pay more attention to the
relevant postmodern concerns, bringing them into focus not just as critiques of modern theory but as potentially illuminative of our experiences of ourselves and of one another. I want to pursue this last alternative – that is, relying not on postmodern perspectives alone, nonetheless
taking seriously some postmodern concerns.

To this end, then, let me acknowledge that what I have described
thus far as a postmodern world of thought may be something of a caricature, despite my caveats regarding the amorphousness of postmodernism as a development in many fields. Even if the assertions of some
postmodern thinkers accord with this view of a postmodern world, they
can be intended as exaggerations, motivated by disenchantment with the

moralistic excesses of some forms of modernist thought; they may be strategies to achieve tolerance of differing views. In any case, it is impossible without gross oversimplification and distortion to ascribe univocal positions to all of the thinkers who have been designated as postmodern. It is no wonder, for example, that Richard Rorty expresses surprise at Sabina Lovibond's inclusion of his writings and Alasdair MacIntyre's along with those of Jean-Francois Lyotard under the term "postmodern." Though Rorty acknowledges some similarities between his thought and that of the other two, he lets stand his demurral: "I am not fond of the term 'postmodernism.'"[7]

Not only are there significantly different agendas among thinkers who may be gathered under the large umbrella of postmodernism, but it is also sometimes difficult to reconcile even within one thinker the various aspects of his or her thought. Rorty, among others, notes internal inconsistencies in much of what is considered "postmodernism," nowhere more apparent than in the mixing of rejections of representational views of knowledge with the rhetoric of "unmasking."[8] I have here neither the occasion nor the desire to adjudicate different interpretations of postmodernist thought. It is clear to me that there are certain tensions and even fissures within it, but I will follow the lines of thought that seem to me useful for discerning whether and how to love in a postmodern world.

First, however, let me identify a basic premise of my own: There are what I will call "locations" in our experience where we can recognize something real and enduring in other beings and something real and enduring in ourselves. There are experiences in which we connect with the "real" beyond us and the "real" within us.[9] That we are able to love in a postmodern world, and how we shall love in this world, can at least be glimpsed in these locations. I will consider only two of them (though there are more): the experience of love and the experience of the suffering of others.

Like postmodern thinkers, I concede the elusiveness of the very notion of "experience." Experience is not a "pure, positivist, nonlinguistic reality that determines the shape of language apart from ideology and culturally systemic shaping."[10] Like premodern and postmodern theorists, I acknowledge that whatever is received is received according to the mode of the recipient. Like postmoderns, I recognize that experience is not self-interpreting; it is constituted for us and interpreted by us within the limits and possibilities of the languages we already have, the worldview we already hold. Our experiences are, therefore, diverse, socially shaped, difficult to understand without some tools of deconstruction. Unlike some postmoderns, however, I allow that there are limits to the meaning of our experiences that are not reducible to the limits of our cultural formation. Something can be given in experience that resists our projection of meaning, challenges our purposes, modifies our language, and changes our understanding. We can make mistakes about what experiences mean. Our very judgments of error, as well as our reflective confirmation of at least partial accuracy, tell us that the reality at the heart of an experience may not always be only the product of our language; left to itself, this reality need not evaporate into nothingness.

EXPERIENCE AND REALITY

Love, as a central concern of human individuals and societies, comes upon hard times when there is less and less access to what is lovable. Certain ways of thinking about love tend to distance us from what is loved, to disallow our contemplating, receiving, and responding to what is lovable precisely as lovable. When, for example, we believe that love should be motivated only by duty, or that, having nothing to do with duty, love counts as love only when it is in the form of unfettered, spontaneous desire, we in significant ways disengage love from the beloved. A duty to love, whether generated by authoritative command or by ineluctable logic, may sustain a preoccupation with loving but not a real nurturance of love (though, of course, duty can also play an important role in both bringing us to love and holding us faithful to a love once it is begun). Desire may disguise itself as love, but in the process miss loving the beloved who is desired (though desire can be both an occasion for love and an important consequence of love). Theories of human affectivity that focus only on duty or desire, rather than on love as a response to what is lovable, can thus undermine the theoretical and practical priority of love. This is what much of both modern and postmodern thought has tended to do, the former by an emphasis on duty and the latter by an emphasis on desire. In both cases, there has been little room to consider the experience of love that I want to identify as a location for an experience of the reality of the self and the other.

A more likely location for both a modern and postmodern sighting of the connection between the self and the other, grounded in something enduring and real, is the experience of suffering, particularly the suffering of others. Almost every philosopher has identified the importance of sympathy and compassion in human relations, and a few have even made these responses central to their moral theory. Schopenhauer, for example, located the ground of moral obligation in what he considered to be natural compassion.[11] Contemporary feminists (whether liberal, socialist, or radical) have tended to begin moral theory with the experience of someone's oppression, the violation of someone's freedom, deprivation of basically needed goods, injury or loss calling for human care, and premature and unnecessary death. Postmodern thinkers have not ignored the stark claims that suffering places on us. Rorty, for example, presents the "liberal ironist" as *noticing* (though not reasoning about) the pain and humiliation of others, experiencing by "imaginative identification" a responsive desire to prevent it and to care for the sufferers.[12]

These two kinds of experience are often closely connected. When we love someone, our attention to their suffering is formed by our love. When individuals or groups suffer, our "noticing" of their wounds can lead us to see them for the first time and perhaps (though by no means necessarily) to love them. But my point is that in these experiences we encounter reality—in others and in ourselves. The point may be clearer if I can describe further the ways in which we are affected by love (of the kind to which I refer) and affected by the suffering of others.

The kind of love I have in mind is the kind that depends on being awakened, touched, tapped, by the lovableness of what is loved. Such love is by no means limited to romantic love; it may, indeed, in some ways characterize all love (though I will not argue that here). Call it Thomas Aquinas's *passio* or Jules Toner's "response" or Irving Singer's "appraisal," it is love that arises or is at least specified by an experience of affective receptivity and response[13] What is loved reveals itself as lovable (as beautiful, valuable in some way), so that love is activated in the one loving. It is at once passion (the other is "received") and action (love is awakened, a responding affective affirmation of the beloved). This is not the only experience that theorists and nontheorists have called "love." There are other important forms or aspects of love, ways in which love expresses itself in our experience; there is love that is commanded, love that is a bestowal of value, love that is the practical exercise of loving deeds in response to the call of duty, love that is an emotional upsurge in search of an object. In all of these forms of love there may be an experience of the self and of what is loved; but where love is a response to the lovableness of the beloved, there the reality of the beloved and the self is experienced as most clear. Since it depends on a perception of the beloved (as well as on all kinds of dispositions that may enhance or obscure this perception), it may be a "mistaken" love. The "reality" at the heart of the experience may be an illusion. Or, as Martha Nussbaum puts it, we may deceive ourselves about what is given in love, "about who; and how; and when; and whether."[14] But the possibilities of error, of illusion and delusion, do not eliminate the possiblities of accuracy, of receiving and responding to what is real. "We also discover and correct our self-deceptions;"[15] at least sometimes we do.

A second location in our experience where we may encounter the reality of others and ourselves, I have said, is our experience of the suffering of others. This is no doubt most apparent in what might be identified as paradigm experiences of suffering – what some have called "tales of terror" and "whirlpools of torment,"[16] where bodies are destroyed, minds ravaged, and spirits broken. These are the sufferings that go on in human history generation after generation—a "voice heard in Ramah weeping" (*Jer* 31:15), peoples subjugated by peoples, families rent asunder, stories of rape and starvation, abandonment, confusion, violence and relentless dying. This is the sort of human pain that Simone Weil named "affliction," differentiating it from "suffering" in the ordinary sense.[17] It is, she said, always both physical and spiritual; it is never only physical (like a toothache that is soon over and gone) but it is also never only spiritual. With this kind of suffering, there is no competition between miseries of the body and miseries of the soul. For affliction when it is spiritual also afflicts, leaves wounds in, the body; and when it is bodily, if it goes on long enough, it always also afflicts the spirit.

This is the kind of suffering that has the power to uproot life; that can be in itself the equivalent of death; that almost always includes some form of humiliation, some social degradation; that has the potential to attack the self—chaining down thoughts to become a "state of mind" that persons can live in sometimes twenty, thirty, fifty years, a lifetime; and in which one's very soul threatens to become its accomplice, pulling to inertia and despair.[18] This kind of suffering, when we see it in others, has the power to grasp us so that we cannot avoid the reality of the sufferers or the reality of ourselves.

To behold acute suffering can, of course, just as well distance us from one another, lead us to build an illusory world in which we mask reality, tempt us to retreat from the claims of others and the intolerable aspects of ourselves. Moreover, if love can be mistaken, so can our perception of suffering be false. I cannot argue that every experience of the suffering of others puts us in contact with what is real in and for the others. Yet we do have some experiences of the suffering of others where their suffering is revelatory, where it holds our gaze inescapably upon what is real.

How we think about and anticipate experiences both of love and of the suffering of others influences the experiences themselves. This is why philosophies have some potential either to facilitate our experiences of the real, or to get in the way—by denying the possibility of such experience or by blunting their starkness with theories that explain them too well. Probably every philosophy holds elements that both facilitate and threaten the kind of experiences I have been describing. I want still to pursue the lines in postmodern thought that shed light on these experiences, that perhaps facilitate them even as they render them problematic.

LOVE'S REQUIREMENTS

Despite the fact that methods of deconstruction tend to undermine notions of a unitary self and dismiss theories of knowledge as presence, there is much in postmodern debates that is useful for exploring our experiences of love and of the suffering of others. This is particularly true of debates about the status of the self and the other, and about the connections between self and other through knowledge and love.

Postmodern critical philosophy is said to have accomplished the death of the self, the end of subjectivity. But the self that is dead is a certain version of the self; it is the self which modern philosophy characterized as disengaged, disembodied, wholly autonomous, and self-transparent. And the subject that has disappeared is the isolated bearer of signs, the conscious knower of clear and certain ideas, the self-governing and self-responsible agent whose task was to instrumentalize body and world.[19] The stability of this subject and self had long ago been shaken by Freud, whose identification of unconscious dimensions of the self divided it and rendered it opaque. The self isolated from the world was challenged by Marx as well, who substituted an active, effective, humanity for the self-sufficient observer. Nietzsche ridiculed the notion of a subject perceiving an objective reality, or an agential self with any core other than its own will to power. Already in the nineteenth century linguistic paradigms began to displace paradigms of consciousness as the subject of knowledge.

Strong lines of postmodern thought have, so to speak, finished the job of erasing an "essential" self, a "true"self, Jacques Lacan, for example, pursued the part of Freud's thought that emphasized radical decentering.[20] Jacques Derrida, Michel Foucault, Julia Kristeva, and Luce Irigaray[21] have all in various ways presented a diffused self, submerged in forces not so much within it as outside of it in society and culture, desiring breakthroughs into new matrices of language, power, and thought. Rorty argues for the rejection of a "core self" in favor of a "web of relations to be rewoven," replacing the notion of a "formed, unified, present, self-contained substance" with a "tissue of contingent relations," stretching into the past and into the future.[22] Oddly enough, postmodernism (as in at least some stages of the thought of, for example, Derrida, Lyotard, and Foucault) offers views both of a decentered, nonoriginary, socially constructed and controlled self, and of a newly released Nietzschean self that is aggressively self-inventive, self-creating, attempting to break all boundaries of theory, obligation, or tradition.

If the "self" is really dead; if there is only process and relation without agency; if there is indiscriminate desire and not real choice of affective response issuing in action; if there are only protean masks and not even a Proteus behind the masks; then there is not much point in asking how we shall love in a postmodern world. Either we will not love in any recognizable sense at all, or we will not be responsible for our socially constructed loves. We will all be like Pixote, moving as in a dream, indifferent to love or compassion, fear or contempt.

But the debates about the self, fueled by postmodern critique, may indeed have given it new life. Three proposals seem to me to be particularly significant in this regard, and particularly helpful in pursuing my question of how we shall love. The three proposals I have in mind are from disparate sources, but they all relate to the issues of the self that have preoccupied modern and postmodern thinkers. I can do no more here than briefly cite them.

The first proposal comes from Charles Taylor's important work not only on the sources of "modern identity," but on the need for a "strong sense" of the self.[23] Taylor argues that the modern understanding of the self as disengaged, representing to itself an objective world which it can instrumentalize, is too "thin" a conception of the self.[24] In opposition to this notion of the self, Taylor proposes a "strong sense" of the self, a sense in which the self is not merely a "bearer or preferences" but a subject of "significance." That is, human persons are beings for whom things matter, have meaning, in a way that accounts for responses of shame, self-esteem, appreciation, love, and so forth. As such, personal agency is more than mere planning, directing, controlling. Here is a self that is not isolated from the rest of the world, not over against what it knows. Here is a self, we can surmise, that can be affected by what is not itself, that can respond with both spontaneity and freedom; a self that is engaged yet not thereby wholly lost as a self.

A second proposal is the one contained in Seyla Benhabib's consideration of what feminism can find useful in postmodern thought. Benhabib distinguishes "strong" and "weak" versions of the postmodern thesis of the death of Man (the death of the subject or self).[25] In the strong version, the subject dissolves into a "web of fictive meaning," becoming "merely another position in language."[26] There is left no trace of autonomy, purposiveness, self-possession, responsibility. The weak version, on the other hand, recognizes that subjectivity is contextually situated, socially structured (by language, narrative, culture); yet the subject is not reducible to heteronomous determination. Selfhood, in this version, is not merely a series of performances, not merely a process without any self-determination. We are, in other words, not only characters in our own stories but to some degree authors as well. Benhabib's point is that feminist theory can align with the weak version of this aspect of postmodern thought, but not the strong; for only the weak version allows room for ongoing critical theory. Whether or not one's concern is for a viable feminism, the weak version of the death of the self seems to accomplish more than the strong. It radically modifies the Enlightenment notion of autonomy (by incorporating the limits of cultural embeddedness), and it opens to new understandings of relationality; yet it does not (against reason and experience) relinquish freedom, intentionality, and accountability.[27]

The third proposal regarding the status of the self is lodged in Edith Wyschogrod's study of the relevance of stories of saints for a postmodern ethic.[28] Wyschogrod's problem is less the social construction of the self than the self-inventive, self-creating notion of "self" that finally is no-self. Postmodernity's "language of desire," "libidinal economy," yields to no boundaries (not laws, not the past, not a charactered self). The decentering of the subject by unlimited desire makes individuation (and hence also unity) of the self impossible; the saint and the sufferer disappear. Wyschogrod's solution to this problem is not to jettison the language of desire but to give it a boundary when it meets the Other. The saint, responding to the Other, achieves selfhood only in relation to the Other. The source of decentering becomes the possibility of new centering; the death of the self yields the life of the self. For Wyschogrod, the saint is the model for postmodern love.

Wyschogrod is not alone in focusing on the Other. While unselfish love is not of much interest to postmodern writers, there are ways in which the modern concern for otherness is advanced by postmodern considerations.[29] Indeed, postmoderns steadfastly privilege otherness, difference, concrete particularity rather than sameness and universality. In a variety of contexts, they do not allow us to turn away from what is different from ourselves, even different within ourselves; that is, they challenge the complacency of our ordinary and familiar interpretations of everything. Barbara Johnson, for example, says of a deconstructionist reading of a text: "a reading is strong...to the extent that it encounters and propagates the surprise of otherness."[30] What deconstruction aims to do is to demystify our familiar understandings, but its goal is not necessarily an infinite regress into nothingness. The surprise that an encounter with otherness can hold is a discovery of error and of an ignorance we did not know we had. Ignorance, in turn, can be not merely a gap in knowledge but an imperative.[31]

If there are, after all, selves in a postmodern world; and if we become selves in relation to others; can we finally answer our questions about love? Probably not yet, at least not without a few more exploratory steps. For one thing, we need to consider more carefully how the self can be *affected* by the Other. The Other is a limit that aids self-definition and self-individuation, but can the postmodern Other awaken love? Can the pain of the Other awaken compassion?

Despite the fact that Nietzsche's influence on postmodernity cuts deeply against receptivity (in favor of active self-making), there are ways in which some strands of postmodern thought are at least amenable to the kinds of experiences of love and of the suffering of others to which I have pointed above. The modern subject cut off from the world is now immersed in the world; no longer preoccupied with self-certainty in settled truth, the subject is freed for relationship. The self has a capacity for being affected by an Other. Against Nietzsche, and against the kind of influences on the self that have to do only with impersonal power, there are some postmodern voices (or at least participants in postmodern discussions) that speak of the importance of sympathy, solicitude, and compassion. As Rorty puts it, pain is nonlinguistic, and not only can we "notice" it but we can respond to it with compassion.[32] Wyschogrod's saints are what they are (and exemplars for the rest of us) because they render themselves vulnerable to the suffering of others. "What is other than the self can affect the self through pain or wounding."[33] For Paul Ricoeur (not, of course, a postmodern in any narrow sense of the term, but in conversation with postmodern writers), solicitude for the suffering of another is a location for relationship that is both receptive and active, receiving and giving.[34]

That we can love in a postmodern world seems to me beyond question, even though there are winds of philosophical thought that blow other ways. As to how we ought to love in this world, however, we have in the end only clues. One of them is to value stories, and through stories to pay attention to the concrete lives of individuals and groups. A second, emerging from the first, is not to suppress difference; to meet the other as really other, not simply as another of myself. A third may be to take seriously the embeddedness of human life—embodiment in all its layers of flesh, of dwelling, of relationships, of culture; to take seriously both beauty and pain, of the body and the spirit, of the individual and the culture. Yet another clue might be to care for potentiality, not only actuality—for what someone has not yet been allowed to be or even think to become, for what has been oppressed or repressed by whatever forces of ignorance or power. And a final clue: across the premodern, modern, and postmodern worlds, never to underestimate the form of decentering that comes from reverence before beauty and compassion before pain.

I began with some stories. They remain as my measure and my challenge. Pixote tells us not only that we have certain possibilities but profound needs; and when these are not met, there comes a contradiction in our being, a wound that cannot remain hidden. Schwartz's "Aria" sings of love's power to awaken to beauty and to bring it to newness; it is the song of the self in a "strong sense," full of yearning for wholeness and union. The woman in the Venezuelan fields will not let us turn from the limits of human endurance, will not let us forget that pain needs no language and responsibility crosses borders that we do not expect.

Do I thus do violence to a postmodern taboo, moving from the arguments of experience to the arguments of principle? Perhaps, though my intention has been to appreciate the contributions and the problems of a postmodern age. In so doing, it seems fair to conclude that we should love in a postmodern world in the same way we should love in any world—where Pixote must not be ignored; where lovers are to heal one another of shame; where the cry of sufferers is not be to silenced. I end where I began, for this is still only a banquet, and our own concrete lives, in whatever our world, remain to be lived.

Notes

1. Delmore Schwartz, "Aria," in *Poetry in Crystal* (Steuben Glass, A Division of Corning Glass Works, 1963), 52. This poem appeared in three different versions in various periodicals. It was designated as part of a sequence of poems entitled "Kilroy's Carnival: A Masque." See *Last & Lost Poems of Delmore Schwartz,* ed. Robert Phillips (N.Y.: New Directions Books, 1989), 7.

2. Margarit Gamio de Alba, "The Indigenous Woman of Central America," transcribed in Leonor Aida Concha, "The Indigenous Woman in Latin America," in *Women in Dialogue,* trans. Ruth Fitzpatrick (Notre Dame, IN: Catholic Committee on Urban Ministry, 1979), 11.

3. For helpful history, mapping, and interpretation of multiple postmodern representatives and themes, see Harry R. Garvin, ed., *Romanticism, Modernism, Postmodernism* (Lewisburg, PA: Bucknell University Press, 1980); Kenneth Baynes, James Bohman, & Thomas McCarthy, eds., *After Philosophy: End or Transformation?* (Cambridge: The MIT Press, 1987), esp. "General Introduction" and Part I, 1–158; Reed Way Dasenbrock, ed., *Redrawing the*

Lines: Analytical Philosophy, Deconstruction, and Literary Theory (Minneapolis: University of Minnesota Press, 1989); Andreas Huyssen, "Mapping the Postmodern," in *Feminism/Postmodernism,* ed. Linda J. Nicholson (N.Y.: Routledge, 1990), 234–77. One key text (but by no means a fully representative one) to which commentators frequently return is Jean-Francois Lyotard, *The Postmodern Condition* (Minneapolis: University of Minnesota Press, 1984).

4. See Iris Murdoch, *Metaphysics as a Guide to Morals* (N.Y.: Allen Lane, The Penguin Press, 1992), 6.

5. Ibid., 185.

6. See in particular Edith Wyschogrod, *Saints and Postmodernism: Revisioning Moral Philosophy* (Chicago: The University of Chicago Press, 1990), xvii–xx.

7. Richard Rorty, "Feminism and Pragmatism," in *The Tanner Lectures on Human Values,* vol. 13, ed. Gretche B. Peterson (Salt Lake City: University of Utah Press, 1992), 13 n. 18.

8. Ibid., 12–13 n. 17.

9. I use quotation marks for "real" to signal the same challenge to a positivisitic sense of "real" that prompted David Tracy to repeat Vladimir Nobokov's "'Reality' is the one word that should always appear within quotation marks." See David Tracy, *Plurality and Ambiguity: Hermeneutics, Religion, and Hope* (San Francisco: Harper & Row, 1987), 47. To repudiate positivism's reality is not (as I hope will be clear in my context) to jettison the real except in the sense of brute facts the knowledge of which requires no interpretation by us.

10. George Levine, "Introduction: Constructivism and the Reemergent Self," in *Constructions of the Self,* ed. G. Levine (New Brunswick: Rutgers University Press, 1992), 6.

11. Arthur Schopenhauer, *On the Basis of Morality,* trans. E. F. J. Payne (N.Y.: Library of Liberal Arts, 1965).

12. Richard Rorty, *Contingency, Irony, and Solidarity* (Cambridge: Cambridge University Press, 1989), 93.

13. See Thomas Aquinas, *Summa Theologiae* I–II 26.2; Jules J. Toner, *The Experience of Love* (Washington, D.C.: Corpus Books, 1968), ch. 5; Irving Singer, *The Nature of Love,* vol. 1, rev. ed. (Chicago: The University of Chicago Press, 1984), ch. 1. These are, of course, not the only writers to describe love in this way, but they offer clear examples of the kind of love in question.

14. Martha C. Nussbaum, *Love's Knowledge: Essays on Philosophy and Literature* (N.Y.: Oxford University Press, 1990), 261.

15. Ibid.

16. The phrases belong to Phyllis Trible and James Crenshaw. See Trible, *Texts of Terror; Literary-Feminist Readings of Biblical Narratives* (Philadelphia: Fortress Press, 1984); Crenshaw, *A Whirlpool of Torment:*

Israelite Traditions of God as an Oppressive Presence (Philadelphia: Fortress Press, 1984).

17. Simone Weil, *Waiting for God,* trans. Emma Crauford (N.Y.: Harper & Row, 1973), 117–25.

18. Ibid., 118–19.

19. For succinct overviews of the "history of the self" in western thought, see Charles Taylor, "Overcoming Epistemology," in Baynes, ed., *After Philosophy,* 464–88; Agnes Heller, "Death of the Subject?" in Levine, ed., *Constructions of the Self,* 269–84; Seyla Benhabib, "Feminism and the Question of Postmodernism," in *Situating the Self: Gender, Community, and Postmodernism in Contemporary Ethics* (N.Y.: Routledge, 1992), 202–41.

20. See Jacques Lacan, *Ecrits: A Selection,* trans. A. Sheridan (N.Y.: W. W. Norton, 1977); Lacan, *The Four Fundamental Concepts of Psychoanalysis,* trans. A. Sheridan (N.Y.: W. W. Norton, 1964); John P. Muller & William J. Richardson, *Lacan and Language: A Reader's Guide to Ecrits* (N.Y.: International Universities Press, Inc., 1982). For an alternate reading of Freud, see Ernest Wallwork, *Psychoanalysis and Ethics* (New Haven: Yale University Press, 1991).

21. I am uncertain whether Julia Kristeva has modified her view of the self in her essay, "Psychoanalysis and the Imaginary," in Levine, ed., *Constructions of the Self,* 285–97. There is some hint here of the possibility of a resurrected subject.

22. Rorty, *Contingency, Irony, and Solidarity,* 41–43.

23. See Charles Taylor, *Sources of the Self: The Making of Modern Identity* (Cambridge: Harvard University Press, 1989); Taylor, *Human Agency and Language: Philosophical Papers,* Vol. 1 (N.Y.: Cambridge University Press, 1985).

24. Taylor, *Human Agnecy and Langauge* I, 97–114.

25. Benhabib, *Situating the Self,* 213–18.

26. Ibid., 214–15. The phrases belong to Jane Flax, who along with Judith Butler, Benhabib is opposing. See Jane Flax, *Psychoanalysis, Feminism and Postmodernism in the Contemporary West* (Berkeley: University of California Press, 1990), 32ff.

27. Postmodern philosophical writings are not without support for Benhabib's "weak" version. Rorty, for example, argues that individuals, while containing within themselves multiple roles, personalities, sets of belief and desire, can nonetheless "harmonize" these various roles, etc. Moreover, such harmonizing, integrating into a "unifying story about oneself," is desirable. Freedom is thereby achieved (though not unfolded as if it always already existed within the self). "Personhood" is a "matter of degree." See Rorty, "Feminism and Pragmatism," 15 n. 22; 25–35.

28. See Wyschogrod, *Saints and Postmodernism,* 233–57. For my own development of some of these ideas, see Margaret A. Farley, "A Feminist Version of Respect for Persons," *Journal of Feminist Studies in Religion* 9 (Spring 1993): 183–98.

29. For a careful history of the development of concern for the Other in twentieth century philosophy, see Michael Theunissen, *The Other: Studies in the Social Ontology of Husserl, Heidegger, Sartre, and Buber,* trans. C. Macann (Cambridge: MIT Press, 1984).

30. Barbara Johnson, *A World of Difference* (Baltimore: The Johns Hopkins University Press, 1987), 15.

31. Ibid., 16.

32. See Rorty, *Contingency, Irony, and Solidarity,* 94. Though I agree with Timothy Jackson that a Christian concept of agape is both fuller and different from anything proposed by Rorty, I think Rorty the "postmodern" may offer more than Jackson finds in Rorty the "liberal." See Timothy P. Jackson, "Liberalsim and Agape: The Priority of Charity to Democracy and Philosophy," *The Annual of the Society of Christian Ethics* (1993), 47–72.

33. See Wyschogrod, *Saints and Postmodernism,* 98 and passim.

34. Paul Ricoeur, *Oneself as Another,* trans. K. Blamey (Chicago: University of Chicago Press, 1992), 190–91. Ricoeur takes pains to differentiate his analysis from that of Emmanuel Levinas, even while he writes appreciatively of Levinas's work in this regard.

20. Church Teaching Authority: Problems and Prospects

John P. Boyle

This chapter first appeared in John P. Boyle, *Church Teaching Authority: Historical and Theological Studies* (Notre Dame, Ind.: University of Notre Dame Press, 1995).

From its beginnings the Christian church has taught. In this book we have traced the historical and theological developments, especially those of the nineteenth and twentieth centuries, which have produced the official teaching by the church about its own teaching authority. Studying the history of such notions as "ordinary magisterium," "*obsequium* of the intellect and will," and "reception" has caused us to look again at the development and the medieval roots of post-Reformation Catholic theology in order to understand the official teaching of today.

Historical study has exhibited the interaction of official teaching with the work of theologians. At times the work of a theologian, Joseph Kleutgen, for example, has found its way into official documents. At other times, theologians have been critical of official formulations—or church officials have been critical of theologians and their work. But for much of the post-Reformation period the work of theologians has reflected common teaching in the church. The period was one in which disagreement with such teaching was not tolerated.

The Second Vatican Council was a time of close cooperation between bishops and theologians, but since the council there has been conflict, some of it highly publicized, and church discipline has been used against some prominent scholars. The 1990 instruction *Donum veritatis* from the Congregation for the Doctrine of the Faith is only the latest in a series of actions by official teachers since Vatican II which attempt both to define and to regulate the activity of theological scholars in the church. Protests against some of these actions and regulations have been published.[1]

In this concluding chapter I will point to theological considerations which underlie both the developments we have traced and the sometimes conflictual situation in which the church now finds itself. I present these considerations in the belief that teaching is a function of the church and therefore a part of ecclesiology. I will argue that different theological understandings of the respective roles of bishops and theologians as teachers in the church have their roots in different ecclesiologies.

THE ECCLESIOLOGY OF VATICAN II: A PARADIGM SHIFT

Teaching is a function (*munus*) of the church. Therefore, in our consideration of the nature and limits of the teaching authority of the church, we need to keep in mind some fundamental characteristics of the church itself. Those characteristics have been set out authoritatively by the Second Vatican Council in the Constitution on the Church, *Lumen Gentium,* published in 1964.

In formulating its teaching on the church, the council set aside the model of the church which had dominated Catholic theology in the counter-Reformation period. Responding to the challenges of the Reformers, counter-Reformation Catholic apologists emphasized the church as a visible institution with a clear hierarchical authority struc-ture which presents divine revelation without error. On this view, the church's hierarchical teachers propose teaching authoritatively and the role of other members of the church is to accept obediently what they teach. This institutional model of the church is often portrayed as a pyramid, with the supreme authority figure, the pope, at the pinnacle of the pyramid and subordinates arranged in descending rank to the base. It was a model well suited to understanding a church which felt itself under siege. This authoritarian, even monarchical, understanding of the church influenced all aspects of church life from the time of the Reformation to the Second Vatican Council.

Lumen Gentium presents quite a different model, though sometimes hesitatingly and not always consistently. The new model found in the council documents is often described simply as a "communion model" of the church, but that term does not appear in the documents of the council, and Avery Dulles[2] has warned against oversimplifying the variety of models which attempt to capture the complex reality of the church.

It is not my purpose here to offer a fully developed ecclesiology. Rather I want to call attention to some principal motifs of the council's teaching about the church in order to further discuss the teaching office. Like the church itself, the teaching office and the mission it discharges is complex.

The constitution *Lumen Gentium* was developed during Vatican II after the council fathers had set aside draft documents presented to them which reflected counter-Reformation Catholic theology only too well. The council's revised teaching documents did not reject the institutional elements of the church, but put them in a way quite different from much official preconciliar teaching or the presentation of a typical preconciliar theological textbook.

Chapter one of *Lumen Gentium* describes the church as a "mystery" or "sacrament." The choice of that starting point is itself a clear signal that the council wished to put primary emphasis not on institutional elements of the church, important as they are, but rather on the church as the reality which makes the God of grace and salvation present in the world. The church is both institution and sacrament; not two realities but one complex reality though which the saving action of Father, Son and Spirit continues among us.[3]

Chapter two of *Lumen Gentium* then turns to another fundamental aspect of the church: the church as a people, the new People of God, which lives in the world of time and space, and is, therefore, a people with a history. This people, with Christ at its head and the Holy Spirit at its heart, shares in the priestly, prophetic, and kingly offices of Christ. Of the people's prophetic office, the council declares that

> The body of the faithful as a whole, anointed as they are by the Holy One (cf. Jn 2:20, 27), cannot err in matters of belief. (n. 12)

This people as a whole is characterized by a supernatural *sense of the faith* when showing universal agreement in matters of faith and morals:

For by this sense of faith which is aroused and sustained by the Spirit of truth, God's people accepts not the word of men but the very Word of God (cf. 1 Th 2:13). It clings without fail to the faith once delivered to the saints (cf. Jude 3), penetrates it more deeply by accurate insights, and applies it more thoroughly to life. All this it does under the lead of a sacred teaching authority to which it loyally defers. (n. 12)

The council goes on to point to the Holy Spirit as the source of charismatic gifts which the spirit distributes "as he will" (1 Cor 12:11) among the faithful. It is for those who preside in the church to judge the genuineness and proper use of these gifts.

It is only after setting out the reality of the church as sacrament and as a people anointed by the Spirit that the council turns to a consideration of the structures of the church, beginning with the hierarchy of bishops, priests, and deacons, then turning to laity and religious. The framework for the discussion of structures—though not explicitly labeled—is very close to the communion model of the church.

THE OFFICES OF CHRIST AND THE TEACHING MISSION OF THE CHURCH

In *Lumen Gentiun,* Vatican II uses the threefold office of Christ as prophet, priest, and shepherd/king as an organizing principle for its discussion of the mission of the church as the People of God (nn. 10–13), as hierarchy (nn. 25–27), and as lay faithful (nn. 34–36). The teaching mission of the church, especially the role of bishops, is discussed most fully in n. 25.

Various texts of the New Testament are recalled in *Lumen Gentium as* the basis of the church's teaching mission. At n.17 the council cites the commission given by Jesus in Matthew 28: "Go, therefore, make disciples of all nations,...baptizing them...teaching them to observe all that I have commanded you" and recalls the words of Paul in 1 Corinthians 9:16, "Woe to me if I do not preach the gospel."

The church is charged with proclaiming the revealed word of God—a theme developed more fully in the Constitution on Divine Revelation, *Dei Verbum.* In its discussion of the transmission of revelation, the council sets out important teaching about the relationship of revelation to scripture and tradition as the channels of the transmission of revelation and the source of the church's certainty about what is revealed. In DV 10, the council says clearly that church teaching authority is not above the revealed word of God but is to serve it by explaining, interpreting, and, if necessary, defending it.

What has been committed to the church and to the vigilance of its teaching office is the "one sacred deposit of the word of God" which is constituted by sacred tradition and sacred scripture (DV 10). In *Dei Verbum* the council says of tradition:

> Now what was handed on by the apostles includes everything which contributes to the holiness of life, and the increase in faith of the People of God; and so the Church, in her teaching, life, and worship, perpetuates and hands on to all generations all that she herself is, all that she believes. (n. 8, Abbot trans.)

It follows that what the church is to teach and to interpret through her teaching office is more than a set of propositions; it is a way of life. At the same time, to speak of 'teaching, life, and worship...all that she herself is, all that she believes" both defines tradition very broadly and includes within the definition things of unequal weight and centrality, things more or less dependent over time upon practical judgments made in differing circumstances. The "life" of the church, for example, seems broad enough to encompass both internal church discipline and the way that Christians comport themselves in the world. Taken in either sense, the internal life of the church and the Christian life itself have taken different forms at various times. That suggests that not everything the church teaches authoritatively must or can be taught irreformably.

The apostolic tradition handed on in the church makes progress through the work of hte Holy Spirit.

The Holy Spirit and the Church

Theological clarity about the work of the Holy Spirit sent by the Father and the Son is fundamental for an understanding of the teaching office of the church.[4] It is the church community which is the Body of

Christ animated by the Spirit of Christ. The church is, in Rahner's phrase, the sacrament of the eschatogically victorious grace of God in Jesus Christ.[5] Therefore *the church,* not just those who are bishops, is the indefectible bearer of the revelation of God in Christ. This is the teaching of the Second Vatican Council, which thus corrected the teaching of Perrone, Franzelin, and of *Humani generis.*[6]

In this community of faith animated by the Spirit there exists, in the view of Heribert Mühlen, a "collective consciousness" of God's revelation in Jesus Christ.[7]

In its teaching on tradition, Vatican II points out that tradition develops in the church, in part through a growth in understanding of realities and of the words which have been handed down. The apostolic tradition, however, includes whatever contributes not only to Christian faith but to Christian life. It follows that there is growth in the understanding of the Christian life too. The discernment of moral norms consonant with the Christian *kerygma* is a collective process, taking place over time within the church community.

This growth of understanding, like other kinds of human knowing, can usefully be thought of in Bernard Lonergan's terms as a "self-correcting process of learning."[8] Such a view seems especially appropriate in the theological context which considers the activity of the Spirit by grace in both the community and in individuals, including the leaders of the community, who must pass judgment on the validity of new ways of understanding or expressing the Christian message. But it also considers the historical realities of human finitude and sin.

THE KENOSIS OF THE SPIRIT

The limits of the work of the Spirit must also be acknowledged, for in coming among us the Spirit takes on certain human limitations.[9] As humanity and divinity in Jesus are, in the words of the Council of Chalcedon, unconfused and undivided,[10] so by analogy is the Spirit unconfused yet undivided from the limitations of the persons in whom he dwells. Mühlen writes of *kenosis* (an emptying) of the Spirit among us analogous to the *kenosis* of the Logos in becoming a human being to which Paul calls attention in chapter two of the Letter to the Philippians.

Moreover, in coming upon Jesus, the Spirit in his anointing has entered into time and therefore into history.[11] Yet he remains unconfused with history, even if inseparable from it. The church cannot dispose of or manipulate the Spirit. The church is not the "continuation of the Incarnation" that Johann Adam Möhler thought it was—with the perilous suggestion of a kind of "communication of idioms" between Christ and the church implied in the phrase.[12] Rather the church shares in the anointing of the Spirit that first came upon Jesus.

There remains therefore an inevitable *eschatological expectation* in the church. For her, the perfection of the gifts of the Spirit is "not yet." But the work of the Spirit goes on in the church in the word, in church office, and in the sacraments.

These are important assertions for a proper understanding of the teaching function. They emphasize the unfinished state of the work of the Spirit in the church and in the world. They emphasize that the church always remains a community of sinners, that with the nature of the church there is always the shadow which Hans Küng has called its "unnature"[13] of human sinfulness and imperfection. The believer and the community of believers can and does suffer from what Lonergan has termed a "scotosis" (blindness) of the intellect and an "impotence of the will."[14] To say that is not to deny the traditional doctrines of the indefectibility and infallibility of the church which are the work of the Holy Spirit in the church; it is only to point out that these doctrines stand in tension with others which assert that the eschaton is not yet. The church's perception and thematization of moral values, like its perception of revelation more generally, are in need of correction and reformulation, especially at the level of specific moral directives. Given the multiplicity of the gifts of the Spirit in the church, the community must be one of ongoing discernment as it seeks a deeper understanding of the faith, a greater penetration of what its Christian commitment implies for its life.

It is entirely consonant with this view of the church as a community of moral discernment with its multiple gifts of the Spirit that some in the church should be called to various offices, including the teaching office, and that they should receive gifts of the Spirt through the reception of the sacrament of Orders. The same kind of transformation of subjectivity which is brought about by the gift of faith and conversion in baptism can be carried further by the work of the Spirit received in this sacrament. Indeed Vatican II emphasized the fundamental role of the sacrament of Holy Orders in its discussion of hierarchical authority.[15]

Therefore there is nothing incongruous in the claim that the college of bishops with the pope at its head possesses, in virtue of the sacrament of Orders and the charismatic gifts of the Spirit appropriate to their role in the church, special insight into the moral demands and implications of Christian life. Such insight can complement or at times correct those of the community. Indeed explicting the implications of the *kerygma* in a continuing *didaché* has been a feature of the life of the church from the beginning.[16] The view of Orders and the effect of the work of the Spirit in the ordained suggested by Scheeben seems sound, as we noted in chapter three. This insight extends to the whole range of things given into the care of the church's authoritative teachers.[17]

Yet the absence in most theological discussions of church teaching authority of any extended consideration of the work of the Holy Spirit, including the Spirit's work in Holy Orders and its link to teaching authority, suggest that there is a serious need for further research on this matter.

What I have been describing, then, suggests a view of the church as *community of religious and moral discernment* in which a dialogue exists between the proposition and explication of the Christian faith and its implications by authoritative teachers and the reception of that teaching by the church community—which also possesses the gifts of the Spirit. It is the experience and reflections of the community which in turn produce further insights and discernment by the community.

The community thus stimulates discernment by the authoritative teachers and a new, perhaps modified proposition of the Christian faith and its implications.[18] Indeed, the limits of the community of discernment cannot be too narrowly drawn, since grace and the gifts of the Spirit are not confined to the institutional limits of the church. And it is an obvious fact of church life in the twentieth century that the church learns from the culture in which it lives (see GS 44).[19]

The relationship of the community of faith and the authoritative teachers has often been conceived in too narrowly juridical terms.[20] The college of bishops was thought of in post-Reformation apologetics in ways that separated it from the community of the faithful—an excess that the Second Vatican Council corrected with its teaching in *Lumen Gentium* about the People of God and the role of hierarchical office.

Officeholders are first of all believers, who have themselves learned the Christian faith from the church community. They do not receive it by special inspiration or some new revelation.

The communion model, which Vatican II began to recover, is far more dialogic than the long-dominant institutional model. The newer model does not at all exclude the possibility of authoritative teaching so fully assisted by the Spirit as to be infallible and demanding of the assent of faith or at least full adherence. The council has pointed out that this protection by the Spirit extends also to the community, which is infallible in believing, so that its assent to infallible teaching will never be lacking. But the same protection of the Spirit can see to it that teaching which is inadequate or even erroneous is not received by the church.[21]

It is the kenotic aspect of the Spirit's presence in the world, the "not yet" dimension of the church's life, that is thus a standing warning against "creeping infallibilism" in the church and a warning, too, against attempts to demand an undifferentiated *obsequium* to every instance of authoritative church teaching. Today it is widely recognized that the church is preserved by the Holy Spirit from corrupting the essential Christian message, but that the church nonetheless has made mistakes. Vatican II itself corrected church doctrine on a number of points.

The Holy Spirit also sees to it that the sinful inclination of human beings do not imperil the efficacy of the church's ministry of word and sacrament: the sacraments give God's grace to those who receive them and do not impede the work of grace (DS 1066); the church's definitive teaching of revelation is preserved from error by the work of the same Spirit (LG 25).

But, as we have pointed out, not every teaching of the church implies the full commitment of its authority and thus the full assurance by the Holy Spirit against human error. In such a case there remains that eschatological not yet and therefore the possibility of error in teaching.

ACCEPTANCE OF CHURCH TEACHING

The possibility of error, even given the possibility of infallible teaching and the day-to-day assistance of the Holy Spirit, implies that the acceptance of church teaching in a particular case could be impossible or at the very least remain an acceptance that is less than total. If that is true, then some traditional terminology used both by theologians and by official teachers is unclear and unhelpful.

In the discussion in chapters four and five of the term *obsequium mentis et voluntatis,* we saw that the use of this terminology tends to obscure the varying degrees of acceptance owed to church teaching. It has long been clear to theologians that the meaning of the term *obsequium* is not univocal, and they developed an elaborate scale of acceptance, ranging from the obedience of faith to simple respect.[22] For all its hesitations, the 1990 instruction of the CDF concedes in principle that at least some day-to-day church teaching may be met with the admission that assent to it is simply not possible. Even rejection of some church teaching may be possible—provided that fundamental respect for the authority of the church is preserved. Not ever refusal of acceptance constitutes unacceptable dissent.

The development of fresh theological language to express the various kinds and degrees of acceptance of authoritative but not definitive church teaching is much needed. This seems especially true in the field of moral theology, in which judgments must be made about matters which are both complex and contingent. As we noted in chapter eight, the CDF instruction (n. 24) makes special mention of such judgments.

It is useful to call attention here to the traditional distinction between "teaching" and "judging." It seems that when church authority studies competing views on a matter of faith and morals and makes a judgment that some views are compatible with Christian faith and others are not, then church authority is committed to a greater degree than in day-to-day teaching and should be heard with greater respect. Nonetheless, "No doctrine is to be understood to be infallibly defined unless it is clearly established as such,[23] and that what is not infallibly taught is, in principle, open to correction.

DOCTRINAL DISCIPLINE AND THE AUTHORITY OF TRUTH

The Second Vatican Council deals with the church's duty to teach as one of the three classic "offices" (*munera*) of the church which parallel the offices of Christ himself as prophet, priest and shepherd/king. The *munus docendi* is a central aspect of the prophetic office, but the church also sees teaching as having a disciplinary and pastoral aspect as well. These appear not only in such regulations as the requirement of canon 812 that all teachers of theology have a canonical mandate but also in the penalties which can be imposed upon those who do not assent to official teaching.

In addition there is a broader and more general disciplinary dimension to the hierarchical supervision of teaching in the church, as Franzelin pointed out. Such discipline appears in the demand of the instruction *Donum veritatis* n. 23 for at least silent submission to church teaching, even when such teaching could be erroneous.

Another facet of doctrinal discipline can be seen in the insistence by church teaching authority on the use of certain terminology to express Catholic doctrine. A prominent modern example is Pope Paul VI's insistence in his encyclical *Mysterium Fidei*[24] on the use of the term "transubstantiation" to describe the change in the bread and wine into the body and blood of the Lord in the Eucharist.

But best known are the occasions on which church authority has imposed penalties, including dismissal from their teaching positions, upon Catholic theologians who have dissented from church teaching. In such cases, is the church protected by the Holy Spirit from acting in error? To the extent that disciplinary action can be said to constitute (on rare occasions) an assertion of revealed doctrine, it falls—arguably we believe—within the secondary object of the infallibility of the church.

But such a statement illustrates a problem: even so vigorous a defender of papal authority as Robert Bellarmine concedes that the pope might err by taking an action that is inappropriate in one way or another.[25] So it could happen that teaching is protected from error at the same time that church discipline is administered badly.

We noted earlier that "discipline" also includes such matters as the approval of liturgical books, books which have been recognized as reflecting church teaching in the formula *lex orandi, lex credendi* (the rule of prayer is the rule of belief), and thus a form of teaching.

I am not suggesting that concern for the unity of the church, which is one of the responsibilities of the episcopal college in particular, will not at times require the exercise of disciplinary authority. In ecclesiology, the challenge is to find the proper balance between polarities, *both* of which are part of the church's structure and life. Michael Place has helpfully reminded us that since the eighteenth century and the work of Pietro Ballerini, great emphasis has been placed upon the role of the pope as the source and defender of the unity of the church. The problem is to see to the demands of unity without suffocating not only the freedom of theologians but the insight into the faith which LG 12 describes as a gift to the faithful from the Spirit.

CHURCH TEACHING AUTHORITY AND THE THEOLOGIAN AS LONER

In this section I want to put the current discussion in a broader context by pointing to an approach different from that which has prevailed in the church much of the time since the mid-nineteenth century. We will consider a view of the relationship between teaching authority and theology and theologians that builds upon a different understanding of the three functions or offices of the church than the one which in fact dominated the period.

In 1837, John Henry Newman, an Anglican priest, published his *Lectures on the Prophetical Office of the Church,* a work at which he had labored from 1834 to the end of 1836.[26] In 1877, now a Catholic, Newman republished the work with an important new preface.

The 1837 lectures discuss Newman's view of the relationship of the episcopal or apostolic office to the prophetical office in the church. The body of theologians is the bearer of the prophetical office in the church and the successor to the New Testament *didaskaloi* (teachers). Newman does not undertake a line-by-line revision of his views in 1877, but the new preface leaves no doubt that his views changed considerably in forty years.

For Newman in 1877 there must be continuing interaction between the prophetical, sacerdotal, and regal offices of the church. There is even a certain priority of the prophetic office over the others insofar as Newman sees that office as the needed corrective to the tendencies of the sacerdotal and regal offices to excess. What is more striking is that Newman ascribes the function of preaching to the apostolic office of bishops, but he ascribes the function of teaching, of doing theology to the *Schola theologorum.* Moreover he says

> Theology is the fundamental and regulating principle of the
> whole Church system. It is commensurate with Revelation,

and Revelation is the initial and essential idea of Christianity. It is the subject-matter, the formal cause, the expression, of the Prophetical office, and as being such, has created both the Regal Office and the Sacerdotal.[27]

Newman has a strong view of the corrective role of the *Schola theologorum:*

...nor is religion ever in greater danger than when, in consequence of national or international troubles, the Schools of theology have been broken up and ceased to be.[28]

Yet, he continues, theology cannot always have its own way:

...it is too hard, too intellectual, too exact, to be always equitable, or to be always compassionate: and it sometimes has a conflict or overthrow, or has to consent to a truce or a compromise, in consequence of the rival force of religious sentiment or ecclesiastical interest; and that sometimes in great matters, sometimes in unimportant.[29]

Much of the 1877 preface is a discussion and illustration of the interaction among the three functions of the church *within* the body of the church as a whole. No function of the church can get along without the others. Yet, religious sentiment and the expedient government of the church sometimes override the interests even of the prophetic function and its principal organ, the *Schola theologorum.*

The notion of the *Schola theologorum* has a role in Newman's famed *Letter to the Duke of Norfolk,* published in 1875. But the *Schola* appears in Newman's letters as early as 1863—and with a meaning that is expansive indeed. The *Schola* is not a group of theologians here or there and much less is it the individual theologian. Rather it is the whole body of Catholic thinkers from the time of the Fathers. It has been said that the notion of the *Schola theologorum* is Newman's application to theology and theologians of Augustine's dictum *securus judicat orbis terrarum,* "the whole world is a reliable judge."[30]

Here I wish only to draw attention to the notion of the active, ongoing interaction among the various offices of the church that Newman depicts. Newman had a lofty view of the role of bishops and of the pope in the church. But he also saw the need for balance among the church's various roles and functions. That balance is not something fixed once and for all; the changing life of the church requires that one function be emphasized at one time and another function at a later one. Newman saw the needs of the Anglican communion as different from those of the Catholic church. The body of Christ lives by changing and adapting.

Newman's view on the relationship of bishops and theologians is in strong contrast with that of Pius IX, set out in the letter *Tuas Libenter* in 1863. Newman was well aware of that and had been able to take the papal letter into account when he wrote his *Apologia pro vita sua* in 1864.[31]

It would not be difficult to extend the list of citations in which the view enunciated by Pius IX was repeated and developed by his successors. Nor would it be difficult to produce citations of respected Catholic theologians who find such claims excessive and the rationale unpersuasive.[32]

The difference of view represented by Newman and Pius IX underlies many present concerns. Theological differences over particular issues of doctrine or practice quickly become arguments about the very constitution of the church if the episcopal office is understood to absorb the teaching function so completely that (as Pius XII put it) all others teach only *vi missionis* (by virtue of a [canonical] mission).[33] Theologians must continue to point out how incongruous such a view is with Paul's enumeration of the gifts of the Spirit in texts like 1 Corinthians 12:28 and with the teaching of *Lumen Gentium* 12 on charisms in the whole People of God. Bishops no doubt have a responsibility for proving and ordering gifts and functions in the church, but it does not follow that such gifts and functions are derived from the bishops. The Holy Spirit breathes where he will.

There is another result of neglect of the diversity of gifts or charisms in the church: the body of theologians which Newman named the *Schola theologorum* simply disappears in favor of an approach which claims that theologians are nothing more than scattered individuals, each one deputed by and subject to episcopal and papal authority as an individual. It is this approach that I have styled "the theologian as loner" in the heading of this section.

That theologians have exercised some collective teaching authority in the long history of the church can hardly be denied. I have already called attention to the medieval triad of *sacerdotium, studium, imperium.*[34] The medieval doctors, especially at Paris but not only there, regularly passed authoritative judgments on the orthodoxy of theological positions. The role of theologians in this function came to a kind of peak in their participation, in numbers significantly larger than that of bishops, in the Council of Constance (1414–1418) and the Council of Basel (1431). But by the time of the Council of Trent (1545–1563), theologians were clearly in a consultative role, although an influential one, and the role of judges of doctrine and decision-makers in matters of discipline was reserved to bishops. At the Vatican Councils I and II, the decision-makers were exclusively bishops, with exceptions only for priests who were superiors general of certain religious orders of men.

The outright denial by popes and bishops of teaching authority to the theologians of the faculty of Paris became very explicit in the seventeenth century, as Jacques M. Gres-Gayer has shown.[35] Further and careful historical and theological studies of the changes from the high Middle Ages to the post-Reformation period are needed if we are to understand how it has happened that theologians in the twentieth century are denied all teaching authority, as a whole body (the *Schola theologorum*), as faculties like that at Paris, or as individuals. Some of this development seems to be rather recent. As we showed in chapter two, Joseph Kleutgen, writing in the mid-nineteenth century, included "the unanimous opinion of theologians" among witnesses to the authentic teaching of the church's ordinary magisterium – though he emphasized the dependence of theologians on the pope and bishops and certainly was not arguing for a teaching authority for theologians apart from the hierarchy.[36]

In the period since Vatican II, the use of the traditional "theological notes" has all but disappeared from theological discussions, and what has replaced them is an emphasis on undifferentiated magisterial authority, i.e., the authoritative teaching of pope and bishops. Today the common or even unanimous opinion of theologians is scarcely ever mentioned as a witness to authentic teaching. In fact there is little mention in church documents of theologians as a group, whether in faculties or as a whole body. Theologians are regarded as individual believers— loners—whose duties to hierarchical teaching authority are no different from those of other believers.

The title of *Donum veritatis* is a case in point: *Instructio de ecclesiali theologi vocatione: An Instruction on the Ecclesial Vocation of the*

Theologian. "Theologian" is singular in both Latin and English. The document recognizes both the problems and the contributions of the theologian and even that there are numerous theologians in the church, but nothing in the instruction suggests that in the twentieth century there exists any equivalent of the medieval *studium* to complement the function of the *sacerdotium.* Newman's vision of the sometimes shifting but still complementary roles of bishops and theologians is absent.

What dominates is the institutional model of the church, with its usual emphasis on juridical, hierarchical relationships with their basis in the institutional structure.[37]

PROSPECTS FOR THE FUTURE

If theological discussion of teaching authority is a part of ecclesiology, fundamental characteristics of the church must also be characteristics of church teaching authority. The Second Vatican Council set in motion a shift from the institutional model of the church to the communion model, which is much used since the council but still being developed by theologians and by official teachers. The discussion of the communion model at the Extraordinary Synod of 1985 and in the May 1992 letter of the CDF is evidence of that.[38] The implication of the model shift are still being worked out.

James Provost has suggested that the communion model supplies principles of legitimate diversity, subsidiarity, and shared responsibility in the life of the church.[39] The communion model should therefore undergird a more dialogic pattern of relationships within the church than did the older institutional model. The development of such relationships, particularly with regard to the exercise of the teaching office, is an urgent task facing both hierarchical church leaders and theologians.

Theological reflection can and must contribute to the development of new patterns of relationships. Such reflection, looking to the charge which Christ gave to the church, will see that faithful teaching of the gospel is one of the foremost tasks of every member of the People of God, because each one shares—though in different ways—in the prophetic office of the church. Fidelity to the gospel message is lived in the church community. To be a Christian is to be a part of the People of God and thus to be a member of the church summoned to fidelity.

The constitution *Dei Verbum* reminds us that revelation has been committed to the church. The church is to proclaim the word of God, to instruct the members of the church on the practical implications of the gospel for the Christian life, to explain and to defend the word of God against attack or misunderstanding. The church is to proclaim the gospel to everyone, mindful of the changed circumstances of modern life so aptly described by the council in its documents on missionary activity, *Ad gentes,* and on the church in the modern world, *Gaudium et Spes.* The latter, at n. 62, looks to theologians as mediators between the church and modern culture.

Catholic belief assigns an important role to the activity of the Holy Spirit given to the church in fulfillment of Christ's promise. The inclination of believers to look to the church for authoritative proclamation of the world of God and reliable interpretation of its meaning is rooted not in admiration for the talents of church members or leaders nor even on the assertion of raw teaching authority by them. Rather it is grounded in faith in the work of the Spirit. It is deference to the work of the Spirit that inclines the believer to accept as true the doctrine of the church in its day-to-day teaching of the word of God and its interpretation of the implications of faith in that word.

But believers also experience the kenotic dimension of the Spirit's coming upon the church; they know the realities of sin and human finitude which can and do lead not only isolated individuals but church leaders to err. That sober reality stands in tension with faith in the Spirit's gifts to the church and with the continued presence of the Risen Lord to the church which permitted Paul to call the church the body of Christ (Rom 12:5 and 1 Cor 12:27) and to speak of the exalted Christ as head of the church (Eph 1:22; Col 1:18).

The work of the Spirit and the presence of the Risen Christ are at the root of a necessary concern for unity in the church, for the Spirit is the origin of that unity and there is but one Lord, one faith, and one baptism (Eph 3–4:5). But we live still in expectation of fulfillment of the end-time, which is not yet.

The work of the spirit is the source of those privileged moments in the life of the church when it is preserved from teaching error, when its sacraments are effective in those who receive them worthily despite the sinfulness of those who minister them. But not every moment is thus privileged in the church's discharge of its office of teaching. Much of the contemporary controversy about church teaching authority is a dispute about teaching which is presented as authoritative but not definitive and thus as making no claim to the fullest protection of the Spirit to preserve it from error.

There are several tensions here, and it is a constant challenge to keep them in a balance which is true to the faith of the church. There is both the active presence of the Spirit to which respect is always owed and the persistent presence of sin in the church which is "always in need of purification"(LG 8). But there is no theological basis for church leaders to suggest that the unity of the church cannot survive differences which result from these tensions and to resort to disciplinary measures to prevent or suppress the differences.

If the more dialogical understanding of the role of church teaching authority is adopted, alternatives to the present inadequate approaches to church teaching and the response owed to it are needed. Some are appearing. For example, at the request of Pope John Paul II, the Pontifical Academy of Sciences carried out a long review of the punishments imposed on Galileo by the Holy Office in 1633. The result is an admission that the church authorities of the time erred. Though the pope's address to the Academy in 1992 speaks only of errors of theologians rather than of the church or curial offices, the 1984 report of the Academy to the pope said that the judges of the Holy Office committed an "objective error" in condemning Galileo.[40] A church "always in need of purification" can and must admit with both grace and candor to other mistakes made before and since 1633. The greatly increased pace of the activity of authoritative church teaching today requires that such admissions be made promptly when they become apparent.

A rethinking of the meaning of *obsequium mentis et voluntatis* is needed. Historical studies suggest that teaching which is not presented as definitive was once understood as more disciplinary than doctrinal and thus had the status of law. Such an understanding has the considerable advantage of avoiding inappropriate claims about the truth-status of such teaching. But the use of legislative authority needs to be restrained by the conviction that the unity of the church cannot be preserved by sacrificing the truth.

Here we can only sketch alternatives to an excessively juridical understanding of teaching authority congenial to an institutional model of the church but not to a communion model. We can still learn something from the medieval jurists. These and other alternatives can avoid Congar's reproach that the claims of the magisterium in modern times seem excessive and unreal.

The resources of Catholic ecclesiology can surely produce a more satisfactory model which will acknowledge the presence and work of Christ and the Spirit in the church, the obedience owed to the revealed word of God, and the respect owed to those charged with teaching by their office, especially the college of bishops. Scholars, to whom the Spirit has given gifts appropriate to their role as mediators between the Christian faith and contemporary culture complement and in important respects enable the work of official teachers while being sustained and nourished by the community.

Yves Congar has articulated this perspective on the relationship of theologians and hierarchical teaching authority in words with which we can conclude:

> We cannot define the dependent condition of theologians only with reference to the "magisterium," even while this retains its truth. In this area as in that of obedience we must not think of the issue just in two terms: authority and theologians. We must think in three terms: above, the truth, the transmitted apostolic faith, confessed, preached and celebrated. Beneath this, at its service, the "magisterium" of the apostolic ministry, and the work or the teaching of theologians, as well as the faith of the faithful. It is a differentiated service, articulated organically, like all the life of the Church.[41]

Notes

1. We trace a number of the regulations put upon theologians in chapter six. Perhaps the best known of the protests was the "Cologne Declaration" signed by 163 scholars from Germany, Austria, Switzerland, and the Netherlands. See the text in *Origins* 18 (1988–1989): 633–634. Scholars from Flanders, France, Italy, and Spain associated themselves in various ways with the declaration or issued statements of their own.

A statement of concerns endorsed by members of the Catholic

Theological Society of America entitled "Do Not Extinguish the Spirit" was published on the 25th anniversary of the close of the Second Vatican Council. The text is in *Origins* 20 (1990–1991): 461–467. Reactions by Archbishop Oscar H. Lipscomb, chairman of the NCCB Committee on Doctrine, and Archbishop John R. Quinn of San Francisco appear at pp. 467–468.

2. Avery Dulles, S.J., *Models of the Church* (New York: Doubleday, 1974: 2nd ed., 1987).

3. A full discussion would consider the reality of the church as a communion (*koinonia*) as well. See the CDF's "Letter to the Bishops of the Catholic Church on Some Aspects of the Church Understood as a Communion" (text in *Origins* 22 [1992–1993]; 108–112). See also Edward Yarnold, "The Church as Communion," *The Tablet* (London) 246 (December 12, 1992): 1564–1565. The role of the Holy Spirit in the church is not given much emphasis in the letter of the CDF.

4. For what follows on the work of the Spirit I am indebted to Mühlen, *Una Persona Mystica.* See also Yves Congar, *I Believe in the Holy Spirit,* 3 vols., trans. David Smith (New York: Seabury, 1983).

5. K. Rahner, *The Church and the Sacraments, Quaestiones Disputatae* 9, trans. W. J. O'Hara (New York: Herder & Herder, 1963), 18.

6. See *Dei Verbum* n. 10. See the conciliar texts together with the reports on the revision process from the Theological Commission in *Acta Synodalia Sacrosancti Concilii Oecumenici Vaticani Secundi* (Vatican Press, 1970–78), 3.3.80–81; 4.1.350–351, 354; and Löhrer, "Träger der Vermittlung," 1.545–587.

7. The notion of a *sensus fidei* or collective consciousness was exploited by J. A. Möhler, *Einheit in der Kirche,* ed. J. R. Geiselman (Darmstadt: Wissenschaftliche Buchgesellschaft, 1957) and after him by Karl Rahner, especially in his treatment of "faith-instinct." See Boyle, "Faith and Christian Ethics," 252–254. See also LG n. 12.

8. See Bernard Lonergan, S.J., *Insight,* 3rd ed. (New York: Philosophical Library, 1970), 286.

9. See Mühlen, *Una Persona Mystica,* 255–256. Chapter seven of LG, "The Pilgrim Church" sets out a view of the church marked by an eschatology which excludes triumphalism.

10. DS 302.

11. Mühlen, *Una Persona Mystica,* 272.

12. See LG 8 which speaks of an analogy between the church and the incarnation.

13. See Hans Küng, *The Church,* trans. Ray and Rosaleen Ockenden (London: Burns & Oates, 1967), 28.

14. *Insight,* 191, 627–630. See also LG 8: "The church, however, clasp-

ing sinners to her bosom, at once holy and always in need of purification, follows constantly the path of penance and renewal."

15. LG, chapter 3. See B. Dupuy, "Theologie der kirchlichen Ämter," in *Mysterium Salutis* 4.2.488–523, esp. p. 517. Dupuy's discussion of the sacramental character is very brief and is undeveloped with respect to the teaching role of the bishop. The view presented here of the relationship of the community to its authoritative teachers resembles the view of the church found in the Agreed Statement by the Anglican-Roman Catholic International Commission dated January 17, 1977 and published in *Worship* 51 (1977): 90–102. See esp., part II which describes the relationship of *episcope* and *koinonia*.

16. See David M. Stanley, S.J., "*Didaché* as a Constitutive Element of the Gospel-Form" *Catholic Biblical Quarterly* 17 (1955): 336–483.

17. See Pottmeyer's comments on Scheeben in *Unfehlbarkeit*, 264–278.

18. While the instruction *Donum veritatis* deals with dialogue between theologians and church teaching authority, which can promote better insights into revelation and the moral law, the approach seems applicable to other qualified persons within the church community. See also GS 43 and canon 212 of the 1983 code.

19. The reality of historical development even in the field of defined dogma has been explicitly acknowledged in the "Declaration in Defense of the Catholic Doctrine on the Church against Certain Errors of the Present Day" (*Mysterium Ecclesiae*) issued by the CDF June 24, 1973, at n. 5. and by the teaching of DV discussed above. See also our discussion of the 1990 instruction *Donum veritatis* in chapter eight.

20. Hermann J. Pottmeyer, who earlier sounded this theme in his book *Unfehlbarkeit*, has returned to it in "Reception and Submission."

21. See LG 25. The same point is made in chapter 2 of *Dei Verbum* on the transmission of revelation.

22. See, for example, the survey of the manualists by Joseph A. Komonchak, "Ordinary Papal Magisterium and Religious Assent," and Bishop B. C. Butler, "*Infallible Authenticum: Assensus: Obsequium:* Christian Teaching Authority and the Christian's Response," Bishop Butler would translate *obsequium* as "respect" (p. 87). "Assent" for him is a special form of *obsequium* reserved for clearly infallible teaching. See also Pottmeyer, "Reception and Submission."

The translators of the *Code of Canon Law: Latin-English Version* (Washington, 1983) published by the Canon Law Society of America rendered the "religiosum intellectus et voluntatis obsequium" of canon 752 as "a religious respect of intellect and will" and the "religiosum animi obsequium" of canon 753 as a "sense of religious respect."

Given the variety of responses that are possible, there is much to commend a phrasing such as "due respect" or "appropriate respect" as the English equivalent of *obsequium debitum*. It is clear even from *Donum veritatis* that due respect is compatible with withholding of assent or even the discreet disagreement with official teaching discussed in chapter eight. New terminology for errant views is also needed.

23. Canon 749 P. 3.

24. *AAS* 57 (1965): 753–774.

25. We called attention to the text in chapter three. See Bellarmine, *Opera Omnia*, 2.87–88.

26. On the dating, see John Henry Newman, *Apologia pro vita sua*, ed. Martin J. Svagli (Oxford: Clarendon Press, 1967), 67.

27. *The Via Media of the Anglicum Church*, 2 vols. (London: Longmans, 1906), 1:xlvii.

28. Ibid.

29. Ibid., xlviii.

30. Paul Misner, *Papacy and Development: Newman and the Primacy of the Pope* (Leiden: Brill, 1976); and see Klausnitzer, *Päpstliche Unfehlbarkeit bei Newman and Döllinger*, 111.

31. See John Coulson, *Newman and the Common Tradition* (Oxford: Clarendon Press, 1970), 131–140.

32. See the discussion in Sullivan, *Magisterium*, 190–204. See also Congar, "A Brief History," 314–331, esp. p. 327.

33. Allocution *Si diligis*, *AAS* 46 (1954): 313–317, citation at 315.

34. See the details in Congar, "A Brief History," 318–321.

35. Gres-Gayer, "The Magisterium of the Faculty of Theology of Paris," 424–450.

36. Kleutgen was careful to note that he had in mind only reputable theologians, the *auctores probati*.

37. There is no body of scholars in the church today acknowledged as playing the role Newman ascribes to the *Schola theologorum*, but theologians and church officials refer to the *auctores probati* (approved authors) for help in determining the meaning of official church teaching or for answers to questions.

Most of the *auctores probati*, like most theologians in the church until recently, were priests or members of religious communities. Most were also males. The tests for being "approved" could take various forms, but included were the publication of widely used textbooks in theology carrying the imprimatur, publications of articles in journals approved formally or informally by church authorities, invitations to serve as theological advisors to church officials and/or institutions.

There existed in the church at least a tacit acknowledgment that a body of theological scholars existed, many trained in the same graduate programs (especially in Rome or the Catholic University in Washington, D.C.), and who were in conversation with one another through their books, lectures, and the like. Most taught in seminaries or in the few Catholic universities.

Since Vatican II, the decline in the number of priests and seminaries and the increase in the number of Catholic scholars teaching in institutions not directly under the control of church authorities has vastly complicated attempts to identify even *auctores probati*—to say nothing of a *Schola theologorum*. Women, including women religious in significant numbers, have entered the professorate, bringing with them new experiences and scholarly interests. Faculties of theology, even in institutions sponsored by churches, are rarely staffed only by persons who are members of the sponsoring church.

Nonetheless, it does seem possible to speak of a body of scholars within the church. Just who they are and what influence they will have in their relations with bishops is undoubtedly one of the issues motivating the efforts by church officials to gain more control over theology and theologians. Persons with scholarly competence, usually certified by a doctorate in theology, and who have a commitment either official or temporary to the service of the church would, I suggest, be the late twentieth-century *Schola theologorum*. Most such persons would be Catholics, but not all. A look at the list of contributors to influential recent works in theology or other sacred science shows that scholars who are not Catholics are a part of many projects undertaken by Catholic institutions or the Catholic hierarchy.

38. Text in *Origins* 22 (1992–1993): 108–112. The text of the "Final Report" of the 1985 Extraordinary Synod of Bishops appears in Xavier Rynne, *John Paul's Extraordinary Synod: A Collegial Achievement* (Wilmington, Del.: Michael Glazier, 1986), Appendix II: 112–132, especially section C on the notion of communion, pp. 122–127.

39. See *The Jurist,* 36, nos. 1–2 (1976): 191–245, a special issue on the theme of communion.

40. The text of the pope's address and the report of Cardinal Paul Poupard, a member of the papal commission appointed in 1981 to study the Galileo case, are in *Origins* 22 (1992–1993): 369–375. A summary history of the work of the commission and further references to sources are in the notes and in marginal material accompanying the texts.

41. Congar, "A Brief History," 328.

List of Contributors

Thomas J. Bouquillon (d. 1902) was a Belgian-born priest who was the first Professor of Moral Theology at The Catholic University of America and the author of *Theologia moralis fundamentalis*.

John P. Boyle is Emeritus Professor in the School of Religion at the University of Iowa.

Joseph M. Boyle, Jr., is Professor of Philosophy at St. Michael's College, University of Toronto.

Francis J. Connell, C.SS.R, (d. 1967) was Professor of Moral Theology at The Catholic University of America and the author of *Outlines of Moral Theology*.

Charles E. Curran is Elizabeth Scurlock University Professor of Human Values at Southern Methodist University.

Henry Davis, S.J., (d. 1952) was Professor of Moral Theology at Heythrop College in England and the author of the four-volume *Moral and Pastoral Theology*.

Margaret A. Farley, R.S.M., is Gilbert L. Stark Professor of Christian Ethics, Yale University Divinity School.

John Finnis is Reader in Law, Oxford University, and Fellow of University College, Oxford.

John C. Ford, S.J., (d. 1989) was Professor of Moral Theology at Weston School of Theology and at The Catholic University of American and co-author with Gerald Kelly of the two-volume *Contemporary Moral Theology*.

Germain Grisez is the Harry J. Flynn Professor of Christian Ethics at Mount St. Mary's College in Emmitsburg, Maryland.

Edwin F. Healy, S.J., (d. 1957) was Professor of Moral Theology at the Gregorian University in Rome and the author of *Medical Ethics*.

John B. Hogan, S.S., (d. 1901) was President and Professor at St. John's Seminary, Brighton, Massachusetts, and the author of *Clerical Studies*.

James F. Keenan, S.J., is Associate Professor of Moral Theology at the Weston Jesuit School of Theology, Cambridge, Massachusetts.

Gerald Kelly, S.J., (d. 1964) was Professor of Moral Theology at the Jesuit Theologate of St. Mary's in Kansas and the author of *The Good Confessor*.

August Lehmkuhl, S.J., (d. 1917) taught moral theology for many years to Jesuits in Germany and was the author of the two-volume *Theologia moralis*.

Richard A. McCormick, S.J., is John A. O'Brien Professor Emeritus of Moral Theology at the University of Notre Dame.

John A. McHugh, O.P., (d. 1950) taught moral theology and other subjects at the Maryknoll Seminary and was co-author with Charles J. Callan, O.P., of the two-volume *Moral Theology*.

Paul E. McKeever (d. 1988) was Professor of Moral Theology at Immaculate Conception Seminary, Huntington, Long Island, and at St. John's University, Jamaica, New York.

Jean Porter is Professor of Moral Theology at the University of Notre Dame.

John A. Ryan, (d. 1945) was Professor of Moral Theology at The Catholic University of America and author of *Distributive Justice*.